FROM
KABUL TO BAGHDAD AND
BACK

FROM
KABUL TO BAGHDAD AND
BACK

The U.S. at War in Afghanistan and Iraq

John R. Ballard, David W. Lamm, and John K. Wood

NAVAL INSTITUTE PRESS
Annapolis, Maryland

Naval Institute Press
291 Wood Road
Annapolis, MD 21402

© 2012 by John R. Ballard, David W. Lamm, and John K. Wood

Library of Congress Cataloging-in-Publication Data
Ballard, John R., 1957-
   From Kabul to Baghdad and back : the U.S. at war in Afghanistan and Iraq / John R. Ballard, David W. Lamm, and John K. Wood.
      p. cm.
   Includes bibliographical references and index.
   ISBN 978-1-61251-022-4 (hard cover : alk. paper) — ISBN 978-1-61251-168-9 (ebook) 1. Afghan War, 2001—-Campaigns. 2. Iraq War, 2003-2011—Campaigns. 3. War on Terrorism, 2001-2009. 4. United States—Military policy—History—21st century. 5. United States—History, Military—21st century. 6. Strategy. I. Lamm, David W. II. Wood, John K. III. Title.
   DS371.412B34 2012
   956.7044'3373—dc23

                                          2012026125

♾ This paper meets the requirements of ANSI/NISO z39.48-1992 (Permanence of Paper).
Printed in the United States of America.

20 19 18 17 16 15 14 13 12   9 8 7 6 5 4 3 2 1
First printing

For the over 3,000 men and women
who gave their lives during the conflict in Afghanistan.

Military service is the ultimate form of patriotism.

Contents

Maps and Figures

Maps

Figures

Preface

The armed forces must have the capability to swiftly defeat adversaries in overlapping campaigns while preserving the option to expand operations in one of those campaigns to achieve more comprehensive objectives. Prevailing against adversaries includes integrating all instruments of national power within a campaign to set the conditions for an enduring victory.[1]

—*The National Military Strategy of the United States of America*, 2004

It seems simple. This book is designed to explain the key strategic and operational actions that marked America's decade-long campaign in Afghanistan; it will pay particularly close attention to the impacts of the parallel campaign in Iraq on the success of the effort in Afghanistan. The book will not only assess the ability of the United States to conduct two nearly simultaneous campaigns in two distant theaters of operations but also take a close look at whether the national command authorities attempted to manage the two as coordinated efforts focused on a single strategic goal.[2] The book also is intended to highlight critical decisions, both political and operational, made during combat operations in the two theaters that dramatically affected the outcome of the Afghan campaign and the ability of the United States to achieve an enduring victory in a nation that has known nothing but war for well over thirty years.

This was certainly not the first instance the United States had been driven to conduct more than one significant military campaign at the same time.

The "Germany First" strategy of the Second World War is well known, and with some study it becomes readily apparent that simultaneous campaigns have been part of nearly every American war since the British decided in 1778 to conduct the Southern Campaign during the American Revolution. Still, the national decision in 2002 to embark upon a second, major military campaign against Iraq will remain both controversial and burdensome for decades, particularly as it most certainly prolonged the development of stability in Afghanistan and severely reduced the flexibility of the United States as the threat in the region grew over time. Regardless of the merits of the decision or the necessity for the attack into Iraq in March 2003, scholars and policy makers should question the real value of conducting more than one military operation at the same time.

Since the end of the Second World War in 1945 the essential character of war has changed.[3] War has incorporated a wide variety of actions over the course of history, so this change has not been unique; what has been significant is the seemingly irrevocable nature of the change due to the loss of preeminence of the nation-state as the primary actor in war and the lack of decisive resolution of the wars that have occurred since 1945. Non–nation-states have engaged in warfare in important ways throughout history, but the role of both the Taliban Wahhabi political movement and the terrorist organization Al-Qaeda in the Afghan campaign was exceptional. Although the sources of the Afghan conflict were not from nation-states, both the United Nations and the North Atlantic Treaty Organization (NATO) strongly endorsed the military response against Taliban-governed Afghanistan.

The use of the term "global war on terror" by the United States has only added to the complexity of this general trend in the changing character of war in the twenty-first century. One can understand why President George W. Bush and key members of his administration began to use the term in late 2001 to indicate the novel nature of the conflict they had been forced to wage against Al-Qaeda. The use of the term "war" incited a whole-of-nation approach, validated the significance of the attacks in New York City and Washington, D.C., and demonstrated in advance the seriousness of the response envisioned. Any effort aimed at Afghan organizations was certain to be global in reach and would ideally become an international response against what was viewed as a common threat to many Western nations.

There being no other convenient moniker, since the effort was clearly seen as opposing terrorist acts, and because no one could rationally support terrorism, it was labeled as a "war on terror," even though terror in itself was but the product of the terrorist acts.

This label seemed understandable and even appealing at the time, but it soon became fraught with difficult challenges. The international nature of the war was confusing to nations that had been fighting terrorists with legal and security tools for years. The status of combatants in Afghanistan from an international legal perspective was overly vague, and of course the attack by the sole superpower on another impoverished nation simply because it was harboring a terrorist organization appeared a gross violation of the new, United Nations–based international order that permeated global thinking at the time. Though a number of coalition partners signed up to assist the United States in the immediate aftermath of the attacks, once the Bush administration linked an "axis of evil" to the war in the president's State of the Union speech in January 2002, some nations began to distance themselves. Once President Bush decided to include Iraq in the overall context of the global war, even normally staunch allies, such as France, reduced their support.

Military theorists and doctrine writers most frequently use a continuum of actions, starting with battles at the tactical level of conflict, to characterize war. Operationally, military activities are grouped into campaigns, which have the same objective but synchronize multiple battles to achieve desired effects on the enemy. Strategies most frequently coordinate the elements of national power (diplomacy, economics, information, law enforcement, and military power) in order to compel other nations to act in certain ways. Thus the effort in Afghanistan was initially envisioned as a single, short, operational campaign to eject Al-Qaeda and destroy its Taliban host while bringing a better quality of life to the average Afghan. What actually occurred was very different indeed, at the tactical, operational and strategic levels, thus, the U.S. war in Afghanistan requires further study so that future such campaigns can achieve better results.

Acknowledgments

This book was inspired by our interaction with numerous Americans, American allies, and Afghans who worked to bring peace and stability to Afghanistan over the past decade. Our work at the National War College and the Near East South Asia Center for Strategic Studies at the National Defense University has allowed us to observe the professionalism and the great hope of so many patriots—all working for improvements in the daily lives of the Afghan people. Particularly after President Obama reconfirmed the importance of the campaign within the vital interests of the United States, their sophisticated questioning led us to explain and, when necessary, to critique the essential elements of such an important national effort. To them this book is dedicated.

Like all our work, this book was also inspired by our family members, our wives, children, and our parents. It was only through their support and sometimes gentle encouragement that this work came to be written.

Although it has benefited from a great deal of government information, this book does not reflect the opinions of the U.S. Department of Defense or the National Defense University, nor does it reflect their policies. The views expressed in this book are ours alone, as are any errors or omissions.

John R. Ballard, David W. Lamm, and John K. Wood
Washington, D.C.

Acronyms and Abbreviations

AAA	antiaircraft artillery
AB	Air Base
ABCCC	Airborne Battlefield Command and Control Center
ACC	Air Combat Command
ACR	Armored Cavalry Regiment
ACTD	Advanced Concept Technology Demonstrator
A-day	day that air combat began
AEF	Air Expeditionary Force
AEI	American Enterprise Institute
AFB	Air Force Base
AFFOR	Air Forces Forward
AFP	Armed Forces of the Philippines
AFSOC	Air Force Special Operations Command
AGM	air-to-ground missile
AIA	Afghan Interim Authority
AIOG	Afghanistan Interagency Operations Group
ALCM	air-launched cruise missile
ALO	Air Liaison Officer
AMC	Air Mobility Command
AMOCC	Air Mobility Operations Control Center
ANA	Afghan National Army
ANG	Air National Guard
ANP	Afghan National Police
ANSF	Afghan National Security Forces

AO	area of operations
AOC	Air Operations Center
AOIG	Afghanistan Interagency Operations Group
AOR	area of responsibility
AQ-I	Al-Qaeda in Iraq
ARCENT	Army Forces, U.S. Central Command
ASOC	Air Support Operations Center
ATA	Afghan Transitional Administration
ATO	Air Tasking Order
AWACS	Airborne Warning and Control System
BANA	battalion of the Afghan National Army
BCT	Brigade Combat Team
BDA	Battle Damage Assessment
CA	civil affairs
CAG	Carrier Air Group
CALCM	Conventional Air-Launched Cruise Missile
CAOC	Combined Air Operations Center
CAP	combat air patrol
CAS	Close Air Support
CBU	cluster bomb unit
CENTAF	U.S. Central Command Air Forces
CENTCOM	U.S. Central Command
CERP	Commanders Emergency Response Program
CFACC	Combined Force Air Component Commander
CFC-A	Combined Forces Command–Afghanistan
CFLCC	Combined Force Land Component Commander
CFMCC	Combined Force Maritime Component Commander
CFSOCC-A	Combined Forces Special Operations Component Command–Afghanistan
CHLC	Coalition Humanitarian Liaison Cell
CIA	Central Intelligence Agency
CINC	Commander in Chief
CJCMOTF	Combined Joint Civil Military Operations Task Force
CJCS	Chairman of the Joint Chiefs of Staff
CJSOTF	Combined Joint Special Operations Task Force
CJTF	Combined Joint Task Force

CMO	civil-military operations
CNN	Cable News Network
COG	center of gravity
COIN	counterinsurgency
COMAFFOR	Commander of Air Force Forces
CONOPS	concept of operations
CONUS	Continental United States
COP	combat outpost
CPA	Coalition Provisional Authority
CSAR	Combat Search and Rescue
CSTC-A	Combined Security Transition Command-Afghanistan
CT	counterterrorism
CTC	Counter Terrorism Center [CIA]
DDR	Disarmament, Demobilization, and Reintegration
DEFCON	Defense Condition
DIA	Defense Intelligence Agency
DIRMOBFOR	Director of Mobility Forces
DoD	Department of Defense
DZ	drop zone
EEOB	Eisenhower Executive Office Building
EFP	Explosively Formed Penetrator
ETT	Embedded Training Team
EU	European Union
EUCOM	U.S. European Command
FAA	Federal Aviation Administration
FAC	Forward Air Controller
FAC-A	Airborne Forward Air Controller
FARRP	Forward-Area Rearming and Refueling Point
FATA	Federally Administered Tribal Areas (Pakistan)
FC	field circular
FLIR	Forward-Looking Infrared
FM	field manual
FOB	Forward Operating Base
FRAGO	fragmentary order
FSK	Forsvarets Spesialkommando
GIRoA	Government of the Islamic Republic of Afghanistan

GPS	Global Positioning System
HASC	House Armed Services Committee
HEYET	Association of Muslim Scholars in Iraq
HIG	Hizb-i Islami Gulbuddin
HIMARS	High Mobility Artillery Rocket System
HUMINT	human intelligence
HVT	high-value target
KMTC	Kabul Military Training Center
I MEF	I Marine Expeditionary Force
I MEF (FWD)	I Marine Expeditionary Force (Forward)
IADS	Integrated Air Defense System
ICRC	International Committee of the Red Cross
IED	Improvised Explosive Device
IGC	Interim Governing Council (Iraq)
IIG	Interim Iraqi Government
IJC	ISAF Joint Command
INL	[State Dept. Bureau for] International Narcotics and Law Enforcement
IO	international organization
ISAF	International Security Assistance Force
ISF	Iraqi Security Forces
ISI	(Pakistani) Inter-Services Intelligence (directorate)
ISR	Intelligence, Surveillance, and Reconnaissance
JAG	Judge Advocate General
JCMB	Joint Coordination and Monitoring Board
JCS	Joint Chiefs of Staff
JDAM	Joint Direct Attack Munition
JEMB	Joint Election Management Board
JFACC	Joint Force Air Component Commander
JOA	joint operations area
JSOC	Joint Special Operations Command
JSOTF	Joint Special Operations Task Force
JSS	joint security station
JSTARS	Joint Surveillance Target Attack Radar System
JTF	Joint Task Force
KHAD	Khadamat-e Etela'at-e Dawlati

LANTIRN	Low-Altitude Navigation and Targeting Infrared for Night
LD/HD	low-density/high-demand
LGB	Laser-Guided Bomb
LIC	low-intensity conflict
LZ	landing zone
MAAP	Master Air Attack Plan
MARFORCENT	Marines Forces Central Command
MASINT	Measurement and Signature Intelligence
MEU	Marine Expeditionary Unit
MEU (SOC)	Marine Expeditionary Unit (Special Operations Capable)
MNC-I	Multinational Corps–Iraq
MND-B	Multinational Division–Baghdad
MNF-I	Multinational Force–Iraq
MNSTC-I	Multinational Security Transition Command–Iraq
MOD	Ministry of Defense
MOI	Ministry of Interior
MRAP	Mine Resistant Ambush Protected [vehicle]
MRE	Meal Ready to Eat
MTT	Military Transition Team
MTW	major-theater war
NAC	North Atlantic Council
NATO	North Atlantic Treaty Organization
NAVCENT	U.S. Central Command Naval Forces
NCO	noncommissioned officer
NGO	nongovernmental organization
NIE	National Intelligence Estimate
NIMA	National Imagery and Mapping Agency
NMCC	National Military Command Center
NORAD	North American Air Defense Command
NSC	National Security Council
NSPD	National Security Presidential Directive
NTC	National Training Center
NTM-A	NATO Training Mission–Afghanistan
NVG	Night-Vision Goggles
OAF	Operation Allied Force
ODA	Operational Detachment–Alpha

OEF	Operation Enduring Freedom
OEF-P	Enduring Freedom–Philippines
OIF	Operation Iraqi Freedom
OMC-A	Office of Military Cooperation–Afghanistan
OMLT	Operational Mentoring and Liaison Team
OPLAN	operations plan
OPT	operational planning team
ORHA	Office of Reconstruction and Humanitarian Assistance
OSCA	Office of Security Cooperation–Afghanistan
OSD	Office of the Secretary of Defense
PDD	Presidential Decision Directive
PGM	Precision-Guided Munition
PDPA	People's Democratic Party of Afghanistan
PLANORD	planning order
POMLT	ANP Operational Mentoring and Liaison Team
PRT	Provincial Reconstruction Team
PSYOP	psychological operation
QDR	Quadrennial Defense Review
QRF	Quick Reaction Force
RAF	[British] Royal Air Force
RC	Regional Command
ROE	Rules of Engagement
RPG	Rocket-Propelled Grenade
RSOI	Reception, Staging, Onward Movement, and Integration [of ground combat power]
SACEUR	Supreme Allied Commander Europe
SAM	Surface-to-Air Missile
SAS	Special Air Service
SEAD	Suppression of Enemy Air Defenses
SEAL	Sea-Air-Land [USN]
SECDEF	Secretary of Defense
SF	Special Forces
SFA	Strategic Framework Agreement (Iraq)
SFG	Special Forces Group
SIGINT	signals intelligence
SIPRNET	Secure Internet Protocol Router Network

SOCOM	Special Operations Command
SOF	Special Operations Forces
SOFA	Status of Forces Agreement
SOLIC	Assistant Secretary of Defense for Special Operations and Low-Intensity Conflict
SRAP	Senior Representative for Afghanistan and Pakistan
SRSG	Special Representative of the (UN) Secretary General
SSR	Security Sector Reform
TACON	tactical control
TACP	Tactical Air Control Party
TAL	Transitional Administrative Law
TF	task force
TLAM	Tomahawk land-attack missile
TRANSCOM	U.S. Transportation Command
TRAP	Tactical Recovery of Aircraft and Personnel
TSC	Theater Support Command
TST	Time-Sensitive Targeting
TTP	Tactics, Techniques, and Procedures
UAE	United Arab Emirates
UAV	Unmanned Aerial Vehicle
UHF	ultra-high-frequency
UN	United Nations
UNAMA	United Nations Assistance Mission in Afghanistan
UNHCR	United Nations High Commissioner for Refugees
UNSCR	United Nations Security Council Resolution
USA	U.S. Army [after a name given with rank]
USAF	U.S. Air Force
USAID	U.S. Agency for International Development
USAREUR	U.S. Army in Europe
USEUCOM	U.S. European Command
USFOR-A	U.S. Forces Afghanistan
USS	United States Ship
USSR	Union of Soviet Socialist Republics
VBIED	Vehicle-Borne Improvised Explosive Device
VTC	video teleconference
WFP	World Food Program
WMD	Weapon of Mass Destruction

Prologue

It was the worst single-day toll for American forces in Afghanistan since U.S. troops entered that country nearly ten years before and one of the largest tolls in a single incident of either the Afghan war or the fighting in Iraq.[1]

Just before midnight on August 5, 2011, a U.S. Army CH-47 Chinook helicopter from special operations aviation Task Force 160 was shot down during an operation conducted against Taliban insurgents in volatile Wardak Province in eastern Afghanistan. The helicopter had been carrying thirty-one American troops (including seventeen elite Navy SEALs, five Naval Special Warfare personnel who supported the SEALs, three Air Force Special Operations personnel, and five army helicopter crewmen) and seven Afghan soldiers; Afghan president Hamid Karzai made the announcement of the tragedy to the world.

The helicopter had been dispatched in response to calls from an American Ranger unit pinned down in heavy combat while attempting to destroy a known improvised-explosive-device cache. The Taliban, after decades of war, understood well that American forces would always attempt to rescue their units in distress, and in Wardak Province that would mean by vulnerable helicopters. The insurgents had lain in wait until they could dispatch the multimillion-dollar helicopter with a simple RPG round and kill the full human cargo of the aircraft. As reports noted at the time, "with its steep mountain ranges, providing shelter for militants armed with rocket-propelled grenade launchers, eastern Afghanistan is hazardous terrain for military aircraft. Large, slow-moving air transport carriers like the CH-47 Chinook are particularly vulnerable, often forced to ease their way through sheer valleys where insurgents can achieve more level lines of fire from mountainsides."[2]

The Navy SEALs killed in the shoot-down were part of the most highly trained unit in the American military, SEAL Team 6 of the Joint Special Operations Command—the same unit that had successfully conducted the brilliant raid that killed Osama bin Laden in his Pakistani hideout only three months earlier. SEALs along with their soldier counterparts in the U.S. Army Special Operations Command were among the troops deployed most frequently to the war-torn country. Some special operators had in fact deployed to Afghanistan ten times in as many years of conflict. They were remarkably skilled and highly dedicated warriors, fundamental to the successes achieved in the war to that point and symbolic of the extraordinary efforts made by America in Afghanistan since the fall of the Taliban government in that country in late 2001.

Despite the horrific loss of life from such elite warriors, in the months that followed the United States continued with its plan to withdraw some 10,000 more troops from Afghanistan by the end of that year, citing security gains and a more capable Afghan army and police. There were then about 100,000 U.S. troops fighting in Afghanistan, more than a decade after the attacks on the Twin Towers in New York City that had started the conflict.

Americans asked how so many highly skilled men could die so far away from their families in a fight that seemed both incongruous and, after the death of Bin Laden, largely insignificant. America had been fighting in Afghanistan for far longer than anyone had anticipated, and the provinces nearest the Afghan capital were still not secure. Was such a cost really justified in a war where victory, by any conventional military standard, seemed at least unlikely?

National treasure can be measured in many ways. Certainly the $444 billion estimated to have been spent by the United States on the war effort in Afghanistan had taken a severe toll on the U.S. economy by 2011.[3] Similarly, the effort to increase stability in Afghanistan had caused a dramatic and lasting downturn in U.S.-Pakistani relations and had harmed the overall image of the United States in the eyes of many in the region.[4] Still, the deaths of so many men at that point in the campaign was a trumpet call for many to ask what more was required to accomplish the war ends so proudly identified in 2001 and how much more blood and treasure could be spent to accomplish those goals in the three short years that remained before the full withdrawal of American forces from Afghanistan was to occur. . . .

This book tells the story of how such precious American treasure came to be offered in operations to quash terrorism in the far reaches of west Asia.

FROM
KABUL TO BAGHDAD AND
BACK

One

Fighting Two Enemies
A Historical Perspective

> The picture is murkier in Afghanistan, the second front
> in the war on terrorism.
>
> —Michael Gerson[1]

The terrorist attacks in New York City and Washington, D.C., on September 11, 2001, ushered in significant changes in the character of American warfare. Some of those changes, such as the creation of a Department of Homeland Security, represented successful responses to international challenges, but at least one change—the decision to conduct preemptive war against likely aggressors—generated one of the most dubious and controversial decisions of the era: the choice made by President George W. Bush to attack Iraq in 2003, while American forces were still engaged in combat in Afghanistan. There is clear evidence to demonstrate that accomplishing the political and military objectives of the United States in Afghanistan, where it was making its primary effort against the perpetrators of the 9/11 attacks, was significantly impeded by the decision to wage war simultaneously against Saddam Hussein's Iraq. America's objectives in Afghanistan were able to be accomplished only after the American forces left Iraq in 2011, after ten years of war. The decision to conduct the war in Iraq while fighting continued in Afghanistan and the impacts of that decision over the decade of combat that followed deserve in-depth analysis.

The Enduring Freedom campaign against the Taliban, coming as it did in response to the attacks by the Al-Qaeda terrorist organization on the World

Trade Center and the Pentagon in September 2001, generated huge international support and a broad coalition of over fifty nations. The operation was an act of collective self-defense provided for under Article 51 of the United Nations (UN) Charter; thus, most experts contend, no UN Security Council authorization was required for its legitimacy. The North Atlantic Treaty Organization (NATO) deemed it an act of collective self-defense under Article V of the Washington Treaty, and the U.S. Congress authorized the operation through its "Authorization for Use of Military Force against Terrorists," signed on September 18, 2001.[2] In contrast, the war in Iraq was never endorsed by the UN Security Council, never saw widespread support from NATO allies, and though it was authorized by Congress in its "Authorization for Use of Military Force Against Iraq Resolution of 2002,"[3] that justification contained language based upon assumptions later proven false.[4]

Under such dissimilar circumstances it should have been difficult for any government to have embarked upon one of the most risky of military strategies—the prosecution of multiple simultaneous military campaigns in separate theaters of war—particularly in that there was no immediacy to the Iraqi threat. History, though too frequently ignored, gives ample evidence of the difficulties associated with such military actions.

In late June 1941, during the Second World War, Adolf Hitler ordered over four million troops of the Axis powers to invade Josef Stalin's Union of Soviet Socialist Republics (USSR), opening a new, 1,800-mile-long eastern front. The offensive was an effort to achieve his primary objective in the war—the expansion of German territory—but it became one of the major mistakes. Though the Germans won some resounding tactical victories and occupied large parts of the most important economic areas of the USSR, they were eventually pushed back from Moscow, and they never mounted another offensive along the strategic Soviet-German front for the remainder of the war. The initial invasion, known as Operation Barbarossa, was the largest military operation in human history in terms of both manpower and casualties.[5]

Operation Barbarossa eventually consumed more forces than any other operation in any other Axis theater of war. Barbarossa brought some of the largest battles, deadliest atrocities, highest casualties, and most horrific conditions of the Second World War. The fighting on that Eastern Front went on for nearly four years. The death toll listed an estimated 7 million Soviets lost in combat or in Axis captivity. The number of Soviet civilian deaths remains contentious, though roughly 20 million is a frequently cited figure. German military deaths are also to a large extent unclear, but some 4.3 million Germans and a further 900,000 non-German Axis forces may have lost their lives either in combat or eventually in Soviet captivity.

Over a century prior, on June 24, 1812, Napoleon Bonaparte had also invaded Russia, with nearly half a million men under arms. He won a significant victory at Borodino and captured the Russian capital of Moscow but left Russian soil six months later, on December 14, with only 22,000 soldiers. The French emperor left nearly 98 percent of his army behind—dead or captured; some 200,000 Russians probably died during the campaign as well. The Russian victory over the French army in 1812 marked a huge blow to Napoleon's ambitions of European dominance. The war on his eastern front was one of the major reasons that the other coalition partner-nations arrayed against him eventually triumphed over Napoleon. His army had been shattered in Russia; morale was low, and the myth of his invincibility had been irrevocably broken. Though it did not mark the end of his long string of victories, the Russian campaign put an end to his reputation as an undefeatable military genius.

In the Second World War case, Hitler had previously attacked into Poland and then into Western Europe to stun and defeat his British and French opponents on his western flank before turning his attention to his primary objective—which was the control of the vast farmlands of the Russian Ukraine and the oil-rich regions near the Black Sea. His judgment called for isolating Russia before destroying its army and controlling its territory. In the French case, Napoleon had another conflict against Britain, Spain, and Portugal ongoing in Spain—which had begun in 1808 and had spawned one of the industrial world's first significant guerrilla wars—but he turned on Russia to compel Czar Alexander I to remain in the French-led continental blockade of the United Kingdom. Russia had reopened trade with Britain that very year.

These are only two of many examples in which major powers, faced with threats from multiple fronts, decided to wage war simultaneously in widely separated theaters in order to accomplish national strategic objectives—that is, of nations that decided to fight two-front wars.[6] Hitler's political objective was the increase of fertile territory needed for the expanding German state; Napoleon had the political goal of knocking Britain out of the war to consolidate Europe within the French Empire. Many nations have made strategically risky choices on multiple fronts in order to accomplish their security objectives. The

Athenians embarked on a Sicilian campaign in 415 BC and changed the dynam-
ics of the Peloponnesian War in ways that favored their opponent, Sparta. The
Romans made similar choices on several occasions, as did the Byzantines, the
Ottomans, the Holy Roman Empire, and the early modern French.

In modern times, during World War I, Germany fought a two-front war
against French, British, Belgian, and American forces on the western front
while simultaneously fighting the Russians on the eastern front, until the Bol-
shevik Revolution of 1917 took Russia out of the war. Given that precedent,
many wonder why Hitler embarked so willingly on a similar strategy in 1941.
During the Second World War the United States too fought a two-front war,
splitting its forces between the European theater, against Nazi Germany, and
the Pacific theater, against Japan. More recently the Israelis have fought several
wars on both their eastern and western borders.

The key question remains: Why would any nation, let alone one that un-
derstands the horrific lesson of the historical precedents and the obvious difficulty of conducting more than one geographically separated major combat
operation simultaneously, actually elect to fight on two fronts at the same
time? Most specifically, given the clear risks, why did the United States in the
first years of the twenty-first century enter into two simultaneous major campaigns in countries so far from its shores—countries that each posed significant threats but were in no way allied with one another? The threats posed by
Afghanistan and Iraq in 2001 were broadly different and certainly could never
have been considered codependent (which might have provided a rational for
near-simultaneous attacks).

The primary explanation offered for the decision to wage war on two
fronts remains the misconception that the fighting in Afghanistan had entered
its last stages and the conviction that the threats posed by Saddam Hussein's
Iraq could not be endured until the level of security in Kabul and other key
areas in Afghanistan was sufficient to permit the redeployment of international
forces. Some have offered the view that the rapid unconventional success enjoyed by the United States in Afghanistan, combined with its hubristic assessment that American forces had been able to decisively defeat the Taliban in a
matter of months, led key American decision makers to believe that Saddam
could be decisively defeated in a similarly short time frame, freeing up the U.S.
military for subsequent combat operations in other nations threatening the
United States (Libya, Syria, and perhaps even Iran).

"As I went back through the Pentagon in November 2001, one of the senior military staff officers had time for a chat. Yes, we were still on track for going against Iraq, he said. But there was more. This was being discussed as part of a five-year campaign plan, he said, and there were a total of seven countries, beginning with Iraq, then Syria, Lebanon, Libya, Iran, Somalia, and Sudan. I left the Pentagon that afternoon deeply concerned," notes retired army general Wesley Clark.[7] Could the United States have imagined that its forces could conduct such operations without becoming involved in the aftermaths of ending regimes? Such a belief certainly flew in the face of most military theorists who valued Clausewitzian ideas about waging war.

American Warfighting

The American way of war tends to shy away from thinking about the complicated process of turning military triumphs—whether on the scale of major campaigns or small-unit actions—into strategic successes. In part, this tendency stems from a systemic bifurcation in American strategic thinking—though by no means unique to Americans—in which military professionals prefer to concentrate on winning battles and campaigns, while policymakers elect to focus on prevailing in the diplomatic struggles that precede and influence, or are affected by, the actual fighting.

—Antulio J. Echevarria II[8]

The events of September 11, 2001, caused much significant change in the United States. Those events certainly demonstrated the impact of globalization and the linked character of modern society, and they forever ended the complacent notion that the United States was safe behind the broad oceans that form its eastern and western borders. Most particularly for this book, however, the fateful attacks on that date abruptly altered the way America thinks about and acts during war. The focus of this analysis is the Enduring Freedom military campaign in Afghanistan, which was both a direct retort to the attacks on 9/11 and part of a larger, less well-defined war against terrorism in general.

This is a book about the way America makes war, how the American military fights and wins battles, and how the entire U.S. government is supposed to outline objectives and frame the circumstances of war to focus all elements of national power toward accomplishing the conditions for victory. The United

States was born in war, and though Americans profess to love peace, it has as a nation now conducted a broad range of wars for a variety of objectives, not always simply for peace. Despite romantic notions to the contrary, America has not always fought for ideal ends or for the most altruistic objectives.[9] Most academic thinking about American warfighting is focused on the Russell Weigley thesis, which places a high priority on fighting with significant force only when vital national interests are at stake, defining clear political objectives, and ensuring that the military is resourced and empowered to employ overwhelming force in conventional combat.[10]

There was a period of maturation in the 1980s in American strategic circles, driven largely by the failures in Vietnam, which led some to reform strategic thinking and place greater emphasis on the coherence and acceptability of strategic options. "After years of self-examination in the wake of Vietnam, U.S. strategic thinking finally reached the conclusion that winning a war really amounts to accomplishing one's strategic objectives."[11] Thus, the Pentagon and the National Security Council began to place greater emphasis on identifying the real goals of military operations. Certainly Operation Just Cause in Panama and Operation Uphold Democracy in Haiti were examples of strong efforts to clearly define national strategic objectives, even in murky circumstances. American efforts in Bosnia followed suit, in an even more complex environment. Perhaps most rational was the decision to minimize the American role in support of a regional partner in the 1999 Operation Stabilise in East Timor.[12]

In 2001, Afghanistan presented the United States with a number of dilemmas. First of all, the fundamental question of national interests in Afghanistan was complex. There is no doubt that two successive American presidents (George W. Bush and Barack Obama) clearly told the American people that fighting in Afghanistan was in the interests of the United States. President Obama said so again on December 1, 2009: "I have determined that it is in our vital national interest to send an additional 30,000 U.S. troops to Afghanistan." In June 2010, Obama recommitted himself to that view publicly, saying, "And what I said last year I will repeat, which is we have a vital national interest in making sure that Afghanistan is not used as a base to launch terrorist attacks."[13] The real issue, however, was not whether protecting America from attack was a vital national interest but whether making Afghanistan a stronger nation (to prevent its use as a launch pad for attacks) was in the interests of the United States. Afghanistan had proven quite immune from international influence throughout its history.

Though complex, those Afghan issues might have been reconcilable had solving them been the only, or even the primary, strategic effort of the United States. Unfortunately, almost from the outset the leaders of the United States began to intermingle the challenging issues presented by terrorists in Afghanistan possessing global reach with the ongoing and nearly intractable problems that America still had with the leader of Iraq, Saddam Hussein. Because the problems became linked, the United States eventually embarked on two near-simultaneous military campaigns[14] designed to fix all the issues in both places at about the same time. America had waged dual campaigns in the past, but choosing to fight two enemies simultaneously was a decision that should have been taken only under the most dire of circumstances.

Two-Front Campaigning in American History

In the ancient world, major campaigns were most commonly fought sequentially. This was largely due to the need of the sovereign, who was frequently also the military leader, to maintain close control over the military forces that were employed on campaign, and partly simply because of the expense and difficulty of coordinating major battles fought out of visual communications range. Over time, commanders developed greater capacities. Some believe the Mongols conducted parallel campaigns in the thirteenth century.[15] Certainly by 1809, Napoleon had changed this historical tendency; his campaign against the Austrians in that year is viewed by some as the first modern war precisely because it included "broad operational fronts in which battles became both sequential and simultaneous" among other innovations.[16]

Americans have had long experience with dual campaigns. The American Revolution took place mostly in the northern colonies until the British understood they might possibly split the weak confederation and, in 1778, invaded the south, eventually to capture Charleston in the spring of 1780.[17] Thus the leaders of the new nation were confronted by the pressure that comes from enemy attacks from two fronts. General George Washington and the leaders of the Continental Congress were forced to divide their meager forces and send new leadership (in the form of General Nathanial Greene) to blunt the British success in the south. Surprisingly, the following year, Washington decided to take advantage of the British southern campaign, turning his attention for the first time from the key cities in the northern colonies and eventually defeating General Lord Cornwallis in the small Virginia port town of York in October 1781. That victory turned the tide of the war.

American leaders also experienced the negative impacts of two simultaneous campaigns in the later stages of the War of 1812, when the British attacked
both Washington and the important port city of New Orleans. Beginning
in March 1813, a British squadron under Rear Admiral George Cockburn
blockaded the Chesapeake Bay and raided towns from Virginia to Maryland in
advance of a march on the American capital, which they took in August 1814.
That same month the British set up a base in Pensacola, Florida, with designs
on the mouth of the Mississippi River. Later in the fall, some eight thousand
British regulars under General Edward Pakenham moved on New Orleans,
which they attacked on January 8 (famously after peace negotiations begun in
early August in Ghent had concluded on December 24, when a final agreement had signed, officially ending the war).

During the American Civil War the early strategy of the North called for
an anaconda-like effort to encircle the poorer, agrarian South. This resulted
quite directly in two major campaigns in separate sections of the country: a
Virginia-focused eastern theater of war, and Mississippi-focused western theaters of war. In perhaps both the best-timed and most accidental simultaneous culmination of effort in U.S. history, the armies of General Ulysses Grant
at Vicksburg in the West and General George Meade at Gettysburg in the
East both defeated their Confederate opponents in the same week in 1863—
sounding the death knell for the Southern cause.

America tried its hand at simultaneous campaigns in very distant theaters
of war during the Spanish American War, when it sent expeditionary forces to
both Cuba and the Philippines in 1898. Admiral George Dewey attacked the
Spanish in Manila Bay only a week after the declaration of war and the U.S.
Army Corps landed near Santiago, Cuba, in the third week of June. In support,
two squadrons of the U.S. Navy, under Rear Admiral William T. Sampson and
Commodore Winfield Scott Schley, respectively, won the battle of Santiago de
Cuba on July 3, destroying the Spanish Caribbean Squadron. Peace came only
a month later.

Most famously, perhaps, the Second World War global strategy called for
attacking and defeating the European Axis powers first, followed later by an
effort to defeat their Japanese allies. Technically, the Pacific campaign actually
preceded, in terms of time, the European combat campaigns, due to the perceived need by the United States to maintain bases and contact with allies in
key areas within the Pacific. To do so, even before America could deploy forces

to Europe, the Pacific Fleet began a series of operations designed to blunt the Japanese advance and keep sea lines of communication open to Australia. Thus by April 1942 the United States and its allies were already fighting a multiple-theater war. "To its credit, the U.S. Navy, drawing from its experience in World War I and anticipating the possibility of a protracted two-ocean war, seriously considered the planning challenges inherent in conducting multidimensional operations over time and across large expanses"[18] and executed such operations extremely well, even under very adverse circumstances in the early months of the war.

By 1944 major sequential naval campaigns commanded by Admiral Chester Nimitz designed to seize advanced bases across the Central Pacific had been timed and sequenced with those of General Douglas MacArthur's Southwest Pacific theater for mutual support in the huge and complex battle for the Philippines. Later they would be coordinated with the aerial campaign conducted by General Curtis LeMay and his XIII Air Force to increase the pressure on Japan in advance of the use of the atomic bomb.

In 1950, as a well rehearsed veteran, General MacArthur conducted simultaneous campaigns on both the western and eastern coasts of Korea, but they were so close geographically that they were clearly mutually supporting. Thereafter, the skill developed in the Second World War seemed to atrophy, and few well-coordinated major campaigns were conducted in the latter half of the twentieth century by American commanders.

So the United States in 2001 was no stranger to the demands of fighting on two widely separated fronts. America had experienced both the benefits and the negative effects of such strategies throughout its history. One can assume then that the key constraints and demands of conducting such difficult military approaches were available for consideration when the United States embarked on its first war in the twenty-first century. The location of that war, however, had its own dominating characteristics. Afghanistan was no easy place to fight and win.

Afghanistan and Modern War: The British Experience

The First Anglo-Afghan War began in 1837, when the British were firmly entrenched in India but fearful of a Russian invasion of India through the Khyber and Bolan Passes in Afghanistan. Russia, for its part, was clearly interested in eastward expansion (see map 1). The following eighty-year period became known as the "Great Game," wherein the British fought two costly wars—the first from 1838 to 1842 and the second from 1878 to 1880—each time attempting to impose their will upon Kabul to reduce the threat from Afghanistan to India. In the first war, the British sent an envoy to Kabul in an effort to form an Anglo-Afghan alliance with Afghanistan's ruling emir, Dost Muhammad, against Russia. Dost Muhammad in return asked for British help in recapturing Peshawar (which had been captured by the Sikhs a few years before). The British refused, and thus Dost Muhammad opened negotiations with the Russians, who had also extended offers to the Afghans. This led the British governor-general in India to fear the worst concerning a Russian invasion of India. The British plan was to install in Afghanistan a ruler who was pro-British (Shuja Shah Durrani) in place of Dost Muhammad.

An army of 21,000 British and Indian troops set out from India in December 1838. After four months the British forces had reached Quetta, through the Bolan Pass, and begun their march to Kabul. They took Kandahar on April 25, 1839. Then, on July 22, in a surprise attack, they captured the heretofore impregnable fortress of Ghazni, which controlled the eastward approach to the North West Frontier Province. Soon after, the British achieved a decisive victory over Dost Mohammad's troops, and he fled with most of his supporters.

The British left only eight thousand troops in Afghanistan, and it soon became clear that Shuja's government could be maintained only by additional British forces. The Afghans resented both the British and the government of Shah Shuja. As time dragged on, the Afghans grew increasingly hostile, as it appeared the British were setting up an occupation. Dost Mohammad returned and attacked the British and their Afghan proxy, but he fared no better this time; he surrendered and was exiled to India in late 1840.

By October 1841, the Afghan tribes were rallying to support Dost Mohammad; and his son, Mohammad Akbar Khan, was threatening the British militarily. By November Kabul was in revolt. The British tried to negotiate with Akbar Khan, while also trying to have him assassinated, but it was Akbar Khan who triumphed and the senior British civilian administrator who was killed in the streets.[19] On January 1, 1842, an agreement that provided for the safe extraction of the British garrison was reached, and days later the British began to withdraw. Their force originally numbered about 16,000 people, only about a quarter of which were military personnel (Indian units and one British battalion, the 44th Regiment of Foot), the remainder being civilian camp

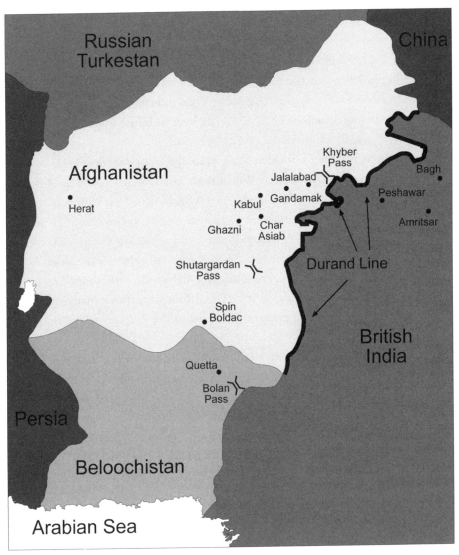

Southwest Asia and the Nineteenth Century Great Game

followers. The British were attacked as they struggled through the snowbound eastern mountain passes and were killed in huge numbers moving along the Kabul River toward Gandamak, where they were massacred. The men of the 44th Foot were all killed except Captain James Souter, Sergeant Fair, and seven soldiers who were taken prisoner.[20] Only one Briton reached Jalalabad. In August 1842, in reprisal, the British counterattacked from Kandahar, pillaged the countryside, seized Ghazni, and advanced back through the Khyber Pass from Jalalabad, eventually defeating Akbar Khan and taking Kabul in September. After having demolished part of the city, they withdrew from Afghanistan; Dost Muhammad restored his authority in Kabul.

In 1878 the British invaded again with about 40,000 men, beginning the Second Anglo-Afghan War.[21] With British forces occupying much of the country, the Afghan ruler, Mohammad Yaqub Khan, signed the Treaty of Gandamak in May 1879. In return for an annual subsidy and assistance in case of foreign aggression, Yaqub relinquished control of Afghan foreign affairs to Britain. British representatives were assigned in Kabul and other key locations, including the Khyber and Michni Passes, and Afghanistan ceded some frontier lands and the city of Quetta to Britain. The British army then started to withdraw, but not before an uprising in Kabul led to the slaughter of the British commander.

Major General Sir Frederick Roberts then led the British back over the Shutargardan Pass into central Afghanistan, where he defeated the Afghan army at Char Asiab on October 6, 1879, and occupied Kabul. Yaqub Khan was forced to abdicate, and the British installed his cousin Abdur Rahman Khan as emir in his place. The Afghan governor of Herat rose again in revolt but was decisively defeated by Roberts on September 1 at the battle of Kandahar, bringing the rebellion to an end. Abdur Rahman signed the Treaty of Gandamak, leaving the British in control of the territories ceded by Yaqub Khan and ensuring British control of Afghanistan's foreign policy and key locations. The British again withdrew.[22]

A third and final Anglo-Afghan War began on May 6, 1919. Its genesis was the assumption of power in Kabul in 1901 by the unreliable and unstable Afghan emir Habibullah Khan. During the First World War, he welcomed a Turkish-German mission in Kabul and sought military assistance from the Central Powers but resisted entreaties from the Ottomans to join against the Allies, attempting to play both sides to obtain the best deal. In 1919 he demanded a seat at Versailles Peace Conference. Habibullah was assassinated in February of that year, and Amanullah, his third son, proclaimed himself emir. Looking to consolidate his power, create a diversion from internal disagreements in Afghanistan, and take advantage of rising civil unrest in India following the Amritsar massacre of April 1919 in northwest India (now Pakistan), Amanullah decided to invade British India with some 50,000 men.

The British army in India, nominally eight divisions, was in poor readiness after the demands of the war in Western Europe, but in May, when Amanullah invaded through the Khyber Pass, he was soundly defeated at Bagh. The British counterattacked toward Kabul, another British command attacked into Afghanistan at Spin Boldac, and Royal Air Force (RAF) bombers attacked Kabul. The war ended with yet another negotiated settlement on August 19, 1919, largely because the British were still preoccupied by the western front in Europe.[23] The British certainly enjoyed tactical successes in the war; however, their troops suffered almost double the amount of casualties of the Afghans, so Amanullah could also claim a victory, and he at least achieved his objectives for the conflict. Though the British were able to get the Afghan government to confirm the Durand Line, established in 1893, as the political boundary between Afghanistan and British India, the Afghans were permitted to abrogate the Treaty of Gandamak and conduct their own foreign affairs as a fully independent state.

One could draw the lesson that the British had accomplished little of what they had identified as the political objectives of their wars in Afghanistan. Although each time they seemed to repulse perceived threats aimed at India, they were repeatedly bloodied and never gained any real control over Afghan affairs (though control outside Kabul often proved tenuous even for many Afghan rulers). One could easily observe that the British "had no exit strategy, and they couldn't sustain their occupation. Countrywide uprisings kept them under ongoing siege"[24] whenever Afghanistan was invaded, which created severe problems.

The United States, in the twenty-first century, had more than the lessons of British history from which to learn about potential war in Afghanistan. It had itself played a key supporting role in a more recent campaign, one that gave the American leadership primary experience with the geography, tribal attitudes, and regional politics of war in Afghanistan.

America's First Experience with an Afghan Campaign:
Helping the Soviets Lose

Though its official start date will likely be debated for years, there can be no doubt that the first American experiences in Afghanistan began not in the twenty-first century but rather in the late 1970s, when the administration of President Jimmy Carter first began to seriously study the possibilities of instability in that region in the context of the Cold War between the United States and the Soviet Union.[25] The relationship between the United States and Afghanistan had never been particularly warm but it took a decisive turn for the worse in February 1979, when the U.S. ambassador in Kabul, Adolph Dubs, was killed in a botched Afghan raid to rescue kidnap victims.[26] The then leader of Afghanistan, Nur Mohammed Taraki, was the leader of the Khalq, a faction within the People's Democratic Party of Afghanistan (PDPA), the Afghan communist party; he had helped overthrow his predecessor, President Mohammed Daoud Khan,[27] in a coup on April 27, 1978. The Taraki government initiated a series of reforms, including modernization of the traditional Islamic civil law, but responded violently to any opposition by the people. Thousands of prisoners were executed, including many village elders and mullahs. Other members of the traditional elite, the religious establishment, and intelligentsia fled the country.[28] Large parts of Afghanistan exploded in rebellion.

Soviet involvement in Afghanistan had begun during the previous century, when, as described above, Russia and Britain were jockeying for influence there. Interest in Afghanistan continued during the Soviet era; Moscow sent billions in economic and military aid to Afghanistan between 1955 and 1978.[29] The Afghan government, having secured a treaty in December 1978 that allowed it to call on Soviet forces, repeatedly requested the introduction of troops in Afghanistan in the spring and summer of 1979 to provide security and to assist in the fight against rebels, known as the *mujahedeen*. Several prominent Soviet politicians, including Alexei Kosygin and Andrei Gromyko, were against any military intervention in Afghanistan, but their recommendations went unheeded.[30]

Eventually the Afghan requests were for regiments and larger units. In July 1979, the Afghan government requested that two motorized rifle divisions be sent to Afghanistan. That same month President Carter authorized American support for the anticommunist guerrillas in Afghanistan, support that would later include arming the Afghan mujahedeen.[31] In September, Deputy Prime

Minister Hafizullah Amin seized power in Kabul, after fighting in the Afghan palace that resulted in the death of President Taraki. For the next two months the Afghan government fell apart as Amin moved against opposition in the PDPA and the rebellion continued to grow all around the country. This chaos eventually resulted in the initial Soviet army deployment into Afghanistan, with Amin's assistance, on December 24, 1979.

The Soviets entered Afghanistan in a two-axis attack supported by air-power and quickly occupied the major urban centers, military bases, and strategic installations in the center of the country. Even so, the Soviet troops had no significant dampening effect on the rebellion. In fact the Soviet invasion, like so many that had preceded it, seemed on the contrary to excite even greater nationalistic feeling and to cause the rebellion to grow.[32] Instead of rapidly establishing a blanket of control as they had been able to do against uprisings in Europe, and though they controlled the main communications routes, the Soviets soon faced a guerrilla war, as the mujahedeen divided into small groups. Almost 80 percent of the country escaped government control; the Soviets could dominate only a few strategic locations.[33]

The Soviet army undertook multidivisional offensives into mujahedeen-controlled areas. For example, between 1980 and 1985 nine offensives were launched into the strategically important Panjshir Valley, but Afghan government control of the area still did not improve.[34] The cities of Herat and Kandahar were always at least partially controlled by the mujahedeen.[35] The Soviets originally envisioned that they would strengthen the Afghan army and provide assistance by securing a few major cities and maintaining the lines of communication around the country, freeing the Afghan army to put down the rebellion, but that never transpired.[36] Hoping to deprive the mujahedeen of resources and safe havens, the Soviets used massive force in response to Afghan guerrilla attacks, destroying villages that they perceived as having given aid to the mujahedeen and forcing local Afghans to flee their homes or die, making it impossible to live in contested areas. They also created an Afghan secret police, the Khadamat-e Etela'at-e Dawlati (KHAD), which was designed both to gather information and infiltrate the opposition.

Despite heavy losses, the mujahedeen were able to resist the Soviets and their Afghan army allies. The mujahedeen was "born in chaos, spread and triumphed chaotically, and has not found a way to govern differently."[37] Combat between the Soviets and the mujahedeen was almost always a local affair, and even after outside support added more sophisticated weapons and a degree of regional coordination made larger battles possible, the basic mujahedeen approach to war was highly factional, episodic, and ephemeral. Olivier Roy estimates that after four years of war there were at least four thousand bases from which mujahedeen units operated.[38] Most of these were affiliated with seven expatriate parties headquartered in Pakistan that served as sources of supply and exercised varying degrees of supervision. Mujahedeen commanders typically led groups of three hundred or so men, may have controlled a few bases of supply, and frequently dominated the activities within districts or subdivisions of provinces. They received aid not only from the United States but also gained large numbers of recruits from sympathetic Muslims around the world, including so-called Afghan Arabs, foreign fighters who were drawn to wage jihad against the communists. Osama bin Laden, a Saudi national, became prominent among them, and many of his followers formed the initial core group of the Al-Qaeda terrorist organization.

The operations of the mujahedeen varied greatly in scope, the most ambitious being achieved by Ahmad Shah Massoud in the Panjshir Valley, north of Kabul. He led at least ten thousand trained troops by the end of the war and even expanded his control from his own Tajik-dominated areas to bring Afghanistan's northeastern provinces under a "Supervisory Council of the North" formed in 1984. Afghan fighters took great pride in their struggle against an overwhelmingly powerful foe, and they did surprising well against the Soviets, year after year.

A 1985 Central Intelligence Agency (CIA) assessment noted that year that the Soviets "have had little success in reducing the insurgency or in winning acceptance by the Afghan people, and the Afghan resistance continues to grow stronger and command widespread popular support."[39] In part, the success of the resistance was due to material support from the United States and other nations. The United States had begun training insurgents and directing propaganda broadcasts into Afghanistan from Pakistan in 1978.[40] In 1981, following the election of President Ronald Reagan, aid for the mujahedeen through Pakistan significantly increased, mostly due to the efforts of Texas congressman Charlie Wilson.[41] In its support of the anti-Soviet opposition the United States was assisted by the United Kingdom, Pakistan, and Saudi Arabia, among others. The United States donated over $600 million[42] in aid every year, with similar amounts coming from the Saudis. The People's Republic of China also sold tanks, assault rifles, rocket-propelled grenades (RPGs), and much more to mujahedeen, in cooperation with the CIA, as did Egypt. Most notably, the CIA provided the mujahedeen Stinger antiaircraft missile systems, which forced notable changes on Soviet tactics due to the importance the Soviets had placed upon heliborne transport in the challenging Afghan terrain.

By 1985 the Soviets had over 108,000 troops in Afghanistan and had accomplished little; the fighting only continued to escalate. In fact 1985 was the bloodiest year of the war for the Soviet Union. That same year, in March, Mikhail Gorbachev came to power in the Soviet Union. "Minimizing his country's involvement in Afghanistan topped his to-do list. Gorbachev had become increasingly impatient with the counterinsurgency against the stubborn U.S.- and Pakistan-backed mujahedeen, which was costing the nearly bankrupt Soviet Union an estimated $2 billion to $3 billion a year. He was prepared to finally and decisively change course."[43] From 1985 to 1987 the Soviet military in Afghanistan focused on the buildup of the Afghan forces and transitioned the Afghans ever more into the lead positions against the mujahedeen—without much success.

In November 1986, Mohammad Najibullah, former chief of the KHAD, was elected president and adopted a new constitution for Afghanistan, but the tide of the war was already turning against him. By mid-1987, when the Soviet Union announced that it would start withdrawing its forces, the mujahedeen was fighting successfully against the Afghan army and their Soviet backers, and its political arm, the Interim Islamic State of Afghanistan, was asserting its legitimacy in the countryside in opposition to the Soviet-sponsored regime of Najibullah. The head of the Interim Afghan Government, Sibghatullah Mojaddedi, even traveled to Washington to meet with the vice president, George H. W. Bush, in the Oval Office.

For the mujahedeen, defeat of the Kabul government was the only solution that could produce peace. Emboldened and sustained by international support, lauded in the world press, and extremely distrustful of negotiations, they had little interest in any form of political compromise and were more than willing to wait out the departure of the Soviet army. The first half of the Soviet contingent was withdrawn from May to August 1988 and the second half from November to February 1989. In order to ensure safe passage the Soviets had even negotiated local cease-fires with mujahedeen commanders, and the withdrawal was generally executed peacefully.[44] The Soviets had lost some 13,000 dead, over 35,000 wounded, and many more stricken by disease; it had also lost over 300 helicopters and some 13,000 vehicles.[45] Objectively, the Soviet Union left Afghanistan in a "coordinated, deliberate, professional manner. . . . The withdrawal was based on a coordinated diplomatic, economic, and military plan, permitting Soviet forces to withdraw in good order and the Afghan government to survive."[46]

Though it "left behind a semi-stable regime, an improved military, and a commitment to a long-term relationship,"[47] the Soviet experience in Afghanistan ended in defeat in the eyes of the world and for some hastened the demise of the Soviet Union itself.[48] Clearly, the Soviet leadership had underestimated the challenges in Afghanistan and not heeded warnings that they should have drawn from the British involvement there over the previous century—lessons of a history their Russian predecessors had helped to make. Afghanistan had proven again to a world power that its terrain was easily to defend and difficult if not impossible to control. The Afghans had shown themselves to be tenacious, divided, but usually locally dominant and almost completely unwilling to compromise their values. With outside support they had humbled a better army and had only grown stronger as the fighting wore on.

As clear as the Soviet defeat was, the myth that Afghanistan was a "graveyard of empires" can be disproved by a wider study of history.[49] Historian Victor Davis Hansen, among others, has argued that although even the ancient Greeks had difficulty subjugating the Afghans, Alexander the Great and his successors did dominate the region for nearly two centuries.[50] And they did so using a relatively small number of forces.[51] Unfortunately, the insights that could have been gained from the ancient Greek experience have largely been lost to history, but the lessons to be learned from the Soviet experience in Afghanistan should have been clear to the Americans who followed them into conflict there.

The United States was a willing participant in the war, fully cognizant of the capabilities of the Afghan resistance and the powerful influences of outside funding and a nearby sanctuary in Pakistan. The CIA and the U.S. Army both did studies of the lessons to be drawn from the Soviet War in Afghanistan, and both studies emphasized the significant negative impacts of political limitations on force size, pressure to minimize personnel and equipment losses, the primitive nature of Afghan infrastructure, and the lack of national Afghan governance capacity as key factors leading to the defeat of a powerful conventional military force. [52] Even so, those same vulnerabilities continued to exact their toll in 2001 when the United States embarked on its own war in Afghanistan.

Even with the paradigm-changing 9/11 attacks, the United States had more than sufficient historical understanding of the complexity of fighting wars against two geographically separate enemies simultaneously to have known that it could make such a decision with only the greatest care. The successful Second World War precedent notwithstanding, American leaders—particularly those who had the recent Soviet experiences in Afghanistan well in mind—should have been reluctant to wage a war against Iraq while the combat operations in Afghanistan had yet to be resolved. As a more detailed analysis in later chapters will reveal, the difficulties and complexities resulting from the decision to invade Iraq before conflict had been terminated in Afghanistan would have lasting and important negative effects on the most powerful nation on earth.

Two

The Attacks of 9/11 and the Decision to Go to War in Afghanistan
A Historical Perspective

The attacks of September 11, 2001, were a shock to the nation but were not the first salvo in what President George W. Bush would eventually label the "War on Terrorism." While the specific nature of the attacks, the use of commercial aircraft, and the prominence of the targets surprised the senior leaders of the United States, many officials had been anticipating some sort of attack on U.S. facilities, most likely overseas, for some time. In reality, the September 2001 decision to go to war in Afghanistan was a natural progression in a series of events that had played out over five years.

The 9/11 attacks were the culmination of a long string of Al-Qaeda attacks on the United States and its allies. In 1996, terrorists had attacked the Khobar Towers, a U.S. Air Force residential complex in Saudi Arabia. Although the subsequent investigation concluded that a Saudi-based terrorist organization, Hezbollah al-Hejaz, with support from the Iranian government, had planned and executed the Khobar Towers attack, some have concluded that Al-Qaeda played a much more significant role. In fact, the 9/11 Commission cites CIA and Defense Intelligence Agency (DIA) analytic reports stating that Osama bin Laden may have been involved in the Khobar Towers plot.[1] William Perry, the secretary of defense when the attack occurred in 1996, said in 2007, "I believe that the Khobar Tower bombing was probably masterminded by Osama bin Laden. I can't be sure of that, but in retrospect, that's what I believe. At the time, he was not a suspect. At the time . . . all of the evidence was pointing to Iran."[2]

On the morning of August 7, 1998, near-simultaneous attacks occurred at the U.S. embassies in Dar es Salaam, in Tanzania, and Nairobi, in Kenya.

The Nairobi bomb blast was spectacular, resulting in more than 200 killed and reports of up to 4,000 injured. In Tanzania, the attack resulted in 11 dead and 85 wounded. While the attacks were ostensibly aimed at U.S. citizens and facilities, only 12 of the nearly 225 deaths were American.[3] In November, 1998 Osama bin Laden was indicted in a U.S. federal court for his role in those embassy bombings.[4] Through the 1990s, the activities of bin Laden and Al-Qaeda were becoming increasingly clear to the U.S. intelligence community.

Initial Salvos, Operation Infinite Reach, and a "Declaration of War"

Following the Khobar Tower bombings, the U.S. government took a much closer look at terrorism. The William Clinton administration began a review of policies, authorities, and directives that culminated in Presidential Decision Directive 62 (PDD 62), "Protection Against Unconventional Threat to the Homeland and Americans Overseas," signed by President Clinton in May 1998.[5] The Joint House-Senate Inquiry lists ten specific responsibilities mandated in the PDD, none of which were offensive or strike capabilities (counterterrorism), and only one of which was tasked to the Department of Defense: protection of Americans overseas (jointly with Department of State).[6] Although PDD 62 laid out a much more comprehensive and integrated approach to terrorism than had previously existed, it did not provide guidance for retaliatory strike planning, offensive preemptive strike planning, or military counterterrorism operations. Less than three months after PDD 62 was approved, Al-Qaeda attacked the U.S. embassies in Tanzania and Kenya, and the shortcomings of PDD 62 became evident to the administration.

In response to the attacks in Africa, President Clinton directed the National Security Council (NSC) and Department of Defense to consider military responses. Based on analysis from the intelligence community that clearly linked Osama bin Laden to the Nairobi and Dar es Salaam attacks and on further intelligence indicating that bin Laden and his top subordinates would be meeting at a specific location in Afghanistan, President Clinton authorized interagency planning for strikes against bin Laden. The operation was code-named Infinite Reach.

On August 20, 1998, the United States launched seventy-nine BGM-109 Tomahawk land-attack missiles (TLAMs) at targets in Afghanistan and Sudan.

The planning for the missile strikes had been detailed and had considered the risks associated with flying missiles through Pakistani airspace at a time when tensions between Pakistan and India were as high as ever. There was considerable concern about alerting the Pakistanis in advance, as credible intelligence linked the Pakistani Interservices Intelligence (ISI) directorate with Al-Qaeda. To preclude the need for notifying the Pakistanis in advance but also to be able to immediately intervene if the Pakistanis detected the missiles and assumed they represented an attack from India, the U.S. vice chairman of the Joint Chiefs of Staff, Air Force general Joe Ralston, arranged to have dinner in Islamabad with General Jehangir Karamat, the Pakistani Chief of Army Staff. If any missiles were detected by the Pakistanis, General Ralston would explain the situation to Karamat and allay any fears of Indian aggression. The Pakistanis did not detect the missiles, flying at almost rooftop levels, and Ralston departed Islamabad as the TLAMs were striking their targets in Afghanistan.[7] While the missiles hit their programmed targets, neither bin Laden nor any senior Al-Qaeda leaders were killed. Nonetheless, the first American salvos had been fired against Al-Qaeda.

Although bin Laden had been explicit in his statements about being at war with the West, President Clinton never declared war on Al-Qaeda, bin Laden, or terrorism. Clinton did, however, make clear that the United States was in a protracted struggle with terrorists. Following the retaliatory strikes in August 1998, President Clinton stated, "A few months ago, and again this week, bin Laden publicly vowed to wage a terrorist war against America." In his radio address on August 22 the president said, "Our efforts against terrorism cannot and will not end with this strike. We should have realistic expectations about what a single action can achieve, and we must be prepared for a long battle." While not placing the United States on a war footing, the Clinton administration was setting the stage for what would later be referred to as "the long war."

According to the joint inquiry following Al-Qaeda's successful embassy bombings, Director of Central Intelligence George Tenet made combating terrorism one of the intelligence community's highest priorities. He increased its emphasis and profile in December 1998 when he circulated a memorandum to senior CIA managers stating, "We must now enter a new phase in our effort against Bin Laden. . . . *We are at war.* . . . I want no resources or people spared in this effort, either inside [the] CIA or the Community."[8]

By the end of 1998, only one agency of the United States was "at war" with Al-Qaeda, and that one agency was underresourced, overstretched, and tasked with other, competing top-tier priorities. Despite the bold statement by Tenet, in December 2002 the joint inquiry would find "that the intelligence community as a whole was not on a war footing before September 11."[9]

Al-Qaeda Ups the Ante

On October 12, 2000, suicide attackers in a small boat made a charge at the U.S. Navy guided-missile destroyer USS *Cole* in the port of Aden, Yemen, ramming the ship amidships. What was speculated to be a shaped-charge warhead connected to a large container of explosives ripped a forty-foot hole at the waterline in the side of the warship. Seventeen American sailors were killed, and thirty-nine were wounded. No speculation surrounded the identity of the attackers—Al-Qaeda quickly claimed responsibility. Bin Laden had been directly involved in the attack's planning, target selection, and financing.[10]

Bin Laden, by now operating in Afghanistan, anticipated—in fact, was hoping for—an American military response. He took precautionary steps to evacuate his training camps in eastern and southern Afghanistan and dispersed his top leadership team in order to minimize the effects of any strikes. To bin Laden's surprise, no U.S. retaliation took place.[11] The Clinton White House, already preparing to turn over to a new administration in a few months, sought both direct evidence of bin Laden's involvement and, more importantly, credible, actionable intelligence regarding bin Laden's location.

"Actionable" intelligence is a high threshold to meet. Having missed bin Laden in the 1998 TLAM strikes, the White House did not want to risk the embarrassment, cost, and frustration of another missile strike that did not result in the death of the terrorist leader. If the United States missed again, or repeatedly, the failures of the world's lone superpower would become a major recruiting tool for Al-Qaeda and boost bin Laden's stature. Besides, most of the credible reporting of bin Laden's whereabouts was hours old at best, making targeting by missiles with a flight time, from offshore and across Pakistan, of ninety minutes or more problematic. In Afghanistan, bin Laden—who for various reasons wanted the United States to attack him—complained about the U.S. failure to retaliate. According to an intelligence source, bin Laden made it clear that if the United States did not attack Al-Qaeda, he would launch an even more spectacular attack.[12]

Despite the lack of actionable intelligence, it was becoming increasingly clear to the intelligence community that Al-Qaeda had mounted the *Cole* attack. President Clinton's frustration, coupled with the increasing intelligence warnings, prompted National Security Adviser Sandy Berger to ask General Hugh Shelton, the Chairman of the Joint Chiefs of Staff, to update and revise any military plans for action against bin Laden and Al-Qaeda. General Shelton had anticipated such a request since Operation Infinite Reach, executed after the 1998 embassy bombings, had failed to kill bin Laden. In fact on August 20, 1998, the day the missile strikes were launched into Afghanistan and Sudan, General Shelton issued a planning order (PLANORD) to the Joint Staff for follow-on strikes. These follow-on plans were revised, expanded, and updated throughout 1998 and 1999 and were eventually code-named Operation Infinite Resolve.[13]

Ultimately the Infinite Resolve plans would include up to fourteen options—various combinations of direct action, strike aircraft, B-2 bombers, missile strikes, covert activity, and diplomatic pressure. Later, U.S. Central Command, by then under the command of General Tommy Franks, added a broader, phased campaign of indefinite duration that included strikes against the Taliban.[14] General Shelton later considered whether more could have been done in the months after the *Cole* attack and before 9/11:

> Pundits contend that we could have done more to capture bin Laden, but was that the case? Were opportunities missed? Did we drop the ball? We had fourteen UBL [Usama bin Laden] capture-or-kill-op plans on the shelf—specific, detailed, fleshed-out, preorchestrated scenarios, ranging anywhere from forces on the ground to armed Predator strikes, to TLAMs—each ready to be executed instantly once we received actionable intelligence that confirmed his whereabouts—and we revised these plans at least once a month.[15]

Despite the detailed planning, no action was taken throughout the remainder of the Clinton administration in response to the *Cole* attacks. Bin Laden's frustration at the lack of U.S. response was growing.

A Diplomatic Approach

While the Joint Staff continued to flesh out military options and the CIA waged Tenet's "war" with limited resources and authorities, the United States began to apply diplomatic pressure to Pakistan and to Afghanistan's Taliban leaders.

The U.S. Permanent Representative to the United Nations, Bill Richardson, made a high-profile trip to Afghanistan in early 1998. Accompanied by Assistant Secretary of State Rick Inderfurth, U.S. Ambassador to Pakistan Tom Simons, and several CIA officers, Richardson met for nearly an hour with the Taliban second-in-command Mullah Rabbani. Richardson pressed Rabbani to turn over bin Laden, but the Taliban would not agree to do so, denying that bin Laden was subservient to the Taliban and claiming that he posed no threat to the United States. In the end, the Taliban walked away with increased legitimacy, having hosted diplomatic talks with arguably the second-highest-ranking diplomat in the Clinton administration.[16]

A year later, in a memo to Secretary of State Madeleine Albright entitled "Pushing for Peace in Afghanistan," Inderfurth lamented, "At the end of the day, we may have to consider the Taliban to be an intrinsic enemy of the U.S. and a new international pariah state. . . . But we could begin to take the steps toward recognition if—and only if—the Taliban takes the steps: getting rid of bin Laden and the terrorist networks; beginning real efforts against the cultivation, processing, and trafficking of illicit narcotics; and improving its respect for human rights in general and treatment of women and girls in particular."[17] Richardson had long since departed the UN ambassadorship, having been replaced by Richard Holbrooke, who in 2010, as President Barack Obama's Special Representative for Afghanistan and Pakistan, would still be dealing with the Taliban, narcotics, and major human rights issues in Afghanistan.

In December 1999 the Department of State again warned the Taliban that it would be held accountable for any future Al-Qaeda attacks. Similarly, General Anthony Zinni, Franks's predecessor as commander of U.S. Central Command, urged General Pervez Musharraf, head of Pakistan's military government, to take strong action against bin Laden. The Clinton administration even went so far as arranging a presidential visit to Pakistan in March 2000—a visit highly desired by Musharraf. Clinton's one-day stopover after a trip to India was the first visit by a U.S. president to Pakistan since 1969. Clinton pressed Musharraf for action against bin Laden and the Taliban and received vague assurances, along with a promise by Musharraf to visit Afghanistan. The United States kept up high-level diplomatic pressure through the summer and into the fall of 2000. Calls to Musharraf from the president and visits by Undersecretary of State Thomas Pickering and the director of Central Intelligence in June failed to move the Pakistanis or influence the Taliban.[18] Almost as a measure of last resort, the United States pushed through United Nations Security Council

Resolution (UNSCR) 1333, renewing the demand for bin Laden's expulsion from Afghanistan and forbidding any nation from providing the Taliban with arms or military assistance. UNSCR 1333 marked the fifth Security Council resolution in three years regarding Afghanistan, the Taliban, and their support for bin Laden and terrorist organizations.

The Taliban simply ignored the warnings, Musharraf was not willing to take a political gamble in Pakistan, and Washington was becoming preoccupied with the upcoming transition to a new president.

A New Team Arrives

The presidential campaign of George W. Bush in 2000 had focused principally on domestic issues. A Bush campaign brochure from 2000 listed six main focus areas: education and schools, Social Security reform, access to health care, rebuilding the military (which Bush described as reliant on aging weapons and failed intelligence), a responsible economic agenda, and across-the-board tax relief—no mention of terrorists or terrorism.[19] Condoleezza Rice, then foreign-policy adviser to the Bush campaign, noted that with no Soviet threat, the United States should refocus on key priorities: "building a military ready to ensure American power, coping with rogue regimes, and managing Beijing and Moscow."[20] Candidate Bush was particularly critical of the Clinton administration for its use of U.S. military in unconventional roles. Bush himself admits that during the preelection debates he stressed that he "would be very careful about using our troops as nation builders."[21]

In a major campaign speech at The Citadel, in Charleston, South Carolina, on September 23, 1999, Bush declared, "Our military is still organized more for cold war threats than for the challenges of a new century." Bush emphasized that U.S. military needed to be "agile, lethal, readily deployable and require a minimum of logistical support."[22] While seemingly prescient, in hindsight, the future president explained at the time that he was concerned about "all the unconventional and invisible threats of new technologies and old hatreds." He went on to list three goals: renewing the bond of trust between the American president and the American military, defending the American people against missiles and terror, and creating the military of the next century. Bush elaborated on his second goal to "build America's defenses on the troubled frontiers of technology and terror" by stating, "Once a strategic afterthought, homeland defense has become an urgent duty." And although Mr. Bush went on to say he would "put a high priority on detecting and responding to terrorism on our soil," it was clear in the speech that his focus was on potential state-sponsored proliferation of missile technology (he specifically mentioned North Korea, Iran, Iraq, and China) and the threats from chemical and biological weapons.[23] Not surprisingly, he made no mention of Al-Qaeda or Osama bin Laden.

The focus, or at least awareness, began to change as the incoming administration's transition team and the president-elect began receiving the detailed intelligence reports from the CIA and key National Security Council staff. According to the 9/11 Commission:

> During the transition, [Richard A.] Clarke briefed Secretary of State–designate [Colin] Powell, Rice, and [Deputy National Security Adviser Stephen] Hadley on Al-Qaeda, including a mention of "sleeper cells" in many countries, including the United States. Clarke gave a similar briefing to Vice President [Richard] Cheney in the early days of the administration. Berger said he told Rice during the transition that she would spend more time on terrorism and Al-Qaeda than on any other issue. Although Clarke briefed President Bush on cybersecurity issues before 9/11, he never briefed or met with President Bush on counterterrorism, which was a significant contrast from the relationship he had enjoyed with President Clinton. Rice pointed out to us that President Bush received his counterterrorism briefings directly from DCI [Director of Central Intelligence] Tenet, who began personally providing intelligence updates at the White House each morning.[24]

During the first week of the Bush administration, Hadley tasked all the members of the NSC Staff to recommend issues that required major presidential policy reviews or initiatives. Clarke, a holdover from the Clinton administration as the National Coordinator for Security, Infrastructure Protection, and Counterterrorism, immediately (the same day in fact, an impressively swift response) sent a memorandum directly to National Security Adviser Condoleezza Rice, jumping over Hadley. The three-page cover memo was noteworthy because, in the second sentence, Clarke stressesd the severity of the issue of Al-Qaeda: "We *urgently* need such a Principals level review on the al Qida [sic] network."[25] Clarke made a compelling argument for an immediate review; however, upon close reading his emphasis seems more on Al-Qaeda threats to U.S. interests in the South Asia and Middle East regions rather than to the homeland. In fact, Clarke recommended that the "principals" (that is, heads of relevant departments and agencies and the most senior advisers) debate whether "the al Qida network poses a first order threat to U.S. interests on a number of regions, or is this analysis a 'chicken little' over reaching."[26] He then went on to state that if the threat was a first-order issue, two elements of the existing strategy needed improvement: going after Al-Qaeda's financing and developing a public information program to counter Al-Qaeda's propaganda. The memo did not explicitly argue for more robust covert operations or military options to attack Al-Qaeda, bin Laden, or the Taliban regime. Finally, Clarke attached to the memo a thirteen-page memorandum prepared in December 2000 by the outgoing Clinton administration as a transition document. The attachment, an interesting assessment of the previous administration's efforts, was entitled "Strategy for Eliminating the Threat from Jihadist Networks of al-Qida: Status and Prospects."[27] There was no indication that Rice took immediate action on either of the memos.

Within the Pentagon, the transition was a painfully slow process and did not lend focus to counterterrorism or Al-Qaeda issues. Secretary of Defense Donald Rumsfeld testified to the 9/11 Commission that he did not recall receiving any briefings about bin Laden from outgoing secretary William Cohen. The Chairman of the Joint Chiefs of Staff, General Shelton, did not brief Rumsfeld on Operation Infinite Resolve plans until February 8, 2001. Additionally, the senior echelon of Rumsfeld's Pentagon was significantly understaffed in the early days of the Bush administration. Deputy Secretary Paul Wolfowitz was not confirmed by the Senate until March 2001, and Undersecretary for Policy Doug Feith not confirmed until July 2001. The position most responsible for counterterrorism issues, the Assistant Secretary of Defense for Special Operations and Low Intensity Conflict (SOLIC), would remain vacant until *after* 9/11. Rumsfeld's initial focus was to flesh out many of the concepts laid out in Bush's Citadel speech, concerning the transformation of the U.S. military and the groundwork necessary to reshape American military policy: confirming new staff, conducting the Quadrennial Defense Review, drafting the Defense Planning Guidance, and reviewing existing contingency plans.

Meanwhile other crises began to test the new administration. In February the attack submarine USS *Greenville,* conducting a demonstration for visiting dignitaries, surfaced beneath the Japanese high school training fishing vessel *Ehime Maru,* sinking the ship and killing nine crew members, including four high school students. On Sunday, April 1, 2001, an American EP-3 reconnaissance aircraft collided with a Chinese fighter jet off the Chinese coast, killing the Chinese pilot. The EP-3 was damaged and landed on the China's Hainan Island, where its crew of twenty-four was detained. After eleven days of intense negotiations, the Chinese released the American crew, and several months later, the United States retrieved the EP-3. These incidents, while significant foreign policy and military issues requiring diplomatic skill to resolve, served to divert attention away from the preferred domestic agenda of tax cuts and education and further delay debate about terrorism, bin Laden, and Al-Qaeda.

By the late spring of 2001 the administration was beginning to catch up. Increased intelligence reporting about Al-Qaeda, including vague references to an impending attack, served to raise the awareness of the president and his national security staff.[28] Hadley and the deputies had also begun to review in detail counterterrorism policies and the contingency plans against Al-Qaeda. The severity of the Al-Qaeda threat was beginning to take hold. In a Deputies Committee (that is, the level below the principals) meeting at the end of April, Deputy Secretary of State Richard Armitage is reported to have stated that the destruction of Al-Qaeda should be the number-one American objective in South Asia, an even higher priority than nuclear weapons control (ostensibly a reference to Pakistan and India).[29] At the same meeting, the deputies resolved to "initiate a comprehensive review of U.S. policy on Pakistan" and to explore policy on Afghanistan, "including the option of supporting regime change."[30] In early June, Hadley circulated a draft National Security Presidential Directive (NSPD) described as an "ambitious program" for confronting Al-Qaeda. The NSPD laid out a multiyear plan that would use all instruments of national power: diplomacy, covert action, economic measures, law enforcement, public diplomacy, and, if necessary, military action. In many ways it was a parallel to the Clinton assessment that Clarke had passed to Rice in her first week as national security adviser. The difference, of course, was that this draft NSPD would be a Bush administration document, if and when approved and signed by the president. The deputies and the principals would spend the rest of the summer debating the document, revising sections, and polishing the final draft. In the meantime, the State Department continued the Clinton approach of démarches to the Taliban, delivering yet another warning on June 27 about "Afghan-based terrorists."[31]

The Principals Committee, chaired by Rice and attended by the secretaries of state and defense, the Chairman of the Joint Chiefs of Staff, the Director

of the CIA, and others, met to discuss Al-Qaeda, bin Laden, and counterterrorism issues for the first time on September 4, 2001. Clarke, in his read-ahead
memorandum to Rice, once again pressed for immediate decisions across a
broad spectrum of counterterrorism actions aimed at Al-Qaeda, ending with
an ominously prescient warning about the risks of further inaction: "You are
left waiting for the big attack [by Al-Qaeda], with lots of casualties, after which
some major U.S. retaliation is in order." After approving for forwarding to
Bush a draft presidential finding authorizing a large-scale increase of covert assistance to the anti-Taliban indigenous forces in Afghanistan, the principals re-
manded the broader Al-Qaeda and counterterrorism issues for further work to
the deputies, who met once again on Monday, September 10, 2001. Central to
their debates was the question of whether the United States should be deliberately involved in the Afghan civil war and the ongoing attempts to overthrow
the Taliban regime. At the September 10 meeting, the deputies agreed upon a
three-phase strategy for the Taliban: first, to send (yet another) high-level envoy
to give the Taliban one last chance to turn over bin Laden and shut down terrorist training activities; second, to continue diplomatic pressure while increasing a covert-action program supporting groups such as the Northern Alliance,
to buy time; and third, to develop a more robust covert-action program to
actually topple the Taliban.[32]

The draft presidential finding for covert assistance and the recommendations of the deputies were still in the throes of bureaucratic processing on the
morning of September 11, 2001. No significant changes to policy and no
updating of the military options had been accomplished since Bush's inauguration nearly nine months earlier.

September 11, 2001

The specific events of September 11 have been well chronicled and do not
need retelling here. The use of airliners as weapons, the nature of the targets,
and swiftness of the attack stood in stark contrast to the crystal-clear, beautiful
early autumn day. Despite the initial shock, the U.S. military and government
immediately went into action.

The first order of business was to establish an air-defense umbrella over
the United States. Almost immediately, the aircraft carriers USS *George Washington* and *John F. Kennedy,* along with five cruisers and two destroyers, all
armed with Aegis combat systems, put to sea to provide an air cap above New

York City and Washington, D.C.[33] The North American Air Defense Command (NORAD) network, thought by some an obsolete relic of the Cold War, went into overdrive to generate combat air patrols (CAP) over major U.S. cities. Despite a total shutdown of civil aviation, it would take weeks before the CAP program was reduced to strip-alert status only.

The carrier USS *Enterprise,* just exiting the Persian Gulf per standing orders, immediately turned around, solely on the initiative of the commanding officer, and headed back to the Gulf. Rumsfeld had placed the entire U.S. military at Defense Condition Three, the first time since the 1973 Yom Kippur war that any part of the U.S. military, let alone the entire Department of Defense, had been placed upon such a high alert status.

In Tampa, the deputy commander of CENTCOM, Lieutenant General Mike DeLong, U.S. Marine Corps, acting in the absence of General Franks, who was traveling out of the country, instructed the staff director of operations, U.S. Air Force Major General Gene Renuart, to stand up the CENTCOM Crisis Action Team as they watched the second plane crash into the World Trade Center.[34]

While it is natural to focus on the military significance of the attacks of 9/11, it's also important to remember that the immediate priorities of the government were domestically focused: organizing federal emergency assistance to New York, Pennsylvania, and the national capital region; tending to the victims; restoring civil aviation; and determining the impact to the U.S. economy and means to reopen the financial markets. The complexity of the issues underscores the total "whole-of government" response required in the immediate aftermath of the attacks, while concurrently it was being determined how and where to respond to the attackers.

President Bush convened the first meeting of the National Security Council via video teleconference (VTC) from Offutt Air Force Base at 3:15 p.m. Eastern Daylight Time. Bush immediately set the tone by declaring, "We are at war against terror. From this day forward, this is the new priority of our administration." He then asked the CIA director, George Tenet, "Who did this?" Tenet replied without hesitation, "Al-Qaeda."[35] Now more than just the CIA was at war; the president and the entire executive branch had taken up the mantle. So did NATO. On September 12, NATO invoked Article V of its foundational treaty—"an attack on one is an attack on all"—and vowed to send any and all assistance needed. Canada, as part of NORAD, was already assisting with the CAPs, and other NATO allies would eventually provide AWACS (airborne warning and control system) and tanker aircraft. Australia quickly invoked the ANZUS (Australia, New Zealand, United States) Treaty's collective-security provision.

It wasn't long before the U.S. Congress supported the president's declaration. On September 14, both the House and the Senate overwhelmingly approved a joint resolution authorizing the president to "use all necessary and appropriate force against those nations, organizations, or persons he determines planned, authorized, committed, or aided the terrorist attacks . . . or harbored such organizations or persons." The joint resolution (signed into law by the president on September 18) went on to state that Congress considered the resolution "specific statutory authorization within the meaning of . . . the War Powers Resolution."[36] While not using the phrase specifically, now even the Congress recognized that the United States was "at war."

Preparations for War

The immediate question surrounding any retaliatory strike was whether any part of the military or the CIA was prepared to act. The CIA and the Defense Department had already been sparring over who would bear the costs of the armed Predator program, and a tacit agreement had been reached for Defense to support new flights run covertly by the CIA out of Uzbekistan in the spring of 2002. The September attacks by Al-Qaeda had accelerated that plan and put new impetus behind the program. But in terms of "boots on the ground," there had been little planning.

The CIA had from time to time been covertly sending teams into Afghanistan to meet with various anti-Taliban factions, principally Northern Alliance leader Ahmed Shah Massoud. Throughout the meetings, Massoud had been frustrated with the meager support he had been receiving from the United States. He was also frustrated that the focus of his CIA interlocutors was almost exclusively on bin Laden and not resolution of the Afghan civil war or the outright overthrow of the Taliban. Bin Laden spent his time in Kandahar, Kabul, or among the various Al-Qaeda training camps in the eastern parts of Afghanistan—all Pashtun areas completely under the control of the Taliban and inaccessible to Massoud's Northern Alliance operatives. On the one occasion in 1999, when Massoud had offered to attack bin Laden's Derunta training complex, the CIA had disapproved the operation for fear of violating the long-standing presidential prohibition on assassinations. On September 9, 2001, Massoud was assassinated by Al-Qaeda operatives. The personal connections between the CIA and Massoud were shattered, but the relationship with other members of the Northern Alliance leadership, such as intelligence director Amrullah Saleh, remained and would prove invaluable in the weeks to come.

Having returned to Washington, President Bush convened a restricted NSC meeting (a pared-down group of only the key principals) on the evening of September 11, followed by two NSC meetings on September 12. The president was focused on Afghanistan, Al-Qaeda, and the Taliban. Others among the "War Cabinet" were debating whether to widen the target list to go after nations that had harbored terrorists or aided them directly—specifically Iran and Iraq, as well as terrorist organizations in Lebanon and possibly Syria. Rumsfeld, Wolfowitz, and others took the broader view, advocating at least consideration of strikes against Saddam Hussein as soon as possible. Others, particularly the outgoing Chairman of the Joint Chiefs of Staff, General Shelton, and Secretary of State Powell, argued for starting more narrowly, with a focus on Al-Qaeda, the Taliban, and Afghanistan.[37] The president deferred debate over the broader definition, essentially prioritizing the "Global War on Terrorism" so as to focus on Afghanistan first. Bush recalls, "Removing Al-Qaeda's safe haven in Afghanistan was essential to protecting the American people."[38]

As a practical matter, it was apparent that only the CIA had any operational capability that was, though limited in size and scope, ready to move quickly. At the afternoon meeting of the NSC, the president approved the already-pending presidential finding to expand CIA covert activities in Afghanistan and to increase paramilitary and financial support to the Northern Alliance.[39] The CIA immediately began planning to reinsert a team into the Panjshir Valley and link up with the Northern Alliance.

General Shelton described the very short list of military options available. Despite the planning that had been done for Infinite Resolve, Shelton told the group, the only off-the-shelf military option was another round of cruise-missile strikes, warning that it would be "just digging holes." Bush's exasperation with the limited military options was immediately apparent: "I don't want to put a million-dollar missile on a five dollar tent," he said.[40] Bush tasked Shelton and Rumsfeld to start working on new plans.

By enthusiastically approving the CIA covert-action plan, the president had, almost without realizing it, put the CIA in the lead and, at least initially, the Defense Department in support. The meetings adjourned on September 12 with no clearly defined "supported-supporting" relationships among the various departments and agencies.

When the NSC reconvened that weekend at Camp David, the CIA had already canceled the pending retirement of its most seasoned Afghanistan and South Asia operative and tasked him to select a team for insertion into Afghanistan. By the evening of September 13, the CIA had begun assembling the team and started planning to reestablish a presence in Afghanistan. The team's mission included convincing the Northern Alliance to cooperate with the CIA and the U.S. military in order to "go after" bin Laden and Al-Qaeda. The CIA team was also tasked to evaluate the Northern Alliance's military capability and determine how to improve its capacity to fight the Taliban.[41] The CIA was moving quickly. According to Bush, "Six months earlier, at my direction, George [Tenet] and the National Security Council had started developing a comprehensive strategy to destroy the al Qaeda network."[42]

By the time the NSC had reconvened on September 15, Tenet was able to brief the president in great detail on his plan to link up CIA paramilitary teams, Afghan warlords, and U.S. Special Operations Forces in order to collect intelligence and mount covert operations against the Taliban. His briefing, in fact, went well beyond the operations in Afghanistan to include details of increased Predator flights as well as high-risk covert operations in about eighty countries worldwide. Tenet was aggressive and persuasive, and Bush enthusiastically supported the director's proposals. The CIA was on the march, having captured the president's imagination. Reflecting in 2010, Bush wrote: "George's [Tenet's] plan called for deploying CIA teams to arm, fund, and join forces with the Northern Alliance. Together, they would form the initial thrust of the attack. By mating up our forces with the local opposition, we would avoid looking like a conqueror or occupier. America would help the Afghan people liberate themselves."[43] There is no record, however, of discussion in those early days of "liberating" the Afghan people.

General Shelton was the last formal briefer. After being taken to task by the president earlier in the week, Shelton arrived prepared with a full briefing that started by identifying three priority targets: Al-Qaeda, the Taliban, and Iraq, stating that Iraq and Al-Qaeda posed strategic threats to the United States. Focusing the brief on Afghanistan, Shelton described three options. The first was to strike Al-Qaeda using the preexisting contingency plan of cruise-missile attacks. Shelton explained that the attack could be launched almost immediately and posed no risk to American troops. It was also unlikely to decapitate Al-Qaeda or topple the Taliban. The second option would build on option one by adding manned bombers for precision, time-sensitive strikes. The third option was to combine cruise missiles, manned bombers, and "boots on the ground." It was understood that option three "was mostly a theoretical option" and that "the military would have to develop the details from scratch." Any deployment of ground forces would take days, if not weeks or months, to execute, given the inaccessibility of Afghanistan and the necessary overflight and support requirements, which would mean diplomatic negotiation. Despite the lack of detail and the challenges of distance, terrain, and diplomatic nego-tiation, Bush clearly favored the decisiveness of a U.S. ground presence.

The Camp David meetings continued to debate whether Iraq should be considered a first-order target in response to 9/11. As the last speaker, Vice President Cheney summed it up: "If we go after Saddam Hussein, we lose our rightful place as the good guy."[44] Bob Woodward, in his 2002 book *Bush at War,* presciently reports Secretary of State Colin Powell's underly-ing concern about Rumsfeld's allusions to fighting in Afghanistan and Iraq at the same time: "Though the U.S. military claims to be designed and equipped to fight two full-scale conflicts simultaneously, Powell thought the Defense Department was overestimating its ability to do two things at the same time from the same command, with the same commander and staff. Military attacks on both Afghanistan and Iraq would be under the jurisdiction of CENTCOM."[45] In retrospect, this was a significant concern that was not given due consideration by the American leadership. In just a few short years Powell's concerns would become reality, but as of September 17, 2001, Bush's strategic vision focused only on Afghanistan: remove the Taliban from power, deny sanctuary to Al-Qaeda, and help a democratic government emerge in Afghanistan.[46]

First Moves

Within a week, the CIA was moving its first team to Central Asia, and the Defense Department had developed its own plans for Afghanistan, building on Shelton's option number three. Rumsfeld pressed CENTCOM commander General Tommy Franks for a creative plan that stressed speed, agility, flexibil-ity, and a light "footprint." Bush received a concept briefing from Franks and

Rumsfeld on September 21 and gave final approval on October 2, exactly a week after the CIA team, without any Special Operations Forces (SOF), had arrived in Afghanistan's Panjshir Valley.

Franks had a four-phase plan: phase I—set the conditions to move forces into the region, linking up Special Operations Forces with CIA teams and the Northern Alliance while simultaneously conducting airdrops of humanitarian daily rations; phase II—conduct initial combat operations with air strikes and limited ground attacks by CIA and SOF embedded with the major Afghan anti-Taliban factions. Phase III was to conduct "decisive operations" using all elements of national power, including up to 12,000 conventional ground troops to oust the Taliban regime and eliminate Al-Qaeda. Finally would come phase IV: "security and stability operations," loosely described by Franks as an "indefinite task" and that President Bush later described as helping "the Afghan people build a free society."[47]

Rumsfeld understood from the beginning that the plans would rely heavily on Special Operations Forces. "A lot of it will be special operations" used to "drain the swamp [the terrorists] live in," said Rumsfeld as the preparations were being made in late September.[48] Rumsfeld changed the name of the operation from Infinite Justice to Enduring Freedom, partly in deference to Islamic scholars who pointed out that for Muslims only God can dispense infinite justice, but also in recognition that the campaign was likely to be a long and complex effort—"It will take years, I suspect."[49]

Renuart was impressed by how much the CENTCOM planners drew from regional experts and past history, particularly the experiences of the British in the nineteenth century and the Soviets more recently. "It was very, very important that we not relearn the lessons of the Russians, that we not get mired in large forces, that we not allow ourselves to be pinned down to big installations that could become easy targets, and that we not be seen as occupiers in the early stages because that would draw the same reactions that the British and the Russians drew." He was impressed by the novel reliance on the Northern Alliance as the proxy ground forces for CENTCOM.[50]

Even prior to the president's approval of Franks' plan, the military had been working around the clock to lay the groundwork for deployment of forces. While the State Department started negotiating access and basing agreements in Central Asia and securing the cooperation of General Musharraf in Pakistan, the military was doing its best to front-load weapons platforms, supplies, ammunition, fuel, and personnel into the CENTCOM area of responsibility. The president signed an executive order on September 14 authorizing the call-up of 35,000 reservists, primarily for the homeland defense mission, Operation Noble Eagle but also establishing a precedent for drawing upon the reserve component and emphasizing to the American people that the nation was, in fact, at war.[51] As much as 235,000 barrels of marine diesel fuel was immediately dispatched to Diego Garcia, and 28,000 gallons of jet fuel was delivered to bases in southern Spain—the staging base for U.S. Air Force air-refueling tankers. On September 14, Rumsfeld issued orders to reposition the C-17 fleet and ordered a full stand-down of the heavy bomber fleet for repairs and upgrades necessary to conduct a long-distance bombing campaign. On September 19, the president approved the deployment of nearly two dozen B-52s and B-1Bs to Diego Garcia, followed shortly by U2 and RC-135 Rivet Joint reconnaissance aircraft.

On the same day that Bush addressed a joint session of Congress and the nation, U.S. Air Force lieutenant general Charles Wald, the Central Command Air Forces commander, departed his headquarters at Shaw Air Force Base, South Carolina, for Prince Sultan Air Base in Saudi Arabia. The United States had recently opened the Combined Air Operations Center, the CAOC, when construction was completed at the end of July 2001.[52] Wald's mission statement was straightforward: "On order, CFACC [the combined forces air component commander, working in the CAOC] provides air support for friendly forces working with the Northern Alliance and other opposition forces in order to defeat hostile Taliban and al Qaeda forces and set the conditions for regime removal and long-term regional stability."[53]

The U.S. Navy was busy repositioning carrier battle groups. USS *Carl Vinson* and *Enterprise* and their groups were already on station in the Persian Gulf, and USS *Theodore Roosevelt* was ordered to deploy from New York on September 18. USS *Kitty Hawk*, homeported in Yokosuka, Japan, departed for the Indian Ocean with only eight of the fifty strike aircraft assigned to her air wing. *Kitty Hawk's* mission was to serve as a "sea-based lily pad" for special operations helicopters supporting the missions in Central Asia.

The major muscle movements had started, positioning bombers and missile-capable warships in the region, but only the CIA was making significant progress in establishing the "boots on the ground" the president wanted. Bush pushed Rumsfeld and the Pentagon, saying, "We are going to rain holy hell on them. You've got to put lives at risk. We've got to have people on the ground."[54]

Still, by September 26 the boots on the ground in Afghanistan totaled seven pairs—those belonging to the CIA team immediately dispatched by Tenet.

Special Operations Forces, the Air Campaign, and Weather

SOCCENT,[55] the Special Operations Forces component of CENTCOM, had been busy working up its subordinate plans to Franks' Operation Enduring Freedom framework. In short order, SOCCENT developed a seven-phase plan for a "U.S.-based insurgency" campaign in Afghanistan.[56] Drawing from existing special operations doctrine for supporting unconventional warfare, the plan envisioned insertion of special operations teams and Air Force Tactical Air Control Teams throughout Afghanistan to link up with anti-Taliban forces. Leaning well forward, Special Forces elements from Fort Campbell, Kentucky, and SOCCENT headquarters in Florida began sending small advance parties to Uzbekistan long before any formal agreement had been made between the U.S. and the Uzbek governments, anticipating the significant coordination and logistical challenges ahead.*

CENTCOM and SOCOM had agreed that the U.S. Army's 5th Special Forces Group (Airborne) (SFG) would provide the bulk of the SOF ground capability for the initial insertions.[57] As the lead SOF element, the 5th SFG's commander, Colonel John Mulholland, was designated the Joint Special Operations Task Force (JSOTF) commander. On October 5, Secretary Rumsfeld personally traveled to Tashkent, Uzbekistan, and secured agreement from President Islam Karimov for the use of Karshi-Khanabad (K2) airfield, a nearly abandoned former Soviet facility. That same day, U.S. military elements began arriving at K2: the 16th Special Operations Wing, of the U.S. Air Force Special Operations Command, with MH-53 Pave Low helicopters critical for combat search and rescue (CSAR) missions; Mulholland's advance party from the 5th SFG; elements of the U.S. Army's 160th Special Operations Aviation Regiment, with MH-47 and MH-60 helicopters; parts of the army's 112th Signal Battalion, for critical global communications capability; and the lead elements of the 1st Battalion, 87th Infantry, from the Army's 10th Mountain Division to provide local security.[58]

---

* For example, to airlift a single Special Forces Group, approximately three thousand men and equipment, would require nearly fifty C-17 cargo aircraft. (Wright, *Different Kind of War,* 61.)

With only the CIA's seven-man team on the ground in Afghanistan and the SOF teams sequestered in Kentucky, the bombing campaign began on October 7, initially striking preplanned targets, only some of which had been confirmed by the CIA's ground team. The first sorties were flown by B-1B and B-52 bombers from Diego Garcia, twenty-five navy attack aircraft from *Carl Vinson* and *Enterprise* in the North Arabian Sea, and two B-2 stealth bombers from Whiteman Air Force Base in Missouri (which flew a combat mission covering approximately 14,000 miles round-trip). Fifty TLAMs were fired from U.S. Navy destroyers and cruisers as well as from two attack submarines, U.S. and British.[59] Initially targeting the Taliban's air-defense capabilities, the missions soon included preplanned targets among the Taliban and Al-Qaeda ground forces. Without good targeting data, confirmed or designated by ground components, the CFACC soon began to run short of targets, and when bombing runs were made, only achieved limited target effects.

Despite the enormously successful efforts by the president and the Departments of State and Defense to build a broad coalition to support military action, overflight rights, and basing access, there remained a reluctance to form a large military coalition. The initial air campaign would be conducted by the United States and only a very few of its closest allies. The senior U.S. military leadership was concerned about the potential for a repeat of the coordination nightmares during Operation Allied Force in 1999.[60] The campaign in Kosovo had been conducted by nineteen NATO allies, each apparently unwilling to subordinate its own interests to the collective mission. The concern about the challenges of coalition warfare was probably well placed, and the problem would return several years later in both Afghanistan and Iraq as an Achilles' heel.

Mulholland and the remainder of the 5th SFG headquarters arrived in Uzbekistan on October 10, three days after the start of the air campaign. Although there was some confusion and poor coordination between CENTCOM, SOCOM, and the Central Intelligence Agency, Mulholland was prepared to begin insertion of Operational Detachment–Alpha teams (ODAs) into Afghanistan as soon as possible. Mulholland's mission statement was broad, allowing the greatest degree of flexibility to the individual ODAs: "Advise and assist the Northern Alliance in conducting combat operations against the Taliban and al Qaeda, kill, capture, and destroy al Qaeda, and deny them sanctuary."[61] His mission was also, interestingly, limited to partnering with the Northern Alliance, meaning that he would be restricted to essentially the northern half of Afghanistan. It also meant he would initially work almost exclusively with Tajiks and Uzbeks and not with the majority Pashtuns, found mostly in the south and east. The south and east would initially be the purview of the Rangers and other higher-end special operations elements. Mulholland had no specified or implied task to "liberate" the Afghans or assist in the establishment of any follow-on Afghan government should the Taliban crumble.

Despite the plans and availability of forces, weather kept the ODAs in Uzbekistan, waiting for an opportunity for helicopter insertion into Afghanistan. The CIA team, code-named Jawbreaker, had been in the Panjshir Valley since September 26 and was anxious for the SOF teams to arrive. The Northern Alliance was anxious as well, as it was increasingly concerned about the limited effectiveness of the bombing campaign without "eyes on target." The CIA had told the Northern Alliance leaders that the ODAs would be bringing laser target-designation equipment—a capability that the CIA was technically not allowed to employ.

Finally, on the night of October 19, the first team from 5th SFG, designated ODA 555, or the "Triple Nickle," was inserted by USAF special operations MH-53 aircraft into the Panjshir Valley. The Triple Nickle would eventually link up with Northern Alliance General Bismullah Khan, an ethnic Tajik, and head south to Bagram Air Base and later to Kabul. ODA 595 followed close behind, landing in the Darya Suf Valley to join General Dostum, an ethnic Uzbek, sixty miles west of Mazar-e-Sharif. The following night, two hundred Rangers from the 3rd Battalion, 75th Ranger Regiment, arrived by parachute on a small airstrip approximately fifty miles from Kandahar. The Rangers secured the airfield for use by other SOF elements for raids and strikes targeted at the heart of the Taliban.[62]

Boots were on the ground, the world had witnessed the long-range strike capabilities of the U.S. military, and the plan appeared to be on track. But there were also some indications of major challenges ahead.

Warning Signs

The start of the air campaign a mere twenty-six days after 9/11 and the insertion of SOF teams shortly thereafter were monumental accomplishments and testimonies to the global reach of the United States. Yet lurking behind these initial successes were warning signs of just how complex the mission ahead would become.

Despite the link-up of the SOF teams with Jawbreaker in Afghanistan, friction remained between the CIA and the Defense Department. Poor communication, at levels ranging from organizations and individuals inside the Beltway to sporadic tactical communications between the Panjshir Valley and the U.S. military elements at K2, contributed to the friction. The teaming of CIA paramilitary and SOF with indigenous forces, literally speaking different languages, further compounded the problem. The real-time linkage of armed Predator video to senior decision makers (and their staff attorneys) in Washington and Tampa caused an entirely new set of coordination challenges.

Although General Franks and CENTCOM clearly had the military lead, there was no forward command-and-control capability, save the small, understaffed JSOTF headquarters set up by Colonel Mulholland outside of Afghanistan. Franks was running most of the operation from Tampa, the air war was being coordinated from Saudi Arabia, the forward element in Afghanistan was from the CIA, the U.S. military forces belonged to U.S. Special Operations Command (SOCOM), and the actual ground maneuver units were indigenous Afghans from the Northern Alliance. And while a broad-based coalition of nearly seventy nations existed on paper, there remained considerable reluctance among the Americans to accept ground forces, even Special Forces, from more than just the closest and longest-standing allies. The question of "Who is in command here?" would ultimately plague operations in Afghanistan for years to come.

The final end state for Operation Enduring Freedom was also not clearly understood. CENTCOM anticipated sustained humanitarian assistance operations and had a single slide-show bullet reference to "set conditions for reconstruction," but nobody was anticipating follow-on nation building or the establishment of a new Afghan government as a task.[63] Only the CFACC had a mission statement that included "regime removal and long-term regional stability." And, outside of the regional experts from the think tanks and the Russian general who had been defeated there, none of the current commanders or planners seemed to fully understand the ethnopolitical and historical complexity of Afghanistan and South Asia.

Bush concedes that he had been wrong about nation building during the 2000 campaign. Bush says that after 9/11 he changed his mind and that "Afghanistan was the ultimate nation building mission." Although "from the beginning [Bush] knew it would take time to help the Afghan people build a functioning democracy consistent with its culture and traditions," there is no evidence that the initial plans for Operation Enduring Freedom included nation-building tasks or objectives. Bush, upon reflection, admitted, "The task turned out to be even more daunting than I anticipated. Our government was not prepared for nation building."[64] Also, the issue of whether or not to broaden the target list to include Iraq and Saddam Hussein was not settled—it remained a deferred decision, at least for the remainder of 2001.

Three

The Opening Gambit
Enduring Freedom and Unconventional Success

Until September 4, 2001, as a result of the Bush administration's initial lack of focus on counterterrorism and Al-Qaeda issues, there was a real dearth of intelligence available across the government about Afghanistan, its people, and the Taliban members who had authority there.[1] And, given that there were no appropriate military plans "on the shelf" that could develop the strategic outcomes defined by President Bush and that there was a significant lack of clarity about what those outcomes really were, the U.S. military had an immense planning task handed to it by the president after his restricted NSC meeting on September 12. As Bush later wrote, "Everything about the country screamed trouble."[2]

Since the United States had largely turned its back on Afghanistan after the Soviets left in 1989, few people in Washington, or in Tampa, Florida, where the military headquarters of Central Command was located, knew much about the area. It was not a priority country in anyone's inbox until September 2001. Even the Taliban and its members were largely opaque to most strategists; many planners understood only that they were "Muslim fundamentalists who sought to return the country to strict Islamic rule using whatever brutality was necessary in the process."[3] Al-Qaeda was somewhat better understood, since analysis had been conducted after the bombing of USS *Cole* in Yemen in October 2000. For example, it was known within the National Security Council staff that Al-Qaeda's 55th Brigade was the principal fighting force within the Taliban.[4] Richard C. Clarke's memo about Al-Qaeda written in December 2000 had noted, "the al Qida network is well financed, has trained tens of thousands of jihadists, and has a cell structure in over forty nations. It is also actively seeking to develop and acquire weapons of mass destruction,"[5] but no real capabilities assessment or order of battle (listing of forces and their organization and major weapons) had been done by the fall of 2001.

The difficulty of military planning for operations in Afghanistan was compounded by the geographic issues of fighting in a country with such varied and challenging terrain, located far from available basing. Afghanistan was landlocked yet located at the crossroads of major north–south and east–west trade routes. The Hindu Kush mountains run northeast to southwest across the country, dividing it into three major regions: a Central Highlands, accounting for roughly two-thirds of the country's area; a Southwestern Plateau, one-fourth of the land; and a smaller Northern Plains area, which contains the most fertile and productive area of Afghanistan. "Most of the country was under Taliban control by 2001 except for some small areas held by Northern Alliance forces in the Panjshir Valley northeast of Kabul and a few scattered pockets of resistance in the northwest of the country."[6] That so few areas were available for reasonably safe operations in a country of 250,000 square miles would severely limit military options, with the possible exception of strategic strikes and limited raids from nearby bases. That limitation and the fact that the CIA was "driving the train" toward an operation that was very different from what the Defense Department might have developed, had it been the lead federal agency, made planning for a campaign in Afghanistan an extreme challenge.

Still, using great diplomatic skill, on September 13 Secretary of State Powell managed to develop agreements with Pakistan for the use of its airspace and overland transit routes from the east.[7] "President Pervez Musharraf of Pakistan had offered the US basing rights at several locations. The largest and most important of these was the Pakistani air base at Jacobabad, Shahbaz AB. Designed as an F-16 base with hardened aircraft shelters, and located three hundred miles southeast of Kandahar, Afghanistan, the base was within reach for USAF Special Operations Forces (SOF) and Combat Search and Rescue (CSAR) assets staging from within the CENTCOM Area of Responsibility."[8] Later similar agreements were made, with the help of Russian president Vladimir Putin, with Uzbekistan, Tajikistan, and with Kyrgyzstan (for the use of its Manas Air Base) in order to deliver forces and operational support into Afghanistan from the north.[9] CENTCOM also deployed maritime forces into the Arabian Sea so that American combat power could be projected into Afghanistan from the south.

The four-phase plan General Franks and his staff eventually developed called for, first, connecting Special Operations Forces with the CIA teams in country; second, conducting an air campaign, including humanitarian air-drops; third, deploying coalition ground forces into Afghanistan to hunt down remaining Taliban and Al-Qaeda fighters; and finally stabilizing the country to build "a free society."[10] Within weeks, by the end of September, special operations soldiers and members of the CIA had been transported to the region and had linked up on the ground with the forces of the Afghan opposition, the Northern Alliance.*

Still, the problem of accurate intelligence on the Taliban and Al-Qaeda forces in Afghanistan remained. The Taliban and Al-Qaeda forces were hard to distinguish from the local population and had the great advantages of being able to intimidate the people and having full knowledge of the terrain. The Americans knew very little about how the Taliban might fight. "A post–September 11 National Intelligence Estimate, prepared as the war in Afghanistan began in October 2001, highlighted how little the Intelligence Community actually knew, including the scarcity of reporting on al-Qa'ida targets. The National Intelligence Estimate went on to describe further the nature of the intelligence gaps."[11] These gaps would only continue to grow as the campaign progressed, leading eventually to some significant mistakes.

CENTCOM Support Structures

None of the desired objectives of the Enduring Freedom campaign could have been accomplished without the significant support structures and regional command relationships that had been built up by CENTCOM over the years since the first Gulf War in 1990. By 2001 General Franks had a series of important bases in the region and had command structures in place that regularly conducted activities all around his area of responsibility.[12]

The strategic military preparations for both Operation Enduring Freedom and Operation Iraqi Freedom had been born in the aftermath of the liberation of Kuwait and had been conducted and refined for nearly a decade

---

★ The Northern Alliance, also referred to as the United Islamic Front or the United Islamic Front for the Salvation of Afghanistan, was an organization that managed to unite all ethnic groups of Afghanistan fighting against the Afghan Taliban and Al-Qaeda. The United Front included Tajiks, Pashtuns, Hazaras, Uzbeks, Turkmen, and other Afghans.

before September 11. Despite the overwhelming defeat sustained by Iraq during Operation Desert Storm in 1990, during most of the decade that followed Saddam Hussein was regularly able to conduct military provocations that the then-commander of U.S. Central Command, General Anthony Zinni, called the "Saddam sine wave." The Iraqi saber rattling seemed to begin just before Thanksgiving and end shortly after New Year's Day, and it resulted in a series of responses, the most notable being Operation Desert Fox in 1998. Because of their enduring frequency, timing, and unpredictability, Saddam's actions had a debilitating effect on U.S. troop readiness and morale and on the patience of the American strategic leadership.

Basing and Engagement

In the late 1990s, General Zinni's plan had been to flatten the "wave" by forward-deploying continual, credible, military force in theater to assure allies and protect American interests in the region. The resulting regional strategy, which harmonized U.S. diplomatic, economic, information, as well as military activities, provided for the dual containment of both Iraq and Iran through a military effort focused on Iraq. To enable these military efforts, the United States and Kuwait signed a ten-year defense agreement in which the Kuwaitis agreed to provide assistance in kind: food, water, and fuel for deployed forces, in addition to a sizeable support package to include housing, school costs, and other benefits to the soldiers and families that were to be stationed in Kuwait. Following the 1996 Iraqi provocation, the Kuwaitis agreed to the rotational deployment of an armored battalion task force on a permanent basis. By 1999 these military activities were becoming routine and were collectively known as Exercise Intrinsic Action, later Desert Spring.

Desert Spring consisted of employing land, air, sea, and special operating force capabilities throughout the Gulf. The ground effort was headed by the U.S. Army Central Command (ARCENT), the commander of which also served as the Combined Land Force Component Commander (CFLCC), providing command and control (C2) for Desert Spring activities from a forward location at Camp Doha in Kuwait. The U.S. Navy Central Command (NAVCENT) and U.S. Marine Forces Central Command (MARFORCENT) directed, respectively, naval and Marine activities from Manama, Bahrain. Scheduled Marine ground-force deployments to Kuwait known as Exercise Eager Mace, provided practice for reception, staging, onward movement, and integration

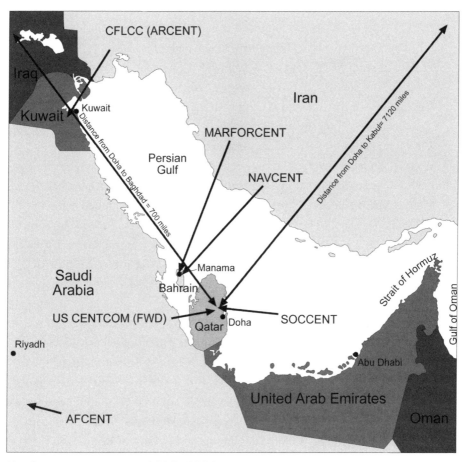

CFLCC (ARCENT)

Iraq

Kuwait

Kuwait

Distance from Doha to Baghdad = 700 miles

Persian Gulf

MARFORCENT

Iran

NAVCENT

Distance from Doha to Kabul = 7120 miles

Saudi Arabia

Manama

Bahrain

US CENTCOM (FWD)

Qatar   Doha

SOCCENT

Strait of Hormuz

Gulf of Oman

Riyadh

Abu Dhabi

AFCENT

United Arab Emirates

Oman

Key Command Locations, 2002–2003

(RSOI) of ground combat power and large-scale over-the-shore training. Combined air forces, primarily from the United States and the United Kingdom, were stationed at Ali Al Jaber and Ali Al Salem air bases in Kuwait and with U.S. Air Force Central Command (AFCENT), whose commander acted as the Combined Force Air Component Commander, located at Prince Sultan Air Base in Saudi Arabia. The CFACC provided command and control for air operations and conducted the air campaign designed to enforce the UN sanctions regime over Iraq, known as Operation Southern Watch. Finally, a Special Operating Forces company was deployed to Camp Doha, Kuwait, with theater SOF headquarters for command and control (SOCCENT) located at Camp Al Salyia, in Qatar. SOCCENT conducted Exercise Iris Gold, a series of continuous interdiction operations along the Shatt Al-Arab and the Arabian Gulf. These activities combined represented a regular way for the United States to impact the region with military forces. It was to be a "shaping campaign" for cultivating local perceptions and maintaining a role in regional affairs; it was also to be a synchronization of national power that would involve, for the first time in U.S. history, the forward deployment of command, control, and support troops on a permanent basis to the Arabian Gulf.

The centerpiece of the U.S. Army Central Command effort was Camp Doha, Kuwait, which served as a logistic hub for American combat power, a mere thirty-five miles from the Iraqi border. It existed for one purpose: the RSOI of ground combat power. Implied in that task was the requirement to maintain and continuously supply the heavy armored brigade of combat vehicles, rolling stock, tools, and ancillary equipment needed by the units that rotated through Kuwait. Additionally, the maneuver space of Kuwait and the capabilities available in Doha allowed U.S. Marine commanders the opportunity to rapidly download equipment from assault vessels, rehearse assault operations, test-fire weapons, refit, and repair before reloading assault ships for deployment elsewhere in theater—a task that would soon be essential for combat operations.

Command Arrangements

The CENTOM Combined Force Air Component Commander was already conducting a regional air campaign focused on enforcing the UN sanctions regime over southern Iraq instituted after the first Gulf War, an operation known as Southern Watch. Air forces assigned on six-month rotations to the Arabian

Gulf to support Southern Watch were both land and carrier based, including aircraft from the U.S. Air Force and naval aviation (Navy and Marine Corps aircraft), as well as some coalition aviation. For nearly six years, these forces had flown nearly a half-million combat sorties without the loss of a single pilot or airframe, denying Saddam Hussein the deployment of offensive military maneuver forces in the southern half of his country. By 2001 the military containment of Saddam Hussein was not in question; but the basing and regional expertise being practiced in the Arabian Gulf added tremendous flexibility to the effort in Afghanistan.

By 2000 the United States and its allies were conducting combined operations in Kuwait, the Gulf, and throughout the region. More importantly, the United States and its Kuwaiti allies had created a robust basing and logistical capability consisting of prepositioned armored vehicles and rolling stock (warehoused on land and afloat), ammunition, and supplies that could enable the United States and its allies to rapidly build up two divisions of combat power with supporting units in theater. The campaign transformed the U.S. military, particularly the Air Force, into an expeditionary force and developed a forward presence that could quickly evolve into a potent joint capability—rapidly deployable anywhere in the region.

Overall joint command and control was conducted from U.S. Central Command headquarters some seven thousand miles away in Tampa. In region, the CFLCC controlled ground operations from Camp Doha. The CFACC conducted continuous air operations out of Prince Sultan Air Base in Saudi Arabia. SOCCENT operated from Camp Al Salyia, in Qatar; and NAVCENT and MARFORCENT directed naval and Marine activities from Manama, Bahrain.

The Northern Alliance, Jawbreaker, Airpower, SOF, and Amphibious Forces

The plan that was employed in Afghanistan was unconventional in concept, both in the level of collaboration among U.S. agencies and in tactical execution. It brought together a host of diverse yet complementary capabilities that eventually had a decisive and rapid effect on the Taliban. It included many parts, but its most essential components were the CIA, military airpower, amphibious forces, and Special Operations Forces.

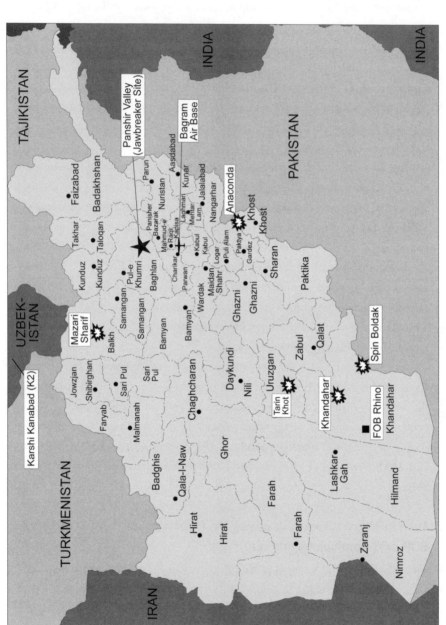

Key Battles in Afghanistan, 2001–2002

Team Jawbreaker—the CIA

Jawbreaker was the code name given to the first CIA team to enter Afghanistan in the aftermath of September 11. It was clear to CIA planners that the key to success in Afghanistan would be to use the indigenous anti-Taliban forces, namely the Northern Alliance, and the some Pashtun tribes, along with U.S. airpower and SOF on the ground. The CIA saw the Northern Alliance as the priority—if the Taliban could be defeated in the north of the country, the south (the Taliban heartland) would have to follow. The first step to any military effort in Afghanistan was for the CIA to link up with the Northern Alliance.

So on September 19, Cofer Black, the head of the CIA Counter Terrorism Center (CTC), directed the deployment of the ten-man CIA team (Jawbreaker) led by Gary C. Schroen to Afghanistan.[13] The team first flew into Uzbekistan on a CIA L100 cargo plane. Then, on September 26, the Jawbreaker team, with three million dollars in cash, flew in a CIA-owned Mi-17 helicopter over the Hindu Kush Mountains into the Panjshir Valley north of Kabul, where they were met by representatives from the Northern Alliance.[14] (See map 2.) The team quickly established a base of operations and secure communications back to the CTC and then met with Muhamed Arif Sawari, the intelligence and security chief for the Northern Alliance.[15]

On the same day that Schroen's team had been ordered into Afghanistan, President Bush gave a speech to a joint session of Congress wherein he laid out the principal demands that the U.S. government had for the Taliban. He also described the campaign to come and the clear-cut distinctions to be made. Bush said,

> The United States of America makes the following demands on the Taliban. Deliver to United States authorities all of the leaders of al-Qaida who hide in your land. Release all foreign nationals, including American citizens you have unjustly imprisoned. Protect foreign journalists, diplomats and aid workers in your country. Close immediately and permanently every terrorist training camp in Afghanistan. And hand over every terrorist and every person and their support structure to appropriate authorities. Give the United States full access to terrorist training camps, so we can make sure they are no longer operating. These demands are not open to negotiation or discussion. The Taliban

must act and act immediately. They will hand over the terrorists, or they will share in their fate. . . . Our war on terror begins with al-Qaida, but it does not end there. It will not end until every terrorist group of global reach has been found, stopped and defeated. . . . And we will pursue nations that provide aid or safe haven to terrorism. Every nation in every region now has a decision to make: Either you are with us, or you are with the terrorists. From this day forward, any nation that continues to harbor or support terrorism will be regarded by the United States as a hostile regime.[16]

On September 27, Schroen and Jawbreaker met with the commander of the Northern Alliance, General Mohammed Fahim; during the meeting Schroen promised Fahim, "You have never seen anything like what we're going to deliver onto the enemy."[17] The Jawbreaker team spent the next week working with Northern Alliance units in northeastern Afghanistan preparing for a ground assault. Meanwhile the National Security Council, the CIA, and CENTCOM worked to put their support together that would facilitate an air campaign to aid the Northern Alliance effort against the Taliban.

Airpower

Enduring Freedom phase-two combat operations began with air strikes on Taliban targets in Afghanistan on October 7, 2001, less than four weeks following the attacks in New York City. The air strikes initially focused on areas in and around the key Afghan cities of Kabul, Jalalabad, and Kandahar. After only a few days most of the known Taliban training sites had been damaged, and the meager Taliban air defenses (largely leftover U.S. Stinger missiles) had been destroyed.[18] The campaign then turned its focus to destroying command, control, and communications targets, which would weaken the ability of the Taliban to coordinate activities.

However, the line of Taliban forces facing the Northern Alliance held firmly through the middle of the month, up to that time no tangible battlefield successes had yet occurred on that front. So two weeks into the campaign, the Northern Alliance leaders asked that the American air campaign focus more on the front lines; the United States redirected its strikes accordingly.[19] This was exactly what the Air Force had been asked to do. Lieutenant General Wald's mission had been clearly stated: "On order, Combined Forces Air Component Command provides air support for friendly forces working with the Northern Alliance and other opposition forces in order to defeat hostile Taliban and al-Qaeda forces and to set the conditions for regime removal and long-term regional stability."[20] Though striking targets thousands of miles away, Wald and his CFACC staff conducted operations from Prince Sultan Air Base in Saudi Arabia.

For Wald, the goal of the initial wave of air attacks had been to gain un-contested control of Afghan airspace, destroying Taliban air-defense capabilities. So the first air sorties had focused on surface-to-air missile sites; early-warning radars; command, control, and communications facilities; airfields; and aircraft. The Taliban air-defense system was unsophisticated but still posed a threat to coalition aircraft with its antiaircraft artillery and surface-to-air missiles. Within days Wald's pilots achieved air supremacy in the skies over Afghanistan. Strikes then began to target Taliban tanks and artillery as well as training facilities in Kabul and Kandahar. By the end of the first week of the air campaign, coalition aircraft had dropped over 1,500 bombs and munitions of various types.[21]

SOF—Army Special Forces

American Special Forces units began arriving at the former Soviet air base near Karshi Kanabad, in Uzbekistan, in the fall of 2001 following a meeting between Secretary of Defense Rumsfeld and the Uzbek president, Karimov, who had agreed to allow U.S. special operators to stage out of Uzbek bases.[22] The 5th Special Forces Group (Airborne) formed the core of Joint Special Operations Task Force North, also called Task Force (TF) Dagger, under the command of Colonel John Mulholland, USA, and operating out of K2. In addition to the 5th SFG, TF Dagger included aviators from the 160th Spe-cial Operations Aviation Regiment and Special Tactics personnel from the Air Force Special Operations Command. Once in place at K2, Task Force Dagger was directed to conduct special operations in support of a number of North-ern Alliance commanders in Afghanistan and to work with them to gain their active assistance in overthrowing the Taliban regime.

> Task Force Dagger planned to quickly establish contact with three of the most powerful of the NA [Northern Alliance] faction leaders, Generals Abdur Rashid Dostum, Mullah Daoud, and Fahim Khan. As-sisted by U.S. air support, each would be encouraged to expand his footholds in northern Afghanistan and to provide a base for follow-on U.S. operations before the onset of winter. Winter in Afghanistan

made mountain passes virtually impassible and even air support was often adversely affected by the winds and storms of the harsh Afghan climate. For political purposes, the Special Forces teams were divided among the various faction warlords as equally as possible, since the United States did not want to give the impression of favoring one of these long-term rivals, now temporary allies, over the other. This policy impacted on the timetable of inserting teams, with some being held up, at times for days, awaiting the successful insertion of another team into a rival's territory. Afghanistan's inherent tribalism and factional splits could never be ignored despite the common enemy.[23]

Task Force Dagger launched its first teams into Afghanistan on October 19–20, 2001. The first twelve-man team infiltrated into northern Afghanistan, to the south of the key city of Mazar-i Sharif, via helicopter, and on October 19 linked up with the local warlord, General Dostum.[24] They quickly began helping Dostum directly by calling in close air support (CAS) from B-1 and B-52 bombers and F-14, F-15, F-16, and F/A-18 fighter-bombers. It was the heavy bombers that finally broke the back of the Taliban defenders, who began streaming in retreat to Mazar-i Sharif and beyond. With the way to victory opened up to him by Special Forces, General Dostum secured the city of Mazar-i Sharif on November 10. The fall of the city was a devastating blow to the Taliban war effort.[25] Mazar-i Sharif and its airport also provided a new hub for the transportation of essential supplies directly into Afghanistan.

Another Task Force Dagger team deployed into northeastern Afghanistan during the night of October 19–20 to contact the Northern Alliance forces dug in on the Shamali Plains just south of the strategic Panjshir Valley, only fifty miles north of the capital city, Kabul, and the stronghold of Ahmed Shah Masood, the revered leader of the Northern Alliance assassinated by Al-Qaeda agents on September 9, 2001. The Northern Alliance forces controlled an old Soviet air base at Bagram, on the plains. The opposing Taliban forces could not penetrate the defensive minefields near the base or attack into the rich Panjshir Valley to the northeast. The team sought out Masood's successors, Generals Fahim Khan and Bismullah Khan. The team linked up with the two Northern Alliance commanders on October 21 at the Bagram air base. They soon found an ideal position from which to call in close air support—the old air traffic control tower at the airfield. "From that location, they could clearly see the Taliban positions in the Shamali Plains spread out before them and immediately began calling in air strikes on the entrenched enemy. From October 21 through November 14, 2001, the Special Forces directed almost continuous CAS missions against the dug-in enemy. The constant air attacks degraded the Taliban/Al-Qaeda command and control, killed hundreds of entrenched front-line troops, and disrupted their support elements. General Fahim Khan was encouraged to begin thinking about an immediate move against Kabul while the enemy was in disarray."[26]

With SOF and the Northern Alliance in direct coordination, the next stage of the air campaign added land- and sea-based fighter-bombers, which began hitting Taliban forces, buildings, and vehicles in pinpoint strikes while other U.S. aircraft began cluster-bombing larger Taliban defenses. AC-130 Spectre gunships and F-15E Strike Eagles from Jaber Air Base in Kuwait, the latter being the first land-based fighters to enter the campaign, joined the fray and began attacking Taliban troop concentrations and vehicles.[27] For the first time in years the Northern Alliance commanders began to see decisive destruction within the Taliban front lines.[28] The Northern Alliance forces soon began to overrun former Taliban positions. In response to the weakening of the Taliban, foreign fighters from Al-Qaeda took over security in some Afghan cities, demonstrating the instability of the Taliban regime. Meanwhile, the Northern Alliance and its Central Intelligence Agency and Special Forces advisers planned the next stage of the ground offensive. In that effort Northern Alliance troops were to seize Mazar-i-Sharif, both to cut the Taliban supply lines and to facilitate the crucial flow of military equipment from the formerly Soviet countries north of Afghanistan. The operation directed against Mazar-i-Sharif was to be followed by an attack on Kabul itself. "The overwhelming majority of ground forces opposing the Taliban in 2001 were Afghan."[29]

Task Force Sword

Task Force Sword, also known as Task Force 11, was Joint Special Operation Command's counterterrorism "hunter-killer" force, with the mission of capturing or killing senior leaders—or "high-value targets" (HVTs)—in both Al-Qaeda and the Taliban.[30] Task Force Sword in Afghanistan was initially structured around a two-squadron component of soldiers and a Navy SEAL (Sea-Air-Land) team, supported by Ranger security teams, NSA, the CIA, and other intelligence specialists.[31] Task Force Sword conducted the first American ground offensive action of the war on October 19, raiding Mullah Omar's Kandahar residence and a remote desert airstrip that would later become known to the world as Forward Operating Base (FOB) Rhino.

> Four MC-130 aircraft dropped 199 Rangers of the 3d Battalion, 75th Ranger Regiment (-) ["minus"—that is, indicating that a battalion or other major element had been detached] onto a desert landing strip southwest of Kandahar, code-named Objective Rhino. Assisted by circling AC-130 gunships, the Rangers quickly secured their objective. Then the soldiers and attached psychological operations (PSYOP) loudspeaker teams moved toward a nearby enemy compound and cleared it without resistance. Having secured the landing zone, they assisted follow-on helicopter-borne forces of SOF soldiers that had additional raids to conduct in the area. In all, the Rangers and SOF soldiers spent almost five and a half hours on the ground, suffering only a few minor injuries. Although the tactical results of the raid were mixed, the Taliban was shown that U.S. forces could strike anywhere and anytime and that no location in Afghanistan was a safe haven any longer.[32]

Task Force K-Bar

Captain Bob Harward, USN, assumed command of SOCENT in Doha, Qatar, in September 2001. His unit was soon redesignated Combined Joint Task Force South, after joining the Special Operations Forces of seven other nations, and later as Task Force K-Bar. Task Force K-Bar was one of the first ground assault teams in the U.S. invasion of Afghanistan, operating from October 2001 until April 2002. After deploying itself directly into southeastern Afghanistan, Task Force K-Bar conducted over forty reconnaissance and surveillance missions, as well as "direct action" operations that killed at least 115 Taliban and Al-Qaeda fighters and captured 107 senior Taliban leaders over a six-month period. Men from Task Force K-Bar also conducted high-altitude observation for other coalition units, numerous raids looking for enemy forces and intelligence, as well as recovery dive operations, boardings of high-interest noncompliant vessels, special reconnaissance, sensitive-site exploitation, destruction of multiple cave and tunnel complexes, apprehension of military and political detainees, identification and destruction of Al-Qaeda training camps, explosion of thousands of pounds of enemy ordnance, and coordination of unconventional warfare operations.[33]

Amphibious Forces—Task Force 58

Given Afghanistan's landlocked nature, few would have thought that amphibious forces would play a large role in combat there. But with the strong, well-developed presence of U.S. forces in the Gulf and Arabian Sea, once overflight and passage rights had been negotiated with Pakistan, CENTCOM forces could project amphibious capability into southern Afghanistan, thus putting pressure on the Taliban from two sides.[34] Navy Special Operations Forces and Marines from Task Force 58 became the essential parts of that southern pincer.

On September 28, the U.S. Marine Corps' 15th Marine Expeditionary Unit (Special Operations Capable), or MEU (SOC), had deployed forces ashore, inside Pakistan, to provide security for CSAR aircraft at the airfield in Jacobabad. On October 7 the 15th MEU and the Amphibious Squadron 1 SEAL detachment established a presence a second forward location, in Shamsi, Pakistan. Then, on October 30, Vice Admiral Charles W. Moore, Commander, U.S. Naval Forces Central Command, and Commander, Fifth Fleet, received a CENTCOM planning order from General Franks to prepare to conduct amphibious raids into Afghanistan. That same day Moore designed Brigadier General James N. Mattis, USMC, as the commander of Task Force 58, entrusting over eight thousand sailors and Marines from the assault ships USS *Peleliu* and *Bataan*.[35]

Initial Success

The Northern Alliance leadership had originally planned a multiday, five-phased operation to take the Afghan capital. However, it soon became apparent that the Taliban had been so badly affected by the U.S. air strikes that their forces could move on the capital more quickly. When the main attack began on November 13, the Taliban forces quickly fell apart. Twenty-four hours later, "to the surprise of the world press and the delight of the Northern Alliance, General Khan's ground forces liberated Kabul without incident. The Taliban and al Qaeda had fled in disarray toward Kandahar in the south and into the supposed sanctuary of the nearby Tora Bora Mountains to the east near Jalalabad. By early December U.S. troops were assisting in a ceremony reopening the U.S. embassy in Afghanistan's capital."[36] With the capture of Kabul, CENTCOM established a Combined Joint Civil Military Operations Task Force (CJCMOTF) "to coordinate the efforts of relief organizations in Kabul and to work to establish Coalition Humanitarian Liaison Cells (CHLCs) in many population centers. The work of restoration had begun even while the campaign to retake the remainder of Afghanistan continued."[37]

Very quickly thereafter, all of the western Afghan provinces, including the city of Herat, fell to anti-Taliban forces. Afghan warlords also returned to power throughout northeastern Afghanistan, and the Taliban was forced back to the northern city of Kunduz. By November 16, the Taliban's last stronghold in northern Afghanistan was under attack by forces of the Northern Alliance. At that point most of the Taliban had been driven back to their original heartland in southeastern Afghanistan near Kandahar. Soon, most of Al-Qaeda and some other Taliban remnants had been forced into a pocket in the Tora Bora area, near the Pakistani border, where they began preparing for a last stand against the Northern Alliance and U.S. forces.

Meanwhile, General Mattis and his Marines were still keeping the pressure on the Taliban in the south. On November 1 Mattis had been directed to "conduct a minimum of three to five raids into Afghanistan over a 30-day period." Later, on November 25, Marines from Task Force 58 commenced operations to establish FOB Rhino (seizing a site previously raided by Task Force Sword), the first U.S. base in Afghanistan, some one hundred miles southwest of Kandahar, to put pressure on the Taliban near its source of major support. General Franks stated, "The purpose of the Forward Operating Base is to give us a capability to be an awful lot closer to the core objectives we seek."[38]

Rhino was the first strategic foothold in Afghanistan and made the prosecution of the ground war in southern Afghanistan possible. While Rhino was being established, fierce battles between Taliban and Northern Alliance troops were still under way near Kandahar. But then the Taliban, realizing that American forces were closing in on them from the north and the south, capitulated, eventually retreating northeast to the mountains around Tora Bora.

Another Task Force Dagger team, ODA 574, deployed into Afghanistan to link up near Tarin Kowt on November 14 with local forces, along with Pashtun militia leader Hamid Karzai, who would later become the interim president of Afghanistan. In early November Karzai had entered Taliban-controlled eastern Afghanistan from Quetta, Pakistan, with a small force of guerrillas. In response, the inhabitants of Tarin Kowt had revolted and expelled their Taliban government. While Karzai was meeting with the town elders, the Taliban counterattacked with some five hundred men to retake the town. Karzai's guerrillas plus ODA 574 deployed to block the Taliban attack, which they repulsed largely due to American close air support.[39] Karzai was later evacuated to safety by the United States.[40] Upon his return, Karzai's forces pushed south toward Kandahar, and on December 7 Karzai was able to gain the surrender of Taliban forces around that key city, "the spiritual and political center of the Taliban movement."[41]

With American CIA and Special Forces teams linked up with the Northern Alliance, and both Kabul and Kandahar being under their control, the first major objectives of the Enduring Freedom campaign had been achieved within the first two months of combat. The next phase, however, required more capacity than the coalition forces then in country could muster. Conventional ground-force operations were needed to occupy key terrain, to root out the remaining Taliban and Al-Qaeda fighters, and to provide the initial security needed for stabilization.

Adapting Command Arrangements

Given the pace of events in Afghanistan, General Franks designated the U.S. Third Army, or U.S. Army Forces Central Command (ARCENT), commanded by Lieutenant General Paul T. Mikolashek, USA, to provide command and control for ongoing operations as the CFLCC. Mikolashek and his headquarters had deployed to Camp Doha, where he officially assumed his new responsibilities on November 20. General Mikolashek's assigned mission was to immediately "direct and synchronize land operations to destroy Al-Qaeda and prevent the reemergence of international terrorist activities in Combined Joint Area-Afghanistan, as well as to conduct humanitarian operations and create conditions for a peaceful, stable Afghanistan."[42]

Therefore on November 30, Task Force 58 units ashore in the Afghanistan Joint Operations Area (JOA) shifted to the tactical control (TACON) of the CFLCC. Task Force 58 remained under operational control of the Combined Force Maritime Component Commander (CFMCC—Vice Admiral Moore was NAVCENT as well). Soon thereafter, on December 3, Task Force 58 received an order from Mikolashek to interdict Taliban supplies flowing along Route 1. The initial intent was to block Taliban and Al-Qaeda forces traveling along the road, but the CFLCC refined his guidance during the upcoming days to "prevent/deny the escape" of Taliban and Al-Qaeda forces from Afghanistan. By the morning of December 14, Task Force 58 had established a second FOB, in Kandahar.

The tempo of operations and numbers of forces in Afghanistan soon convinced General Mikolashek to position a command-and-control node closer to the actual fighting. Mikolashek wanted to deploy his entire headquarters to the fight, but permission to do that was denied by Franks. CFLCC asked instead for the equivalent of a division tactical command post to serve as the CFLCC (Forward) headquarters, which would operate initially from the forward operating base at K2 in Uzbekistan. On November 25, the 10th Mountain Division, at Fort Drum, New York, commanded by Major General Franklin L. "Buster" Hagenbeck, received orders to deploy its headquarters to Central Asia for the mission (joining elements of the division already in the theater), it became CFLCC (Forward) on December 12, at Karshi Kanabad.

"The mission of CFLCC (Forward) was to command and control Army forces, less Special Operations forces, in the Combined and Joint Area of Operations, Afghanistan (CJOA). General Hagenbeck's first priorities were to ensure support for ongoing Special Forces operations, to oversee repair of the damaged airstrip at Mazar-e Sharif, and to open a ground line of communications into that key city."[43] The headquarters also worked with Uzbek officials and General Dostum to open the Freedom Bridge near Terrnez, Uzbekistan, clearing a critical pathway for the smooth flow of supplies and humanitarian aid from Central Asia into northern Afghanistan. Humanitarian aid and military supplies were critical components of the next stages of the fight. These command-and-control and logistical steps greatly facilitated the posturing of coalition forces for future operations and for the stabilization of the northern portion of Afghanistan.

The Tora Bora Assault

The Americans had been looking for Osama bin Laden since September 11. Later it would become known that he had been in both Kandahar and, on November 8, in Kabul[44]—both of which had been taken back from the Taliban. He then fled to Jalalabad, in eastern Afghanistan. By November 14, the CIA was receiving reports that the Al-Qaeda leader was in Jalalabad, giving pep talks to an ever-growing entourage of fighters. CIA team chief Gary Berntsen dispatched an eight-man team to the city, which was "crawling with fleeing Taliban and Al-Qaeda fighters."[45] Before the CIA team could get there, however, bin Laden and Ayman Al Zawahiri had fled north to Tora Bora.

Tora Bora, the "black cave," is a stone complex situated in the White Mountains of eastern Afghanistan, near the Khyber Pass. It was suspected to be in use by Al-Qaeda and the location of bin Laden's headquarters, as well as a cache for ammunition. On December 3, a CIA team and Special Forces operators from Task Force Sword were inserted to develop intelligence in support of a subsequent operation to destroy the complex and take the enemy fighters. On December 5, the Northern Alliance took control of the low ground below the mountain caves from Al-Qaeda fighters. The Americans called in Air Force bombers to take out selected targets, which forced the Al-Qaeda fighters to shift to higher fortified positions and dig in for a decisive battle. "As the fighting got underway, bin Laden initially sought to project an easy confidence to his men. Abu Bakr, a Kuwaiti who was at Tora Bora, said that, early in the battle, he saw bin Laden at the checkpoint he was manning. The Al-Qaeda leader sat with some of his foot soldiers for half an hour, drinking a cup of tea and telling them, 'Don't worry. Don't lose your morale, and fight strong. I'm here. I'm always asking about you guys.'"[46] It seemed that the Americans had a good chance of taking bin Laden out of the war.

Unfortunately a dispute was raging among American officials about how to conduct the battle. By late November, Hank Crumpton, the overall CIA coordinator for activities in Afghanistan, was beginning to fear that bin Laden might try to escape from Tora Bora. "He explained this to Bush and Cheney personally at the White House and presented satellite imagery showing that the Pakistani military did not have its side of the border covered. CIA Director George Tenet remembers Bush asking Crumpton if the Pakistanis had enough troops to seal the border. 'No, sir,' the CIA veteran replied, 'No one has enough troops to prevent any possibility of escape in a region like that.'"[47] Still, Crumpton thought the United States should try, by adding even more troops.

On the evening of December 3, one CIA member of Berntsen's team, a former Delta Force operator who had gone deep into Tora Bora, came to the Afghan capital to brief the lay of the land. He told Berntsen that taking out Al-Qaeda would require a Ranger battalion. "That night, Berntsen sent a lengthy message to CIA headquarters asking for eight hundred Rangers to assault the complex of caves where bin Laden and his lieutenants were believed to be hiding, and to block their escape routes. Crumpton says, 'I remember the message. I remember talking not only to Gary every day, but to some of his men who were at Tora Bora directly and their request could not have been more direct, more clear, more certain: that we needed U.S. troops there. More men on the ground.'"[48] General Franks disagreed and continued to depend on the local tribesmen and their few supporting members of Task Force Sword to do the job. He said at the time that there was no proof bin Laden was at Tora Bora (later reports discounted that view).[49] As the Northern Alliance advanced up through the difficult terrain, on December 12 and 13 some Al-Qaeda forces negotiated a truce with a local militia commander to give them time to surrender their weapons. Bin Laden was apparently still in the area on those dates—the same days that General Franks was in the Pentagon briefing Secretary Rumsfeld about his Iraq plan.[50] In retrospect, some believe that the truce was a ruse to allow bin Laden to escape.

The fighting flared again later, possibly initiated by an Al-Qaeda rear-guard action designed to buy time for the main force to escape through the mountains into the tribal areas of Pakistan. Once again, tribal forces backed by U.S. special operations troops and air support pressed ahead against fortified Al-Qaeda positions in caves and bunkers scattered throughout the mountainous region. British and German commandos accompanied the few American operators in the attack on the cave complex. By December 17, the last parts of the cave complex had been occupied and their defenders overrun. No massive bunkers were found, only small outposts and a few minor training camps.[51] Osama bin Laden was not found at Tora Bora.

Later, the failure to take the leader of Al-Qaeda out at Tora Bora became a cause célèbre. People involved, from both the CIA and Task Force Sword, argued that CENTCOM missed the chance to end the war that December. Peter Bergen proposed that Tora Bora may have been the first instance where Iraq issues negatively impacted the campaign in Afghanistan. Bergen wrote of the causes for failure at Tora Bora in 2009:

> Then there was Iraq. In late November, Donald Rumsfeld told Franks that Bush "wants us to look for options in Iraq." Rumsfeld instructed the general to "dust off" the Pentagon's blueprint for an Iraq invasion and brief him in a week's time. Chairman of the Joint Chiefs Richard Myers would later write, "I realized that one week was not giving Tom and his staff much time to sharpen" the plan. Franks points out in his autobiography that his staff was already working seven days a week, 16-plus hours a day, as the Tora Bora battle was reaching its climax. Although Franks doesn't say so, it is impossible not to wonder if the

labor-intensive planning ordered by his boss for another major war was a distraction from the one he was already fighting.[52]

Still the international coalition led by the United States and its Northern Alliance allies had much to be proud of by the end of December 2001. "With the capture of Kabul and Kandahar and the destruction of organized resistance in Tora Bora, Afghanistan was now in effect liberated. It had taken fewer than sixty days of concentrated military operations and only a few hundred soldiers to seize the country from the Taliban and its terrorist allies."[53]

Diplomatic and Humanitarian Efforts

The Bonn Agreement

Since the Taliban had been the de facto government of Afghanistan, by the end of the year the country was effectively without government at the national level and was only poorly served by provincial and local governments. Understanding this and acknowledging its responsibility to assist in the development of a new government, the international community sponsored a conference of twenty-three prominent Afghans in December 2001, in Bonn, Germany, to develop a plan for governing the country. Key members of the Afghan delegation included General Abdul Rahim Wardak, a Pashtun who as a mujahedeen resistance leader had fought the Soviets during the 1980s and would become defense minister; Yunus Qanooni, a Tajik protégé of Ahmad Shah Massoud; and Mirwais Sadeq Khan, another future minister and son of Ismail Khan. Other participants included representatives of the four major Afghan opposition groups, including the Northern Alliance but not the Taliban. Observers to the meeting were representatives of neighboring and other involved countries, including the United States.

As a result of the agreement, signed on December 5, 2001, the Afghan Interim Authority (AIA), to be made up of thirty members headed by a chairman, was created, with a six-month mandate. Hamid Karzai was named the AIA chairman. That mandate was to be followed by a two-year Transitional Authority, after which elections were expected to be held. The Transitional Authority was to facilitate the work of a constitutional *loya jirga*[54] tasked with preparing a constitution. The document granted authority to the Special Representative of the UN Secretary General (SRSG), then Lakhdar Brahimi, to "use his/her good offices with a view to facilitating a resolution to the impasse or a decision" if the Interim Administration or the Special Independent Commission (for establishing the emergency *loya jirga*) failed to support the work of developing a new Afghan constitution. The agreement also called for the creation of an independent Supreme Court of Afghanistan and requested voter registration and census support from the UN, with a view toward holding national elections (not specifically addressed in the agreement). One of the sections of the Bonn Agreement called for the establishment of a NATO-led International Security Assistance Force.

On December 20, the UN Security Council passed United Nations Security Council Resolution 1386 (2001), authorizing the establishment of an International Security Assistance Force (ISAF) to help the Afghans maintain security in Kabul and its surrounding areas.[55] "The United Kingdom (UK) assumed the lead for providing command and control (C2) for ISAF and appointed Major General John McColl to command the organization. By early 2002, eighteen other nations had pledged military forces to this command, which began operations that winter."[56] Then on December 22, in Kabul, the internationally recognized administration of President Rabbani handed power to the new Afghan Interim Authority, established in Bonn and headed by Chairman Karzai. The SRSG moved to Kabul to commence his work in support of the new Afghan administration. At the same time, the first of the ISAF troops were deployed in country, under British control.

Humanitarian Efforts

With the reduction of fighting in most areas of the country, international relief organizations were able to increase their efforts to help the Afghan people. The World Food Program (WFP) delivered some 114,000 metric tons of food in December, enough to feed six million people for two months. By December 20, approximately $358 million of the nearly $662 million being sought for UN relief work in Afghanistan had been received. While the WFP had achieved 81 percent of its funding requirements, UNHCR had secured only 59 percent of its anticipated needs.[57] As is common, international funds were being donated mostly for emergency relief, very little for reconstruction efforts in the war-torn country. To increase the flow of international assistance an International Conference on Reconstruction Assistance on Afghanistan was held in Tokyo on January 21 and 22, 2002.[58] The conference was attended by representatives of fifty-eight countries and included interim chairman Karzai, as well as his minister for foreign affairs, Abdullah Abdullah. Addressing the conference, Secretary-General Kofi Annan said such assistance would require

$10 billion over a ten-year period, including $1.3 billion to cover immediate needs for 2002.[59] It was only a start to the long-term effort to reconstitute the country after so many years of conflict.

These efforts to recreate the Afghan state and support its development seemed very logical at the time, but they unfortunately covered over an important fact about Afghanistan. "Afghanistan had a very different history and conception of the state. It was based on a model of state power and sovereignty in which rulers sought direct control of urban centers and productive irrigated agricultural lands, together with the lines of communication that linked them. Inhabitants in poor geographically marginal areas were left to fend for themselves as long as they did not challenge state authority."[60]

> When the United States entered Afghanistan in 2001 after the defeat of the Taliban, it and the international community gave priority to establishing a stable government in Kabul. Its Afghan interlocutors used the opportunity to lobby for a highly centralized government. They argued that without firm control from the center, Afghanistan would split apart because of ethnic and regional differences. In fact, no faction had ever proposed dividing the country on ethnic or regional lines. . . . The enthusiasm for restoring a highly centralized government was confined to the international community and the Kabul elite that ran it.[61]

This fundamental misunderstanding of the Afghan state would come to plague the international effort there in many ways.

Iraq Mission Development Begins

By December 2001, the tide of war in Afghanistan had clearly turned. Although the conflict was far from won, and in fact the contest in Tora Bora was beginning to go off course, General Franks in Tampa and several senior officials in the Pentagon were already turning their attention to the other potential adversary in the so-called war on terror. Secretary Rumsfeld had reminded Franks not to forget about Iraq back in the early days in September 2001[62] but seems to have not returned to the subject until the end of November, when he asked General Franks to develop a commander's concept for potential combat operations in Iraq. Franks quickly became deeply embroiled in that task, devoting ever more time to Iraq issues, though combat in Afghanistan continued.

The Enduring Freedom campaign was related indirectly to the potential conflict with Iraq in four important ways. First, both Afghanistan and Iraq are within the Central Command area of responsibility; thus General Franks and his staff would be responsible for operations in both countries and would have to manage all associated actions and activities, including deployment, resupply, and coordination of intelligence assets needed in both. Second, concurrent operations in both countries would frequently stretch sparse military assets beyond their normal operating capabilities. This was particularly true of airborne reconnaissance and Special Operations Forces. (Many such units would eventually serve in both countries, and some portion of what was learned during a deployment and in combat in one area could often contribute to an increase in proficiency when the unit was eventually assigned to the other country, but the operational environments in Afghanistan and Iraq were often very different.) Third, both were associated with the war on terror (although the conflict in Afghanistan was directly related to the attacks of September 11, making Operation Enduring Freedom central to prosecution of the war on terrorism, whereas any war in Iraq would have a much more tenuous link to terrorism). Finally, some policies designed for one country did eventually affect the conduct of operations in the other, either because people assumed the two operating environments were more alike than they were or because it became too difficult to develop different policies for concurrent operations. One example of this problem was the development of heavier, fully armored combat vehicles for Iraq that were insufficiently mobile for effective use in Afghanistan.[63]

General Franks seems to have focused only intermittently on the Iraq problem until December 4, when he gave his first Iraq briefing to Secretary Rumsfeld.[64] Franks was concerned about many aspects of the plan for operations in Iraq, but dominant among his concerns were the possibility of terrorist safe havens and the potential for the use of weapons of mass destruction (WMDs). After careful consideration of the matter, Franks proposed making regime change and removal of Saddam's WMD capability the main objectives of any military undertaking in Iraq.

During his initial VTC with Secretary Rumsfeld, Franks formally advanced several critical assumptions concerning a conflict with Iraq in order to establish in his own mind that he fully understood the mission and scope of operations. Franks specifically asked the defense secretary if removing the Saddam Hussein regime from Iraq was the correct objective, and he sought (and received) confirmation that the key mission requirements would include ending Iraq's capacity to threaten its neighbors with either conventional forces or WMDs.[65] Franks seemed to feel that the version of the war plan that was then current at CENTCOM (numbered 1003-98), a plan honed by his predecessor, General Zinni, did not reflect the current balance of forces between Iraq and the United States and had not benefited from the most recent lessons learned in Afghanistan. Franks therefore set out to have his staff conceive a new plan that would better reflect the current military balance of power between Iraq and the United States and also incorporate the lessons learned in Afghanistan.

General Franks felt that the 1003-98 plan was "based on Desert Storm–era thinking" and was "troop-heavy,"[66] probably because he had just witnessed the current capability of Special Operations Forces combined with modern airpower in Afghanistan. So the force totals listed in the existing plan were among the first areas slated for revision. Franks wanted a smaller, faster plan—like what had worked for Afghanistan. In particular, he was concerned about the amount of time it would take to deploy sufficient forces to accomplish his mission in Iraq, without completely sacrificing the element of surprise and placing forces at risk of counterattack from the Iraqi military (as they had been during Operation Desert Shield in Iraq in 1990).

When Franks next formally briefed Rumsfeld he had already cut the size of the force and had begun to focus more on speed than on combat power. After presenting his initial ideas in the VTC to Rumsfeld and Chairman of the Joint Chiefs of Staff, General Meyers, he went on to present the basic framework for operations in Iraq to the president at Bush's ranch in Crawford, Texas, on December 27. Franks felt his one-on-one meeting with the president was something of a test; apparently President Bush gained a feeling of trust for Franks, for he seemed very supportive of the general's ideas afterward.[67]

All of this took place as the campaign in Afghanistan was making crucial steps forward. There can be no doubt that the CENTCOM staff was overtasked during December trying to conduct one war while secretly planning for another. We will never know for certain if either campaign might have been executed better had they not been executed concurrently, but few doubt that Enduring Freedom failed to gain and retain the full attention of its commanders that it deserved in the winter of 2001–2002. The shifting of CENTCOM's attention from Afghanistan significantly increased the risk that the mission would not be accomplished as effectively as it deserved.

The Shift to More Conventional Operations

Once the fighting around Tora Bora had ended, it became obvious to commanders on the ground that the character of the combat operations in Afghanistan needed to change, in order to focus on the stabilization of the country.

> The goals and strategy of Operation Enduring Freedom underwent several revisions during the course of the war—actually, during its first three weeks. This turbulence reflected the difficulty of finding a strategy that could reconcile the administration's immediate war aims with a set of broader, longer-term strategic considerations—such as stability in Afghanistan and in the region surrounding it. During the war's third week it became clear that there was no such strategy available, and this posed a choice: either the United States would have to accept the prospect of a longer war or set aside some of its broader stability concerns. Given the potential political risks associated with any long-war scenario, this was an easy choice to make: the broader concerns were set aside.[68]

The choice in favor of short-term goals over longer-term accomplishments did not last long in Afghanistan, but it did have some negative implications, among which was the failure to develop a vision for conflict termination that could match the goal of keeping Al-Qaeda out of Afghanistan thereafter. Within a matter of weeks the Taliban and Al-Qaeda had been reduced to isolated pockets of fighters.[69] By mid-December, U.S. Marines under the command of General Mattis had secured Kandahar Airport; the Taliban capital was in the hands of the Northern Alliance, and in the north and east of the country other key cities, such as Kabul and Mazar-i-Sharif, were also free of the enemy. Conventional forces from the 10th Mountain and 101st Airborne Divisions were arriving in sizable numbers to augment the nascent Afghan security forces. By the end of December it was clear that the strategy then in use in Afghanistan would have to evolve if it was to have any real impact on the country itself.[70]

Fighting in 2002: Operation Anaconda

With the establishment of a new interim government in Afghanistan, the coalition had begun to build up its convention forces to focus on the stabilization effort in the country in 2002. U.S. forces established their main base at Bagram

Air Base, just north of Kabul. Kandahar airport also remained an important American site. Several outposts were established in eastern provinces to hunt for the remaining Taliban and Al-Qaeda fighters. The number of U.S.-led coalition troops operating in Afghanistan soon passed ten thousand.

Following the Tora Bora battle, intelligence analysts began searching for the remaining pockets of enemy forces throughout Afghanistan. Troops from Task Forces K-Bar and Sword hit a number of potential enemy locations south and west of the Tora Bora Mountains. Soon the focus of American intelligence-collection efforts shifted toward that area as well, particularly Paktia Province and the Gardiz-Khowst-Orgun-e triangle. The people in that area were Taliban sympathizers and were reported as tolerating the continued presence of Al-Qaeda fighters.[71] Indications were growing that there was a major concentration of enemy forces remaining in the Shahi Kowt Valley, southeast of Gardez.

The Shahi Kowt Valley runs north to south just to the west of a major mountain range about one hundred miles south of Kabul, near the Pakistani border. There are two main approaches to the valley, one from the northwest and the other from the southwest, around two major ridgelines just to the west and northwest of the valley. These major terrain features dominated the two approaches to the valley. Much of the valley is approximately 8,000 feet in elevation, with the surrounding peaks exceeding 11,000 feet. The valley was surrounded by formidable terrain, making the area difficult—nearly impossible—to isolate.[72] Estimates of enemy strength in the valley varied widely, from some two hundred to nearly a thousand.

Initially, Task Force Sword considered the option of attacking into the valley using only Special Forces teams leading the few hundred Afghan military forces they had trained. However, as the number of enemy assessed to be operating in the valley began to increase, Sword asked for planners from conventional units. By mid-February a total of six Special Forces (SF) "A Teams" of twelve men each, three SF command-and-control elements, three other special operations task forces, and a U.S. infantry brigade of three battalions were involved, along with nearly a thousand Afghan military in units trained by the Special Forces.[73] As the size of the American forces grew with the estimates of the enemy in the valley, on 15 February the planning effort for, and command and control of the forces involved in, the operation was given by General Mikolashek to his CFLCC (Forward), General Hagenbeck, as commander of a new Combined Joint Task Force Mountain (CJTF Mountain),[74] which was formed at the Bagram airfield on February 21, 2002.[75]

In response to continued enemy activity, on March 2, 2002, American and Afghan forces launched Operation Anaconda. According to General Franks, of the two thousand coalition troops involved about half were Afghan forces, whose primary mission is to block Al-Qaeda and Taliban forces from leaving the area. Some eight to nine hundred U.S. troops were involved in the initial combat operations, along with about two hundred special operations units from international partners (Australia, Canada, Denmark, Germany, France, and Norway) in the U.S.-led coalition. The bulk of the U.S. forces involved were from the 10th Mountain Division and the newly arrived 101st Airborne Division, based at Fort Campbell, Kentucky.[76]

"Operation Anaconda's scheme of maneuver called for isolation and encirclement of the valley area, followed by converging attacks to destroy Al-Qaeda forces. A mixture of Afghan militia, U.S. and coalition Special Operations, and conventional forces would establish three sets of concentric rings astride enemy escape routes before the main strike into terrorist defenses in the valley."[77] The plan called for close coordination of five different task forces—some of them including Afghan and coalition forces, using seven blocking positions, closing on the enemy from four different directions, all in the extremely demanding terrain of the Shahi Kowt Valley—by a divisional headquarters (that of Hagenbeck's 10th Mountain).

The attack was delayed for several days by bad weather. On D-day, 2 March, things started to go wrong almost immediately. The main effort, the combined Afghan–Special Operations Forces holding group known as Task Force Hammer, under the command of an Afghan, Zia Lodin, suffered a truck accident and then got bogged down in its approach before being hit by friendly fire from a circling AC-130 that killed one American, Chief Warrant Officer Stanley L. Harriman, and wounded three others.[78] Air support was poor throughout the day at a variety of places on the battlefield, but its lack of effectiveness was particularly detrimental to the Afghans, whose morale suffered in the face of continuous, strong enemy fire from excellent observation sites on the mountain heights. Bad weather rolled in, cutting off important second waves of helicopter-borne troopers from the 101st Division's Task Force Rakassan.

Unexpectedly, and though facing overwhelming numbers of coalition forces, the enemy fighters stood their ground. Due to their superb observation sites, "enemy mortars were particularly effective"[79] against the 10th Mountain Division's 1st Battalion, 87th Infantry, whose soldiers were trying to occupy battle positions known as GINGER and HEATHER. "Much of the enemy fire against the attempt to establish GINGER and HEATHER was coming from the nearby village of Marzak, just to the northwest of the positions. After repeated overflights of the town by unmanned aerial vehicles revealed enemy fighters but no indications of civilians, General Hagenbeck declared the village hostile and directed air strikes onto the town. A series of bombing runs virtually obliterated the village."[80]

The battle continued for another eighteen hours, with twenty-eight U.S. soldiers suffering injuries, before CJTF Mountain withdrew slightly and repositioned its forces farther south in the face of unexpectedly strong enemy fire. The heaviest American casualties occurred later, at about 0300 on March 4, during an effort to establish two observations posts above the enemy, when a Navy SEAL, Petty Officer 1st Class Neil Roberts, was knocked from an MH-47 Chinook helicopter and was captured and (though it was not then known) killed.[81] Later in the early morning, a second helicopter returned under fire and dropped troops near where Roberts had fallen, and then two more helicopters (one of which was shot down) were dispatched to the same "hot zone"; six more Americans died in that firefight attempting to rescue Roberts.[82] Americans now call this engagement the battle of Roberts Ridge.[83]

Operation Anaconda would continue for a total of nineteen days. From March 5 to March 9, U.S. forces continued to move down the eastern ridgeline while the Commander Zia Task Force fought for control of one of the two major ridgelines, known a s "the Whale," and the valley floor, known as Objective Remington. Al-Qaeda and Taliban fighters were still trying to launch small counterattacks. By March 9, CJTF Mountain had taken Objective GINGER, dominating Objective Remington, and had isolated the Whale, using airpower. From March 7 to March 12 the fighting gradually was reduced to dealing with remaining snipers. Zia's task force finally took control of the Whale and the valley floor on March 12. Finding the entire operation highly successful, General Franks, declared Anaconda officially over on March 19.[84] Only a few months later, the battle would become the focus of a great deal of criticism.

What Went Wrong in Anaconda?

Although Al-Qaeda lost many of its most experienced and most aggressive fighters in this operation, in truth, it was far from fully successful. According to the official U.S. Army history of the war:

For the first time in the war, the Al-Qaeda had indeed stood and fought. They had occupied well-camouflaged, dug-in fighting positions with overhead cover and large stocks of food and ammunition. They had excellent forward observation posts that provided early warning and observation for placing well-targeted mortar and artillery onto any coalition forces coming into the valley. The initial U.S.-led Afghan ground attack failed in part due to poor air support, a lack of artillery, and, most damning, a more numerous and aggressive enemy than anticipated. Despite focusing all available intelligence collection assets, including many highly sophisticated national assets, on a relatively small square of ground in Afghanistan, the United States was still unable to gain an accurate picture of enemy size, strength, and intentions.

All that was true, but even larger problems were behind the failure to smash the last large pocket of Taliban and Al-Qaeda resistance in 2002. The command structures in place at the time did not give General Hagenbeck operational control of all the forces involved in the fighting. He elected not to employ his own artillery in Afghanistan. Air support was poor largely because CENTCOM air force components had not been effectively included in the planning and execution of the operation. The command structures inside CENTCOM and those designed for operations inside Afghanistan were confused and poorly coordinated.[85] These shortfalls were quickly corrected, but the coalition had learned an important lesson about the tenacity of the adversary it was fighting in Afghanistan.

Balanced Early Success, But Overconfidence

By late March of 2002, despite the frustrating end to the battle at Tora Bora and the high casualties experienced during Anaconda, most people around the world considered Operation Enduring Freedom a resounding success; most in fact expected that Osama bin Laden and his Al-Qaeda organization would soon be rolled up and that some semblance of calm might even return to the region. In reality the situation was quite different. The effects of the operation were assessed at the time in this way:

> 3,000 to 4,000 Taliban coalition troops are dead. . . . [A]pproximately 7,000 Taliban and foreign troops were prisoners as of 15 January; most of the top Taliban leadership has survived the war and eluded capture; many are in Pakistan and seeking to re-integrate into Afghanistan; of

more than three dozen Taliban leaders on the Pentagon's "wanted list," more than 12 have been killed, injured or have defected. At least eight of the 20 top Al-Qaeda leaders and aides pursued by the Pentagon in Afghanistan are believed dead. Eleven training camps affiliated with Al-Qaeda, and many other Al-Qaeda facilities in Afghanistan, have been destroyed or overrun."[86]

Analyst Carl Conetta later wrote, "Translating these achievements into qualitative terms: the Taliban have been driven from power in Afghanistan, fragmented as a political force, and widely discredited as an ideological movement. Nonetheless, many members and veterans are likely to reassume a role in the Afghan polity—some as provincial insurgents, others as members or even leaders of other formations. Al-Qaeda infrastructure and operations in Afghanistan have been destroyed, a substantial proportion of their core cadre have been attrited, and their capacity to act globally has been disrupted significantly—although perhaps only temporarily."[87] Conetta also observed, "Taliban have been driven from power and Al-Qaeda has been scattered to the hills, but Afghanistan has not come to rest in a stable place."[88]

Though the operational concept employed in Afghanistan had been quite unconventional, General Franks and his CENTCOM staff had directed the campaign from Tampa, largely as they had practiced during Exercise Internal Look in November 2000 and in Exercise Lucky Sentinel the previous spring. Enduring Freedom demonstrated a relatively unique American approach to combat, driven largely by the circumstances of the terrain, time, and distance in Afghanistan.[89] Though Osama bin Laden and many of his supporters were later found to have escaped from the Tora Bora pocket, the operation in Afghanistan was a successful example of the integrated employment of special operations, strategic firepower, and indigenous forces to topple a repressive regime. Nonetheless, the ability of those same forces and their arriving NATO/ISAF allies to restore stability to Afghanistan had yet to be proven. Overall, Enduring Freedom operations up to the spring of 2002 had shown balanced early success but indications of overconfidence. Though Anaconda's weaknesses were largely tactical, in retrospect, the battle also showed that CENTCOM could not effectively manage intense efforts for both Afghanistan and Iraq.

The Advent of "Shock and Awe" for Iraq

Before the fighting in Afghanistan was completely finished, as has been seen, General Franks and his staff were asked to redirect the focus of their efforts to possible operations against Saddam Hussein's Iraq. Many of the lessons learned in Afghanistan would change how the planning and fighting in Iraq were conducted, but with each passing day the actions connected with Iraq took priority and dominated decisions. The effort in Afghanistan soon slipped to second place among the key policy makers in Washington.

By the end of January 2002, General Franks and his staff had developed what they called a "generated start" plan for an invasion of Iraq. It was a generated start because for the first time in recent history, America was to go to war on its own time line, without a specific provocation, and with some degree of secrecy (which was required in order to employ force effectively against the Iraqi regime). Due to the time required to mass a decisive amount of force near Iraq, the early-deploying phases of any generated-start operation would be fraught with risk. One of Frank's early recommendations was that the United States triple the amount of forces it had stationed in Kuwait, using the ongoing effort in Afghanistan as a cover. Secretary Rumsfeld reminded Franks that no decision for war had been made and that the United States could not even signal such a possibility without a presidential decision, but he approved Franks' recommendation, along with an increase in the Gulf region's support infrastructure.[90]

Franks outlined four phases of operations for his concept, two of which were a deployment phase of some six months and a "phase four" posthostilities effort that would take "years not months" to complete.[91] The total number of troops envisioned at this point was about 400,000. After Franks had outlined three broad approaches to the amount of force to be employed (including a unilateral option without allies), President Bush closed the discussion by noting, "We don't know what kind of weapons they've developed, and we don't know Saddam's intentions . . . but we do know he has used WMD before. . . . We can not allow weapons of mass destruction to fall into the hands of terrorists. I will not allow that to happen."[92]

With that guidance and concurrence on its basic concept, over the spring of 2002 the Central Command staff continued to hone its plan, in concert with component-command staffs from the four services. As the plan matured it began to take on characteristics of a new warfighting approach that had been pioneered by a group of retired senior officers in the mid-1990s. This construct, named "Shock and Awe" (after their book),[93] emphasized shattering the cohesion of an enemy force with rapid-tempo operations, much like the impact of the highly mobile Wehrmacht on the French forces in 1940. It fit well into the desire by Rumsfeld, Franks, and others in the Pentagon to reduce the number of forces in the plan but still achieve a decisive effect.[94] During February, March, and April 2002 Franks would brief Rumsfeld several times, and each time the number of forces in the plan would be reduced. The expectation was that the lower number of troops would facilitate surprise and rapid deployment, while the technological advantage held by American forces would fill the resulting gap in force-on-force firepower ratios.

In subsequent briefings Franks discussed a deployment phase of only four months to develop a force of 160,000 troops for the main assault. Although this was a significant reduction in the forces needed to oust Saddam Hussein, the posthostilities phase of Franks's plan still envisioned some 250,000 men and women.[95] Meanwhile, a study indicated that the ideal time for any attack would be in the winter months of January, February, or March, when the Iraqi army would be at its lowest state of readiness.

On March 21, General Franks convened his component commanders to conduct a rehearsal of the plan as it then stood in the Warrior Prep Center, near Ramstein Air Force Base, Germany (the site and the wearing of civilian clothes provided excellent operations security). During that meeting he was able to reveal the seriousness of the president's intentions and to work face to face with his key leaders. The planning effort up to that point had been highly classified and compartmented (labeled "top secret," code word "Polo Step"), and the meeting provided the first forum for all the key players to work through the intricacies of the plan and their mutual support needs. During the meeting, Franks discussed his concept to confront Saddam with multiple crises at the same time—attacking from several directions, including Turkey in the north, Kuwait in the south, and from the air. This was very much in the style of Shock and Awe. The air component commander, Lieutenant General T. Michael Moseley (who had replaced General Wald in November), argued for a longer air campaign; the land forces component commander, Lieutenant General Mikolashek, proposed starting his attack before the air assault, in order to surprise the Iraqis. Mikolashek also voiced concerns about the numbers in the plan.[96] Mikolashek was also running the ongoing fight in Operation Anaconda, so he had every reason to be concerned about the coordination of air and ground forces in an even larger campaign. The Central Command component commanders debated the sequencing of the attacks, and Lieutenant General Mikolashek, though very preoccupied by events in Afghanistan, continued to voice concerns about key elements of the plan;[97] however, no one questioned the logic of attacking Saddam Hussein while combat continued in Afghanistan. The rehearsal discussion among key commanders should have addressed the daunting challenges of fighting two campaigns in the same theater.

Franks conducted another briefing with the president on May 11, 2002; by that time the CENTCOM staff had come up with a way to help hide the increasing activity around Iraq by spiking air activity in the no-fly zones to desensitize the Iraqis. Moseley and his air planners had also developed an inside-out air attack scheme that would help keep the Republican Guard out of Baghdad so the Iraqi capital would not become another Stalingrad—where massive urban casualties had been inflicted in World War II.[98] The plan was much improved, yet on May 23 the president still stated publicly that there were "no war plans on my desk" for a war with Iraq.[99] Most Americans believed that his full attention and the efforts of his senior military officials were directed at the fighting in Afghanistan. Those serving in Afghanistan soon sensed that the truth was very different.

Four

Iraq and the Iraqi Freedom Campaign
Shift of National Strategic Focus

For the sake of peace in the world and security for our country and the rest of the free world . . . and for the freedom of the Iraqi people.
—President George W. Bush[1]

A fter the fall of Kabul in 2001, the tide of war in Afghanistan had clearly turned in favor of the United States. Though that conflict was still ongoing, General Franks in Tampa and several other senior officials in the Pentagon were soon shifting their attention to other potential adversaries in the American "war on terror," principally Iraq. In the immediate aftermath of 9/11, President Bush had asked his intelligence staff to find any shred of links between Al-Qaeda and Saddam Hussein.[2] According to journalist Bob Woodward, Bush became convinced of Saddam's involvement within six weeks.[3] Secretary of Defense Rumsfeld had reminded Franks not to forget about Iraq back the early days in September 2001;[4] the secretary returned to the subject just after Kabul fell to the coalition in November, asking the Central Command commander to develop a concept for potential combat operations in Iraq. As we have seen, Franks became increasingly embroiled in that planning task during December, devoting ever more time to Iraq issues even as significant combat operations in Afghanistan continued, some 1,400 miles from Baghdad.

Directing the regional combatant commander to shift any of his attention from events in Afghanistan indicated that a significant change in mind-set had already begun, very soon after the coalition found such rapid success in Operation Enduring Freedom. The fall of Kabul seemed to justify what many in Rumsfeld's Defense Department saw as the triumph of more modern, high-technology forces over third-world opponents. That this was a mistake would become painfully obvious in time, but its immediate impact was twofold. First, the operations in and around Tora Bora, in Afghanistan, where the United States found its best early chance to kill bin Laden, did not receive the full attention of the Defense Department or Central Command, and bin Laden escaped.[5] Second, after the fall of Kabul the baseline assumptions upon which the campaign in Iraq was founded included an insidious false emphasis on speed instead of mass in the Iraqi battlefield. Despite the problems in Anaconda, Secretary Rumsfeld, Franks, and others seemed to believe that the advances of technology in the American military finally allowed warfare without large numbers of troops.

While Franks and his CENTCOM staff were focusing most of their attention on Iraq, the United Nations was passing UNSCR 1386, which confirmed the Afghan Interim Authority as the legitimate government in the country and created the International Security Assistance Force to lead in the security efforts there as envisaged by the Bonn Agreement.[6] Although ISAF was initially chartered only to secure Kabul and its surrounding areas from the Taliban, Al-Qaeda, and factional warlords and to support the eventual establishment of the new Afghan Transitional Administration (ATA), its establishment portended that the United States would soon have a reduced role in Afghanistan.[7] Both of these actions helped persuade Franks and many around the world that the U.S. effort in Afghanistan had reached a fundamental turning point. Though a great deal had been accomplished in Afghanistan, there was still much more needed to ensure that the Taliban and its Al-Qaeda partners could not someday regroup and return to Kabul. Still, America, in its hubris, turned its attention elsewhere.

The "Axis of Evil" and President Bush

In January 2002, President Bush had addressed the American people in his annual State of the Union address and introduced a new strategic construct that would play a large role in all aspects of American international relations in the coming year. He said,

Iraq continues to flaunt its hostility toward America and to support terror. The Iraqi regime has plotted to develop anthrax and nerve gas and nuclear weapons for over a decade. This is a regime that has already used poison gas to murder thousands of its own citizens, leaving the bodies of mothers huddled over their dead children. This is a regime that agreed to international inspections then kicked out the inspectors. This is a regime that has something to hide from the civilized world. States like these, and their terrorist allies, constitute an axis of evil, arming to threaten the peace of the world. By seeking weapons of mass destruction, these regimes pose a grave and growing danger.[8]

It seemed to many people around the world that Afghan campaign was receding in importance and that President Bush was ready to expand his national counterterrorism efforts elsewhere. Indeed, by the end of that same month, General Franks had developed his new, "generated start" plan for an invasion of Iraq.[9]

Meanwhile on Tuesday, February 5, calling on his countrymen to "take each other's hands" to rebuild the nation, interim Afghan leader Hamid Karzai raised Afghanistan's new flag over the presidential palace. With a new government and new leader in place in Kabul, and a new international force mandated for security, the campaign in Afghanistan seemed clearly on the path to resolution—after less than six months. But in any war, nothing is certain until the end; only two weeks later, before dawn on February 16, ISAF soldiers suffered their initial casualties when a post in Kabul came under attack. Soldiers of the British 2nd Parachute Battalion returned fire. The following week saw the first units of a new Afghan army starting to train in Kabul. Then, in late March, the Security Council voted to create the UN Assistance Mission in Afghanistan (UNAMA) for a period of one year.

Despite appearances and what many in Washington wanted to believe, war is fundamentally unpredictable, and the campaign in Afghanistan was not yet resolved. Operation Anaconda in the Shahi-Kowt Valley in early March 2002 had clearly shown that to be true. The Taliban had been strong enough there to launch a counterattack against the coalition forces, with what later information suggested was of five hundred to a thousand fighters.[10] Some five hundred Taliban fighters had been eventually killed in the fighting—more than in all but the largest of battles to be fought in Iraq.

A New National Strategy of Preemptive Attack

In the late spring of 2002, President Bush revealed a new national strategy, calling for America to "take the battle to the enemy, disrupt his plans, and confront the worst threats before they emerge."[11] This "preemptive attack" strategy radically changed the national approach of the United States toward global threats.[12] The basic tenets of this new strategy were that the United States could no longer sit back and wait for attacks to unfurl across the sea but must proactively analyze and act to prevent attacks from reaching its shores. General Franks conducted another briefing with the president on May 11, 2002; by that time, as we have seen, the CENTCOM staff had come up with a way to help hide the increasing activity around Iraq by spiking air activity in the no-fly zones to accustom the Iraqi force fluctuations. Through the summer of 2002, while events in Afghanistan continued to unfold, General Franks and the CENTCOM staff rarely stopped working on the plan for war in Iraq. By August the pressure from the White House was so great that Franks told his commanders that they needed to be ready attack in Iraq on a moment's notice. As Army Chief of Staff General Eric Shinseki noted in October 2002, "from today forward the main effort of the U.S. Army must be to prepare for war with Iraq"[13]—and so it was. The campaign in Afghanistan had slipped to "yesterday's news."

Unfortunately progress in Kabul remained uneven at best. It was at that point, October 27, that the top UN envoy in Afghanistan, Lakhdar Brahimi, told the UN Security Council that the Karzai's government did not have the power to deal with the underlying problems that were the cause of Afghanistan's security issues and that there would be no long-term security in Afghanistan until a well-trained, well-equipped, and regularly paid national police force and national army were in place.[14] With that sober news, the United Nations had agreed to an extension of the UN mission in Afghanistan and to a command shift for ISAF in February 2003.

Postconflict Planning—National to Operational

Although postconflict concerns for the invasion of Iraq had been discussed from the very first briefings between Central Command and the president, the question of which government agency would direct American activities after the fall of Saddam was not formally determined until January 24, 2003, only weeks before combat operations began. During a National Security Council meeting on that date the president determined that the Defense Department would direct activities in the immediate aftermath of Saddam's removal. Soon thereafter, President Bush signed National Security Presidential Directive 24,[15] specifying the responsibilities for managing a postinvasion Iraq. Very quickly after that determination of postconflict responsibility, Secretary Rumsfeld's staff developed the concept for the Office of Reconstruction and Humanitarian Assistance (ORHA), which was to manage such activities in Iraq. The NSC assigned a senior director and an executive group to oversee Iraq policy implementation, but that organization left the planning and implementation tasks to the Defense Department (DoD).

As the official U.S. Army history of the war states, "Despite the misgivings about nation-building, the DoD did commit resources to the planning of post invasion operations. In retrospect, however, the overall effort appears to have been disjointed and, at times, poorly coordinated, perhaps reflecting the department's ambivalence toward nation-building. Franks did not see postwar Iraq as his long-term responsibility. He later wrote that he expected a huge infusion of civilian experts and other resources to come from the U.S. Government after CENTCOM completed the mission of removing the Saddam regime. Franks' message to the DoD and the Joint Chiefs was, 'You pay attention to the day after, and I'll pay attention to the day of.'"[16]

The Final "Five Attacks Plan" and Back to the Future: Cobra II

With a final, resourced plan ready for execution, all that was required were the final unit deployments, positioning for the assault, and the execute order from the president of the United States. Very little could have stopped execution after January 2003. Strategic timing issues drove much of the final preparations for the attack into Iraq; the training cycles of the defending Iraqi forces, the negative effects of hot weather on coalition forces, the availability of strategic reconnaissance assets during the winter lull in Afghanistan, and the desire to keep international pressure on Saddam meant that the thrust north out of Kuwait needed to be set in the early spring of 2003. Military planners can always use more time to refine their efforts, particularly in cases such as the 2003 invasion of Iraq, where they were effectively planning one major campaign while continuing to fight another some 1,300 miles away. However if combat operations were to be ordered, the campaign had to start early enough to avoid the summer heat, and CENTCOM expected forty-five days of high-intensity combat. Therefore the force needed to be postured and ready early in the year.

Once all the details of the plan were synchronized, the initial attack into Iraq was scheduled to begin forty-eight hours after an ultimatum for Saddam and his sons to depart was issued by President Bush. That set D-day for Operation Iraqi Freedom as March 19, 2003. As the evening of March 19 arrived, everything was set in the Kuwaiti desert south of Iraq. President Bush communicated with each of General Frank's component commanders[17] in a secure video teleconference to ensure each one had what he needed to begin the assault. After confirming that everything was in place, he directed, "For the sake of peace in the world and security for our country and the rest of the free world. And for the freedom of the Iraqi people, as of this moment I will give Secretary Rumsfeld the order necessary to execute operation Iraqi Freedom."[18]

Unexpected Encounters: The Problems of Combat on the Cheap

The initial push to break through the Iraqi defenses went much better than expected, as did the movement to control the Rumaylah oil fields; the Iraqi military was largely caught off guard by the coalition axis of attack. The attack was commanded on the ground by army Lieutenant General Dave McKiernan, using two major subordinate commands, one Marine and one Army: I Marine Expeditionary Force (I MEF), under Lieutenant General Jim Conway, and V Corps, under Lieutenant General William Wallace. (The major tactical commanders were Major General Jim Mattis of the 1st Marine Division and Major General Buford Blount, USA, of the 3rd Infantry Division.) Very quickly, however, it became obvious to the leaders on the ground that a real paucity of operational intelligence about Iraqi units and their leaders left coalition commanders uncertain about the locations and intentions of the Iraqi forces. As the penetration grew deeper it also became clear that the expectation of the type of Iraqi resistance expected had been far from accurate.[19] Though the coalition forces that penetrated early into Iraq met with great success—even greater than expected, in fact—when they were opposed it was most frequently by Saddam Fedayeen militia forces, who mounted an irregular-force battle of hit and run, without uniforms or the cohesive "conventional structure" that the coalition had anticipated. This hit-and-run tactic did not bode well for the continuing advance deeper into more inhabited areas of Iraq, particularly as the militia tended to use civilians as shields.

The main V Corps attack through southwestern Iraq along the Euphrates River toward Baghdad was spearheaded by the 3rd Infantry Division (3rd ID) and its commander, "Buff" Blount. His division was to secure the corps advance base at Talil air base, then press north toward Najaf and Karbala. Unfortunately, what the army troopers found at the small town of Samawah changed their plan. They took the bridges over the Euphrates River easily enough, but once they pushed into the town they were immediately counterattacked by the Saddam Fedayeen in significant numbers. Where they had expected flowers and a parade, they found a vicious fight.[20] Lieutenant Colonel Terry Ferrell commanding the 3rd Squadron, 7th Cavalry Regiment told General Blount over the radio, "This is nothing like we planned to fight."[21]

As Blount's forces began to punch against isolated strongpoints all along the western side of the Euphrates, Saddam Hussein came to believe that his forces were defending successfully in the southwest and staving off the coalition attack. In reality, Blount's division was still racing north toward Saddam's capital, nearly as fast as his huge, fuel-inhaling tank engines could stand. Saddam was so convinced that he was holding his own against the coalition that he sent messages to the French and Russians asking them to stop efforts to gain a cease-fire; he may even have thought he was winning the war.[22]

At that point in the campaign the effects of the big "A-day" air-plan attacks were still to come, and although much of Iraq's infrastructure was off-limits to the coalition air planners (as a result of lessons during the previous campaign), the full weight of the coalition attack was far from obvious.[23] At that point too, the real motive force of the attack—speed, which would be the tool of choice to unhinge the Iraqi government—had yet to be fully employed.[24] The American public knew very little of the fighting at this early stage; General Franks was supremely confident; Saddam Hussein was confused; and his generals were far, far out of touch.

General Mattis and his 1st Marine Division in their supporting attack had passed through Nasiriyah and were racing north along two axes: Regimental Combat Team 1 (RCT-1) on Iraqi Route 7 toward Kut, and RCT-5, followed by RCT-7, on Route 1 up between the two rivers toward Diwaniyah and Hillah. The Marines of RCT-5 attacked into Diwaniyah on the 26th and were soon fighting northward through the cities and towns at the junction of Routes 7 and 17.

The lead brigades of the 3rd ID had continued north after dealing with Samawah, and by March 25 they were poised to take Najaf. Intelligence sources

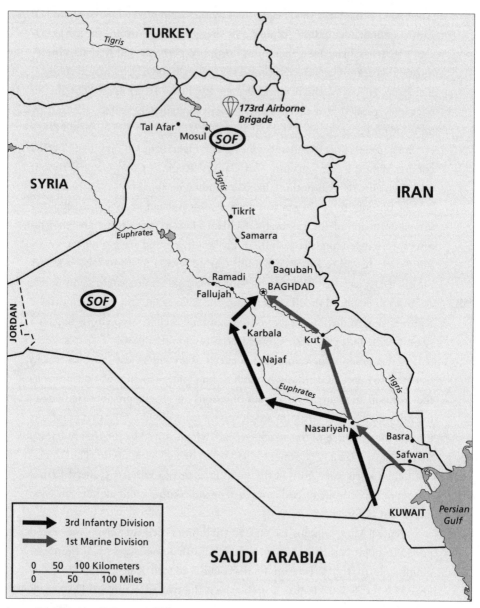

Iraq: the Initial Iraqi Freedom Campaign

indicated to General Blount that the Saddam Fedayeen militias were reinforcing in Najaf and, even more surprising, had displayed a willingness to attack
out from the city against the American forces.[25] Najaf was not only quite a
large metropolitan area but one of the most holy cities in Islam; severe "fires"
(that is, air and artillery strikes) restrictions had been imposed in order to safeguard the religious sites in the city center. General Blount decided to isolate
Najaf rather than attack it; the 3rd ID did so by the 27th, but the fighting even
around the city took many by surprise.

Then, on March 27, General McKiernan issued an order to halt the advance into Iraq. General Wallace and Blount had encountered more opposition than expected on the left of the coalition attack, and the Marines had
encountered more of the same moving up in the center. Even more discon-
certing to McKiernan and his staff was the fact that the enemy was fighting
a different kind of war that had been foreseen, something more akin to an
irregular delaying action than a conventional fight. McKiernan developed the
impression that an operational pause was necessary—perhaps for a few days.[26]
Unfortunately the decision to halt occurred at nearly the same time that the
media was reporting negatively about the progress of the campaign, quoting
General Wallace as saying, "The enemy we're fighting is different from the one
we'd war-gamed against."[27] Coinciding as it did with the decision to pause,
such ideas upset both General Franks and Secretary Rumsfeld. The pause and
the overly confused international media coverage contributed to Saddam Hussein's belief that he could still win the conflict.[28]

Driving Forward: The Escarpment and Kut

General McKiernan released the 3rd ID to attack north toward Karbala on the
first of April.[29] Karbala was a real concern. If there was a place where the Iraqi
forces were likely to defend against the attack route of the division, it was at
the Karbala Gap, a plain between the Euphrates and a lake about twenty miles
to the west—and that was also the place many feared Saddam might likely
employ his chemical weapons.[30] Thankfully no major forces were blocking
the Americans, and the Saddam Fedayeen militia commander in Karbala had
arrayed his forces to the south and southeast of the city, away from the route of
march of the 3rd ID's vehicles.

It is likely that Saddam Hussein had never believed that Americans would
attack Iraq with the goal of ending his regime. Based upon a belief that his

French and Russian diplomatic partners could dissuade America from all-out war and what he perceived as an American tendency to give up before facing extreme casualties, Saddam assumed that President Bush could at most attempt to control the Shia-dominated areas of southern Iraq. But the speed of the American forces quickly sealed the fate of the Iraqi regime. Saddam and his generals had no idea that their opponents could move forces toward Baghdad at the speeds that were evident over the last two weeks of March. "Such movements were simply beyond their understanding of military operations and logistics capabilities."[31] The speed advantage that General Franks had pressed on his subordinates for the sake of tactical success had indeed been a major contributor to the strategic success of the campaign.

Penetrating the "Red Zone"

By April 3, three weeks into the invasion, coalition forces had crossed through the suspected "red zone," where they feared Iraqi counterattacks with chemical weapons, and had moved into the distant outskirts of Baghdad.[32] Once the coalition forces got close to the city, General McKiernan issued an order assigning the Tigris River as a boundary between the two American forces, giving the Marines the eastern zone of Baghdad as an objective to control. V Corps and the MEF were to grip the city from the west and southeast, respectively, and gradually move in, forcing the defending Iraqi forces into untenable positions in the city and then attack them with precision air and artillery fires.

General Blount pressed his division attack directly into the Baghdad International Airport. Then a task force from the army's 64th Armored Regiment executed a raid, later called "Thunder Run,"[33] to rupture the remaining Iraqi defenses. The next day, April 7, Blount conducted a second armored raid, deeper into downtown Baghdad, and occupied and held one of Saddam Hussein's palaces in fierce fighting. Blount's men did not exfiltrate; they stayed downtown, and the raid became a dagger thrust into the heart of the Ba'ath regime. Saddam was no longer in control.

The Marines too maintained the momentum of their attacks toward the city center. All three Marine regiments crossed the Diyala River on April 5 and pressed toward eastern Baghdad.[34] Three days later, with approval from Lieutenant General McKiernan, they advanced into Baghdad itself. When the

Marines seemed to encounter only limited opposition, they continued their advance deeper into the city.[35]

The Marine sector included Baghdad's Firdos Square, with a huge statue of Saddam Hussein at its center. Late in the day on April 9 the Marines rolled in, to finally be met in Iraq only by cheering crowds. The local Iraqis promptly decided to topple the statue (with the Marines' help). Within hours of the palace seizure by the 3rd ID and with television coverage of the crowds in Firdos Square spreading throughout the globe, U.S. forces ordered Iraqi forces within Baghdad to surrender.

Catastrophic Success

As operationally successful as the initial phase of Iraqi Freedom was, grounds for important criticism remain. In particular, it became clear that efficiency in modern battle cannot mean doing only enough to defeat the enemy forces. The major shortfall in execution of the conventional phase of Operation Iraqi Freedom was the coalition's inability to properly assess the impact of its own highly successful synergistic attack on an opponent trained for a much more methodical battle. In fact, the American forces so far exceeded the expectations of most planners that their senior commanders were unable to control the catastrophic results of their own impact on Iraq. They were unable to effectively transform their combat power after April 10 so as to develop some practical control over the wide array of activities in Iraq—particularly response to looting by the population—needed in order to control events throughout some semblance of a transition to stability operations. As strong as the coalition was between March 20 and April 10, it quickly lost its influence over events in Iraq, and it lost control by the last week of April, when the Iraqis rose up to destroy almost every vestige of the Ba'ath Regime.

Anticlimax: The Lost Year of the Coalition Provisional Authority

The Operation Iraqi Freedom plan called for the rapid turnover of responsibility in Iraq to retired general Jay Garner and an organization he put together, the ORHA. In practice, the transition from primarily conventional combat operations to what was considered to be posthostilities activities in Iraq was fraught with difficulty. First, ORHA was on the ground in Iraq for only a few weeks before it was superseded by a new organization, the Coalition Provisional

Authority, led by Ambassador Paul Bremer. Secondly, the U.S military was given very clear guidance by the secretary of defense to begin a drawdown of forces as quickly as possible. Finally, the Iraqi expatriates who had been identified to lead Iraq in the immediate post–Saddam era were woefully disorganized and inadequate to the task. When combined with significantly greater destruction in Iraq and a general loss of civil order in the major Iraqi cities, these factors made April and May 2003 a critical and unfortunate turning point in the campaign.

General Garner and his staff had developed a plan for the posthostilities effort. They were clearly a pickup team, without much practice working together, but they were all committed to the task of restoring Iraq's essential services. Garner and his team had planned to partner, ministry by ministry, advise, and assist the Iraqis in reforming their government and quickly getting their country back on its feet.[36] The problem was that by the time Garner and his advance team got to Baghdad, seventeen of the twenty-three Iraqi ministries were completely dysfunctional—due to the chaos that followed the end of the Ba'ath regime.[37] Upon their arrival on April 18, it was immediately obvious to the ORHA staff that conditions in Baghdad were much worse than they had expected.

The first blunder of the postconflict phase was the general failure to stop the looting throughout Iraq. The Bush administration had far underestimated the anger of the Iraqi people against the Ba'ath Party and the effects of the economic deprivation wrought by the interwar economic sanctions regime. The Iraqis basically stole everything that was suddenly no longer under state management, from the copper wiring in state buildings to storehouses of food and fuel, to the treasures of the national museums. Military commanders on scene in Iraq wrestled with the dilemma of trying to halt the looting, but General McKiernan never implemented martial law; that omission basically restricted the American forces from interceding to stop the Iraqis from looting.[38]

The military in Iraq was depending upon Garner to accomplish the greatest part of the posthostilities mission, and yet he was finding that his ability to influence the essential levers of governance in Iraq was grossly insufficient. Each time he met with Iraqis, Garner promised a cooperative and relatively short effort to reestablish governance and prosperity in Iraq. He had no idea how short his experience in Iraq was to be.

Without any prior notice to Garner, former ambassador Paul Bremer was assigned by President Bush to serve as the senior American official and lead a new effort to help shape Iraq.[39] Bremer was to head a new organization, the Coalition Provisional Authority, or CPA, with the mission to "restore conditions of safety and stability, to create conditions in which the Iraqi people can safely determine their own political future, and facilitate economic recovery, sustainable reconstruction and development."[40] The CPA had many of the same weaknesses as ORHA, plus it had a leader who knew very little about Iraq or its people. The Pentagon leadership clearly indicated that it considered that success had been achieved in Iraq when it ordered General Mc-Kiernan and his CFLCC staff to depart for Kuwait in June 2003. Wallace was replaced by the newly promoted Lieutenant General Ricardo Sanchez, who assumed the senior military command in Iraq, soon designated as Combined Joint Task Force 7 (CJTF-7). Sanchez was tasked to build and operate a joint and combined headquarters responsible for the theater-strategic, operational, *and* tactical levels of war.[41]

At the same time that the most crucial element of military command was changing in Iraq, its next higher headquarters, Central Command, was also undergoing a change of leadership. General John Abizaid was named as its new commander on July 7, 2003, immediately following the retirement of General Franks.[42] It was a very peculiar time for a commander to retire and be replaced by another leader, who, though certainly as well qualified, had different approaches and a different philosophy of leadership.

Bremer Assumes Control

Ambassador Bremer's first official act upon arrival in Baghdad was to issue CPA Order Number 1, "De-Ba'athification of Iraqi Society," which ended all functioning of the Ba'ath Party in Iraq; his second major order, the "Dissolution of Entities," resulted in the formal dismissal of the Iraqi army and police. Both orders were discussed in Washington, and both in retrospect were mistakes.[43] They were not mistaken ideas, but they were executed in manners that made them counterproductive to the rapid development of a new Iraqi government and society.

CPA Order Number 1 was issued to ensure no one in Saddam's regime had any claim to power in Iraq and to ensure that the stranglehold of the Ba'ath Party over Iraqi society was broken forever. Many key officials expected the order would really only affect the senior levels of the party membership, but since Iraqi expatriates were charged with enforcing the order within Iraqi society and they chose a very strict interpretation, it effectively cast out every official of any importance in the country, including teachers and the lowest-level ministry employees. It resulted in the widespread loss of bureaucratic expertise to the new nation of Iraq throughout 2003 and 2004. Bremer also wanted to destroy the underpinnings of the Iraqi regime, "to demonstrate to the Iraqi people that we have done so and that neither Saddam nor his gang is coming back," so he sent to Secretary Rumsfeld on May 19 a proposal for the disbandment of the security forces; Bremer received permission from the secretary before briefing President Bush and subsequently signing the order on May 23.[44] The problem was that formally disbanding the army and the police put thousands of the most capable potential insurgents among Iraqis out of work and put the only effective means of controlling Iraqi society out of reach for months, if not years.

August 2003—The Insurgency Begins in Earnest in Iraq

Even if Al-Qaeda had had no significant present in Iraq in the summer of 2003, the remnants of the regime and the decentralized organization of the Saddam Fedayeen (which had never been completely destroyed in combat) could have embarked upon a strong campaign to combat the efforts of the coalition in Iraq. In addition to the network itself and the obvious will of newly unemployed former party and security officials and their subordinates to carry on the fight, there was a general understanding that the Americans were ill suited to prolonged irregular combat, as had been frequently pointed out on the basis of the experience of the U.S. military on Somalia in 1993. There is also evidence to support an early reinforcement of the efforts of the "dead-enders" (as administration members would call the insurgents) by other Sunni Muslim supporters, including members of Al-Qaeda.

The Sunni areas of Iraq—primarily the "Sunni Triangle," encompassing Ramadi, Fallujah, the area northwest of Baghdad, and that northward to Tikrit—had yet to really be subjugated by coalition forces. What forays had been made into these larger cities were relatively limited in duration and were never comprehensive enough to ensure that anticoalition elements did not simply squirm out of the hands of coalition units and into the countryside.

On August 19, the UN headquarters in Baghdad was bombed and its Special Representative, Sergio Vierra de Mello, killed. Ten days later, on August 29, another bombing, of a major mosque complex in Najaf, killed the leader of the main Shiite faction in Iraq,[45] Mohammad Baqr Al Hakim.[46] Within a month, the insurgency had demonstrated that it could kill some of the most influential people in the country deep inside places that should have been safe for them. That kind of insurgency was not haphazard and was not disorganized. From September onward, more and more key leaders in Iraq and the United States would realize that the coalition was not simply fighting dead-enders and criminals loosed by Saddam but instead a much more organized and lethal network of enemies of the new Iraq.[47]

The Bremer Plan for Sovereignty

Ambassador Bremer embarked upon a plan for the transition to Iraqi sovereignty that included creation of a Governing Council, a constitution, and election of a new government. Bremer and his staff worked relentlessly to make such a transition happen, but it was difficult going. On November 15, the Governing Council and Bremer concluded an agreement on the timetable and agenda for the drafting of a new constitution and afterward the holding of elections under that constitution. That agreement also included a target date for transition back to Iraqi control—June 30, 2004. The dominant question was whether a constitution could be drafted quickly enough to hold elections in Iraq before the end of the following June. That would have been doubtful in a peaceful Iraq, and the country was anything but calm by the winter of 2003.

The coalition was still conducting security operations and searching relentlessly for Saddam Hussein. The Iraqi leader's sons, Uday and Qusay, had already been discovered and killed by the soldiers of the 101st Division and Special Operations Forces in a house in Mosul on July 22, but the coalition searched for Saddam for over four more months until on December 14, 2003, he was captured at a farmhouse near Tikrit. Pictures of the former leader, bearded and dirty from his period in hiding, thrilled people around the world.

But by that time, the security situation had already transitioned from old-regime dead-enders to another enemy. On November 2, 2003, insurgents had shot down a Chinook helicopter outside of the city of Fallujah, killing seventeen soldiers and wounding eighteen others—it was the deadliest day of the war to date. Another helicopter was shot down near Tikrit on November 7, killing four more soldiers. Bremer voiced concerns privately with President Bush that the military leaders in Iraq did not seem to have a strategy to win against this new threat; he also noted that holding elections would be difficult in such an uncertain environment. Still, he pressed for maintaining the June 2004 goal for sovereignty in the face of some who still lobbied for an immediate handover.[48]

The Iraqi insurgency was a diverse conglomeration of groups, including former Ba'athists as well as criminals and foreign fighters. "The most ardent of the groups was clearly the faction initially known as al–Tawhid wal–Jihad, led by Jordanian Abu Musab al–Zarqawi. It was Zarqawi who had perpetrated the bombing attack of the UN headquarters in Baghdad in August. Through the fall he made more contacts and recruited more members to his group, aided by the general lack of security and the unemployment of so many Iraqis—particularly Sunnis, who felt completely disenfranchised. Consequentially, Zarqawi came to be recognized as the regional 'emir' of Islamist terrorists in Iraq without having sworn fealty to bin Laden."[49] Whatever the strength of his ties to bin Laden, in October Zarqawi changed his group's name to Al-Qaeda in Iraq, or AQ-I. His faction would become over the following two and one-half years the most significant threat to the Iraqi state.

Major Combat in Iraq Continued: Fallujah I

Once the American military realized that its service in Iraq was not going to be completed with the fall of Saddam Hussein, it had to consider how to maintain forces in both Iraq and Afghanistan over an indeterminate period of time. The Pentagon had to devise a way of deploying large units into Iraq on a rotational basis for a long-term commitment while maintaining pressure on the Taliban, nearly 1,300 miles to the east. The forces that had arrived in the March time frame in 2003 were retained in Iraq until they could be replaced in the same month of 2004. This established the first of what would become annual transitions among American commands in Iraq, during the early spring of each year.

While Bremer and his staff were working to keep what was now called the Governing Council together, figuring out how to pay the new Iraqi police force and reintegrate Sunnis into the political process, drafting the Transitional Administrative Law (TAL),[50] and developing priorities of work for the massive $18.6 billion appropriation for Iraqi reconstruction, the U.S. military was trying to adjust to this new, ill-defined phase of the war. American casualties averaged forty deaths every month in early 2004, but the military leadership still expected improved stability in the spring; it wholly underestimated the growing anger and capability of the opposition in Iraq.

In a signal turn of the tide of war, four Blackwater contract employees ventured into the restive city of Fallujah during the morning of March 31. They were ambushed by insurgents and killed; their bodies were burned and later hung from the girders of the old bridge leading west out of the city. The incident horrified the world and directly altered the pace and conduct of counterinsurgency operations in Iraq.

The killings resulted in an assault on the city by U.S. Marines (in an operation known as Vigilant Resolve), and as with any combat operation in urban terrain, a toll on the civilian population was nearly unavoidable. Those casualties had a profoundly negative effect on the international media, the work of the CPA, and the effectiveness of the new Iraqi council. By April 8, with bombs still being dropped in Fallujah, even senior officials in Washington were questioning the rationale of the fight. Iraqis in Baghdad very quickly urged restraint and began negotiations with the insurgents. Bremer directed a temporary halt in order to reduce the perceived civilian damage. By April 13, high-level negotiations had started, and the operation to destroy the insurgents in Fallujah was effectively on hold. By April 22 a cease-fire was in effect in the city.

From late April onward the situation in Fallujah remained increasingly uncertain. The insurgents inside the city reinforced their presence, using mosques and hospitals as defensive positions; some analysts believed they would use the local residents as human shields if combat resumed. The insurgents clearly understood that civilian casualties and U.S. attacks on mosques and other normally restricted targets played in their favor in the international media. Great political pressure began to be applied to cease any further combat and seek a negotiated settlement. The police in Fallujah, who were never very supportive of the coalition, began to side more and more with the insurgents gathering in the city. By June the city was no longer open to American patrols.

These confrontations made life for Bremer and the CPA much more difficult, but the political progress in Iraq continued, albeit at a more irregular pace through the spring; although the crisis in Fallujah nearly tore the IGC apart, Bremer and his staff managed to keep it together long enough to develop the plan for an Interim Iraqi Government (IIG). Bremer diplomatically crafted a power-sharing structure for the IIG that would give each of the three major religious groups in Iraq a seat at the leadership table in Baghdad. On June 28 the CPA turned over full sovereignty to the IIG in a surprise move two days prior to the announced date of turnover of sovereignty. That same day, Ayad Allawi assumed power as prime minister and leader of the new Iraqi government. With the reestablishment of Iraqi sovereignty, the United States appointed a new ambassador to Iraq, John D. Negroponte, and also changed the military command structure in Iraq, naming General George Casey, the son of a general killed in combat in Vietnam, to take the command and bring the war to an end.

The Afghan Campaign Continues—March 2002 to December 2003

> In March 2002 Afghanistan appeared to be a nation ready to rise from the ashes of Taliban rule.
>
> —Donald P. Wright[51]

As America invaded Iraq, operations in Afghanistan continued, still focused on rooting out the remnants of the Taliban. In late March 2003 the Security Council had extended the UN assistance mission in Afghanistan for another year, to see the country through to general elections. In the middle of April, as noted above, with the security situation still far from improving, at the request of Germany and the Netherlands, the two nations leading International Security Assistance Force at that time, NATO agreed to take command of ISAF in August.[52] So as the Ba'ath Party was falling from power in Iraq, international partners were still willing to renew their commitments to the Afghan mission.

Border security remained an increasing concern. On April 22, 2003, President Karzai traveled to Islamabad to discuss border disputes, terrorism, and exchanges of prisoners with President Musharraf of Pakistan. Many in the Afghan government still viewed Pakistan, which had both nurtured and actively supported the Taliban, with real concern; it was known that Pakistan was harboring Taliban fugitives—either tacitly or actively.[53]

But continuing attacks by rebels as well as deadly factional fighting within the country still posed serious threats to the future of Afghanistan, and the Afghan government had only just launched its training program to create a 50,000-strong national police force and a border police force of some 12,000, with a goal of restoring order in the country with domestic forces by 2008.

Interior Minister Ali Jalali was a key proponent of this initiative; he also inaugurated an Afghan Human Rights Department, aimed at curbing abuses by Afghan police forces, and pushed the Afghan government to construct a number of police stations on the Iran-Afghanistan border in order to curb the illicit trade in drugs and protect border security forces. At the same time, the Afghan Disarmament, Demobilization and Reintegration Program, designed to disarm some 100,000 former combatants and integrate them into civilian life, was delayed because Afghan authorities were unable to make crucial Defense Ministry reforms.

Meanwhile General Hagenbeck was attempting to gain a better understanding of the situation and develop plans for future operations in Afghanistan. After visiting many of the locations of active operations in the country during the spring of 2002, "Hagenbeck and his staff began framing this new approach, which represented the first attempt by a senior coalition command to articulate the overall direction for the military campaign in Afghanistan since U.S. Central Command (CENTCOM) published the original OEF campaign plan in November 2001."[54] A key question remaining was the extent to which the United States was willing to rebuild Afghanistan.

As the spring turned to summer in 2002, the remaining Taliban forces fled to the rural regions of the four southern Afghan provinces that formed their heartland: Kandahar, Zabul, Helmand, and Uruzgan. "The United States continued to track leads concerning the locations of Osama bin Laden and Taliban leader Mullah Mohammed Omar but did not know where the two key enemy leaders were hiding."[55] In the wake of Operation Anaconda, General Hagenbeck developed plans for an operation known as Mountain Lion to keep the pressure on and to produce an environment wherein the Afghan *loya jirga* could meet to start the development of a new government in the country.

The Pentagon also requested that British Royal Marines, highly trained in mountain warfare, be deployed to Afghanistan to assist with the clearing operations in such difficult terrain.[56] The Royal Marines conducted a number of missions over a period of several weeks, with varying results. The surviving members of the Taliban, who during the summer of 2002 probably numbered in the hundreds, avoided combat with the coalition forces and their Afghan allies and melted into the caves and tunnels of remote Afghan mountain ranges or crossed the border into Pakistan.

Following Anaconda, the U.S.-led coalition conducted a series of tactical actions designed to demonstrate the coalition's ability to operate in a variety of places throughout Afghanistan. A secondary objective was to improve security to support the convening of the *loya jirga* scheduled in June. CJTF Mountain believed it had to prevent all Taliban and Al-Qaeda attacks to ensure the political process moved forward.[57] As a part of these actions, coalition forces took the lead in conducting Operation Jacana, from May to July 2002, with, notably, Royal Marines of 45 Commando as well as some U.S. forces, Australian Special Air Service (SAS) troops, and the Norwegian Forsvarets Spesialkommando (FSK) also participating.[58]

The Jacana operation began in mid-May, following a Taliban ambush on a SAS patrol. The Australians called in a U.S. air strike, which killed some of the enemy. Then 45 Commando was inserted to destroy the Taliban force that had exposed itself in the ambush. During subsequent actions in the area several caves and bunkers containing arms, ammunition, and supplies were found and destroyed. Over a hundred mortars, a hundred antitank weapons along with hundreds of RPGs, antipersonnel mines, rockets, and artillery shells and thousands of rounds of small-arms and antiaircraft ammunition were discovered during the operation.[59]

Command Changes in Afghanistan

When the 10th Mountain Division headquarters had initially deployed to Afghanistan in late 2001, its role had been to serve as the forward headquarters for CFLCC, the headquarters belonging to CENTCOM that oversaw all coalition ground-force operations throughout the combatant command's area of responsibility (AOR). The division, in turn, would command all land forces inside Afghanistan. Both the operation in the Shahi Kowt Valley in November 2001 and Anaconda in the following spring had illustrated command and control deficiencies with this structure as the effort grew in Afghanistan. When the focus of effort began to shift to include civil-military operations (CMO), the commander needed to coordinate at many more levels—interfacing with coalition partners, the UN, and other international organizations, as well as providing political and diplomatic assistance to the new Afghan government. (The UN had passed Resolution 1401 establishing UNAMA in order to create an administrative framework that would bring order to the international humanitarian assistance and reconstruction efforts in Afghanistan as well.) With all these tasks evolving, Hagenbeck understood that more coordinating authority would be needed if the U.S. command structure was to succeed.

General Franks had also been coming to realize he needed a commander on the ground who could better interface at senior levels. In fact as early as February 2002 Franks had asked the commander of the U.S. Army's XVIII Airborne Corps, Lieutenant General Dan K. McNeill, USA, to travel to Afghanistan to assess the situation. All these factors, in addition to the pull of Iraq planning across every facet of CENTCOM, soon resulted in the creation of a new Combined Joint Task Force (CJTF-180) built around McNeill's corps in Afghanistan. Even as that command was being created however, McNeill was informed of a problem as significant as the remaining enemy he might face:

According to McNeill, General John Keane, the army vice chief of staff, told him, "Don't you do anything that looks like permanence. We are in and out of there in a hurry." In addition, McNeill would have to do all these things under an informal troop number ceiling of seven thousand U.S. servicemen and women in Afghanistan. In this way, the military leadership in the Pentagon reinforced the importance of the force cap and the imperative of preventing the coalition from becoming enmeshed in a long campaign. The problem that lay in front of McNeill was how to attain coalition military objectives in Afghanistan with a limited force and a limited amount of time. McNeill recalled that while senior military and civilian officials never gave him a carefully crafted mission statement, it was clear they wanted the coalition forces to do two things: continue operations to kill or capture the Taliban and al-Qaeda forces that might still reside in Afghanistan and supervise the creation of Afghan security forces.[60]

Doing all of these things well in combat conditions was a tall order. Also, McNeill would not even have the use of his full staff in Afghanistan. "General Shinseki and General Keane directed him to leave half of his corps headquarters at Fort Bragg, North Carolina, in case the Army had to use corps' units like the 82nd Airborne Division to react to terrorist strikes or mount other campaigns that loomed on the horizon. McNeill believed that both senior officers at that time suspected the United States was moving closer to war in Iraq and wanted to retain the capabilities of the XVIII Airborne Corps headquarters for that contingency."[61] At least the 10th Mountain Division was a normal part of his XVIII Corps, and McNeill knew General Hagenbeck well.

The deployment of the new CJTF-180 began in May 2002 as the Jacana operation was being conducted. "CJTF-180's lines of effort were: 1) tactical combat operations, 2) the establishment and training of the ANA, 3) support to the ISAF, 4) civil-military operations, and 5) information operations." During the period from June 2002 to June 2003, CJTF-180 reorganized to fight with its new approach but conducted only one major combat operation. This was largely because by the time the new CJTF staff was ready to operate, the planned *loya jirga* and the coming winter season limited its ability to plan and execute multiple major offensives.

> On June 11, 2002 the AIA convened the loya jirga; approximately two thousand Afghans, chosen from slates of provincial party candidates or appointed based on membership in specific religious or political organizations, arrived in Kabul and began deliberations about the future of Afghanistan. Although traditionally participants in loya jirgas were exclusively male, the Loya Jirga Commission, established by the Bonn Agreement to oversee the 2002 meeting, ensured that 160 women were among the thousands that convened in Kabul. The delegates deliberated for several days before agreeing to the establishment of an ATA with Hamid Karzai as interim president. A week later, Karzai had completed forming his cabinet. While observers noted that the new government featured too many military leaders, especially those from the Northern Alliance, the loya jirga had served the purpose set at Bonn to put Afghanistan on the path toward a democratic future.[62]

Following the *loya jirga*, for a week beginning on August 18, CJTF-180 conducted its only major operation of the year. More than two thousand U.S. and coalition forces, including units form the newly arrived 82nd Airborne Division, conducted Operation Mountain Sweep in the former Al-Qaeda and Taliban areas of southeastern Afghanistan. Mountain Sweep continued the operation Mountain Lion efforts to search out Al-Qaeda and Taliban forces and gather information about the terrorist organizations. The Operation included five combat air assault missions and resulted in the discovery of five separate weapons caches and two caches of Taliban documents.[63] The operation took place mainly around the villages of Dormat and Narizah, south of the cities of Khowst and Gardez. Coalition forces detained ten persons during the operation.

Some would claim that more should have been done by McNeill and CJTF-180 that summer. Hy Rothstein has noted that "the Taliban was in such a state of panic and confusion in 2002 that securing the countryside would have been met with little if any opposition. Simply stated, much of Afghanistan was ripe for establishing traditional governance and security structures once the Taliban was out of the way."[64] But the focus of the Bush administration was on Iraq planning and no one in Washington was pushing for more American resources in Afghanistan, so the emphasis shifted to getting the Afghans to help themselves. The official Army history of the war noted:

> Unquestionably, the most important decision came in the spring of 2002 when Coalition leaders reached the conclusion that the great majority of their forces would not be departing Afghanistan anytime soon. Despite the victory in the Shahi Kowt Valley, the new Afghan state was still in its infancy and required nurturing if it was to endure. With Coalition strategic success contingent on the survival of this nascent state, officials in the United States and Europe began planning a new campaign that demanded security missions to prevent the military and political resurgence of the Taliban as well as reconstruction operations and programs to train Afghan security forces. With the decision to extend the Coalition presence in Afghanistan came a change in command structure and force levels. These transitions essentially ended the campaign that centered on Special Operations Forces (SOF), which had defined the first 6 months of operations and initially made Operation ENDURING FREEDOM (OEF) appear as a unique conflict. After spring 2002, conventional units would become the core of the Coalition's presence, even as the nature of the conflict in Afghanistan retained characteristics that many would describe as unconventional.[65]

Civil-Military Operations in Afghanistan

"Some in the Bush administration were initially concerned specifically about limiting expectations for nation building, which was not a Presidential priority in the first Bush administration, especially after its main focus shifted to preparation for war in Iraq. Progress was slow but steady, and the Taliban appeared to be relatively dormant. Kabul remained calm. After more than two decades of war, many believed that peace had come to the Hindu Kush."[66]

With the establishment of CJTF-180 came a stronger emphasis on helping the Afghans develop and govern the country. "U.S. joint military doctrine in 2001 defined CMO [civil-military operations] as those activities 'that establish, maintain, influence, or exploit relations between military forces, governmental and nongovernmental civilian organizations and authorities, and the civilian populace in a friendly, neutral, or hostile operational area in order to facilitate military operations, to consolidate and achieve operational U.S. objectives."[67] This broad definition appeared to allow coalition commanders an open approach to CMO without committing their limited assets to a true "nation building' effort that American senior officials wanted to avoid."[68] Brigadier General David E. Kratzer, deputy commander of the 377th Theater Support Command, had been appointed by General Mikolashek to lead the civil-military effort back during the winter of 2001; he was to return to Afghanistan as the commander of the Combined, Joint Civil-Military Operations Task Force of CJCMOTF.[69]

Even with the creation of an additional command to conduct CMO, in early 2002 there remained significant limitations on the process for funding projects and serious concerns about its utility and risks; the deployment of the CJCMOTF worried senior coalition leaders that the campaign might be veering off course. Kratzer recalled that in 2001 General Franks had "told me directly, with his finger in my face, that I would not get involved in nation building."[70] Kratzer's first obstacle was to develop a way to access funds for the construction and humanitarian projects the Afghans needed. Initially he had no authority to fund his mission; but by April he had successfully argued his case and gained the authority to control the funding he needed. "By May 2002, on the eve of the arrival of CJTF-180, CJCMOTF had used $2.56 million to support a diverse set of projects that included the refurbishment of roads, bridges, schools, and medical facilities."[71]

To assist the Afghans and yet stay away from nation building, the CJCMOTF had established Coalition Humanitarian Liaison Cells[72] to coordinate the aid deliveries of nongovernmental organizations working in Afghanistan. Still, "in some cases, rather than coordinating aid delivery, the CHLCs became agencies that directly provided assistance on the ground, especially in emergencies and in regions that were not secure."[73] Although the negative impact of such employment was a tendency for the nongovernmental organizations not to work with the CHLCs, it had a very positive effect as well. "The CHLC concept proved so successful that it inspired the creation of experimental Joint

Regional Teams, which would later evolve into Provincial Reconstruction Teams that would be subsequently deployed throughout Afghanistan."[74]

CMO would not work without security, which required both continued military operations and the development of a much more capable Afghan security force. In February 2002 General Kratzer also took the title of Chief of the Office of Military Cooperation–Afghanistan (OMC-A). In early 2002 this office represented the main thrust of the coalition's effort to assist the new Karzai government through the improvement of the police and army in the country. This effort was similar to the capacity-building actions of the Multinational Security Transition Command Iraq (MNSTC-I) but received far less funding for what was in reality a similarly daunting problem.

This activity occurred within the greater context of the international effort to reestablish Afghanistan's military, police, and judicial organizations. In early 2002 the United States joined Germany, Italy, Japan, and the United Kingdom in an agreement on what was called Security Sector Reform (SSR). Germany took the lead in reform of Afghan police forces and created a comprehensive five-year training program focused on tactics, criminal and narcotics investigations, traffic control, and Islamic law. . . . Italy, with assistance from the United Nations and the United States, undertook reforms of the justice system. . . . Japan led the Disarmament, Demobilization, and Reintegration (DDR) project, officially called the Afghan New Beginnings Program. The DDR program intended to convince regional militias to disband and either join the ANA or find other jobs.[75]

Action continued on the operational side as well. For a week beginning on August 18, more than two thousand U.S. and coalition forces, including units from the newly arrived 82nd Airborne Division, conducted Operation Mountain Sweep in the former Al-Qaeda and Taliban strongholds of southeastern Afghanistan. Mountain Sweep continued the Operation Mountain Lion effort to search out Al-Qaeda and Taliban forces and gather information about terrorist organizations. The operation included five combat air assault missions and resulted in the discovery of five separate weapons caches and two caches of Taliban documents. The operation took place mainly around the villages of Dormat and Narizah, south of the cities of Khowst and Gardez. Coalition forces detained ten suspected Taliban members during the operation.[76]

On September 5, 2002, a car bomb was detonated in downtown Kabul, killing more than thirty Afghans; on the same day AIA President Hamid Karzai was the target of an assassination attempt, prompting him to replace his Afghan bodyguards with U.S Special Forces. Such activities in the national capital, supposedly under the security umbrella of ISAF, caused many to question the effectiveness of security there. On October 30, the UN Secretary General's Special Representative in Afghanistan, Lakhdar Brahimi, informed the Security Council that in his view, "Security remains a priority concern for the people of Afghanistan. Sporadic fighting continues to erupt from time to time, particularly in the north, the south-east and, to a lesser extent, the west. The Government does not yet have the means to deal in an effective manner with the underlying problems which are the cause of such threats to security."[77]

On November 6, 2002, rival factions in northern Afghanistan began turning in their weapons as part of a UN–monitored program to curb violence. More than 120 assault rifles and some artillery pieces were seized from soldiers loyal to Abdul Rashid Dostum and others loyal to Ustad Atta Mohammad in the Sholgara District, southwest of Mazar-i-Sharif. The next day, near Khost, elements of the 82nd Airborne and Special Forces soldiers seized 5 107-mm rockets aimed at a U.S. airfield in southeastern Afghanistan. The U.S paratroopers then swept through four areas northeast of Khost, seizing weapons that included 28 mines, 76 hand grenades, 147 rocket-launched grenades, 62 launchers, and more than 500 5.62-mm rounds. Five men were taken to Khost for questioning.[78] Intermittent fighting continued in the area through early December.

During the same period, U.S officials were pushing the Afghan government Defense Commission, made up of Afghan officials and warlords, to build up the country's army to 70,000 troops within two years. At that time, Afghanistan's national army comprised only one thousand men and was woefully inadequate even to defend key areas of the country. The shortfalls in army capacity only encouraged local warlords to operate their own militias, a fact that was often a source of friction between leaders and the government in Kabul.

Reconstruction work to help the Afghan people continued apace. On November 10, as part of an international effort, work began on rebuilding the major highway that runs around the periphery of the country. The project was expected to cost $250 million, two-thirds of it pledged by the United States, Japan, and Saudi Arabia.[79] The 750-mile portion of the roadway, which goes from Kabul through Kandahar and then to Herat, had been built in the 1960s with U.S. funds but had been largely destroyed during the Soviet occupation and the civil war that followed it. The United States was not stingy with its financial support during this phase of the conflict. In mid-November, Congress passed legislation authorizing $2.3 billion in reconstruction funds for Afghanistan over four years, plus another billion to expand ISAF.

In response, at the end of November the Security Council voted unanimously to extend the International Security Assistance Force in Afghanistan for a year, with Germany and the Netherlands jointly taking over its command for the next six-month rotation of command. ISAF was then about 4,800 strong and operated only in Kabul. About 9000 U.S. troops were still in Afghanistan as part of the coalition.

The Evolution of the Provincial Reconstruction Teams in Afghanistan

On August 28, 2002, Colonel George P. Maughan of the 360th Civil Affairs Brigade (based in Columbia, South Carolina) took the reins of the CJCMOTF and strengthened the command's focus on reconstruction efforts. Maughan created and implemented a national government–level ministerial team of fifteen civil affairs (CA) soldiers who worked within key areas of Karzai's provisional government, including the Ministries of Finance and Education.[80] Then, in the spring of 2002, the leaders in the CJCMOTF turned to a new type of organization, to be known as regional or provincial reconstruction teams, that might be able to link key personnel from the Defense Department, Department of State, the U.S. Agency for International Development (USAID), and other key reconstruction stakeholders who could review a project nomination together, with regional context in mind, and thereby rapidly reduce the nomination-to-implementation cycle.[81]

The idea was introduced to Hamid Karzai, but, according to Interior Minister Ali Jalali, Karzai preferred the term "Provincial Reconstruction Teams," because he did not like the connotation of the term "regional." For Karzai, that term suggested that the teams would work for regional leaders, and he did not want to empower the men who had been warlords in the past and now sought to retain their military strength and independence from the Kabul-based government.[82] Provincial Reconstruction Teams (PRTs) would become one of Enduring Freedom's greatest contributions to the transition from combat to stabilization.

In September 2002 Lieutenant Colonel Michael Stout, an experienced CA officer, arrived from an assignment at the United States Institute of Peace to do a study on the effectiveness of the CJCMOTF. During the visit, he discussed the lack of an authorized political-military (pol-mil) plan for Afghanistan with the CJTF staff. Ideally, a pol-mil plan could guide the coalition in its efforts with the new government of Afghanistan. Stout had an unsigned draft of such a plan with him; it would soon become the authorizing document for the PRTs.[83]

The pol-mil plan for Afghanistan had been created earlier in 2002 by the U.S. State Department director of the Political-Military Bureau for Contingency Planning and Peacekeeping, under the management of Mr. Dennis Skocz. In December 2001 Ambassador James F. Dobbins, who was serving as the U.S. Representative to the Afghan Opposition in 2001, directed Skocz's department to produce this document—similar to one he had commissioned it to do for him when he served in Kosovo.[84] The plan featured a Kabul-centered approach that emphasized political and economic long-term viability for Afghanistan following the collapse of the Taliban.[85]

Pol-mil plans help coordinate the interagency efforts of the governments involved in a campaign. "A well-constructed plan clearly assigns elements of national power—military, economic, diplomatic—to specific objectives and should serve as the cornerstone of the combatant command's or joint task force's campaign plan. Most importantly, in the long term, it is the key transition document for strategic, operational, and tactical operations. Simply put, the POL-MIL Plan is a roadmap for assisting countries like Afghanistan to achieve political and social stability."[86]

Lieutenant Colonel Stout's knowledge of the pol-mil plan and his experience turned his temporary duty in Afghanistan into a much larger mission. General McNeill and his staff identified Stout as the expert they needed to establish the PRTs while providing a logical transition strategy that would shift the burden of the reconstruction from the Defense Department to the Department of State. Stout's initial task was to establish the first four PRTs, the first three in the towns of Gardez, Bamian, and Konduz. According to Stout, the pilot PRTs were intended "to flesh out the concept for the CJTF Commander and figure out what it should look like. . . . [W]e had a USAID representative that was going to be embedded with the PRT, we had a Department of State representative that was going to be on the ground assigned to the team, and then, most importantly, there was a representative from President Karzai's government."[87] The PRT then was the "linchpin in that transition,"[88] teaming up the military reconstruction agencies with representatives from State, USAID, and the Afghan government.

> The first three PRTs were established in early 2003 with the U.S. as the lead country for each. President Karzai requested the first team be established in an unstable area to help extend the reach of his government, and he chose Gardez where the inaugural PRT opened in January, 2003. The Bamian PRT, located in that north-central city, opened on March 2, 2003. Finally, the Konduz PRT began operations on April 10, 2003. On July 10, 2003 the first non-American-sponsored PRT located in the northern city of Mazar-e Sharif opened with the United Kingdom serving as the lead country.[89]

Lieutenant Colonel Carl E. Fischer recalls that in late 2002, when CJTF–180 requested five to six hundred additional combat-arms soldiers to serve on the security elements for the PRTs, those requests came back denied, because, he contends, of the demand for combat units—specifically U.S. Army infantry battalions—to support Operation Iraqi Freedom (OIF). Combat in Iraq thus meant that no forces were available to help secure the PRTs in Afghanistan.[90]

The PRT concept was a crucially important step forward in the coalition campaign. In addition to representatives from the CJCMOTF, each of these PRTs was to include at least one representative each from USAID, State, and, if possible, the U.S. Department of Agriculture. A representative from the Afghan Ministry of the Interior also served on each team to help mediate and guide interactions with the local population. This pairing of Defense and State officials in the field was progressive, but it also became a recruitment challenge, because civilians in such agencies as the State Department could not be easily deployed into combat zones.

Still not everyone involved in the Afghan reconstruction effort readily accepted the PRT concept. Some members of international organizations (IOs), nongovernmental organizations (NGOs), and even some representatives of the U.S. State Department had serious objections to the structure and intent of the teams, most frequently because they brought military officers closer to field reconstruction projects. Deborah Alexander, USAID field program manager for Afghanistan in 2002, also voiced concerns about the PRTs: "I like the regional team concept . . . I think the work they've done has been terrific. I'm happy that the Civil Affairs teams are expanded, but I'm not happy that there is an expansion of other military forces. I'm real concerned about how this is going to be perceived because I think if I have my finger on the pulse, I think it's going to be seen as an occupation, that these military regional teams are going to be seen as taking over their country."[91]

Selling the concept would take time, but the PRT eventually demonstrated its worth both in Afghanistan and later in Iraq, where a similar approach was instituted after 2005. Despite the fact that the logistical, transportation, and security needs of the PRTs took resources away from security operations, Major General John Vines, then-commander of the 82nd Airborne Division in Afghanistan recognized the utility of the teams and concluded that they made a positive overall contribution to the campaign even in the first months of their operations.[92]

As the PRT concept evolved, the CJCMOTF continued to fund and enable a variety of Afghan reconstruction projects. "As of 1 January 2003, CJCMOTF had received 492 project nominations and had approved 305 funded projects valued at $14,020,986. CJTF-180 at that time was in the process of transferring 26 approved projects with an estimated value of $1.722 million to NGOs or other agencies for execution."[93] Another commentator observed, "By early 2003 the types of projects assumed by coalition forces and the civilian aid community spanned a wide spectrum, ranging from MEDCAP projects such as a clinic in Kandahar that treated 1,400 civilians to the large scale renovation of the Avecina Pharmaceutical Plant, which not only made medicine available but also laid the groundwork for employment of hundreds of Afghans."[94] CJTF-180 still had much more to do to accomplish the objectives of the campaign in Afghanistan, but the growth of the overall reconstruction effort, and particularly the introduction of the PRTs, moved the command closer to the planned transition to stability operations run by the Afghans themselves.

ISAF and Afghanistan

ISAF was a critical part of the security equation in Afghanistan. The initial ISAF headquarters had been based around the British 3rd Mechanized Division, commanded by Major General John McColl. His headquarters had arrived in Kabul in December 2001, and until the force expanded beyond Kabul in 2003, ISAF consisted of roughly division-level headquarters and one brigade covering the capital, the Kabul Multinational Brigade. The brigade was composed of three battle groups and was in charge of the tactical command of deployed troops. ISAF in the early phase of its operations did not include any American forces. Its headquarters served as the operational command and control center of the mission, even though the individual contingents of the force retained national command chains and were therefore often not as responsive as other elements of the coalition in Afghanistan.

The command of ISAF originally rotated among different nations on a six-month basis. However each time a rotation neared the end of its term, a new lead nation had to be secured, which proved increasingly difficult. To solve that problem, command was turned over indefinitely to NATO on August 11, 2003. This marked NATO's first deployment outside Europe or North America. In February 2002, eighteen countries were contributing to the force. It was expected to grow to 5,000 soldiers over the year, and in June 2002 Major General Hilmi Akin Zorlu of Turkey took command of ISAF. During his period in command, the number of Turkish troops increased from only about one hundred to 1,300. By November 2002, ISAF consisted of some 4,650 troops from over twenty countries, still under Turkish command and still focused only on the area around Kabul. Then on February 10, 2003, Lieutenant General Norbert van Heyst took command of ISAF on behalf of Germany and the Netherlands. His deputy was Brigadier General Bertholee of the Netherlands. Their mission headquarters was formed from the 1 German/Dutch Corps (1GNC) and included staff members from the United Kingdom, Italy, Turkey, and Norway, among other nations.

On August 11, 2003, Lieutenant General Goetz Gliemeroth of Germany took command of the first ISAF mission under the command of NATO. On October 13, United Nations Security Council Resolution 1510 permitted ISAF to conduct missions outside of Kabul for the first time. Later that month, 230 German soldiers were deployed to the region of Kunduz, marking ISAF's first operation away from the Afghan capital.[95] Overall ISAF was an effective tool to develop security in and immediately around the Afghan capital, and it actively demonstrated the resolve of the original international coalition formed in the wake of the September 11 attacks, but in comparative terms it was a relatively weak force with a weak mandate. Some even laughed that ISAF stood for "I Saw Americans Fighting."[96] That would change as the campaign grew more complicated and the enemy returned to contest the ground in Afghanistan in greater numbers.

Problems and Progress in Afghanistan, April 2003–December 2003

Back in mid-April, a U.S.-Afghan patrol had been attacked by militants; air support had been called in, and five members of the enemy group had been killed.[97] Unfortunately only two days later, 4 Canadian soldiers were killed and 8 others wounded by a friendly-fire incident involving two F-16s over Tarnak Farms, near Kandahar.[98] Then on July 1, in central Uruzgan Province, a U.S. B-52 struck suspected Al-Qaeda and Taliban cave and bunker complexes, while an AC-130 gunship strafed several nearby villages. U.S. officials believed the villages were legitimate targets, but 48 civilians were killed and 117 were injured at a wedding party. The pilots thought the aircraft had come under attack from people on the ground, although no antiaircraft weapons were found.[99] This was not the first such incident of Afghan casualties, but it was significant enough that it started a trend of Afghan objections to continued bombings that would grow in volume and in significance over time. Over the summer, coalition soldiers continued to press the enemy in Tarin Kowt, Kabul, Jalalabad, Khost, Asadabad, and several other locations.

In July President Karzai had issued the decree to convene a five-hundred-member *loya jirga* on October 1, 2003, to approve a draft of the country's new constitution. The process of improving governance in Afghanistan was a crucial part of making the country inhospitable to terrorists, but no long-term improvements in governance could be established unless and until the security situation in the key areas of the country could be stabilized. Unfortunately security remained uncertain in many parts of Afghanistan at that point in the war. For example, during the same month, coalition forces killed up to two dozen insurgents in a combat operation near Spin Boldak after dozens of heavily armed rebel fighters attacked a border post nearby. After the battle, the insurgents simply escaped across the border into Pakistan.

The importance of the sanctuary in neighboring Pakistan was becoming even more obvious. General Richard Myers, chairman of the Joint Chiefs of Staff, noted in an interview that "the largest threat to Afghanistan's new government comes from across the border of Pakistan."[100] The Pakistani leadership was not oblivious to the problem. A few months later, in a speech to his officers, Musharraf admitted that some anti–Afghanistan government activity was coming from within the Pakistani border, noting, "Certainly everything is not happening from Pakistan but certainly something is happening from Pakistan."[101]

At about the same time, in the Zormat Valley, in Paktia Province, about a thousand soldiers of the Afghan National Army, together with coalition troops, deployed in Operation Warrior Sweep, which was the first major combat operation for the new Afghan army. Later in the summer Afghan National Security adviser, Zalmay Rasul, Pakistani general Ashfaq Parvez Kayani, and General Vines agreed in a meeting to establish a communications hotline to improve coordination of security activities among the three nations. Border control points were eventually established as well, but the enemy forces confronting ISAF still seemed to travel between the two countries at will.

More effort was required. On September 7, President Bush announced he would ask Congress for an additional $87 billion for U.S. efforts in Iraq and Afghanistan (although only $800 million of that immense total was earmarked for Afghan reconstruction). Later, on the 23rd, Bush addressed the United Nations General Assembly appealing for more support for the effort in Afghanistan. President Karzai addressed the assembly the next day and specifically called for a broader international military presence in Afghanistan and an extension of ISAF beyond the Kabul area. German chancellor Gerhard Schroeder reinforced for the General Assembly the point that Afghanistan's political reform needed sustained international support to succeed. Accordingly on October 13 the UN Security Council voted unanimously to expand the ISAF mission beyond Kabul. (Some coalition partners were already starting to have second thoughts—Canadian Prime Minister Jean Chrétien made it clear that same month that Canadian troops would not be sent beyond Kabul, despite the Security Council appeal.) President Bush also announced that Zalmay Khalilzad, then his special envoy in Afghanistan, would be the new U.S. ambassador in Kabul.

Notwithstanding renewal of the international commitment to security in Afghanistan and national elections looming, military actions remained the central focus of coalition effort in the country. Operation Mountain Resolve began in Nuristan and Kunar Provinces in early November 2003. Parts of the

22nd Infantry Regiment of the 10th Mountain Division conducted a "hammer and anvil" combat operations, in conjunction with the Combined Joint Special Operations Task Force (CJSOTF). The 22nd Infantry "hammer" was to push up the Waygal River Valley in an effort to drive Al-Qaeda and Taliban forces north against the "anvil" of the CJSOTF forces. The effect on the Taliban was uncertain, but the terrain punished the infantry forces and allowed most of the enemy to escape the anvil.

Then on December 6, the U.S. military launched its biggest ever ground operation of the war to date, code-named Avalanche, across eastern and southern Afghanistan. Over two thousand soldiers were involved, including four infantry battalions as well as soldiers from the Afghan National Army and militia. The operation was designed to disrupt militant activity in the southeastern provinces of Afghanistan and to establish conditions for the provision of humanitarian aid. It captured more than a hundred suspects and accomplished little else; it resulted in the deaths of only ten Taliban fighters; two soldiers from the Afghan National Army were killed. ISAF seemed to be shadowboxing.

In late December, Lieutenant General David W. Barno, USA, a veteran of the 75th Ranger Regiment, arrived as the new coalition commander in Afghanistan; he quickly outlined changes in the operational strategy to improve security conditions around the country. Among Barno's intended improvements were better coordination of U.S. military and political efforts and more focused operations, bringing conventional and special operations forces together to isolate Taliban and Al-Qaeda forces from the population.[102] Barno didn't wait long to act.

Five

Fighting Two Wars

The Afghan Campaign as
a Secondary Theater

It's important for Americans to know this war will not be quick and this war will not be easy. . . . The battles in Afghanistan are not over.
— President George W. Bush[1]

With only very few exceptions, the active campaigning season in Afghanistan ends with the onset of winter and begins again only in the spring. Still, no significant operations were conducted in Afghanistan in the spring or the summer of 2003, even with the pace of events continuing in Afghanistan, since most of the nations of the coalition were completely absorbed by the prosecution of the initial phases of the Iraqi Freedom campaign. America's most exclusive assets—reconnaissance, surveillance, refueling, and counterterrorism units—were all drawn into the vortex of the attack on Iraq as well, so there was precious little capacity in the Afghan theater while Saddam Hussein's government was being toppled in Iraq.

In the summer of 2003, the coalition actually began drawing down its forces in Afghanistan, just as it had begun doing in Iraq. General McNeill, the CJTF-180 commander, began transitioning to a mission focused principally upon humanitarian assistance and support to the new Afghan government; a downsized, U.S.-led Combined Joint Task Force 180, commanded by Major General John Vines (the commander of the 82nd Airborne Division), took control of operations. Vines' headquarters was located at Bagram Air Base, forty miles north of Kabul, and provided command and control for the over 11,000 troops from nineteen nations remaining in country.

This new CJTF structure was a significant reduction in capability from the four-hundred-man headquarters that had existed in Afghanistan during the previous year. Operational and tactical missions once performed by a corps headquarters were assigned to a division headquarters of less than two hundred people. The military span of control for the CJTF was daunting: one division-sized headquarters attempted to conduct security and reconstruction efforts across a nation the size of Texas with a population of 31 million.[2] Even more worrisome was the fact that only one army brigade was responsible for the entire battle space. Complicating matters further, the special forces, civil-military operations, aviation, and logistical commands operating in Afghanistan reported directly to the CJTF at Bagram, not through the brigade commander, who frequently had to deal with the consequences of operations conducted by special operating forces of which neither he nor the CJTF had been unaware.[3]

The reason for the drawdown in forces was clear: CENTCOM was "under enormous pressure not to over commit resources to Afghanistan to make sure everything possible was available for Iraq."[4] Not surprisingly this change had a detrimental impact on the effectiveness of the new CJTF; General Vines admitted that he could no longer focus on the tactical aspects of the campaign.[5] Instead he found that he had to focus his effort on many of the same coordination duties previously handled by General McNeill—such as coordinating CMO, Afghan capacity building, and governance.

The Combined Joint Civil Military Operations Task Force's Afghan National Army (ANA) training program with the Afghan government was a high priority. Without Afghan security forces in place, the government in Kabul could not extend its authority throughout the country and few reconstruction projects would succeed. The CJCMOTF was also continuing its efforts to build Afghan capacity in other important ways. By late 2003 it had supervised all four newly created provincial reconstruction teams, the "two American teams at Gardez and Konduz, a British post in Mazar-e-Sharif, and a New Zealand mission in Bamian. All four PRTs were in relatively quiet areas."[6] At that time, there was only one PRT in the volatile eastern provinces of Afghanistan, at Gardez, and there was no PRT presence in the more volatile southern part of Afghanistan, where reconstruction was needed most. Establishment of four more PRTs had been planned for the spring of 2004, but even eight was far short of what was actually required. Finally the new CJTF-180 commander also had to begin working much more closely with the American Presidential

Special Envoy to Afghanistan, Zalmay Khalilzad, and meeting with Afghan political officials such as Karzai, with whom he talked several times a week.[7]

The U.S. embassy country team in Kabul was in no better shape than its military counterpart, largely because the State Department's need to fill required positions in Iraq was even more urgent than the Defense Department's. Following the ouster of the Taliban, a U.S. Liaison Office in Kabul had reopened on December 17, 2001, with Ambassador James Dobbins serving as director. The United States recognized the Afghan Interim Administration only on December 22, 2001, when the latter assumed the authority to represent Afghanistan in its external relations. The U.S. embassy then officially reopened, on January 17, 2002, with former ambassador to Syria Ryan Crocker as chargé d'affaires; Crocker departed Kabul on April 3, 2002, and was replaced as ambassador by Robert Finn, who in turn left the post August 1, 2003. Zalmay Khalilzad officially presented his credentials as ambassador on November 28 and would retain the position until June 20, 2005. In the summer of 2003, the embassy at Kabul was critically short of manpower and staffed with a mix of soon-to-retire Foreign Service Officers and very young acolytes just learning their craft.

Coordination between the embassy, the U.S. military, and the other American interagency partners (such as the Justice and Commerce Departments) was further hampered by the geographic distance between Bagram and Kabul. Unity of effort suffered; the military C2 situation was in flux; and over time, the continuing toll of "kinetic" military operations risked alienating the Afghan people due to collateral damage affecting civilians.[8] Even more ominously, August 2003 proved to be one of the deadliest months since operation Enduring Freedom began, with more than 220 Afghan soldiers and civilians killed by Taliban forces.[9]

"Despite the best coalition efforts, the enemy had found ways to regroup and retaliate. Pockets of enemy forces found safe havens in the mountains of Afghanistan, along the border with Pakistan, and inside Pakistan itself, especially in and around the city of Quetta, where the Taliban leadership found refuge and began to reorganize, plan future operations, and recruit new members to fill their depleted ranks."[10] The security situation in Afghanistan was not getting any better. In fact, in mid-2003 a Taliban mullah had stated, "We have the American forces and the puppet regime of Karzai on the run. They will collapse soon."[11] With the United States trying to downsize its forces and the Taliban resurgent, a change in approach was required.

The New COIN Approach

To establish the conditions for permanent change in Afghanistan, coalition leaders realized that the operational end state required non–combat-oriented, nation-building operations. Unfortunately with combat operations in Iraq placing huge demands on the force, it was apparent that the U.S.-led effort was neither structured nor resourced to handle the operational counterterrorism threat plus the reconstruction of Afghanistan.[12] Fortunately the arrival of two senior leaders, the newly designated Ambassador Khalilzad and Lieutenant General David W. Barno, in October 2003 shifted the campaign dramatically from a counterterrorism-focused operation to a true coalition counterinsurgency (COIN) campaign.

The main effort for this new COIN campaign was to be political development: the successful Afghan presidential election in the fall of 2004 and the parliamentary elections in the summer of 2005. But progress was also to be made in a number of other key areas, such as the development of the Afghan economy and security-sector reform. Importantly the leadership of and synchronization for this COIN effort came from a uniquely structured U.S. country team that seamlessly blended diplomatic, informational, economic, and military means.

Starting in the fall of 2003, the U.S. interagency effort in Afghanistan gained unprecedented policy authority for the conduct of the campaign. This was not a planned bureaucratic outcome but rather the by-product of the fortunate political conditions that being an "economy of force" campaign provided. Iraq consumed Washington's attention, and Washington could focus on only one crisis at a time. As a result, from late 2003 through the summer of 2005 the coalition effort thrived on a series of planned strategic successes, focused on the Afghan presidential election in the fall of 2004, and worked toward the parliamentary elections the following year. This integrated U.S. counterinsurgency strategy in Afghanistan was the work of an integrated civilian and military team—senior leaders who made it their business to be in continual dialogue and discussion with Bush administration policy makers, members of the international coalition, and nongovernmental organizations. In rebuilding one of the world's most devastated countries, this was simple pragmatism. They could not afford to be at cross-purposes.[13]

Before General Barno took command of the effort in Afghanistan, General John Abizaid, CENTCOM commander beginning in July 2003, directed that an additional three-star headquarters be created in Kabul to focus on political-military affairs and build necessary relationships with Karzai's government and ISAF.[14] These had become tasks critical to the overall effort, and the CENTCOM commander believed that a headquarters dedicated to working at these levels would give the Afghan government the attention and support it required.[15] On his arrival General Barno began assembling a "pocket"[16] staff of six officers, the core of a new strategic headquarters for Operation Enduring Freedom, to be named Combined Forces Command–Afghanistan (CFC-A).[17] General Vines and his CJTF-180 would work for General Barno, managing the tactical fighting.

Because the important coalition and Afghan leaders were located in Kabul, Barno sought to establish CFC-A there. Locating the new headquarters in Kabul was a strategic decision that paid significant dividends: "The benefit of physical collocation of senior military and diplomatic leaders and their staffs cannot be overemphasized; nearly all other lessons learned were influenced by physical proximity and its beneficial effect on personal interaction and coordination. Being in the same place allowed more agility and speed in dealing with rapidly developing crises."[18] Barno's office was only two doors from Ambassador Khalilzad's; the commander being physically in the embassy signaled to military officers in CFC-A that the command was to focus on all elements of national power. At the same time, this close proximity allowed Khalilzad and Barno to build a true interagency team.

The resulting coordination structure was a distinct break from traditional country-team structures. In Kabul the political and military efforts were structurally fused inside the embassy, allowing extremely rapid interagency decision making within the country team, in contrast to Washington, where non-Iraq decisions often took time. From a military perspective, the belief that the military headquarters should have been somewhat removed from the capital, in part to avoid entanglement in the political complexities of Kabul's international embassies, special envoys, ISAF units, the UN's UNAMA, and NGOs, was a valid one. However Barno's mandate was not tactical but strategic, and he realized that to make progress in Afghanistan he had to embrace this free-wheeling, confusing, and sometimes counterproductive mix of organizations as essential to his mission. Despite the warning that "Kabul will consume you," Barno thrived in the environment.[19]

The development of a counterinsurgency strategy to synchronize coalition military, civilian, and Afghan governmental activities began shortly after

General Barno's arrival. Lakhdar Brahimi requested that he develop a plan to address the deteriorating security situation in the south and east of the country.[20] "The UN was responsible for devising and implementing a plan to hold Afghan presidential and parliamentary elections beginning in 2004. However, due to increasing violence that specifically targeted UN election trainers, it was becoming clear that the UN would be unable to extend its reach into significant parts of the Pashtun southern half of Afghanistan. Moreover, a strong Taliban offensive was expected in the spring of 2004, which would further threaten the elections and thus undermine the 'roadmap' set forth by the international community in the Bonn Process."[21]

The CFC-A staff concluded that there were three conflicts occurring simultaneously in Afghanistan.[22] The first was a kinetic conflict pitting the coalition and Afghan government forces against Al-Qaeda and related terrorist organizations. They operated primarily in the southern and southeastern provinces along the Afghan–Pakistan border. "The second conflict centered on insurgent networks including the Taliban and the Hizb-i Islami Gulbuddin faction (HIG). Pockets of remaining Taliban tended [to] locate near Kandahar in the south and the adjoining provinces of Zabul, Oruzgun, and Ghazni, and along the Pakistani frontier, where they had training bases and other facilities."[23] Although the HIG, the Taliban, and Al-Qaeda were different organizations, there were indications by the fall of 2003 that their leaders were interested in collaborating.

Finally, the third conflict was the struggle to prevent "centrifugal forces,"[24] resulting mostly from regional militia directed by warlords who did not support the new central government and sought to disrupt the peaceful transition to democracy. These regional leaders maintained armed forces despite the Disarmament, Demobilization, and Reintegration (DDR) program, led by the Japanese under the Bonn Agreement. Former mujahedeen and Northern Alliance leaders like Abdul Rashid Dostum and Ismail Kahn had tacitly given their support to the ATA, but they continued to become embroiled in violent feuds that threatened to pull the Bonn process apart. Other organizations, such as groups of poppy producers and criminal groups, also undermined the authority of the Afghan government either directly or indirectly.[25]

Given this analysis, General Barno and the CFC-A staff formulated an innovative approach to address these conflicts. The first step was to identify the center of gravity (COG) for the campaign. Barno viewed the CJTF-180 campaign between summer 2002 and fall 2003 as too exclusively focused on defeating the enemy; he specifically identified the population of Afghanistan as the center of gravity of his effort. Barno felt that "anything we did that jeopardized the population's support for that effort, the population's support for their government or for the degree of hope which they all had for their future, that put the entire mission in Afghanistan at risk."[26] So for Barno success meant that population's gradually assisting the efforts of the coalition and Afghan security forces to eliminate the threats they posed. He said, "In our emerging strategy, I viewed the tolerance of the Afghan people for this new international military effort as a 'bag of capital,' one that was finite and had to be spent slowly and frugally."[27] The coalition had to help preserve this capital rather than expend it.[28]

With that strategic center of gravity in mind, Barno and his staff developed a counterinsurgency campaign strategy based upon five interagency pillars: "Defeat Terrorism and Deny Sanctuary," "Enable the Afghan Security Structure," "Sustain Area Ownership," "Enable Reconstruction and Good Governance," and "Engage Regional States."

The first pillar called for operations and actions that placed continual pressure on the enemy. While Special Forces teams would continue their search

The CFC-A Campaign and Its Five Pillars

for Al-Qaeda senior leaders, the coalition would conduct full-spectrum operations: a mix of combat operations targeting insurgents, negotiations among rival groups, and reconstruction missions. The second pillar, Enable the Afghan Security Structure, encompassed the effort to rebuild the Afghan National Army and the Afghan National Police. The third pillar, Sustain Area Ownership, represented the most important and dramatic change in the way U.S. military units were to operate under Barno. He directed that the CJTF move away from a series of "raids" launched from bases and mandated the creation of areas of operation (AOs) for ground task forces.[29] For the first time in the Afghan campaign, ground forces were to remain in place for extended periods of time, familiarizing themselves with the local population and key leaders.

The fourth pillar, Enable Reconstruction and Good Governance, was a product of area ownership. Here PRTs were designed and fielded to build Afghan infrastructure and government institutions. Governance projects focused on democratic elections and development of the ATA, both of which also undermined the strength of regional militia leaders and poppy growers. Finally, the fifth pillar, Engage Regional States, required CFC-A to operate as a subregional commander responsible for diplomacy with bordering nations, such as Pakistan, Tajikistan, and Uzbekistan.

To operationalize this approach, General Barno delegated responsibility for specific pillars to his subordinate commands. CJTF-180 would bear the burden for the security operations and reconstruction efforts that supported the first, third, and fourth pillars. The Office of Military Cooperation-Afghanistan would focus on the second pillar. The CFC-A commander and staff, working in concert with the American embassy, pursued the initiatives at the center of pillar five.[30]

Barno also understood that his resources were, and would remain, limited. In late 2003 there were 14,000 coalition troops reporting to CFC-A. By the summer of 2005 that number would increase to nearly 20,000. While tactical units were spread quite thin, CFC-A never requested additional units (with the exception of short-term deployments for election preparations); Barno unequivocally asserted, "I was very comfortable with the troops I got. . . . I felt very comfortable having that many forces in country and being able to accomplish the mission in the environment we had there."[31]

General Barno's confidence about his force levels derived from the fact that CFC-A would not use coalition maneuver units to secure Afghan communities; instead, the maneuver units could clear the enemy out of an AO and win the support of the population, allowing the ATA to hold the area. Coalition maneuver units would be assisted by increasingly competent and dependable Afghan security forces as well as a growing number of PRTs. This multifaceted and synchronized approach would ensure that the population remained in support of the coalition and the Afghan government and that its support would prevent the enemy from returning and regaining a foothold.

The CFC-A campaign plan linked the three "wars" and five pillars together with twelve interagency lines of effort, representing a whole-of-government approach incorporating diplomatic, informational, military, and economic elements of coalition power. In Barno's view, the campaign plan was an evolving document whose assumptions were to be continually challenged. The result was a coalition and Afghan interagency campaign plan, fully synchronized with Ambassador Khalilzad's action plan for the attainment of strategic goals and objectives.[32]

The Enemy Has a Vote

After managing to evade U.S. forces throughout most of 2003 and 2004, the Taliban gradually began to recoup its numbers and begin preparations to launch the insurgency that Muhammad Omar had promised during the Taliban's last days in power.[33] In 2003 small, mobile camps were established along the border with Pakistan by Al-Qaeda and Taliban fugitives to train recruits in guerrilla warfare and terrorist tactics, including suicide attacks against Americans.[34]

The first sign that Taliban forces were regrouping came on January 27, 2003, when a band of fighters allied with the Taliban and Hezb-i-Islami were discovered and assaulted by U.S. forces at the Adi Ghar cave complex north of Spin Boldak. Eighteen rebels were reported killed, and no U.S. casualties were reported. The site was suspected to have been a base to funnel supplies and fighters from Pakistan.[35] Some American experts already knew that the Taliban and its associated groups were posturing for a renewed conflict. Barnett Rubin, a specialist on Afghanistan at New York University, noted in the spring of 2003, "The general idea that was being put forward . . . is that the Afghan military, backed by U.S. forces, is engaged in mopping up some remnants of the past— that is not true. . . . They [the Taliban] are now organizing for a new offensive, and they are still getting some support from Pakistan. Even if Pakistan is not cooperating directly, it is not cooperating in efforts to end the support that is coming from Pakistani territory."[36]

Major bases, a few with as many as two hundred men, were created in the mountainous tribal areas of Pakistan by the summer of 2003. The Pakistani military stationed on the border seemed unwilling to prevent such infiltration, and Pakistani military operations proved of little use. During September 2004, the Taliban began a recruitment drive in Pashtun areas in both Afghanistan and Pakistan in order to launch a renewed conflict against the Karzai government and the coalition. Most of the recruits were drawn from the *madrassas,* or religious schools, of the tribal areas of Pakistan, from which the Taliban had originally arisen.

As the summer of 2003 continued, the attacks gradually increased in frequency in the "Taliban heartland." Dozens of Afghan government soldiers, employees of subgovernmental organizations, humanitarian workers, and several U.S. soldiers died in the raids, ambushes, and rocket attacks. Besides using guerrilla attacks, Taliban fighters began building up their forces in Dai Chopan, a district in Zabul Province that straddles Kandahar and Uruzgan, at the very center of Taliban strength.[37] Dai Chopan is a remote and sparsely populated corner of southeastern Afghanistan composed of towering, rocky mountains interspersed with narrow gorges. Taliban fighters decided it would be the perfect area to make a stand against the Afghan government and the coalition forces. Over the course of the summer, perhaps the largest concentration of Taliban militants since the fall of the regime gathered in the area, up to a thousand guerrillas. Over 220 people, including several dozen Afghan police, were killed in August 2003 as Taliban fighters gained strength.[38] As a result of the increases in enemy activity, coalition forces began preparing offensives during the winter and early spring of 2005 to root out the remaining rebel forces. In late August 2005, Afghan government forces backed by U.S. troops and heavy American aerial bombardment advanced upon Taliban positions within the Dai Chopan area. After a one-week battle, the Taliban forces were routed, with up to 124 killed.[39]

The Taliban gradually reorganized yet again and reconstituted its forces over the winter, preparing for a summer offensive in 2005. It established a new mode of operation, gathering into groups of around fifty to launch attacks on isolated outposts and convoys of Afghan soldiers, police, or militia and then breaking up into groups of five to ten to evade subsequent offensives. U.S.

forces in the strategy were only attacked indirectly, most frequently through rocket attacks on bases and the use of improvised explosive devices (IEDs) on roadways. To coordinate the Taliban strategy, Mullah Omar named a ten-man leadership council for the resistance, with himself at the head. Five operational zones were created, each assigned to a different Taliban commander (Mullah Dadullah, for example, was placed in charge of Zabul Province operations).[40] Taliban groups were "financially assisted by Al Qaeda through extremist groups in Pakistan, and 'some elements within Pakistan's security agencies are turning a blind eye.'"[41] Al-Qaeda forces in eastern Afghanistan concentrated their attacks on American forces, frequently using elaborate ambushes that were beyond the ability of most Taliban units.

Executing the Campaign

Despite the long and difficult list of tasks to be performed by the coalition, the real hallmark of the international leadership from 2003 to 2005 was the maintenance of strategic focus in the execution of the campaign. Here the main effort for the coalition and international community emerged from an initial request made by Lakhdar Brahimi a few months before—asking how to set the conditions for and execute successful Afghan presidential and parliamentary elections in the fall of 2004 and summer 2005, respectively. All CFC-A and CJTF operations, including the deployment of the 22nd MEU in the spring of 2004, supported this objective.

On April 15, 2004, General Vines and his 10th Mountain Division CJTF-180 were replaced by the 25th Infantry Division, commanded by Major General Eric T. Olsen, and CJTF-180 was renamed CJTF-76. While the relationship between Barno and Olsen was not a particularly warm one, staff officers in both CJTF-76 and CFC-A worked extremely well together. Relations between Barno and Khalilzad remained superb. The UN effort in Afghanistan was then headed by a new special representative to the Secretary General, Jean Arnault. Along with a few key Afghans, that small group of international leaders led the planning and execution for the first Afghan election. Most importantly they led the entire effort from the rear. In the eyes of Afghans, it would be their own government and the Afghan people who would deliver the elections.[42]

To conduct the presidential election in October 2004, the initial task facing the coalition was to secure the difficult eastern and southern portions of the country so that UN and other international and subgovernmental organizations could conduct and monitor election training. Additionally, at some point prior to the election, an independent UN team would make a security assessment that would determine UN participation in the election process. The immediate objective was to ensure the UN that the security situation, emergency procedures, Afghan election infrastructure, and even UN command and control of the election process were prepared. The U.S. election planning group met on a weekly basis for months, and as the election neared it would meet nearly every day. Additionally, the U.S. planners met weekly with UN and international election officials at the UN headquarters.

To secure the election process, which included securing UN election workers conducting training, CJTF-76 began executing a counterinsurgency strategy, rapidly establishing area ownership of the Afghan battlespace. This required assigning every inch of ground to a commander. Major General Olson organized the CJTF into six task forces, three of which maintained direct area ownership of most of Afghanistan. Two brigade task forces were assigned to the most dangerous areas in Afghanistan: TF Thunder, commanded by Colonel Gary Cheek, in Regional Command (RC) East; TF Bronco, commanded by Colonel Richard Pedersen, in RC South; and a cavalry headquarters, TF Longhorn, commanded by Colonel Phillip Bookert, in the west. As General Barno explained, "This approach mirrored New York City's successful policy in the 1990s of holding police captains responsible for reducing crime in their precincts. Like New York's captains, Olson, and his commanders, now 'owned' their areas and were responsible for results."[43] Area ownership meant that for the first time in the war, unit commanders had defined areas, clear sets of challenges, and direct responsibility for long-term outcomes. Previously, units had owned no battlespace except the ground they were on during an operation's duration, often only two or three weeks long. Over the long term, battlespace had been "owned" only by the CJTF-180 in Bagram, and no subordinate unit had sustained responsibility for outcomes in any specified area. This concept had had profound implications. Now, rather than pass through an area intent on simply routing an enemy on the basis of intelligence derived at a faraway operating base, units operated in their own distinct territories for up to twelve months. Commanders now had the opportunity to become experts in their areas, build personal relations with tribal elders and key government officials, and most importantly, convince the population that they were there to stay.[44]

While maintaining area control, extension of the reach of the central government was fundamental to helping Afghanistan become a nation that embraced the rule of law and that entrusted its elected government with a monopoly on violence. Both Afghans and the coalition had to deal with the perception, and often the reality, that the power of the nation's legitimate institutions seemed to grow weaker with every kilometer of distance from Kabul. Effective local government remained a problem, and traditional tribal and clan cultures continued to hold powerful sway throughout much of the countryside. The primary coalition interagency instrument designed to address this challenge was the PRT.[45]

Provincial Reconstruction Teams were eighty-to-one-hundred-person interagency organizations normally posted to provincial capitals. Early in the CFC-A campaign, they typically comprised a security force, medical and logistics components, a civil affairs team, a command-and-control element, and senior representatives from the Afghan Ministry of Interior, U.S. Department of State, USAID, and in certain areas, the U.S. Department of Agriculture. The PRT presence in an area was a catalyst for change. It signified the international and Afghan commitment to bettering the lives of the people through improved government support. To integrate and set priorities for the PRT effort, a multinational PRT executive steering committee in Kabul, cochaired by the Afghan minister of interior, then Ali Jalali, and the CFC-A commander, met on a quarterly basis.[46]

The PRT became a powerful counterinsurgency weapon to win Afghan "hearts and minds." With allocated Commanders Emergency Response Program (CERP) funding, which reached nearly $100 million in fiscal year 2005, a commander could address pressing civil needs with a minimum of bureaucracy and work with the Afghan population to significantly improve their lives. By the end of 2003, four PRTs were operating in largely safe areas: Gardez, Konduz, Mazar-i-Sharif, and Bamian. Beginning in 2004, CFC-A accelerated the formation of an additional eight by disassembling the CJCMOTF headquarters in Bagram and assigning its civil affairs experts to form the new PRTs in the field. These additional PRTs were deployed to the south and east of Afghanistan, so when the snows melted in the spring of 2004 newly deployed PRTs could be confronting the Taliban across the most contested areas. By the spring of 2005 there would be a total of nineteen PRTs in Afghanistan.[47]

By placing lightly defended PRTs in the dangerous southern and eastern areas of Afghanistan, General Barno was assuming a significant operational risk.

While he knew that the PRTs had little ability to defend themselves with small arms against a determined enemy, he also realized that the enemy knew that twenty minutes after a distress call, any PRT in southern Afghanistan could have combat aircraft with bombs overhead and a rapid-reaction force right behind it. In General Barno's analysis, the 2001 offensive that toppled the Taliban had produced a healthy respect for American airpower that allowed CJTF-76, among other things, to conduct small patrols far from bases in relative security. PRTs similarly benefited from air support and leveraged it regularly.[48] In the end, however, it was Barno who directed the bold move of rapidly expanding the PRT effort.

Playing Politics and "Warlords"

From the start, the Afghan strategy was a coalition strategy. Due to the lead-nation concept agreed to in Bonn in 2002, almost all U.S. plans, policies, and operations required close coordination with the four other "lead nations" contributing to the effort. While the United States conducted the lion's share of counterterrorism and kinetic counterinsurgency operations, as well as supporting the development of the Afghan National Army and paying the lion's share of the costs, other nations did accomplish key tasks. Japan was the lead for the disarmament of warlords, Great Britain headed counternarcotics operations, Germany worked on developing the Afghan National Police, and Italy invested in judicial reform.[49] Additionally the CFC-A conducted close and continual coordination with the ISAF, which controlled all operations in Kabul and northern Afghanistan as of August 2003 and would control western Afghanistan as well by the end of 2005.

Extending the reach of the central government was fundamental to success in Afghanistan. In the eyes of the Afghans, the elected government had to embrace the rule of law if it was to be trusted with a monopoly on violence. As former Afghan interior minister Ali Jalali often stated, "Afghanistan is a strong nation, but a weak state."[50] Even President Hamid Karzai recognized the populist nature of Afghan society and its tradition of local rule. While CJTF tactical combat and PRT operations were aimed primarily at the insurgents in the south and east of the country, a unique strategic opportunity afforded itself two months prior to the presidential election that would help assert the legitimacy of the Afghan government.

On August 15, 2004, Ismail Khan became embroiled in a violent fight with another local warlord, Amanullah Kahn, in the city of Shindand, some ninety miles south of Herat.[51] Ambassador Khalilzad was ready to take quick strategic advantage of a bad tactical situation—the opportunity to neutralize two powerful warlords, an informational theme that would resonate with the Afghan population in 2004. Hamid Karzai, although the nominally elected as the president of Afghanistan, had very little real power outside of Kabul, and putting an end to the infighting between the two warlords would clearly reinforce his authority. It would also counter the sentiment that the Afghan government did not own a monopoly of power inside its own borders and could not protect its citizens from insurgents, warlords, or even coalition forces, particularly special operations.[52] So Khalilzad directed CFC-A to develop a plan to remove both warlords and bring them to Kabul. Within twenty-four hours, the 1st Reserve Corps of the ANA, stationed in Kabul, was alerted and boarded U.S. military aircraft. The corps deployment involved seven hundred soldiers augmented by three hundred Afghan police. Backing the deployment was a considerable U.S. maneuver and logistical effort consisting of Special Forces, heliborne forces, and logistical support from the CJTF.

Coalition forces rapidly seized the old Soviet air base at Shindand, separated the militias, and placed Amanullah Kahn in government custody. In only thirty hours the ANA and ANP also seized all of Ismail Kahn's heavy weapons and began moving them to a containment site in the vicinity of the commercial airport at Herat. After two days of civil violence by Ismail Kahn's cronies, which damaged the UN offices in Herat, the entire episode was concluded. After spurning Karzai's offers for a few weeks to give up his position and move to Kabul to join the government, Ismail Khan finally relented and was named to the cabinet post of minister of energy in the Karzai government. Amanullah Kahn was not so fortunate and was placed under house arrest in Kabul.[53]

The ANA deployment to Shindand in August 2004 indicated that with U.S. support the Afghan National Army had made useful progress since its establishment. At the end of 2004, it was an ethnically balanced national army consisting of some 24,000 soldiers, trained by a rotating U.S. National Guard brigade known as Task Force Phoenix. By 2007 it would grow to nearly 50,000 troops. General Barno noted, "From 2003 to 2005, no ANA formations were defeated or broke in combat engagements. Moreover, ANA units showed notable discipline during intense civil-disturbance operations—operations for which they had not been specifically trained."[54]

On the other hand, the operation in Herat indicated that the Afghan National Police (ANP) force was probably two full years behind the army in its development. Under the Bonn Agreement, Germany was the lead nation for the training of the ANP. The German effort focused on the training of individual police officers, not police units. Consequently the ANP units required the close supervision by the ANA to be effective. As the presidential election approached, CFC-A worked on a number of issues to improve the effectiveness of both the ANA and the ANP.[55]

To prepare the ANA for the critical mission of securing polling stations for the upcoming Afghan national election, then looming four weeks away, CFC-A purchased nearly $2 million worth of riot-control helmets, body and face shields, and cell phones to ensure reliable commercial communications. Additionally the CJTF provided military police training for the ANP in Kabul and also began integrating ANP units into the overall election security plan. The ANP would provide "inner ring" security at the polling places—a tactic very similar to what had been successfully done in Iraq in January 2005. On July 12, 2005, just prior to the Afghan parliamentary elections, the Office of Military Cooperation–Afghanistan officially assumed responsibility for the U.S. role in reforming the Afghan National Police force and was renamed as the Office of Security Cooperation–Afghanistan (OSC-A).[56]

Fall 2004—Support for the Presidential Election

As the elections approached, CFC-A prepared a comprehensive security plan that incorporated not only the tactical and operational security plan that the CJTF was developing for the polling stations and regional counting houses but also ensured that the Afghan Joint Election Management Board (JEMB) and UN command-and-control efforts were rehearsed and exercised. Unfortunately neither the U.S. embassy nor CFC-A had the authority to provide the infrastructure that would be required to ensure that the JEMB and the UN headquarters could actually "run" an election. Despite this shortfall CFC-A provided $4 million to the JEMB and UN, for security barriers, fiberoptic cabling, and cellular phones for local polling places and to award contracts to securely move ballots from remote polling stations to regional countinghouses.[57]

During the last week of September CFC-A, CJTF-76, the JEMB, and the UN completed an election rehearsal, and the following week CFC-A hosted a final election briefing for the government of Afghanistan and the international community. The briefing laid out in great detail the concentric-ring plan to secure 22,000 Afghan polling stations and some 5,000 countinghouses and command-and-control nodes, beginning with the ANP, followed by the ANA, with coalition forces and airpower "over the horizon."[58] On October 9, with 55.4 percent of the votes and three times more votes than any other candidate, Hamid Karzai won the first democratic election in Afghan history. Twelve candidates received less than 1 percent of the vote. More than 70 percent of Afghanistan's nearly 12 million registered voters cast ballots, including millions of women. The election was a tremendous success and further bonded the U.S. country team, the international coalition, and the Afghan government.[59]

With the election completed, many rank-and-file Taliban began to realize that the ballot box, not violence, might be the future of Afghanistan. Many in this group began to approach Afghan tribal elders and coalition forces directly, in attempts to reconcile with the Afghan government. CFC-A and the CJTF planned a set of operations to exploit that situation. CJTF-76 developed an "allegiance program," which General Barno immediately recommended to Ambassador Khalilzad. In two days Khalilzad gained approval from the newly elected Afghan president to initiate a program through which Taliban fighters could rejoin Afghan society.

The command quickly developed not only a reconciliation program for former Taliban but also planned and executed a program that released nearly eighty detainees a month from the detention center at Bagram. The psychological impact was enormous.[60] Here the Afghan government played a significant role in providing oversight for the program; in collaboration with village elders who served as "parole officers," CFC-A began the process of reintegrating former fighters into Afghan society. The effort not only helped bring Afghans back together but created distrust among the Taliban, producing seams and fissures that the coalition could exploit.[61] By the winter of 2005 the CFC-A, working in concert with the Afghan National Security Council, had produced the Tachim-e Solh reintegration program, entirely run by Afghans.[62]

Building a New Afghan Security Force with Embedded Teams

Another key component of the coalition effort in Afghanistan was building the Afghan security forces. Little heralded yet crucial to long-term stability in the country, the U.S.-led effort to build the national army and police under-girded almost every other undertaking in the security sector. In the early days it was directed by the CJCMOTF. Brigadier General Krantzer not only com-manded the CJCMOTF but had by February 2002 also taken on the title of chief of the Office of Military Cooperation–Afghanistan. That office's goal was "to establish working relationships with key individuals within Afghanistan's nascent Ministry of Defense to accomplish overall objectives established by the Bonn Agreement within the greater context of the international effort to reestablish Afghanistan's military, police, and judicial organizations."[63]

The American role in the security sector reform (SSR) process was to rebuild the Afghan National Army into a professional fighting force loyal to the democratically elected government of Afghanistan. This was a very popular concept, because by quickly establishing indigenous security forces, CENT-COM could hand off responsibilities for security to the Afghans and with-draw many of the American forces. But in early 2002 Afghanistan's police and army were essentially nonexistent. In March 2002 UN Secretary General Kofi Annan had recognized this and declared that the entire Bonn Agreement agen-da largely depended on the establishment of effective Afghan security forces. "Proper management of the security sector," Annan asserted, "is the necessary first step toward [Afghan national] reconciliation and reconstruction; indeed, managing this sector may be considered the first reconstruction project."[64]

The obstacles on the path to a new army were significant. In addition to the remnants of the Taliban, Afghanistan faced threats posed by warlords, who in early 2002 controlled whole regions of the country. Ali A. Jalali, Karzai's interior minister that year, regarded the growing problem with warlords as inseparable from the fundamental issue of Afghan sovereignty. The AIA's lead-ers could ill afford to have the new Afghan political process come to resemble the historical patterns of the previous decades. "Given the lingering security threats from the Taliban and al-Qaeda as well as the continued presence of regional leaders who had retained their own military forces after the fall of the Taliban regime, the creation of a new ANA was not just about the legitimacy of the ATA but concerned its very survival."[65]

So on May 1, 2002, OMC-A had committed U.S. soldiers in Afghanistan to the training of Afghan recruits and the formation of ANA units.[66] The key to the OMC-A plan at this stage was making the U.S. Army's 1st Battalion, 3rd Special Forces Group (1/3rd SFG) responsible for training the ANA and Afghan border-guard battalions.

Upon his arrival in Afghanistan, General McNeill took charge of the OMC-A, revised the blueprints and roadmap for the ANA's development, and attempted to further the DDR program to defuse the serious threats posed by the numerous militias that still existed outside the control of the ATA.[67] That roadmap that was eventually developed was based on building an army of about 70,000 Afghan soldiers. In December 2002 Hamid Karzai endorsed that number in a presidential decree that established the basic framework for the ANA.[68] The plan called for the formation of the ANA in three phases, each of which would take approximately two years.[69] In Phase I, to be completed by June 2004, three milestones would be reached: the first battalions of the ANA would be formed into what OMC-A called the Central Corps, based in Kabul; the Ministry of Defense would be established; and Afghanistan would have a functioning Border Command that safeguarded its frontiers. The mission of the Central Corps was to serve as a counterbalance to regional leaders and conduct security operations independent of coalition forces.[70] Phase II, which would end in June 2006, would see the completion of the Central Corps so that it could secure the capital, as well as the early steps of creating a small air force. The final phase was intended to end in June 2008 with the completion of a fully functioning Ministry of Defense and some regionally based corps. Between 2002 and 2004, OMC-A planned to train and equip some twenty-four army battalions.

"OMC-A's plans met Afghan realities and by late summer 2002 some of the inertia in the ANA effort began to erode the optimism initially held by many in both the coalition and the ATA."[71] On August 29, 2002, for example, Afghan finance minister Ashraf Ghani stated that the lack of the presence of the central government's military force made the population uneasy. Ghani asserted, "We are in danger of losing the confidence of the Afghan people. Historically, this means that they take security into their own hands, and the country [descends into anarchy] and the leaders are hanged. I do not know how far along we are in this cycle, but I will be honest that I am not getting a full night's sleep lately."[72] The finance minister and others were essentially reacting to the slow growth of the Afghan army.

The 1st Battalion of the ANA (1st BANA) graduated with 308 new soldiers on July 23, 2002. The 2nd ANA Battalion followed on August 14, 2002, with 300 additional soldiers coming from the Kabul Military Academy. However, problems in housing and specialized training led to difficulties in making those first units capable of conducting operations. Worse was the attrition inside these initial units. The original OMC-A plan was to train 602 soldiers per battalion. But desertions quickly made that goal unattainable.[73] Eventually the ATA and coalition leadership agreed to combine the Afghan National Guard forces, trained separately by British units, with the 1st BANA in an effort to mitigate the attrition rates.[74]

On October 3, 2002, the 3rd BANA graduated with 358 soldiers after experiencing the loss of only 8 men during its training.[75] While the 1st and 2nd BANAs had received no advanced training after their initial basic course and were not yet conducting operations, the coalition worked hard to give the 3rd BANA specialized classes that would prepare it for combat as soon as possible. Eventually, the 3rd BANA became the first operational unit of the ANA when it began conducting security operations in Paktia Province on February 4, 2003.[76]

Building the first three battalions of the ANA was frustrating, because the primary recruiting base for the ANA was the thousands of militia members in Afghanistan. Inducting these men—many of whom were former mujahedeen or Taliban supporters—into a new army did not automatically make them loyal to the central government. Most of these individuals had formerly sworn allegiance to individual commanders or warlords not a distant political leader whom they had never seen in person.

The Growth of OMC-A and the Creation of CJTF Phoenix

In October 2002 Major General Karl Eikenberry, USA, became the chief of OMC-A. By that point, the task of growing the ANA was well under way. Three infantry battalions had already been trained, and two more—the 4th and 5th BANAs—had begun the training process. OMC-A was planning to initiate the training for seven more BANAs between late October 2002 and June 2003.[77] Eikenberry concluded, "The mandate [to build the ANA] was clear and it was a central task, but it is also fair to say that up until that time there had been few resources committed."[78] This point was driven home in December 2002 when Eikenberry visited the Kabul Military Training Center (KMTC) on the eastern side of the city and found the conditions deplorable for both the new Afghan soldiers and their American advisers. He later recalled that the food and the sanitary conditions were terrible and there was no heat inside the barracks. Eikenberry remembered thinking, "This is the Valley Forge of the Afghan National Army."[79]

This reaction came with the realization that creating a new military institution that could protect the nation of Afghanistan from foreign and internal threats was going to be a long and arduous process. Success for OMC-A would require more than just the training and equipping of light infantry battalions. Instead Eikenberry and his command were really in the business of constructing an entire military structure, to include the Ministry of Defense, a general staff, and all the other institutions and facilities that normally protect a nation.

To accomplish all of these tasks, Eikenberry realized that he needed a much more robust headquarters staff and more capability. As the project grew larger than training small, tactical units, the coalition's reliance on American Special Forces and other allied units as trainers proved no longer feasible.[80] Eikenberry turned to coalition partners for assistance with ANA training in the fall of 2002, when he asked for the British to conduct the training for noncommissioned officers (NCOs). Later the French army began conducting officer training for the ANA. Small contingents from the Romanian, Bulgarian, and Mongolian armies assisted by forming mobile training teams (MTTs) that provided instruction on how to operate and maintain Soviet-designed weapons and equipment.[81] These MTTs were flexible and responsive—they paved the way for much of the future ANA training.

In the spring of 2003 Eikenberry decided to create a new task force that would serve as the central core of trainers for the ANA. That organization took the name CJTF Phoenix, to signify the rebirth of Afghanistan's professional army. For the new CJTF, Eikenberry turned to the U.S. Army's conventional forces, and the U.S. Army assigned an augmented infantry brigade, the 2nd Brigade, 10th Mountain Division, to provide a headquarters and training teams. The 2nd Brigade started training the ANA during the summer of 2003; however, it did not deploy with all of its units—the 2nd Battalion, 14th Infantry Regiment (2-14 IN) deployed in support of Operation Iraqi Freedom that spring instead. CJTF Phoenix then began training with an augmented brigade headquarters and one infantry battalion—a force of approximately one thousand soldiers.[82] In the fall of 2003, the 2nd Brigade was designated for deployment to Iraq as part of Operation Iraqi Freedom. The coalition then arranged for the 45th Infantry Brigade of the Oklahoma Army National Guard to provide the manning for CJTF Phoenix beginning in November 2003. This move marked the first major commitment of a brigade-size Reserve Component force in Enduring Freedom.[83]

OMC-A further revised the approach the coalition would take in training the ANA by directing CJTF Phoenix to organize its effort into MTTs and embedded training teams (ETTs). The general concept dictated that the MTTs would conduct initial training for all ANA soldiers at Kabul Military Training Center (KMTC). Specialized training for infantry subunits would occur afterward. Then the MTTs would leave, and the ETTs, consisting of ten to fifteen soldiers who would live with the ANA battalions and mentor them during actual operations, would arrive and take responsibility for the next phase of the unit's development. This program was a critical innovation in the coalition's effort to build the ANA.

In December 2003 Major General Craig Weston, USAF, relieved General Eikenberry as head of the OMC-A. During the summer of 2004, the 76th Infantry Brigade, Indiana Army National Guard, commanded by Brigadier General Richard Moorhead, relieved the 45th Infantry Brigade as the core of CJTF Phoenix. Assisting the 1,000 soldiers of the 76th Brigade were approximately 500 additional Army National Guardsmen from fifteen other states, along with detachments of U.S. Marines and USAF officers and airmen. France, Germany, Romania, Canada, New Zealand, the United Kingdom, and Mongolia also provided military trainers for CJTF Phoenix.[84] By September 2004 the expanded CJTF Phoenix had successfully trained nearly 15,000 ANA soldiers and the Afghan Ministry of Defense (MOD) had activated regional commands in Kandahar (the 205th ANA Corps) and Gardez (the 203rd).[85] In addition to maintaining ANA Central Corps (201st ANA Corps) headquarters in Kabul, by year's end the Afghan MOD had activated two more regional commands at Mazar-i Sharif (209th) and Herat (207th).[86]

In light of OMC-A's success in training the ANA, during 2005 CFC-A requested that OMC-A develop a comprehensive plan for conducting comparable Afghan National Police training. Although German forces had developed and were now running the ANP Academy, they were seriously limited by inadequate funding and a shortage of personnel. Therefore the OMC-A staff prepared a detailed plan for restructuring the ANP training program.[87]

Among the many clear successes of the Enduring Freedom campaign, the effort to build the ANA and later the ANP stand out as both crucial and innovative. Techniques developed in Afghanistan were also used in Iraq, and vice versa. Both efforts were crucial to the development of functional nation-states and the important capacity of any government to control the use of force within its borders.

Changes in Leadership and in Course

On May 3, 2005, a cold and rainy day in Kabul, Lieutenant General Karl Eikenberry returned to Afghanistan and assumed command of Combined Forces Command–Afghanistan from General Barno. In his change-of-command remarks Eikenberry pledged "to follow in General Barno's footsteps . . . to work together, build security forces and support the rebuilding of Afghanistan." He also noted that the command would "work with the Afghan government to support the upcoming parliamentary elections." He ended his remarks by stating, "Our mission will continue in the same direction[:] . . . working with the United Nations, coalition forces, and most importantly, the Afghan government."[88] However almost immediately he made it clear that the command's new focus would be the "Afghan security sector" and NATO expansion. When the new commander was asked if the NATO transition plan was based upon conditions on the ground, he replied that there was an agreed transition calendar that the command would keep.[89] But Eikenberry had a different approach in mind; he made immediate changes to the schedule, focusing more time with the CFC-A staff and much less time with the country team. Eikenberry also moved several members of his staff back from the embassy, effectively ending the high level of interagency coordination Barno had achieved with Khalilzad.[62] The new commander stated that he had read the campaign plan and did not find it very "elegant."[90] His comments about the campaign plan to his British deputy, Major General Peter Gilchrist, were blunt: "This is ridiculous. That is like a Soviet Five-Year Plan. We won't have any of that."[91]

Later that month Ambassador Khalilzad also began his transition to become the new U.S. ambassador to Iraq. His replacement in Kabul would be Ambassador Ronald Neumann. Although the U.S. country team in Afghanistan had begun to produce significant results, it was now being dismantled—the embassy was being "normalized."[92] With the departure of Khalilzad and Barno by the summer of 2005, the unique interagency teamwork and embassy structures were abolished. A more traditional—and some would say less dynamic—embassy emerged. While this made career diplomats and military officers more comfortable, the decision-making process that resulted was too bureaucratic and reliant on Washington to be effective in Kabul. As operational demands in Iraq increased from 2005 to 2006, U.S. senior leadership began to signal that it was time to reduce the U.S. troop presence in Afghanistan and to have NATO gradually assume command of military operations in Afghanistan.

The Coalition Response in 2006—ISAF to the Fore

We are faced with a full-blown insurgency.

—Ahmed Rashid[93]

From January 2006, ISAF took responsibility for operations in southern Afghanistan, to help the Afghan National Army fight the increasingly violent militant groups based around the Pakistan border and curb the drugs trade that funded them. The British 16th Air Assault Brigade (augmented by Royal Marines) formed the core of the force in the region, but 2,300 Canadians and nearly 2,000 Dutch troops participated, as well as smaller contingents from the other nations, including Australia and Denmark. ISAF's focus in southern Afghanistan was to develop enough security and form PRTs, with the British leading in Helmand Province while the Netherlands and Canada would lead similar deployments in Orūzgān and Kandahar Provinces, respectively. Local Taliban figures with fifty to seventy fighters voiced opposition to the incoming force and pledged to resist it.[94] In 2006 southern Afghanistan saw the worst violence in the country since the ousting of the Taliban regime in 2001. About nine hundred people were killed—half died in May alone.[95] The Taliban were "ambushing military patrols, assassinating opponents and even enforcing the law in remote villages where they operate with near impunity."[96]

ISAF launched operation Mountain Thrust on May 17, 2006, with the purposes of rooting out the Taliban forces in the area. Daily firefights, artillery bombardments, and allied airstrikes turned the tide of the battle in favor of ISAF forces, but never with complete results, even though "military operations are followed with an increased security presence and aid programs designed to win back local support."[97] More than 1,100 Taliban fighters were killed and almost 400 captured in the operation, a month and a half long. Still, the operation did not manage to quell the Taliban insurgency.

In July 2006 control of the international forces in southern Afghanistan was passed to NATO, under the overall command of British General Sir David J. Richards. The regional command in the south was led by Canadian General David Fraser. Following Fraser, in November 2006 Dutch Major General Ton van Loon took over Regional Command South for a six-month period from the Canadians.

The Canadian forces, under NATO command after the end of July, launched Operation Medusa in an attempt to clear the areas of Taliban fighters once and for all. The fighting during Medusa led to a second, and even more fierce battle in the town of Panjwaii. There, daily gun battles, ambushes, and mortar and rocket attacks met the Canadians.[98] The Taliban were reluctant to give up the area, and after being surrounded by the Canadian forces they dug in and fought a more conventional battle with an estimated 1,500 to 2,000 fighters. After weeks of fighting, the Taliban were eventually cleared from the Panjwaii area, and Canadian reconstruction efforts began. NATO reported it had killed more than 500 suspected Taliban fighters.

Another major NATO offensive, called Operation Mountain Fury, was launched in September 2006 to clear Taliban rebels from the eastern provinces of Afghanistan. Mountain Fury included several smaller operations as well. The fighting was again intense, with numerous of coalition casualties and heavy Taliban losses. Along with the Canadians and Dutch, the British were major contributors to the expanded NATO mission in the area. By late 2006 around five thousand British personnel had been deployed to Afghanistan, particularly in Helmand Province, the location of some of the heaviest fighting.

The fighting for NATO forces was intense throughout the second half of 2006. As planned, the NATO forces began reconstruction efforts after major combat of Operation Medusa had ceased, but the British and Canadians still encountered more fierce combat. The situation in RC West deteriorated over time, with the worst Taliban activity taking place in Badghis, in the far north, and Farah, in the southwest. On September 18 Italian special forces of Task Force 45 and airborne troopers of the Trieste Infantry Regiment of the Rapid Reaction Corps (composed of Italian and Spanish forces) took part in Operation Wyconda Pincer in the districts of Bala Buluk and Pusht-i-Rod, in Farah Province. The Italian forces killed at least seventy Taliban during the fighting.[99]

The Canadian involvement in Mountain Fury was stepped up when they mounted an operation of their own called Falcon Summit on December 15, 2006. During the first week of Falcon Summit, massive Canadian artillery and tank barrages were carried out in a successful attempt to clear pockets of Taliban resistance. Eventually the Canadians gained control of several key villages and towns that had been Taliban havens, such as Howz-e Madad.[100] NATO was successful in achieving tactical victories over the Taliban and denying areas to them, but the Taliban were certainly not completely defeated, and NATO had to continue such operations into 2007.

Consternation

The 2006 push by ISAF was actually the third stage of a planned assumption of control in Afghanistan by NATO that had been proposed by Marine General James Jones, the Supreme Allied Commander Europe, in February 2004. Jones had developed the plan to advance the alliance but also to free up American forces for the troubled effort in Iraq. Once again the U.S. national imperative favored the effort in Iraq. Under the Jones plan, operations in Afghanistan were to be turned over to NATO, based upon a four-stage plan. In Stage 1, NATO assumed control of Regional Command North in October 2004; during Stage 2, NATO assumed control of RC West in September 2005; Stage 3 called for NATO to assumed control of RC South, as it had did in July 2006. Finally, in Stage 4, NATO had assumed control of RC East in October 2006.[101] As CFC-A was supporting the expansion of NATO into RC West, it had already become clear that NATO lacked the infrastructure to support the logistical, rotary-lift, and medical assets needed to adequately expand even into that relatively small and operationally less challenging region, let alone to begin to untangle the vast support requirements needed in Regional Command South, where the combat demands might also be significant. What was most surprising to the CFC-A staff, however, was that the CENTCOM commander felt that if NATO went into Afghanistan, a significant number of American troops might go home or be diverted to Iraq.[102] There seemed to be little interest in keeping up the American pressure at CENTCOM in Tampa once NATO began to take responsibility.

Despite the problems with NATO troop and support commitments, many felt that the Atlantic Alliance was so damaged by the European disagreement over Iraq that it was compelled to support Operation Enduring Freedom.[103] While numerous senior NATO leaders were briefed by CFC-A that the situation in Afghanistan was extremely fragile and required commitment, flexibility, and at times overwhelming combat power, few seemed to understand the scope of the problem at hand. NATO senior political and military leaders provided their counterparts back in Brussels a view much different from what had been briefed. To further compound the problems of maintaining pressure on the Taliban while NATO was phasing in, the United States announced that NATO would assume complete responsibility for all combat operations in Afghanistan by midyear and that the American troop strength would be reduced by 2,500 by the spring of 2006.[104] Words carry meaning, however unfortunate, and these words reinforced a long-standing Taliban message that the United States was an "unreliable partner" and would soon be leaving Afghanistan.[105]

By the end of 2006 the security situation on the ground, particularly in the volatile south, was deteriorating rapidly. Many of the coalition of NATO countries, each with its own national interests in mind, began to make demands of the Afghan government and of each other. The violence and diplomatic chaos caused a great deal of finger-pointing but did little to advance a coalition military effort that was by that time hamstrung by cumbersome command and control and a disunity of effort.[106]

Security Declines in Afghanistan

As a result, Taliban and Al-Qaeda gathered strength, changed tactics, and significantly increased both their capabilities and their attacks. Overall security incidents increased from 900 in 2004 to 5,000 in 2006; IED detonations increased from 352 in 2004 to 1,536 in 2006; and coalition troop fatalities increased from 58 in 2004 to 191 in 2006.[107] In response ISAF commanders burned rapidly through the "bag of capital" that represented Afghan tolerance for ISAF operations as the total tonnage of bombs dropped in Afghanistan increased from 86 tons in 2004 to an incredible 2,644 tons in 2006. The lesson is clear: to maintain political will for the ISAF campaign at home, commanders were attempting to drive down casualties by the generous application of airpower.[108] As violence continued to increase, by 2006 NATO troop contingents became divided into those who fought (the Americans, the British, the Canadians, and Italians) and those who did not fight (the French, Germans, Dutch, and Spanish), mainly due to restrictions or "national caveats" imposed by their political leadership.[109]

To further compound the problems associated with combat operations, in July 2006 NATO assumed control of all combat operations in Afghanistan. The ISAF commanders who followed, beginning with General Richards, had to contend with a C2 bureaucracy that made it extremely difficult to command or control anything.[110] The military command numbered 26,000 troops. An additional 10,000 Americans served under U.S. national control (support and

SOF), complicating "hard knock" coordination. The twenty-six NATO PRTs deployed across Afghanistan reported to a headquarters different from those of the ground maneuver units that operated beside them in the same battle spaces. From 2006 to April 2007 the senior U.S. military commander was once again a two-star division commander located at Bagram, but unlike his CJTF-180 predecessor was responsible only for Regional Command East.[111] Operational responsibility for Afghanistan resided in Brunssum, the Netherlands, three thousand miles away. By April 2007, an American four-star general was to command ISAF, but he would report only through NATO channels. Both the Supreme Allied Commander, Europe, and the commander of U.S. Central Command directed forces in Afghanistan that reported separately up two chains.[112]

With the advent of NATO military leadership in 2006 there was still no comprehensive strategy to guide the U.S., NATO, or international effort. Interagency and international unity of purpose was substandard at the end of 2006 as coalition partners acted in their national self-interest. For not only did the U.S. country team change, but the entire international effort in Afghanistan dramatically shifted from a U.S.-led effort that placed progress in Afghanistan first to a North Atlantic Treaty Organization effort that placed its own existence and success first.[113]

Six

The Casey Strategy in Iraq, from Fallujah to Tal Afar

As the situation in Afghanistan was starting to worsen, one should expect that the primary theater of war, Iraq, would at least be improving; however that case was hard to make. On June 1, 2004, General George Casey had assumed command in Iraq from Lieutenant General Sanchez and set up a new senior organization in Baghdad named the Multinational Force–Iraq (MNF-I). Casey knew Washington's policies in Iraq well, and he arrived in Iraq to exert new command influence and to stimulate more aggressiveness in order to finish the war. Casey's goal was to encourage the Iraqis to take ownership of their problems and accept responsibility for their own security. As the senior military commander in Iraq, he would focus on supporting the political development in the country, training Iraqi forces, limiting the role of American forces, and transferring the burden for providing security to Iraqi forces. Meanwhile the new U.S. ambassador in Iraq, John Negroponte, could focus on building and strengthening the Iraqi government led by Prime Minister Ayad Allawi and help motivate the Iraqis to hold elections.

Within the military realm in Iraq, two other major headquarters were also created, under the overall strategic direction of MNF-I: Multinational Corps–Iraq (MNC-I) and Multinational Security Transition Command–Iraq (MNSTC-I). MNC-I would run the day-to-day operational war in Iraq, focusing primarily on defeating terrorists and rooting out the insurgency, while MNSTC-I would focus on the training and development of the Iraqi security forces, police, army, navy, and air force. Lieutenant General David Petraeus, who had commanded the 101st Airborne Division during the initial invasion phase of Iraqi Freedom, returned to Iraq to set up and command MNSTC-I. This new command structure seemed to be focused appropriately on the key requirements of the war in Iraq. Casey could focus on the overall strategy and support the military functioning of the American pol-mil effort in the country, while the commanders of his two subordinate commands could focus on fighting and training.

In mid-2004, Sunni opposition to the new government, and certainly to the MNF forces, was anticipated and well understood by most people working on the development of the new Iraq. What was potentially much more dangerous and what concerned them more, however, was the slow but clear growth in Shia opposition to the coalition and the Iraqi Interim Government. That opposition was made clear in Baghdad in the continuing strife in the slums of the largely Shia area known as Sadr City as the summer passed. It became even more dangerous with the growing demands of Shia resistance leader Muqtada al-Sadr and his demonstrations in the holy city of Najaf in late July and early August.

Sadr's anticoalition Mahdi Militia had conducted various armed activities intended to intimidate local security forces and anyone else who would aid the new Iraqi government—this was a serious threat to any expectation of a rapid establishment of security in Iraq. Sadr's spokesman called for revolution and claimed that his supporters controlled four provinces in the country.[1] When attacked by members of the Mahdi Militia, the police in the city of Najaf called for Iraqi army support. Later U.S. Marines from the 11th MEU were also called in by the provincial governor;[2] this brought the coalition directly into conflict with al-Sadr and his Shia militiamen. When the fighting continued to escalate, the provincial governor, Adnan al-Ziruffi, ordered the local Iraqi National Guard and police forces to seal off Najaf in response to reports that busloads of Mahdi Militia were traveling from Baghdad to fight there.

Some thought the use of such force would intimidate al-Sadr and dampen his continued antigovernmental rhetoric, but in fact his followers grew ever more militant as additional pressure was applied. Outside of al-Sadr's actions, that part of Iraq had been relatively quiet, but in reaction to the significant threat posed by the antigovernment Mahdi Militia, the 11th MEU was soon called upon. It was directed to conduct full-scale offensive operations in order to defeat al-Sadr's forces in Najaf and restore normal civil authority in the city. Over the following weeks, in the first sustained urban combat since in Fallujah the previous April, coalition forces under the tactical control of the 11th MEU commander, Colonel Tony Haslem, destroyed or expelled the well-entrenched elements of the Mahdi Militia from Najaf, and they did so without damaging the holy Imam Ali Shrine and mosque complex. Perhaps most importantly, the fighting in Najaf showed a new Iraqi military capability for the first time, in the form of one battalion of the new Iraqi Civil Defense Corps that participated in the fighting.

Fallujah II—Operation Al Fajr

Unfortunately in May 2004, after the failure of the first Fallujah operation to calm the restive city, insurgent and terrorist activity inside Fallujah only grew more intense with each passing week. By the time the fighting ended in Najaf, MNF-I had realized that the growing problem in Fallujah might not be soluble by negotiations alone and that plans for a second military assault needed to be developed. The second Fallujah operation would include an effort to split the enemy from its popular support base, as well as a parallel, reinforcing effort designed to draw the civilian population out of the city in advance of the fighting, thus reducing civilian casualties and better revealing enemy forces so as to give precision targeting a greater role in the operation. The insurgent leadership could have had no doubt that the attack would come, but constant probing in the shaping phases—that is, preliminary operations to "shape" the conditions in the battlespace—helped convince them that the main attack would come again from the south and east, as had been the case in Vigilant Resolve.

Attaching the "Blackjack Brigade" from the 1st Cavalry Division, the First Marine Expeditionary Force, which was responsible for al-Anbar Province and the city of Fallujah, cut all the roads leading to Fallujah from the east, then moved a task force including the Iraqi 36th Commando Battalion up the peninsula west of the city to effectively seal it off. Once the city was surrounded, the main combat forces of the 1st Marine Division moved into place on the northern edge of Fallujah. Beginning on November 8, the second fight for Fallujah, known as Operation Al Fajr, employed overwhelming force by integrating Army, Marine, and Iraqi battalions and attacking with two regiments side by side from north to south through the city.

The assault was spearheaded by Army mechanized and armored battalions, followed up by infantry, a tactic that combined the shock effect of the armor with the large numbers of "boots on the ground" required for urban combat. The Iraqi soldiers facilitated the clearing of sensitive sites, such as mosques. The MEF also fully integrated airpower as well as numerous tactical sensors and Special Operations Forces (whose snipers were particularly valued). The fighting in Fallujah was up-close, vicious, unpredictable, and very manpower intensive. Some buildings in the city were cleared multiple times. Tanks were used often and with telling effect. Indirect fires (i.e., "spotted" by observers who could see the target) from 155-mm artillery positioned less than five kilometers away in Camp Fallujah occurred on a daily basis during the heaviest periods of fighting. Bulldozers were used on several occasions to push the walls of buildings in on stubborn defenders. Insurgents, for their part, used armor-piercing bullets and even sewed grenades inside their clothing to kill and maim coalition troops at every opportunity.

The initial objectives of the attack were secured early, and the entire city was under MNF control after four days of very hard fighting. Although small pockets of determined, even suicidal insurgents would continue to fight for nearly a month, the I MEF staff began to transition to local Iraqi control during the first week of combat. The city needed to be secure and made safe, essential services had to be restored to at least minimal levels, and the residents of the city had to regain some semblance of normalcy in their lives before all the goals of Al Fajr would be met. The basic concept of the operation depended upon a series of transitions—from combat to restoration of security and essential services, to resettlement and return to local control by an Iraqi municipal government. The city of Fallujah was opened for resettlement on December 23, 2004, only six weeks after the initial assault.

Prime Minister Allawi wanted to show the Sunnis that they would be cared for at least as well as the Shia populations in other areas of Iraq, so Al Fajr generated significant host-nation leadership. The prime minister had to be personally involved on many occasions, due to the sensitive nature of the fighting in the primarily Sunni province and the massive funding required to rebuild and repair the city. Fundamental questions of emergency law and reestablishment of police capability also required a high level of governmental involvement, particularly as several of the ministers were reluctant to cooperate with each other. Still, reconstruction of essential civic service sites, battle-damage compensation (including reimbursement for damaged homes), and funding for new economic development initiatives were already apparent in early 2005.[3]

The First Free Iraqi Elections: A Measure of Success and Missed Opportunity

On January 30, 2005, the Iraqi people went to the polls to chose representatives for the transitional 275-member Iraqi National Assembly. The voting was the first general election in newly sovereign Iraq, and it marked an important step in the transition from the interim structures established under the CPA to true Iraqi institutions. President Bush and other leaders around the globe hailed the event as a crucial step toward the future. The result was an overwhelming victory by the Shia United Iraqi Alliance party, largely because Sunnis in Iraq still felt alienated and threatened by insurgents and as a result were mostly afraid to vote. This gave the Shia parties a license to develop the new government in their own fashion and significantly restricted any Sunni input within the national government for years.

For the MNF, January 2005 had been important as the first free national election in recent Iraqi history had been held, the insurgency in Fallujah had been destroyed, the Shia militias in Baghdad and the south of Iraq had been rendered docile, and General Casey and his staff had successfully managed security in Iraq under the authority of a sovereign Iraqi government. Casey and Ambassador Negroponte had formed an effective team, and the MNC-I operational effort (soon to be commanded by Lieutenant General John Vines, formerly commander of the CJTF in Afghanistan) had demonstrated its value. The key issue remaining was how to transition Iraq to full Iraqi control.

The Casey Strategy

The MNF-I strategy under General Casey can be summarized as "buildup and transition to Iraqi forces." It had been developed under the hand of Casey's predecessor, General Sanchez, and although Casey approved it and directed its execution in August 2004, it was not well adapted to the situation in which the coalition found itself as the months passed in Iraq. A well-respected counterinsurgency analyst, and later Pentagon official, Kalev Sepp notes that the strategy "did not talk about what you had to do to defeat an insurgency. It was not a counterinsurgency plan."[4]

In 2005 the strategy was being put into practice through military operations designed to disrupt the flow of foreign fighters and insurgent support into the country while simultaneously training Iraqi troops to fill the security vacuum in the center and north of the country.[5] In 2005 this was being accomplished using two primary levers: the MNC-I lever of tactical, kinetic operations (still decentralized into five subregional commands aligned with the Iraqi provinces and one focused on Baghdad)[6] and a Multi-National Security Transition Command Iraq lever focused completely on the development of the Iraqi security forces (military and police).[7]

MNSTC-I, commanded from June 2004 to September 2005 by Lieutenant General David Petraeus, was responsible for developing, organizing, training, equipping, and sustaining the Iraqi security ministries (Ministry of Defense and Ministry of the Interior [MOI]) and their associated Iraqi Security Forces (ISF). The ISF included not only traditional military and police units but also the border patrol and special site security units that were separate parts of the Iraqi security force system. It also had to develop Iraq's security institutions and build the associated infrastructure, such as training bases, police stations, and border forts required to provide security at the national level in Iraq. MNSTC-I did this primarily by associating American military advisory teams within the individual Iraqi units that were being developed and by managing the equipment purchases and training regimes of the units themselves. Because Ambassador Bremer had disbanded the Iraqi security forces, Petraeus and his subordinates had to create entire units instead of simply retraining parts of the Iraqi security force structure that the coalition called back into employment. As with everything the coalition found in Iraq in 2003, the Iraqi security forces were far less effective than had been assumed prior to the invasion; the job of MNSTC-I was very challenging in technical terms and had the added complication that the units and their advisers were often put into combat situations well before their skill levels matched the requirements of modern warfare.

Therefore it was the MNSTC-I mission that was truly fundamental to the U.S. strategy for victory in Iraq. Only after MNSTC-I accomplished its mission to train the ISF could the Iraqis become capable of defeating the insurgency and taking responsibility for maintaining security within the country. As the ISF became capable, the coalition would be able to reduce the number of its troops in Iraq and withdraw. The flaw in this concept lay in the core problem of developing security forces in a country plagued by open warfare (of a kind that had already manifested itself as an insurgency), rampant criminal activity, and increasingly frequent internecine fighting between the major social factions.

Lack of an effective strategy was not the only issue plaguing the American effort in Iraq at the time. Political progress was just as important to the future of Iraq as controlling the insurgency, and yet in the spring of 2005 John Negroponte was appointed director of national intelligence by President Bush. Negroponte returned to the United States, leaving Iraq without a U.S. ambassador until Zalmay Khalilzad's arrival in Baghdad from Kabul four months later. During the summer of 2005 the newly elected Iraqi government had to draft a new national constitution and make preparations for the first elections of a national assembly in the winter. This was a crucial period, requiring a great deal of mentorship in the difficult pathways of democracy. Although Khalilzad had worked wonders in Afghanistan and knew the National Security Council staff well, the improvement of governance in Iraq suffered a serious loss of momentum in the critical summer months.

Meanwhile in the aftermath of the serious defeats suffered in the preceding months, the insurgency as a whole adapted and began shifting its strategy away from actions designed to damage coalition military forces and bases and toward assaults on the population of Iraq. This shift was certainly in part a reaction to the powerful blows it had suffered at the hands of Casey's forces, but it was just as much a purposeful shift away from attacks on the strengths of the coalition toward actions that would sow fear and discontent among the Iraqi people—who had already suffered far too long under conditions of Ba'athist oppression, twenty years of intermittent warfare, and economic sanctions.

The Case of Tal Afar

In the spring of 2005 Colonel H. R. McMaster arrived in Tal Afar with his 3rd Armored Cavalry Regiment (3rd ACR). McMaster was both a combat veteran (having been awarded the Silver Star during Desert Storm) and a military intellectual (author of the prize-winning book *Dereliction of Duty*).[8] The 3rd ACR and its commander initially approached their second Iraq tour of duty in Tal Afar with a typical, mostly kinetic mind-set—focused on killing insurgents. This was understandable, for "when they arrived . . . the city was largely in the hands of hard-core Iraqi and foreign jihadis, who, together with members of the local Sunni population, had destabilized the city with a campaign of intimidation, including beheadings aimed largely at Tal Afar's Shiite minority."[24] McMaster later admitted, "When we first got here, we made a lot of mistakes. We were like a blind man, trying to do the right thing but breaking a lot of things."[9]

The difference was that under McMaster the 3rd ACR listened, learned, and adapted to the situation in the city, always keeping in mind that they needed to develop security in Tal Afar for the longer term, whatever the details of the MNF-I mission. Even though Tal Afar was largely controlled by Sunni extremists who were aiding Al-Qaeda in Iraq, the officers of the 3rd ACR realized that their heavy-handed approaches were not helping. Eventually they began to talk with the local leaders, spending "forty or fifty hours a week with sheikhs from Tal Afar's dozens of tribes: first the Shiite sheikhs, to convince them that the Americans could be counted on to secure their neighborhoods; and then the Sunni sheikhs, many of whom were passive or active supporters of the insurgency."[10]

This effort was not new in Iraq—members of the coalition had worked with the Iraqi population in the late spring and summer of 2003 (particularly in the north) and sporadically thereafter, but because they shifted around the country the American units rarely developed the affinity needed to make real inroads and develop trust. The Marines had recently developed good working relationships with the local leaders in al-Anbar Province, but overall, the civil affairs–oriented approach was not common, largely because it was difficult, slow, and decidedly "unmilitary." In Tal Afar, one of the American commanders, Lieutenant Colonel Chris Hickey, committed himself to that different approach with McMaster's support. "In painstakingly slow and inconclusive encounters, each one centering on the same sectarian grievances and fears, Hickey tried to establish common interests between the Sunnis and the Shiites. He also attempted to drive a wedge between nationalist-minded Sunnis and extremists, a distinction that, in the war's first year or two, American soldiers were rarely able to make; they were simply fighting 'bad guys.'"[11] George Packer noted, "At the highest levels of the Administration, the notion of acknowledging the enemy's grievances was dismissed as defeatist. But in Tal Afar I heard expressions of soldierly respect for what some Americans called the Iraqi resistance."[12]

Despite progress beginning to be felt in the civil-relations approach, the problem in Tal Afar worsened to the point that it required the application of combat power. In September the 3rd ACR executed Operation Restoring Rights, attacking with nearly equal numbers of Iraqi troops (approximately five thousand soldiers from the 3rd Division of the ISF) "into the oldest, most dense part of the city, which had become the base of insurgent operations; there were days of heavy fighting, with support from Apache helicopters shooting Hellfire missiles.[13] "Most of the civilians in the area, who had been warned of the coming attack, had fled ahead of the action (unknown numbers of insurgents escaped with them)."[14] The destruction was significant, but not nearly as bad as Fallujah had experienced the previous November.

Because the ACR had managed to establish useful working relationships before the assault, McMaster was able to fully integrate his forces inside the city to hold his combat gains. "After McMaster's offensive, Hickey and a squadron of a thousand men set up living quarters next to Iraqi Army soldiers, in primitive patrol bases without hot water, reliable heat, or regular cooked meals."[15] Both American and Iraqi units helped with the restoration of security in Tal Afar; Packer noted, "The American patrol bases around the city stand next to Iraqi Army battalion headquarters; this allows for daily conversations among counterparts in the two armies and frequent sharing of information. The Americans are not just training an Iraqi Army; they are trying to build an institution of national unity before there is a nation."[16]

The results of Restoring Rights were far-reaching; not only did conditions improve in Tal Afar, but other American officials took note of the tactics used to developed the rapport in the city. While on an inspection tour of Iraq for the secretary of state, Philip Zelikow happened to visit McMaster and the 3rd ACR in Tal Afar.[17] When asked about the concept of the obviously successful approach in the city, McMaster informed Zelikow that his approach had been to clear out the insurgents, hold the terrain, and then begin to build up the city. Zelikow, who had been searching for a way of explaining the unclear strategy in Iraq, was sufficiently impressed to pass on the vision to Rice, who used the analogy in her next testimony before Congress on October 19, 2005.[18] "And that's the origin of 'clear, hold and build'—developing that as a catchphrase would just help people internalize that there's a strategy, and here's what it means."[19]

General Casey was taken aback by the secretary of state's testimony; he didn't think it matched his own strategy in Iraq.[20] Donald Rumsfeld also disagreed. In his eyes, the coalition forces were not in Iraq to build a nation but only to provide security for the developing Iraqi government and its forces.[21] Still, despite arguments at the top over whether Operation Restoring Rights was a true reflection of the U.S. strategy in Iraq, there was no doubt that individuals and units within the Army could learn and adapt on their own.

Problems and Progress with the Iraqi Security Forces

In September 2005 General Petraeus departed MNSTC-I for another command at the U.S. Army's Combined Arms Center at Fort Leavenworth, Kansas. By the end of his command tour, Iraqi army and police were being employed in combat, countless reconstruction projects had been executed, and hundreds of thousands of weapons, sets of body armor, and other equipment had been distributed in what was described as the "largest military procurement and distribution effort since World War II," at a cost of over $11 billion.[22] The year before, Petraeus had written an article for the *Washington Post* outlining the progress being made by MNSTC-I in building Iraq's security forces. In it he had made very clear the many challenges associated with the training and equipping effort: "Although there have been reverses—not to mention horrific terrorist attacks—there has been progress in the effort to enable Iraqis to shoulder more of the load for their own security, something they are keen to do."[23]

Some of the challenges involved in building security forces had to do with accomplishing this task in the midst of a tough insurgency. The command was also plagued by allegations of corruption. Two years later, the *Washington Post* would state that according to a government report, MNSTC-I "lost track of about 190,000 AK-47 assault rifles and pistols given to Iraqi security forces in 2004 and 2005 . . . raising fears that some of those weapons have fallen into the hands of insurgents fighting U.S. forces in Iraq." The same article quoted an official in the Government Accountability Office who said that the weapons distribution was "haphazard and rushed and failed to follow established procedures."[24]

Among the key elements of the effort in Iraq, the performance of the MNF in building the Iraqi security forces and the efforts of MNSTC-I were particularly important. The ISF included some 100,000 members in October 2004; that number increased to 130,000 in January 2005 and stood at 160,000 in June of the same year. By the time General Petraeus departed the number was over 200,000. However, building an army requires more than assembling units and equipment. The real proof in the effectiveness of MNSTC-I was not the simple number of units under arms but the effectiveness of the Iraqi forces across the span of all their missions: military, police, and security. Assessments of Iraqi efficiency vary, but overall there was a clear and increasing growth in the ability of the Iraqi units to shoulder the real burdens of the war after December 2005. The plan was showing improvement, but the insurgency was not abating.

Maturation of the New Iraqi Government

The new Iraqi constitution was drafted by members of a committee during 2005. Unfortunately, due to the Sunni boycott of the January 2005 elections, there would be very little Sunni input into the drafting of a constitution that could well determine the future of all Iraqis. The drafting and adoption of the new constitution was not easy, because sectarian tensions heavily affected the process. The deadline for the draft was extended four times due to lack of consensus on key religious language. Also, to the end, many Sunni leaders were split as to whether to support the constitution. Fortunately the biggest Sunni block, the Iraqi Accord Front, did finally support the document after receiving promises that it would be reviewed and amended to take into account their views. Under this key compromise, brokered before the referendum by Zalmay Khalilzad, it was agreed that the first parliament elected under the new constitution should sponsor a constitutional review to determine whether any portion of the constitution should be amended. Any amendments agreed would have to be ratified by a referendum similar to the one that originally approved it. After this understanding was reached, the Sunni-majority Iraqi Islamic Party agreed to support the referendum on October 15, 2005.[25] After the balloting, Electoral Commission officials stipulated that 78 percent of voters backed the charter and only 21 percent opposed it. Of the eighteen Iraqi provinces, two recorded no votes, which was only one province short of a veto. Rejection votes in three of Iraq's provinces (most likely Mosul, al-Anbar, and Salahaddin, those with Sunni majorities) would have required the dissolution of the assembly, fresh elections, and the recommencement of the entire drafting process. Still, even with controversy, the development of a new constitution for all Iraq was a fundamental step forward in governance of the new nation.

Following the first post-Saddam national elections in January and ratification of the constitution in October, a general election was held on December 15 to select a permanent 275-member Iraqi Council of Representatives. Because of the huge number of political entities in Iraq, the legislative elections took place under a list system, with voters choosing from a list of parties. Two hundred thirty seats were apportioned among Iraq's eighteen governorates. The additional 45 seats were allocated under a complex system to those parties whose percentages of the national vote total exceeded the percentage of the 275 total seats that they had been allocated. Women were required to occupy 25 percent of the 275 seats. Voter turnout was high, and the level of violence during polling was relatively low. The election produced a government headed by Nouri al-Maliki, the secretary general of the Islamic Dawa Party. Maliki was a Shiite who had opposed Saddam before escaping into exile in 1979; afterward he had lived in Jordan, Syria, and in Iran before returning to Iraq, where he had worked on the de-Ba'athification committee before being elected to the transitional national assembly in 2005 and then helping to write the new constitution. The new government was not fully representative of the Iraqi people, but the election did demonstrate further progress toward a functioning Iraqi state.

2006: Descent into Chaos in Iraq

> Iraq came pretty close, I think, to just unraveling in the course of that year.
>
> —Ambassador Ryan Crocker, September 11, 2007[26]

The success of the December 2005 provincial elections in Iraq generated a great deal of optimism among American officials as 2006 began. The accomplishments of the coalition seemed to be making a difference in restoring security in Iraq, and particularly in several of the key towns and cities (such as Fallujah, Basra, Tal Afar, and Mosul) daily life was returning to a more normal state. Many expected that the new members of the Iraqi provincial governments would contribute still more to the stability in Iraq and that the coming year might actually justify a reduction in U.S. forces, as the Iraqi security forces grew in number and capability.[27] Tragically all these rosy expectations were to be incinerated in 2006 in a series of horrific sectarian clashes and car-bomb explosions.

Several suicide bombings were conducted in Iraq in 2005 in the midst of Shiite religious celebrations, causing numerous casualties, but none of those attacks was as significant as the February 22, 2006, bombing of the Shiite "Golden Mosque" in Sunni-inhabited Samarra, in Saladin Province. That attack largely destroyed the golden dome of the mosque and touched off nation-wide Shiite reprisals against Sunnis. For most, it is considered to have sparked the Iraqi-on-Iraqi violence that approached civil warfare from the bombing until late in 2007. The climate of chaos that resulted from these multiple, re-tributive attacks seemed to indicate that Iraq was on a downward spiral, with little hope for recovery.[28]

Most analysts attribute the Samarra bombing to AQ-I; the bombing cer-tainly seemed to support the goals of Zarqawi and his organization. On several occasions, even President Bush seemed to imply that with the bombing of the Golden Mosque, Zarqawi had succeeded in his goal of destabilizing Iraq and discrediting the new Iraqi government in the eyes of its people. Indeed by early 2007, most U.S. officials saw AQ-I as the driving force behind the insurgency, even though AQ-I had strategic goals very different from those of its minority partners in the contest against the coalition and the Iraqi govern-ment.[29] Major bombings inspired by AQ-I constituted only a small percentage of overall attacks in Iraq (which in early 2007 numbered about 175 per day), but they garnered a huge part of the international media coverage and were most influential in dampening the expectations of the American people con-cerning victory in Iraq. Most of the U.S. combat deaths resulted from roadside bombs and munitions most likely employed by local Sunni insurgents.[30]

By October 2006 the Office of the United Nations High Commissioner for Refugees (UNHCR) and the Iraqi government estimated that more than 365,000 Iraqis had been displaced since the bombing of the Golden Mosque. No one had any accurate idea of how many Iraqis had been killed by their neighbors over the same period.[31] Department of Defense estimates of sectar-ian violence and deaths by execution in Iraq between February and July alone were that some 4,800 lives had been lost.[32] It was a period of horrible vio-lence and almost daily press coverage of explosions and killings all around the country. At the same time, when the Iraqi security forces were supposed to be taking primacy in Iraq, they were being rent by sectarian divisions.

During this period also the Iraqi government had been expected to make great steps forward to resolve key domestic political issues in the country, yet by the spring of 2006 there was no prime minister in Baghdad to oversee this effort. A new Iraqi government had been selected in the general election held on December 15, 2005, but the Iraqi Council of Representatives was slow to form and develop procedures. Most importantly, it took six months of negotiations to form a "government of national unity" between the parties that had received the majority of votes: the United Iraqi Alliance, the Iraqi Accord Front, the Kurdistani Alliance, and the Iraqi National List. It was only in May 2006 that a functioning government was formed under the leadership of Maliki.

SOF and the Death of Zarqawi

Over the three years since the invasion, the role of Special Operations Forces had grown in Iraq. Initially the Special Forces had served as adjuncts to the conventional assault on Saddam's military, but as the campaign shifted into a counterinsurgency mission, their unique capabilities had become increasingly important, and their numbers in Iraq had grown accordingly. By 2006 most of the American special mission units that performed direct action, strategic reconnaissance, and counterterrorist operations were either already in Iraq, had just returned from combat in that country, or were preparing to fight under MNF-I control in the future. Lieutenant General Stan McChrystal masterminded the hunt for terrorists and commanded the Joint Special Operations Command in Iraq under General Casey. General McChrystal worked creatively to improve the integration of SOF into conventional operations and to maximize conventional force support for his own counterterrorist and intelligence-gathering operations. He also develop innovative ways of improving the "fusion" of intelligence and shortening the senor-to-shooter linkage to make special operations missions more effective and successful in the hunt for terrorists.[33]

The most significant achievement of the special operators in Iraq was the identification and killing of the head of AQ-I, Abu Musab Zarqawi, outside Baquba in June 2006.[34] "Before his death, Zarqawi had largely established as AQ-I's strategy an effort to provoke all-out civil war between the newly dominant Shiite Arabs and the formerly preeminent Sunni Arabs. Zarqawi apparently calculated that provoking civil war could, at the very least, undermine Shiite efforts to consolidate political control of post-Saddam Iraq."[35] Had Zarqawi been successful, his strategy could have pushed the United States to leave Iraq by significantly undermining public support for the war effort, leaving the Maliki government in Iraq vulnerable to continued AQ-I and Sunni insurgent attacks.

Although Zarqawi had come to symbolize the link between the core of the Al-Qaeda movement under Osama bin Laden and the ongoing antigovernment insurgency in Iraq, his death did not cause the demise of AQ-I (which simply took a new leader). Neither did it end the fighting, which had largely shifted to sectarian violence and Iranian-supported attacks on the MNF by the time he was killed. Still, the death of Zarqawi was a significant proof of Special Operations Forces capability and the improvement of intelligence fusion in the campaign. In its wake a number of other insurgent leaders were located and captured, striking AQ-I a severe, if nonmortal, blow.[36]

Just as Zarqawi was dying in the bombed rubble of a simple Iraqi house, President Bush was at Camp David, in Maryland, listening to criticisms of the Iraq strategy; in response he decided to make an unannounced visit to Baghdad to meet with Maliki and get a sense how the war progressing and how the new Iraqi government was functioning. Bush seemed to be pleased with what he saw and heard in Baghdad, saying in a public statement, "I assured them [the Iraqi leaders] that we'll keep our commitment; I also made it clear to them that in order for us to keep our commitment and be successful, they themselves have to do some hard things. They themselves have to set an agenda. They themselves have to get some things accomplished."[37] Bush returned from Baghdad with renewed faith in the war effort but also seeming to sense that the Iraqi government was in trouble.

Together Forward

The Multinational Corps command in Iraq passed to Lieutenant General Pete Chiarelli in 2006; like Barno in Afghanistan, once in command Chiarelli was not slow to begin operations in Iraq designed to increase security as the new Iraqi government was being formed in the face of growing sectarian violence. In March he started Operation Scales of Justice in Baghdad. This operation significantly increased the size of the forces in the Iraqi capital and netted some eight hundred suspected insurgents in its first two months, but it didn't seem to make a dent in the overall violence in Iraq. Then in the summer of 2006, MNF-I launched a new major operation that was designed to fully integrate Iraqi security forces into a more broadly representative coalition, with Iraqi forces taking a more prominent role; it was known as Together Forward.

Operation Together Forward was directed by Prime Minister Maliki and was to be led primarily by Iraqis, with coalition support. Beginning on July 9,

Multinational Division–Baghdad soldiers supported by Iraqi security forces killed or captured over four hundred suspected insurgents, conducted some 32,000 combat patrols, and seized numerous weapons and ammunition caches. On August 7, MND-B soldiers and the ISF began Phase II of operation Together Forward, designed to further increase security and reduce violence in and around the capital. The goal of Phase II was to capitalize on the progress made during Phase I and give Iraqi forces a chance to operate with more autonomy than previously. In support of Phase II, 6,000 additional Iraqi forces were to be sent to Baghdad, as well as about 3,500 soldiers of the 172nd Stryker Brigade Combat Team. But only two of the planned six Iraqi battalions were committed to the operation, and that insufficiency in Iraqi forces was seen as a reason for the operation's lack of overall success. The coalition was able to clear certain areas of insurgents, but the combined MND-B and ISF force was unable to keep the insurgents and militia members from funneling back into them.

A second major operation, Together Forward II, was executed in August of 2006. As in its predecessor, the coalition forces were to move into neighborhoods, clear them of extremists, and hold them while building up essential services and infrastructure to better support the needs of the local population. Unfortunately Together Forward II placed a far greater emphasis on the pace of clearing operations than on holding and rebuilding.

The Iraq Study Group Report, directed by James A. Baker III and Lee H. Hamilton and published in December 2006, determined that recent operations in Iraq had been failures. Among the several recommendations of the report was that "changes in course must be made both outside and inside Iraq."[38] It also argued that "the United States should significantly increase the number of U.S. military personnel, including combat troops, imbedded in and supporting Iraqi Army units. As these actions proceed, we could begin to move combat forces out of Iraq."[39]

Another Strong Current: Change in Ramadi

The two battles for Fallujah in 2004 had driven Al-Qaeda in Iraq from that city. But even though certain sheikhs and imams within the Iraqi resistance began backing the political process after the reopening of Fallujah, AQ-I simply shifted its emphasis to the neighboring provincial capital of Ramadi, which it came to call "the Capital of the Islamic State of Iraq."[40] AQ-I could offer money, jobs, social mobility, and an ideological appeal—jihad against the infidel—to potential supporters, whereas the national government in Baghdad was offering nothing to al-Anbar Province. Also, sectarianism allowed AQ-I to assume a role as the protector of the Sunnis in a new Iraq that seemed dominated by Shiites. Continued violence in Ramadi, a city whose mostly Sunni citizens had always been hostile to the coalition and had refused to vote in the January 2005 national elections, pushed al-Anbar Province nearly into the category of "the impossible win." Marine intelligence analysis repeatedly said that the coalition effort was untenable in al-Anbar, yet in 2006 even that extreme prognosis began to be reversed, unexpectedly and for a surprising reason.

In an episode that sets a classic example for any future insurgency effort, the horrific acts of AQ-I in Ramadi and other areas inside Iraq began to exceed even the extremely high tolerance of Iraqis, who had been made nearly immune to pain by years of repression.[41] There had been an attempt at reconciliation in late 2005; in November a conference with the resistance had been held that offered government support for tribes that worked with the new government; and elements of the al-Anbar resistance had worked to secure the December 2005 elections. In retaliation, over the following three months AQ-I killed many of the key leaders of the tribes that had attended the conference and punished anyone found to be cooperating with the government or the coalition. By the early spring, tolerance for AQ-I in Ramadi had lessened significantly.

"It is true that al-Qaeda has become unwelcome in the city," a leading Ramadi sheikh said in February 2006.[42] "Al Qaeda still insists that it is justifiable to kill any Iraqi linked to the Government, including local Sunni policemen, an ideology increasingly rejected by local residents who want a stronger Sunni representation in the security forces." The previous month, an AQ-I suicide bomber had stepped into the line during a recruiting drive for Iraqi police at a glass factory, the only industrial site in the city, killing more than fifty people and wounding at least sixty more. Al-Qaeda claimed credit for the attack and was immediately condemned by Sheikh al-Miklif, whose tribe constituted 40 percent of the provincial population around Ramadi and which stood to gain the most from the jobs that had been made available. Abu Musab al-Zarqawi was still the leader of AQ-I, but he was losing popularity in the only area of Iraq he seemed to rule. "There is a hatred for Zarqawi in Ramadi now," a resident said. "People are exhausted by what he has done. Six months ago he was still accepted, though not 100 percent. Now we see him continue to target locals and their sons and kill our leaders, and we reject him totally."[43]

I MEF and its commander at that time, Major General Richard Zilmer, developed a plan for another major operation during April and May, and the American brigade in Ramadi surrounded the city with checkpoints, but the main part of the operation was delayed until the new Maliki government was formed in late May. Progress in security was still tied to political progress. Throughout the spring, the new commander in the Ramadi area, Colonel Sean MacFarland, USA, of the Army's 1st Brigade, 1st Armored Division, conducted increasingly aggressive operations in the city, aided by growing support from locals. In June his brigade conducted operations to clear neighborhoods in the city and then to establish outposts to hold the ground taken from AQ-I. His operations were so successful that the insurgents temporarily halted their attacks. They soon resumed, and MacFarland continued his efforts, working methodically through the city, neighborhood by neighborhood, but even by August he seemed to have made little tangible progress.

As 2006 progressed Sunnis all over central Iraq suffered under more and more attacks, until they began to realize that they could not defeat both their own Shia countrymen (or deny them the support they were receiving from Iran) and the coalition, even if they remained aligned with Al-Qaeda. With the U.S. public seemly demanding an American withdrawal of forces, the Sunnis were soon confronted with an even more stark reality—they would be decisively defeated in any future civil war without the moderating presence of the coalition forces. So over the summer three rural tribes outside Ramadi started to back the fledgling Iraqi police.[44] Eventually Sheikh Abdul Sittar Eftikhan al-Rishawi ad-Dulaimi of the influential Abu Risha tribe publicly switched sides and began to work with the new Iraqi government forces and the coalition. While he had likely been profiting from the black market, and some of his tribesmen had certainly been active insurgents, Sheikh Sittar had grown so angry at AQ-I that he began to pressure other tribal leaders to change sides as well.

Then in August another local sheikh, Khalid Illiyawi, was killed by AQ-I, which refused to return his body in time for a proper Muslim burial—an unforgivable insult. That act seemed to tip the balance, pushing even more local tribal leaders off the fence and against AQ-I. The following month, twenty-three Sunni tribal leaders in al-Anbar, led by Sheikh Sittar, formed an "Anbar Salvation Council."

President George W. Bush
(Department of Defense)

General Tommy Franks with Secretary Donald Rumsfeld (Department of Defense)

President Hamid Karzai (U.S. Navy photo by PO1 Mark O'Donald)

Lieutenant General (later General) Dan McNeill
(Department of Defense)

Lieutenant General David Barno with Secretary Rumsfeld and
Ambassador Zal Khalilzad (Department of Defense)

Ambassador Khalilzad
(Department of Defense)

Lieutenant General (later Ambassador) Karl Eikenberry with
Secretary Robert Gates (Department of Defense)

General David McKiernan (Department of Defense)

President Barack Obama (U.S. Air Force photo by TSgt. Jeromy K. Cross)

General Stanley McChrystal (Department of Defense)

General David Petraeus and President Obama (Department of Defense)

General John Allen (ISAFMedia Photo)

As al-Qaeda's fighters tightened their grip on Ramadi, they became increasingly repressive and challenged the tribal leaders' power. Soon they were kidnapping and beheading innocent people as part of a campaign of extortion and intimidation. Some sheikhs fled to Jordan and Syria. Sheikh Sittar's father and three brothers were killed, his father during the holy month of Ramadan, and he says he has himself survived several kidnap attempts. This summer a fellow sheikh was ambushed and beheaded by Al-Qaeda supporters, who piled insult on injury by keeping his body so it could not be buried immediately, as demanded by custom. "We began to see what they were actually doing in al-Anbar province. They were not respecting us or honouring us in any way," said Sheikh Sittar, speaking through an interpreter. "Their tactics were not acceptable." During the late summer he began enlisting his fellow sheikhs in a movement called the Sahawat or Awakening, whose goal is to drive Al-Qaeda from al-Anbar province.[45]

The Salvation Council recruited some thirteen thousand young Sunnis from around al-Anbar Province to help provide security in Ramadi, Fallujah, and other provincial cities. Sittar told an American reporter, "They brought us nothing but destruction and we finally said, enough is enough."[46] The coalition leaders in al-Anbar understood the potential of the Salvation Council and committed themselves to additional work projects that gave tribal leaders the ability to offer to fence-sitters patronage and salaries that could offset financial offers from AQ-I. Over the fall and winter months the Awakening movement gained even more adherents and started to give AQ-I real competition for dominance in several locales.

Some twenty insurgent leaders were killed by tribesmen through the fall months; AQ-I was struggling to maintain dominance against the growing tribal security movement as 2006 drew to a close. Then on November 25 some three dozen members of AQ-I attacked the small Albu Soda tribe living on the outskirts of Ramadi in an area known as Sufia, on the road between Ramadi and Fallujah. The tribe had not joined the Awakening, preferring instead to maintain neutral, but even neutrality angered AQ-I, and it attacked the tribe fiercely in retaliation. Members of the tribe notified a local Iraqi army unit of the attack, the Iraqi unit notified Colonel MacFarland, and he directed one of his battalions to immediately join in the defense of the Albu Soda tribe.[47] Once the American forces helped repulse the attack, the Albu Soda tribe flipped completely to support the coalition. "It was like liberated France," said Mac-Farland, and tips began to flow in and the streets of Ramadi opened up for the MNF-I forces.[48]

By the end of the year, the security situation in al-Anbar Province had shifted in obvious ways toward the coalition. The Iraqi government demonstrated that it was willing to give tribes greater power and allow tribal access to the black market; Baghdad even permitted the al-Anbar tribal leaders to control the local police and the Emergency Response Unit that had been created in Ramadi. With the arrival of a new Fallujah police chief, Colonel Faysal, AQ-I intimidation within that city diminished significantly. Finally, late in the year the Albu Issa tribe began to actively fight AQ-I. "Sheikh Sittar and U.S. commanders believe that the tide is turning in their favour.'Most of the people are now convinced that coalition forces are friends, and that the enemy is al-Qaeda,' the 35-year-old Sheikh claimed in his first face-to-face interview with a Western newspaper. . . . 'Al-Qaeda is now on the run,' said the local coalition commander, Colonel Sean MacFarland."[49] The tribes had rejected their former alliance with AQ-I and had switched sides to become the "counterinsurgency overseers" in al-Anbar Province.

Insufficient Progress in Iraq

Even with the changes in the security situation in al-Anbar Province in late 2006, however, the overall situation in Iraq was probably worse than it had been at the beginning of the year. The level of violence and the lack of neighborhood security in Baghdad were particularly significant. The benchmark of the Casey Strategy—the development of the Iraqi army—was also doubtful at best. *The Iraq Study Group Report*[50] noted,

> By the end of 2006, the Iraqi Army is expected to comprise 118 battalions formed into 36 brigades under the command of 10 divisions. Although the Army is one of the more professional Iraqi institutions, its performance has been uneven. The training numbers are impressive, but they represent only part of the story. Significant questions remain about the ethnic composition and loyalties of some Iraqi units—specifically, whether they will carry out missions on behalf of national goals instead of a sectarian agenda. Of Iraq's 10 planned divisions, those that are even-numbered are made up of Iraqis who signed up to serve

in a specific area, and they have been reluctant to redeploy to other areas of the country. As a result, elements of the Army have refused to carry out missions.[51]

The report went on to list a number of other important shortfalls, including lack of leadership, equipment, personnel, and logistics support.

Perhaps even more significantly, the Iraqi government was still driven by sectarian agendas, characterized by inefficiency, and dominated by Shia officials whose loyalties to the new Iraq seemed to be less strong than their devotion to other, often tribal interests. As a result the Iraqi government was "not effectively providing its people with basic services: electricity, drinking water, sewage, health care, and education."[52] In many sectors of the Iraqi economy, production in late 2006 was below prewar levels, and in Baghdad the situation was even worse. It was an untenable situation during a still-active insurgency.

Forcing Change in Iraq

In late 2006 General Casey was doing his level best to execute his 2004 military strategy in Iraq, which was based upon recoiling coalition force units into ever fewer U.S.-run bases while building capacity within the Iraqi security forces. At the time, however, popular opinion in the United States about the conduct of the war was changing in a way that had a profound effect on operations in Iraq. In part this change was due to the casualty rate among U.S. forces in Iraq, which was rising steadily in the fall of 2006. October of that year was in fact the sixth-deadliest month of the war, with 106 American lives lost in combat. "Total attacks in October 2006 averaged 180 per day, up from 70 per day in January 2006. Daily attacks against Iraqi security forces in October were more than double the level in January. Attacks against civilians in October were four times higher than in January. Some 3,000 Iraqi civilians were killed every month."[53] To most Americans the cost of the war—especially the human cost—was exceeding the gains being made. It seemed that even after the death of terrorist leader Zarqawi in June 2006, the sectarian violence he had stoked with the bombing of the Golden Mosque in Samarra the previous February was steadily escalating, to the point that the government in Baghdad could do little to stop it. Calls for the ouster of Secretary of Defense Rumsfeld had begun to be voiced around Washington as early as the previous April.[54]

The U.S. military was not unaware of these anxieties. As a proactive organization, the Joint Staff in the Pentagon, under the hand of its chairman, Marine General Peter Pace, began to study alternate strategies for the Iraq campaign in the summer of 2007. That effort gained new immediacy when General Casey came to realize that he could not reduce the force in Iraq to twelve brigade equivalents, given the widespread civil unrest evident in Iraq. Then the November congressional elections in 2006 were a disaster for the Bush administration, bringing in a new Democratic majority in both houses of Congress and serving as a referendum on the war. Unbeknownst to the American people, Secretary Rumsfeld had submitted his resignation the day prior to the elections, with the coming congressional defeat obvious, and the president formally and publicly accepted Rumsfeld's resignation the day after the results of the election were announced, naming former deputy director of the CIA Robert Gates as the new defense secretary. Not only had Gates been deputy National Security Advisor for Bush's father during the Gulf War, but he had recently served as a member of the Iraq Study Group, which had sought new ways of enhancing security in Iraq. In general he was well informed on matters of strategy and was a skilled decision maker.

With a new defense secretary at the helm in the Pentagon[55] and Democrats in the House of Representatives clamoring for an end to funding for the war, in late November the president began a fairly open-minded search for new options in Iraq. He met with key members of the diplomatic corps at the State Department, as well as with a group of "Iraq experts," including generals and historians, on December 11. Two days later he met with the members of the Joint Chiefs of Staff in the Pentagon; this meeting "in the tank" with the Joint Chiefs revealed a decidedly negative mood among the military senior leadership of the United States.[56]

The following day, December 12, yet another report on Iraq, by the American Enterprise Institute (AEI), was released by its authors, Frederick Kagan, Kenneth Pollack, and General Keane. Notably among the many more pessimistic reports on the conflict, the AEI report called for a change in military strategy in Iraq, observing that "the basis of the Abizaid-Casey strategy is twofold: American forces in Iraq are an irritant and generate insurgents who want to drive us out of their country, and the Iraqis must be able to create and maintain their own stability lest they become permanently dependent on our military presence. Both of these arguments contain elements of truth, but realities in

Iraq are much more complex." The AEI report specifically recommended a large and sustained surge of U.S. forces to secure and protect critical areas of Baghdad.[57]

The report and its recommendation were highly controversial. At a time when most Americans were looking for a way to end the conflict and Congress appeared adamant that funding for the war was to be curtailed significantly, the AEI report envisioned an increase in military forces in Iraq—seemingly completely counter to the idea that America needed to shift the burden of combat onto the Iraqi forces. The report was lucid and persuasive, but if the president was to consider its adoption, he had not only to face the inevitable criticism of those who understood that increasing forces would increase casualties (at least in the short term) but also to admit that the strategy he had so strongly advocated over the previous twenty-four months would not bring the desired result. It was a decision requiring significant moral fiber and risking a great deal of political capital.

Iraq Strategy Culmination: The Loss of Presidential Confidence

Although there were expectations that President Bush would announce a change in the Iraq strategy in December 2006, he did not make a formal announcement until January 10, 2007. In a speech to the nation from the White House, President Bush outlined the four key components of "The New Way Forward in Iraq."[58] Underlying these components was a continuation of the policy to "let the Iraqis lead" but also a decision that there would be a new effort to put down sectarian violence and bring security to the people of Baghdad. During his speech the president announced the deployment of "more than twenty thousand additional American troops to Iraq." It was clear that President Bush had actually made the decision and had already directed the Pentagon to execute the plan at an earlier date. The delay of the speech until the second week of the year had enabled the advanced deployment of troops of the 82nd Airborne Division, which were already arriving in Baghdad as the president spoke.

This decision to increase the troop level in Iraq was both historic and courageous. With his administration losing support and the ability to influence the public debate on the war, President Bush chose to commit more forces, and likely suffer more casualties, in order to achieve decisive victory in Iraq. At the time, most Americans expected the administration to back out of Iraq on a specific time line or to simply declare that its major objectives had been accomplished and then depart without regard to the conditions on the ground. (All four key objectives originally announced for the war could have been justifiably considered accomplished at the time: Iraq now had a weak but functioning democratic government, reasonably secure borders, and was a single, unitary state that could defend itself from external aggression.) But President Bush chose the more difficult route. Shortly thereafter he dispatched a new "command team" to Iraq, installing Ryan Crocker as ambassador and General David Petraeus as commander of MNF-I.

Crucial Month in Iraq: December 2006

The month of December brought more than just the president's decision to change the strategy in Iraq. It was perhaps the most momentous if least-heralded month of the long war. In Iraq a new commander of MNC-I, Lieutenant General Ray Odierno, USA, concluded that General Casey's concept would not produce victory; he therefore decided, at the risk of his career, to engender support for the changed operational approach. December 16, 2006, the counterinsurgency doctrine manual that Generals Petraeus and Mattis had labored so long and so well to produce—*Counterinsurgency,* Field Manual (FM) 3-24—was finally published, giving the entire U.S. military a new playbook for COIN operations and validating what many younger officers were discovering, mistake by mistake, at the tactical level in Iraq.[59]

According to General Odierno, on December 19 "the coalition captured some mid-level Al-Qaeda leaders just north of Baghdad. Upon them was a map that clearly depicted al Qaeda's strategy for the total and unyielding dominance of Baghdad, betting that control of Iraq's capital and its millions of citizens would give them free rein to export their twisted ideology and terror. Indeed, did operate with impunity in several areas surrounding the capital that we call the 'Baghdad Belts,' using these sanctuaries to introduce accelerants of violence. This strategy was similar to the way in which Saddam Hussein employed his elite Republican Guard forces to control the city. It was clear to us that Coalition forces would need to clear AQ-I from these belts and deny these enemies safe havens in order to control Baghdad."[60] The map and the importance of the "Baghdad Belts" became key to the new operational concept General Odierno was developing with his staff.

The new secretary of defense also took a much more aggressive stance than anyone expected in December 2006, traveling to Iraq in his first days in office. During a visit to Baghdad on December 20, Secretary Gates met with Iraqi Minister of Defense Abdul Qadir, along with Generals Pace, Abizaid, and Casey, to discuss the way ahead in Iraq. Then, finally, on the next to last day of the year, Saddam Hussein mounted the gallows where he had sent so many others to die and was hanged. The year 2007 would be a very different one in Iraq as well.

Seven

Parallel Campaigns

The common perception among the nonmilitary community is that the United States did not embrace a counterinsurgency doctrine until the release of Field Manual 3-24, *Counterinsurgency,* by the commander of the U.S. Army Combined Arms Center and the Marine Corps' Deputy Commandant for Combat Development and Integration, then–Lieutenant Generals David Petraeus and James Amos (as the successor to Lieutenant General James Mattis) in December 2006. Another common misperception, often repeated and almost considered gospel, is that the U.S. military, and in particular the army, deliberately and systematically avoided thinking about counterinsurgency doctrine in an attempt to bury the ghosts of Viet Nam. David Petraeus himself is said to have contributed to this myth, despite his own study and writing on counterinsurgency over the course of his entire career. Neither of these widely held misconceptions is true.

The U.S. military has a long tradition as a thinking, professional, and self-assessing organization. The American military has perhaps the most aggressive and broadest system of continuing education and training in the world. Officers in the U.S. Army, for example, spend about four and a half years in professional education and training—more than 20 percent of their careers—between the time they are commissioned as second lieutenants and when they pin on the eagles of a full colonel. A significant percentage of the officer corps attends fully funded, full-time graduate education programs, and many of the remainder obtain advanced degrees on their personal time. Our military challenges its officers and noncommissioned officers to think and reflect between deployments and to invest in advancing the collective knowledge of their profession. These opportunities and expectations were the norm rather than the exception for the cohort of leaders that have shaped and shifted doctrine over the last decade.

Opening Intellectual Salvos

As early as 1984, following his experiences in Grenada in Operation Just Cause, John Abizaid was tasked by the Vice Chief of Staff of the Army, General Maxwell Thurman, to study the Israeli incursion into Lebanon. Not specifically a counterinsurgency, the Israeli incursion was nonetheless a "small war," with many of the attributes the United States would find problematic over the next twenty-five years. Unfortunately Abizaid's study focused primarily on the initial rapid (and successful) Israeli attack into Lebanon and ignored the much more difficult, and perhaps unsuccessful, prolonged occupation by the Israeli Defense Forces. The preoccupation with the purely military aspects of such incursions would become a theme of sorts of the military thinkers, at the expense of the much more costly and intractable follow-on stabilization and constabulary actions.[1] Fortunately Abizaid had an opportunity several years later, once again at the behest of General Thurman, to return to Israel and the Lebanese border. It was made clear to Abizaid that the Israeli occupation was not succeeding; he told Thurman that the Israelis' oppressive tactics were inflaming the situation, emboldening the oppressed Shiites, and radicalizing the local population. In short, an overreliance on purely military force was losing the conflict for the Israelis.[2]

Although through the 1980s the United States was involved in Latin America supporting both insurgencies and counterinsurgencies, the military's role frequently was overlooked—or suppressed—by the institutional focus on regaining the conventional "big war" prowess many leaders thought had been lost as a result of Viet Nam. The Army in particular had invested billions into the development of the National Training Center (NTC), an industrial-scale laser-tag facility covering a thousand square miles of the Mojave Desert, where literally hundreds of tanks and infantry fighting vehicles, artillery, attack helicopters, and close air support could go toe to toe with highly trained mock Soviet forces. The large-scale conventional training was necessary to take advantage of the increasing capabilities of the newest generations of Abrams tanks, Bradley fighting vehicles, and Apache attack helicopters, which could cover vast distances at unprecedented speeds. Having the equipment alone wasn't enough to deter the Soviets, but demonstrating the ability to fully capitalize on the hardware's potential and exploit the AirLand Battle doctrine of the 1980s undoubtedly played a part in hastening the fall of the Soviet Union. During the same period, the Marine Corps invested heavily in the Twentynine Palms training facility, another thousand-square-mile piece of desert in southern California. The success of the NTC and Twentynine Palms led to the creation of the light-forces-focused Joint Readiness Training Center in 1987 at Fort Chafee, Arkansas (later moved to and expanded at Fort Polk, Louisiana) and the very small but highly symbolic Combined Maneuver Training Center in Hohenfels, Germany, in 1988.

Despite the focus on conventional war, parts of the military, particularly the Special Operations Forces, stayed involved in irregular warfare, support to insurgencies, and counterinsurgency. U.S. Southern Command had responsibility for many of these operations. Forward-looking officers, such as the U.S. Southern Command (SOUTHCOM) chief, General Jack Galvin, continued to prod the Army to think beyond the conventional training models and challenged the military to maintain at least some core competency in what became known as "low-intensity conflict."

In 1986 Galvin published an article in the U.S. Army War College journal *Parameters* entitled "Uncomfortable Wars: Toward a New Paradigm." Galvin attempted to nudge the Army toward thinking not just about doctrine for the small wars he was waging in SOUTHCOM's AOR but also about what types of future conflicts the Army would be called upon to prosecute on the nation's behalf. "It is that form of war, a synthesis of conventional and guerilla warfare, with greater importance accorded the societal dimension, that appears a likely model for the future," wrote Galvin. He went on to describe "population-centric" warfare, a phrase later made popular by General Stanley McChrystal in Afghanistan. Galvin stated, "In each case in high- or low-intensity conflict, the struggle involves interaction between three elements: the government (with its armed forces), the enemy, and *the people*."[3]

Galvin was also an officer with nearly forty years in the Army, and he knew all too well the speed at which such an institution embraces change. He (or his ghostwriter, a young aide named David Petraeus) saw the challenge of moving the institutional army in a new direction: "Changes do occur within the walls of our military cloister, but usually only when preceded by the long process of consensus building, in which more time is spent overcoming resistance to change than in examining new ideas."[4] Galvin was attempting to accelerate the process.

Around the same time, the U.S. Army Command and General Staff College, in many ways the service's intellectual center, issued Field Circular (FC) 100-20, *Low Intensity Conflict.* Interestingly the FC never directly refers to the army's experiences in Viet Nam; in fact, there is not a single mention of Viet Nam or Southeast Asia in the entire publication. But it nonetheless draws from the doctrine that existed at the end of the Viet Nam War and was technically still in effect. The Field Circular provides some overarching doctrinal guidance for tactical and operational commanders in a low-intensity environment. The introduction defines the environment in terms familiar to forces deployed for Operations Iraqi Freedom and Enduring Freedom (OIF and OEF): "Low-intensity conflict (LIC) is a limited politico-military struggle to achieve political, military, social, economic, or psychological objectives. It is often protracted and ranges from diplomatic, economic, and psychosocial pressures through terrorism and insurgency. LIC is generally confined to a geographic area and is often characterized by constraints on the weaponry, tactics, and the level of violence. LIC involves the actual or contemplated use of military capabilities up to, but not including, combat between regular forces."[5]

The FC is organized into four main sections: I. "Foreign Internal Defense" (including insurgency, counterinsurgency, security force operations, and foreign internal defense operations); II, "Terrorism Counteraction"; III, "Peacekeeping Operations"; and IV, "Peacetime Contingency Operations." Presciently, the Command and General Staff College circular reminds the reader that "FID [foreign internal defense], terrorism counteraction, and peacetime contingency operations can be found at all levels of conflict. These general categories are not mutually exclusive, but often overlap."[6] In other words, there is no single prescriptive doctrinal formula for fighting a counterinsurgency.

Following the experiences in Grenada, Panama, and SOUTHCOM's other operations, the military did publish some new doctrine. The Army and Air Force jointly issued Field Manual 100-20/Air Force Publication 3-20, *Military Operations in Low-Intensity Conflict,* in December 1990. Stating that "low intensity conflicts have been a predominant form of engagement for the military over the past 45 years" and would likely to continue to be "for the foreseeable future," the manual went on to describe the "four major types of operations typically found in LIC—support for insurgencies and counterinsurgencies, combating terrorism, peacekeeping operations, and peacetime contingency operations."[7]

It is instructive to look at the 1990 manual from the perspective of the current day, following a decade of intervention in Afghanistan and Iraq. FM 100-20 describes "Low Intensity Conflict Imperatives" as "Political Dominance" (where the political objectives drive military decisions at every level from the strategic to the tactical), "Unity of Effort," "Adaptability," "Legitimacy" (further described as "the central concern of all parties"), and "Perseverance." Recognizing that counterinsurgency requires a robust "Internal Defense and Development Strategy," the doctrine describes such a strategy as having four main components: "Balanced Development" (political, social, and economic progress), "Security" (protect the population), "Neutralization" (separate the insurgents from the people), and "Mobilization" (support for the government). Finally, FM 100-20 goes on to describe the four necessary principles for low-intensity conflict and counterinsurgency warfare: "Unity of Effort," "Maximum Use of Intelligence," "Minimum Use of Violence," and (building a) "Responsive Government." It is hard to view the 2006 publication of FM 3-24 as new and revolutionary, let alone the first doctrinal publication on counterinsurgency in more than twenty years.[8] Perhaps Galvin was correct. The military, at least at some levels, was resisting the necessary changes, despite thinking (and publishing doctrine) about the new ideas.

Experience and Necessity

The reality is that the United States has never fully abandoned "small wars," and the military has never deliberately purged itself of capabilities and doctrine associated with low-intensity conflict, counterinsurgency warfare, or foreign internal defense. The United States has a long history of engaging in various forms of counterinsurgency warfare. One could argue that the Indian wars that lasted through much of the nation's formative years were collectively a form of counterinsurgency. Viet Nam is of course the most debated war in COIN terms. Other, less frequently examined operations could also fall in the category of low-intensity conflict, if not outright counterinsurgency operations: Grenada and Panama (1980s), Lebanon (1983), Somalia (1993), and other, smaller assistance missions. The larger point here, however, remains that made by General Galvin. The military, and in particular the large, bureaucratic institutional services and Department of Defense, were resistant to change.[9] True change was to be born of necessity when U.S. forces were sent to secure the nation's interests.

Shortly after 9/11, the U.S. Special Operations Command Pacific formed Joint Special Operations Task Force (JSOTF) 510 to assist the government of the Philippines pursue the Islamic terrorist group Al-Harakat al-Islamiya, better known as the Abu Sayyaf Group. The small but highly capable Special Operations Forces Task Force would be very successful in building partner capacity in the armed forces of the Philippines, supporting the legitimate and elected government, building local governance and rule of law, and improving infrastructure in the remote southern Philippines. In many ways, what became Operation Enduring Freedom–Philippines (OEF-P) was a vindication of the doctrine as written in 1986's Command and General Staff College FC 100-20 and 1990's Field Manual 100-20.

While the scale of operations and the circumstances presented to the Special Operations Forces in the Philippines were radically different than the cases in Iraq or Afghanistan, the success met in OEF-P was an indicator of both the validity of doctrine as it existed in 2001 and the flexibility and adaptability of the SOF community. The JSOTF returned to its roots to build a campaign plan, acting "by, with, and through" the host Philippine government and forces. "By, with, and through" would not emerge as a foundation principle of the operations in Afghanistan until late 2009, but the approach was on full display, and successful, in OEF-P as early as 2002. OEF-P planners, under the guidance of Brigadier General Donald Wurster and then-Colonel David Fridovich, built upon and improved a COIN model first put forth by Professor Gordon McCormick in 1994. OEF-P planners visualized a diamond, with the four apexes being the people (the center of gravity), the government, the insurgents, and international actors.[10] Within the diamond were represented the "internal environment" and the "external environment." Each of the four corners interacted with and influenced the others. Undergirding the diamond model were six principles:

- Consider popular support the center of gravity
- Enhance government legitimacy and control
- Focus on people's needs

- Target insurgent safe havens, infrastructure, and support
- Share intelligence (especially HUMINT, intelligence from human agents and sources)
- Develop indigenous security forces.

OEF-P was conducted along three interconnected lines of operation: building the Armed Forces of the Philippines (AFP); focused civil-military operations, led by the AFP, with government agencies; and Information Operations.[11] These three lines of operation are unsurprisingly similar to those employed later in Iraq (under both Generals Casey and Petraeus) and in Afghanistan throughout Operation Enduring Freedom's history. In particular the focus on building the Iraqi and Afghan national security forces became the main pillar of U.S. strategies in both theaters. But the OEF-P experience offers a caution as well. Colonel Greg Wilson, a veteran of OEF-P and author of a thoughtful article in 2006, states, "By itself, however, just building the host-nation's capacity to capture or kill insurgents will not guarantee victory. The United States must employ a holistic approach that enhances the legitimacy of the host-nation government and its security forces in the eyes of the local populace."[12] In fact Wilson perhaps falls a bit short in his warning, as the term "legitimacy" has broad applicability and includes such issues as the rule of law, dispute resolution, basic humanitarian subsistence requirements, and a minimal economy. His bottom-line warning is spot on, though: simply building host-nation security force capacity has not been sufficient.

Despite the successes of the government of the Philippines, the AFP, and JSOTF-510, U.S. forces remained engaged in the southern Philippines for over ten years. Such sustained presence and assistance reinforces what has become common knowledge about COIN: it is difficult to define "victory," and COIN requires persistence and patience, sometimes over more than a decade. What is most interesting, though, is that the basic tenets for successful COIN were in place by 2002 and, upon reflection, the principles and doctrine developed and employed by JSOTF 510 are highly consistent with FM 3-24, published some four to five years later by primarily Iraq veterans.[13]

Afghanistan

Half a world away from the Philippines, the U.S. efforts in Afghanistan were transitioning from the initial success of Operation Enduring Freedom's unconventional CIA-SOF fight against the Taliban and Al-Qaeda to a less defined, essentially security-assistance mission. Previous chapters have described the transition from CJTF-180 and the formation of Combined Forces Command–Afghanistan in late 2003. The transition, as we have seen, was not seamless or particularly smooth. The competing demands of the U.S. effort in Iraq loomed large. According to General McNeil's successor in Afghanistan, Lieutenant General John R. Vines, U.S. Central Command was "under enormous pressure not to over commit resources to Afghanistan to make sure everything possible was available for Iraq."[14] The idea of "overcommitment" to Afghanistan implies that the U.S. government would at least "sufficiently commit" to the theater in order to meet the needs of the mission. Such a dedication of resources—including the sustained focus of the senior political leadership—was not to be forthcoming. Instead Enduring Freedom became the "economy of force" theater, making it, in the simplest of terms, the theater to "not lose" rather than to "win."

The arrival of General Dave Barno as commander of CFC-A brought a fresh look at counterinsurgency doctrine as the organizing principle for OEF. Although the Provincial Reconstruction Teams had begun under General McNeill's tenure with CJTF-180, the civil-military coordination and cooperation was accelerated, as we have seen, under Barno and the newly arrived U.S. Ambassador Zalmay Khalilzad. The CFC-A focus shifted from an enemy-centric approach to a population-centric approach as early as mid-2003, the same period that OIF was basking in the success of the lightning assault on Baghdad and the relative calm that immediately followed. Barno's campaign plan, similar in many ways to the OEF-P model being successfully employed by JSOTF-510 in the southern Philippines, comprised five pillars:

- Defeat terrorism and deny sanctuary
- Enable Afghan security structure
- Sustain area ownership
- Enable reconstruction and good governance
- Engage regional states.

All five pillars supported the center of gravity—the Afghan people.[15] Elements of Command and General Staff College FC 100-20 and Field Manual 100-20 were clearly evident in Barno's approach. His population-centric focus presaged Field Manual 3-24 by several years. Barno's COIN approach would face many difficulties and would be challenged by an increasingly complex command arrangement (particularly as the United States sought to off-load Afghanistan to NATO) and by increasing demands from the Iraq theater, further pushing OEF into the economy-of-force possture.

Counterinsurgency doctrine was existent in the early years of both OEF and OIF, but it was also evolving, fed along the way by the publications and thinkers already mentioned. No tectonic shift suddenly occurred with the publication of Field Manual 3-24 in December 2006. So if the doctrine was already maturing, why wasn't it effective in the field? Or if it was effective at the tactical level, why weren't results seen at the operational and strategic levels?

Parallel but Disjointed Campaigns

By late 2006 the effort in Iraq was in dire straits, at least at the political level in Washington. The campaign in Afghanistan was almost totally an afterthought, as politicians, military leaders, and academics focused on the increasingly worsening conditions in Iraq. But the situation in Afghanistan was not improving either, and in many ways it had stagnated. In December 2007 Chairman of the Joint Chiefs of Staff, Admiral Mike Mullen, put the issue in plain English in congressional testimony: "In Afghanistan, we do what we can, in Iraq, we do what we must." Mullen's statement prompted House Armed Services Committee Chairman Ike Skelton to state, "I find it troubling that our ongoing commitment in Iraq prevents us from dedicating resources in Afghanistan beyond what is necessary to prevent setbacks, as opposed to what is required to realize success."[16] Mullen was finally stating what many had known for several years—the administration's highest priority was Iraq. Skelton's statement summarized what many, including those inside the Bush administration, were equally concerned about. Indeed the level of violence was such, and the sense of despair in some corners so prevalent, that the president and his senior advisers had few good options. Two parallel campaigns, neither of which was fully resourced, were in many ways consuming each other. By late 2006 the Bush administration had made a choice: surge in Iraq and continue to hold in Afghanistan, as an economy-of-force theater.

But the surge decision did not in and of itself denote a high-level embrace of a new COIN doctrine. Much has been made of Secretary of State Condoleezza Rice's testimony in October 2005 declaring the strategy in Iraq as "clear, hold, build."[17] In fact Rice's statement, derived, as we have seen, from Ze-likow's observation of McMaster's localized success in Tal Afar, Iraq, conflated tactical doctrine with top-level political-military strategy. In fact, "Clear, Hold, Build" was only one of three major components of the "National Strategy for Victory in Iraq" released by the White House on November 30, 2005, and it addressed only the security sector. The other two, and equally important, components were a political track and an economic track.[18] General Casey wanted to continue to focus on building the Iraqi security forces and transferring responsibility to the Iraqis, whether the internal political realities supported such a transfer or not. Casey did not prioritize population-centric security and stabilization efforts. Despite Secretary Rice's declaration of a "new strategy," Casey remained in command in Iraq until February 2007, fifteen months after Rice's congressional testimony, without changing his overall campaign plan, until President Bush replaced him with General David Petreaus.

Operations in Iraq

Upon taking command in Iraq, General Petraeus brought new focus at the strategic level. Although his influence was clearly felt all the way down to the battalion level, the corps commander in Iraq was actually the coordinator and orchestrator of the operational and tactical actions in the country, and he had to be fully committed to any new strategy for it to succeed. The new multinational corps commander who had just taken charge of operations in Iraq in December 2006 was Lieutenant General Ray Odierno, who had formerly been the commander of the 4th Infantry Division in the Sunni Triangle in 2003.

Odierno's arrival in Baghdad in December 2006 was much more important than anyone believed at the time; after all, several other highly capable corps commanders had preceded him in Iraq, and none of them had managed to make a significant difference in the actual prosecution of the war.[19] The difference was that Odierno (who had a reputation for being tactically aggressive) took time to study the actual situation in Iraq for the first forty-five days after his arrival. Many thoughtful strategists subscribe to Karl von Clausewitz's dictum that understanding the war one is fighting is a prerequisite for successful execution, yet few actually study the nature of the conflict that they are dealing with in its early stages, before they become completely absorbed by the chaos of war.[20]

General Casey had tasked Odierno with conducting operations in such a way as to break the cycle of violence then tearing Iraq apart and to bring sufficient stability to the country so that the Iraqi government could begin to develop enough political progress to solve Iraq's long-term problems. So the mission given Odierno and his staff was not new, but it was combined with the idea that in the process he would have to cut the U.S. force in Iraq by as much as one-third.[21] It would have been a challenge for any commander to accomplish Odierno's assigned mission, and many had already tried; to do so with fewer troops would be even more difficult.

Thankfully, in carefully studying conditions in Iraq, Odierno and his staff found a new way of looking at the problem. For Odierno, reducing the violence required more than kinetic attacks on insurgents; he saw that at the same time he had to secure the population if he had any hope of stopping the horrific cycle of attacks and reprisals. His team recognized that although previous efforts to clear Baghdad of insurgents had met with some success, these gains were temporary, because the coalition forces were not committed to holding the areas they had cleansed of insurgents; once they departed, the enemy moved right back in to punish people who had befriended the coalition soldiers.

Unfortunately, holding the key areas in Iraq (including many sectors of Baghdad) would require not only a change in the FOB-based approach then in execution but also many more troops than he would inherit, and everyone in Iraq and even most in the White House had been talking only about troop reductions over the past two years.[22] The Casey troop-reduction strategy assigned to Odierno was called the "Bridging Strategy"; some might have called Odierno's new idea a bridge too far, but in December 4, 2006, when he was formally briefed on the Casey plan, Odierno was not afraid to do something almost completely different, even if his approach was bound to rankle his boss.

When Secretary Gates visited Iraq in December, very soon after taking office, General Odierno lobbied him for a troop increase. Gates, who had been a member of the Iraq Study Group, recommended to President Bush too that he order a temporary troop increase to help stem the violence. President Bush, as we have seen, announced what came to be known as "the surge" in January 2007 and ordered five additional combat brigades to Iraq.

Tactical commanders were already improving their working relationships in Iraq on the basis of their combat experience and in accord with the ideas codified in the new FM 3-24; General Odierno was already planning to use more forces; and General Petraeus was taking over the strategic leadership of the war—as a result of all this the conflict turned slowly but decisively in a new direction in the early months of 2007. Petraeus took command of MNF-I from General Casey in the Al Faw Palace in Baghdad on February 10, 2007. The change of command marked a clear change in both the leadership of the Iraq war and the strategy that would be the driving force behind the coalition effort in Iraq. But change at that level would take time and had to be based upon Iraqi political improvements in governance, as well as tactical efforts to end the insurgency.

General Odierno and his team had already decided that creating stability in Iraq required more than just greater resources; it required a change in mind-set. They determined that the coalition forces had to make the protection of the population a first priority, creating safe neighborhoods and markets and allowing Iraqis to go about their daily lives. They also decided that the coalition needed a more balanced approach in its targeting of extremists, and they were convinced the Iraqi government could no longer give Shiite militia groups freedom to commit extrajudicial killings.[23] As the additional brigades began to arrive in the first months of 2007, the coalition forces also began moving out of large bases and into small outposts in population centers all across Iraq, especially in and around Baghdad.[24]

During a series of early offensives commanded by Odierno, MNC-I forces also renewed the emphasis on providing essential services, encouraging local governance, and separating "irreconcilables" from individuals willing to make peace with the legitimate government of Iraq. While conducting these initial operations, General Odierno also worked to deepen growing alliances with groups of "concerned local citizens" that had agreed to work with his forces to bring security to their neighborhoods. The "Awakening," as discussed in chapter 6, started in al-Anbar Province in 2007 and began to spread across much of the country. Many of who took part in the Awakening were former insurgents who had rejected the program of violence and chaos wrought by AQ-I and decided instead to support the new Iraqi government. Later they came to be known as "Sons of Iraq."

Operation Fardh al-Qanoon, or Enforcing the Law, began on February 13, 2007. Fardh al-Qanoon was significantly different in concept than either Operation Together Forward I or Together Forward II of the previous year, insofar as it reflected the new emphasis on security for the people identified by General Odierno's study the preceding winter. It also took advantage of the fact that Major General Joseph Fil's 1st Cavalry Division was now on its second tour in Iraq, this time as the headquarters for Multinational Division–Baghdad; almost all of its commanders were veterans of combat in Iraq. Fardh al-Qanoon featured troops living in the neighborhoods, interacting with residents, and gaining real human intelligence about the insurgent threat. MNC-I forces moved out of their forward operating bases in and around Baghdad, into smaller joint security stations (JSSs) and combat outposts (COPs) located in every neighborhood covered by the operation. In the COPs, coalition forces, Iraqi police, and units of the Iraqi army shared the same living conditions and worked together to execute better coordinated security operations.

During Fardh al-Qanoon, the "Clear, Hold, and Build" strategy of 2005 and 2006 was replaced with a new "Clear, Control, and Retain" strategy. This new strategy focused on controlling and retaining neighborhoods to provide real, lasting security for the population and also preventing enemy reinfiltration. Once safe, those neighborhoods were turned over to Iraqi forces, which were augmented by embedded American advisory teams, and the American combat units were shifted to oversight roles. The new Fardh al-Qanoon approach also placed greater emphasis on rebuilding essential services and on long-term investment in neighborhoods and their supporting political and economic institutions than had been the case in the past. Perhaps most significantly, since Prime Minister Maliki had been converted to the idea that the militias were a major threat, during Fardh al-Qanoon coalition forces conducted operations against extremist elements inside the Shia-dominated Sadr City area of Baghdad, which had previously been forbidden territory—a situation that had contributed to the failure of the 2006 operations in Baghdad.

The first of the surge brigades arrived in Baghdad in February 2007 at the start of the Operation Fardh al-Qanoon. That same month, additional U.S. and Iraqi forces were shifted into Baghdad from other towns in Iraq. Eventually seven U.S. combat brigades conducted operations as part of the MND-B during Fardh al-Qanoon. Once deployed into the city, individual U.S. battalions were paired with Iraqi brigades and assigned to work together within a structure of ten districts that spanned Baghdad.

The New Command Team in Iraq

The arrival of General Petraeus reset the strategic military approach of the coalition in Iraq, but it was less than half of the change needed at the national level if the new strategy was to have long-term results. General Petraeus knew well that his relationship with the new ambassador in Iraq and their collective relationship with Prime Minister Maliki would be crucial to sealing the success of any operational leverage that General Odierno might be able to develop in the aftermath of Fardh al-Qanoon. Luckily the new ambassador, Ryan Crocker, was an old Middle East hand and probably the finest possible choice for the position. Crocker had served in three other Middle Eastern posts as ambassador (Lebanon, Kuwait, Syria), as well as, most recently, Pakistan, in South Asia. He had worked as a member of the "Future of Iraq Project" back in 2002 and had served as the deputy assistant secretary of state in the Near East Bureau before being assigned to Islamabad. Indicative of his energy, once named to the post in Baghdad Crocker flew directly to Iraq, even before being ceremonially sworn in by Secretary Rice in Washington.[25]

Once Ambassador Crocker arrived on March 29, he and General Petraeus determined to act always as a team—particularly when meeting with Prime Minster Maliki.[26] The two American leaders were different temperamentally, but they shared many interests, most of all a fierce commitment to finding solutions for the problems in Iraq. The two worked out of offices located side by side in the Al Faw Palace and would redesign the new U.S. embassy in Baghdad so that it would be the case there as well. General Petraeus understood full well that doing his job effectively required political improvement in Iraq; indeed, many of the key benchmarks that would be used over the coming year to judge success in the war were strictly in the Iraqi domestic arena and almost completely out of his direct control.[27] He was determined to work as seamlessly as possible with Crocker to inspire and push the Iraqi government toward needed reforms and domestic quality-of-life improvements.

June—Operation Phantom Thunder

A series of operations under the overarching title of Phantom Thunder was launched on June 16. Phantom Thunder demonstrated the first full employment of all of the surge forces newly arrived in Iraq and also marked the combat debut of the new MNF-I team of Petraeus and Crocker. The operation was designed to protect the Iraqi people, ease reconciliation among the religious sects, defeat AQ-I and other extremists, and continue to develop the Iraqi Security Forces.

All five brigade combat teams in MND-B operated inside Baghdad, and a sixth brigade combat team operated in Taji, north of the city, to seal off a major insurgent exit route. The focus of all these operations was clearing the Baghdad districts of Adhamiya, Rashid, and Mansour, where sectarian fault lines existed and most of the violence inside the city had taken place. The initial results of these linked operations inside Baghdad were mixed—some districts showed progress, while others remained violence prone—but progress was evident. By the end of June over 750 people had been detained, more than 150 insurgents had been killed, and some 125 caches had been found, and 300 IEDs and 7 VBIEDs (vehicle-borne improvised explosive devices) had been neutralized.[28]

The initial offensives in 2007, the first major efforts to secure both Baghdad and its belts, showed flaws in the coalition's approach but also revealed slow progress. In two follow-on operations conducted later the same year, the deficiencies were corrected and obvious momentum began to build. The third offensive was known as Operation Phantom Strike; it was conducted for several weeks starting in mid-August, with the goal of having coalition and Iraqi forces maintain pressure on AQ-I operatives and other insurgent groups as they were flushed from sanctuaries in the capital. General Odierno's fourth major offensive was to be labeled operation Phantom Phoenix; it would begin just weeks before his departure in February 2008 and would be designed to pursue the enemy from Baghdad into Diyala Province, provide essential services, and jump-start provincial government improvements in less-contested areas.[29]

The surge also added some four thousand Marines to the fight in al-Anbar Province. These additional forces demonstrated renewed commitment to that province and encouraged Sunni Salvation Council members to continue recruiting volunteers to help secure their towns. Added to the effect of new facilities projects and improvements in the local economy, these efforts convinced the residents to increase even further their cooperation with the coalition forces (primarily by revealing insurgents and their safe houses) in order to help reduce violence. "U.S. commanders even offered a $300 to $350 per month wage and additional training to the Sunni volunteers recruited by the Council for security duties. These volunteers came to be known as the 'Sons of Iraq.' By 2008 there are some 75,000 Sunni Sons of Iraq throughout the country."[30]

As early as June 2007, at the beginning of the surge, General Petraeus had called security improvements in al-Anbar "breathtaking." He and other commanders were able to walk freely in downtown Ramadi, which had been a major battleground only months before. General Petraeus later testified that that al-Anbar Province could be turned over to provincial Iraqi control by July 2008.[31] The positive trends observed in al-Anbar encouraged other anti–Al-Qaeda Sunnis to join the Awakening movement. In May 2007 a Salvation Council of tribal leaders was formed in Diyala Province. Beginning in early 2007 the town of Amiriyah was slowly stabilized through the emergence of former Sunni insurgents cooperating with the coalition as a force called the "Amiriyah Freedom Fighters." These fighters claimed to have expelled AQ-I from their neighborhoods. Even neighborhoods in Baghdad began to undergo similar transformations. The employment of the COPs and JSSs, in partnership with the ISF, combined with the willingness of a population to come forward with information about AQ-I, brought the Iraqi capital in late 2007 to the point where 75 percent of its districts were considered secure. Prime Minister Maliki said on February 16, 2008, that AQ-I had been largely driven out of Baghdad.[32]

Although the augmentation of the force in Iraq was the centerpiece of the new strategy, it was not the only significant factor in the decisive change in the situation that eventually brought success. The effort in Iraq was conducted both in depth and in breadth, and it fully engaged both conventional and Special Operations Force activities to produce a synergistic effect on the enemy.[33] This comprehensive approach to counterinsurgency—simultaneous, large-scale operations to strike multiple enemy concentrations and bases of support while continually focusing on protecting the populace and reconciling with those willing to make peace with the government—led to dramatic decreases in attacks through Iraq. "In December 2006, coalition forces were sustaining more than 1,200 attacks per week, and the civilian death toll for the month was over 3,000."[34] By late September 2007, there had been a 50 percent decrease in the number of attacks in Baghdad. The decrease in car bombs, mortar, and rocket attacks was even greater than 50 percent.[35] When Odierno and his team finished their tour in February of 2008, civilian casualties were down 70 percent and attacks on coalition forces had dropped to their lowest levels since 2004. In the Baghdad security districts specifically, ethnosectarian attacks and deaths had decreased by 90 percent. The situation in Iraq had been "utterly transformed."[36]

Thus the main focus of effort in 2008 in Iraq would be improving governance in the provinces, passing several critical national laws, developing a process for reconciliation, and beginning the task of identifying how the coalition would depart from Iraq—and doing all these things while maintaining upward trends in security across the country. The unique problem that would menace all of these goals was the growing influence—both political and military—of Iran in Iraqi affairs.

General Odierno relinquished command of MNC-I in Iraq in February 2008 and was replaced by Lieutenant General Lloyd Austin and his staff, of XVIII Airborne Corps.[37] Odierno had been nominated to become the Vice Chief of Staff of the Army but was soon chosen instead to succeed General Petraeus in Iraq. After a short return to Fort Hood, Texas, he assumed command of MNF-I in September 2008, just as General Petraeus moved to take command of the U.S. Central Command in Florida. Ambassador Crocker remained at his post in Baghdad, again teamed with Odierno. Thus, a couple of related decisions enabled Petraeus, Odierno, and Crocker to maintain their strategic partnership and continue to shepherd Iraqi security into 2008.

The Second Front

By the time Petraeus took command in Iraq, NATO had assumed command of nearly the entire military operation in Afghanistan. There were now two parallel, but distinctly different and diverging, campaigns under way in Iraq and Afghanistan. In a deliberate move by Washington, the United States in 2005 began, as we have seen, pressing NATO to take an ever-increasing role in Afghanistan, despite knowing that NATO would bring fractured command and control, tremendous challenges to unity of effort, and a diffuse political agenda wherein each of the twenty-six NATO members, along with the sixteen non-NATO partner nations, would pursue its individual interests. But transferring overall operational command to NATO would, at least in theory, relieve Washington of much of the day-to-day running of the effort in Afghanistan.

The parallel but disjointed nature of the efforts manifested itself in many ways. With the two campaigns being run by the same geographic combatant command and the preponderance of forces in both theaters coming from the United States, one would think that the approaches—the campaign plans— would be more similar than not. In truth it was as though OIF and OEF existed in different universes. By early 2007 the management and oversight structures for the two commands at the White House, National Security Council, State

Department, Defense Department, and CENTCOM were all different. That is, even the management and interagency-coordination structures within each level were different between Iraq offices and Afghanistan offices. And it was not just a matter of main effort versus economy-of-force effort—wholesale management practices were dissimilar.

Even in areas that would seem to easy to align, parallel efforts led to wholly different management structures. Provincial Reconstruction Teams are a good example. The PRTs in Afghanistan reported through a military chain of command, were essentially military-centric organizations, and were the management responsibility of the Department of Defense (for the U.S. teams at least.) The PRTs in Afghanistan, only about half of which were American, had not evolved much since first introduced. In Iraq the PRTs had evolved rapidly and eventually were of several configurations. Almost all of the Iraq PRTs were American, and responsibility for them in Washington fell to the State Department.

At CENTCOM large operational planning teams (OPTs), which melded operations, plans, logistics, personnel and other staff functions, had been established for both Iraq and Afghanistan. But almost as soon as the transition from CFC-A to NATO-ISAF was complete, the CENTCOM Afghanistan OPT stood down, and its personnel were reallocated to the Iraq effort in Tampa. At the Joint Staff, separate deputy directorates within the Strategic Plans and Policy Office (J-5) had oversight of political-military affairs for the respective wars. Although located within a hundred feet of each other, the two offices, each headed by an army colonel, rarely if ever compared notes or worked joint actions. Such coordination was left to the three-star J-5 himself, and it usually consisted of directing the Afghanistan products and proposed plans to more closely mirror the Iraq team's output. Day-to-day operational oversight was the responsibility of the Director of Operations (J-3). The J-5 operated on the second floor of the Pentagon, the J-3 in the restricted-access National Military Command Center in the basement. While there was ongoing, daily coordination between the officers of the J-5 and the J-3, the offices were not integrated. Attempts by the J-3 to consolidate the J-3 and J-5 Iraq and Afghanistan efforts into a single task force—one that would include J-2 (intelligence), J-4 (logistics) and other J-code offices and be headed by the J-3—did not come to fruition until the creation of the Pakistan-Afghanistan Coordination Cell in mid-2009. Earlier attempts to consolidate were resisted by the bureaucracy or were just too cumbersome to put in place when the focus was split between Iraq and

Afghanistan. The resistance wasn't a fight over doctrine or strategy but simply the inertia of a long-standing bureaucracy.

At the Office of the Secretary of Defense (OSD) level, the focus was similarly diffuse. Oversight for the Iraq efforts was the responsibility of the assistant secretary of Defense for International Security Affairs, but Afghanistan fell to the newly created assistant secretary for Asia and Pacific Security Affairs. Large portions of the war effort, particularly for Afghanistan, fell to diverse offices including the assistant secretary for Special Operations and Low Intensity Conflict, the deputy assistant secretary for Counternarcotics, and a deputy assistant secretary–level office dedicated solely to management and recruitment of the coalitions for Iraq and Afghanistan. Further compounding the confusing wiring chart were offices at both OSD and the Joint Staff devoted to NATO affairs and management. Perhaps the best-integrated offices were those of the OSD-Comptroller and Joint Staff J-8 responsible for development and defense of the budget and fiscal allocation. In the eyes of most of the rest of the Defense establishment, the comptroller and J-8 were united in their scrutiny of every new proposal and in their propensities to say "no" as the opening policy position. The fragmented structure cannot be blamed on Secretary Rumsfeld alone, as the organizational construct, despite some minor reorganization, persisted after Secretary Gates replaced him in late 2006.

The State Department was no better. Although significantly smaller and more streamlined than the Defense Department, State was perhaps even more bureaucratic and territorial. Iraq issues fell to the Middle East Bureau, while Afghanistan, naturally, was part of the South and Central Asia Bureau. Each war had a special "coordinator" position, but with no autonomy and almost completely reliant on the regional bureau staff. Special functions and oversight fell outside the regional bureaus to functional ones, such as the Bureau for International Narcotics and Law Enforcement (INL), with oversight of not only counternarcotics issues for Afghanistan (frequently competing with the much-better funded DoD counternarcotics office) but also with oversight of the Afghan National Police development program (for which DoD was holding the U.S. military responsible, through the Combined Security Transition Command–Afghanistan). State's Bureau of Politico-Military Affairs had oversight of sales and transfers of military equipment. The State Department's office of the coordinator for counterterrorism (State CT) looked into some aspects of funding for terrorist organizations as well as counternarcotics-related funding. Throughout this same period, the authorized but not funded Office of the Coordinator for Reconstruction and Stabilization hovered on the margins. Finally, and in many ways summarizing the broader schizophrenic and fractured nature of the interagency, the U.S. Agency for International Development had oversight of much of the reconstruction and development projects in both Iraq and Afghanistan, but it was constantly wrestling with its identity. Neither a separate agency nor a fully subordinate bureau of the State Department proper, USAID had to constantly fight for a seat at the table for policy and strategy debates while being routinely criticized for pursuing its own disconnected agenda.

The intelligence community suffered from many of the same issues. The National Intelligence Council did serve as a sounding board and coordinator to a large extent across the intelligence community. However the intelligence community was as turf conscious as any of the departments previously described and had significant internal organizational issues never fully resolved by the creation of the Director of National Intelligence position.

At the National Security Council staff level, by 2006 a single office was responsible for Iraq and Afghanistan; it was headed by Meaghan O'Sullivan. Having served in the Coalition Provisional Authority in Iraq with Bremer, O'Sullivan had made a name for herself and moved on to serve as the Senior Director for Iraq at the NSC. By 2006 O'Sullivan had been promoted to Deputy National Security Advisor for both Iraq and Afghanistan and reported directly to the National Security Advisor, Steve Hadley. O'Sullivan led a relatively small staff focused primarily on Iraq, but with a senior director for Afghanistan and a single subordinate director devoted to Afghanistan policy matters.

In the case of Afghanistan, the state coordinator for Afghanistan (the dual-hatted deputy assistant secretary for Afghanistan and Pakistan) and the NSC's senior director for Afghanistan co-chaired the Afghanistan Interagency Operations Group, or AIOG. The purpose of the AIOG was to coordinate issues across the interagency and to tee up policy actions for the Deputies Committee. Attendees at the weekly AIOG meetings ranged from deputy assistant secretaries from State or Defense to senior or midgrade representatives of Defense (OSD-Policy), the Joint Staff (J-5), Treasury, Justice, the U.S. Trade Representative, and the Department of Agriculture. On occasion the U.S. ambassador to Kabul would attend if he were in town. But most of the weekly meetings were attended by action officers, not policy makers. The agenda for the AIOG meetings was largely set by the co-chairs and was a mix of tasks sent from the Deputies Committee to items of particular interest to the cochairs or sent from the embassy. The AIOG was collegial and collaborative, but the co-chairs had little direct tasking authority. Policy issues could languish for months unless the deputies issued specific "taskers" linked to a formal NSC Deputies Committee meeting or if a particular crisis erupted requiring immediate interagency coordination.

In the last quarter of 2006, as the Bush administration was consumed with the situation in Iraq as well as with the American midterm elections, several high-profile "strategy reviews" were undertaken. Besides the independent and bipartisan Iraq Study Group, Secretary Rice had set up an internal policy review in the State Department, and the chairman of the Joint Chiefs of Staff, General Pace, had convened a group of experienced colonels to review in depth the Iraq war and make recommendations for adjustments to policy and strategy. At the same time, Steve Hadley tasked a very small and secret group on the National Security Council staff to begin looking at changes in Iraq strategy, and in particular to consider what would become "the surge." By November, the president had established a separate formal review, directed Deputy National Security Advisor J. D. Crouch to run that group and to complete its recommendations in two weeks.[38]

As seemed to be the norm by 2006, the administration followed with an Afghanistan version of a strategy review. Led by Meaghan O'Sullivan but executed primarily by her senior director for Afghanistan, Tony Harriman, the review assessed the progress made against what was essentially the same strategy for Afghanistan that had been in place since late 2003. While the review was thorough, much time was spent on determining whether specific projects were on track or whether allocated funds were being spent according to congressional rules. Little time was spent debating the underlying assumptions or challenging whether the major goals and lines of operation were in fact correct. While there was some discussion of the resources available, there was no deliberate exercise to determine if the established goals had been resourced to the levels necessary to achieve success in a reasonable period of time.

While the president would soon ask Congress for additional funds for increases in troops and reconstruction in Afghanistan, there was still an underlying, but not necessarily articulated, understanding that the Afghan theater would continue to make do with the leftovers from Iraq. Ultimately the 2006 Afghanistan strategy review endorsed the existing plan, while asking for additional resources. The priority remained bolstering the security sector, primarily through the incremental growth of the Afghan National Army, and through continued expectation that NATO, in command of the entire geographic area of Afghanistan since October 2006, would provide additional forces despite a well-established pattern of falling short of the requirements set by the military commanders.

By early February 2007 there was a growing concern about the trends in Afghanistan. Although the strategy review of late 2006 had not proposed any major shift in policy or strategy, there was a consensus that the situation was continuing to deteriorate. The United States reassumed command of the theater when General Dan K. McNeil, the commander of CJTF-180 in 2002, returned to take over as ISAF commander from Britain's Sir David Richards during the first week of February. McNeil's return was more than just the standard rotational arrangement between the United States and the United Kingdom. His return, as a four-star, was a not-so-subtle indication that the United States wanted to instill more unity of effort among the allies and stem the deterioration of the security conditions. In fact, when the British learned in 2006 that McNeil would assume ISAF command as a four-star, they quickly announced the appointment of Richards, then a lieutenant general, to the "acting" rank of general. (He reverted to lieutenant general upon his handover to McNeil and his return home, to be permanently promoted to general a year later when he became Commander in Chief, Land Forces.) Regardless of the coalition politics surrounding the matter, raising the ISAF command to a four-star billet was an early indicator that the United States and major NATO allies were not comfortable with the direction of the Afghan war. Simply elevating the ISAF command position was obviously not going to solve the problems in Afghanistan, however, and the strategy review completed in 2006 did not set a new course or make radical change. In fact the review essentially concluded that ISAF, the Afghans, and the international community simply needed to improve the execution of the existing strategy.

Donald Rumsfeld claims that he tried but only marginally succeeded "to turn the NSC's attention to Afghanistan in 2006."[39] Here he means that the actual statutory members of the NSC, the principals, as the NSC staff was busy with the internal but somewhat superficial strategy review just mentioned. By

January, a month after Rumsfeld's departure from the Pentagon, Bush's senior advisers realized that Washington was consumed by the Iraq debate, the Iraq Study Group recommendations, and the fallout from the 2006 midterm elections. In an effort to acknowledge that the United States had an ongoing commitment to the war in Afghanistan and to announce additional resources for the theater, President Bush gave a speech at the American Enterprise Institute in mid-February 2007. His intention was to cast a spotlight on the Afghan efforts, but he first had to address the situation in Iraq. After noting that "one of the interesting things that I have found here in Washington is there is strong disagreement about what to do to succeed [in Iraq], but there is strong agreement that we should not fail," Bush noted wryly that the Senate had voted unanimously to confirm Petraeus as the senior commander in Iraq but that the House might vote against the strategy (by denying the funding and resources required). The president jibed, "This may become the first time in the history of the United States Congress that it has voted to send a new commander into battle and then voted to oppose his plan that is necessary to succeed in that battle."[40]

But the real purpose of the speech was to discuss Afghanistan. While there was no radical change to the U.S. strategy in the theater, there was no doubt that the situation was not as optimistic as the administration had been portraying. Bush described a litany of improvements that had been achieved in Afghanistan since September 11, 2001. All of his points were valid: improvements in education (particularly for girls), successful elections, improved infrastructure, and improvements in access to basic health care. All of the achievements were noteworthy, but the security situation was deteriorating, and at an increasing rate.

Bush described five key goals in Afghanistan:

1.   Increase the size and capability of the Afghan National Security Forces
2.   Strengthen the NATO forces
3.   Help President Karzai improve provincial governance and develop the rural economy (with particular emphasis on PRTs)
4.   Reverse the increases in opium poppy cultivation
5.   Fight corruption.

These five goals were not new or different from the long-standing U.S. strategy for Afghanistan. Since 2002 the United States had set out a comprehensive plan that amounted to nation building and focused on three main pillars: security, governance, and economic development. Also, the five goals outlined by Bush were consistent with the pillars established in Barno's campaign plan of 2003, which emphasized building the ANSF, improving reconstruction and good governance, and engaging the regional players

Bush's speech was consistent with the 2003 CFC-A campaign plan, not some significant, or even nuanced, improvement. The president declared, "There has to be political development, and tangible evidence that a government can provide opportunity and hope," but he provided no indication of any political strategy other than continued strong support for President Karzai and the important reconstruction work done by the PRTs. He declared the U.S. strategy as "robust and important" and then went on to announce that he had requested Congress to appropriate an additional $11.8 billion over two years to fund the strategy and that he had extended the tours of 3,200 U.S. troops in country.[41] He also explicitly linked administration support to President Musharraf and Pakistan as an important component of the Afghanistan strategy, but without providing any specifics on how cooperation with the Pakistanis would or should play out. The strategies for both Iraq and Afghanistan both had elements of nation building—the endeavor the Bush team had explicitly spurned in the 2000 presidential campaign and the early months of the administration. The president had recognized that to secure Afghanistan against a return of the Taliban and keep it from becoming a safe haven for Al-Qaeda some degree of nation building was required.

The same day as the president's speech the White House released a fact sheet stating that the "clear goal" of the United States was to "help the people of Afghanistan defeat the terrorists, and establish a stable, moderate, and democratic state that respects the rights of its citizens, governs its territory effectively, and is a reliable ally in the War on Terror." The second stated purpose added an unequivocal charge to conduct nation building: "to help President Karzai defeat our common enemies and help the Afghan people build a free and successful nation."[42]

Not surprisingly, nowhere in the president's speech or the fact sheet was any indication as to whether the increased funding and the marginal extension of the 3,200 soldiers were what the commander and the ambassador actually needed or had requested in order to accomplish the mission. And there was no indication that the president had concluded that he needed to improve execution within his cabinet and NSC staff.

Congress was still paying attention, at least the House Armed Services Committee. In June a small interagency team went to the Hill to give a closed briefing to the HASC. Although billed as a briefing, the meeting was conducted more like a hearing, though without the public or the press in the room. The areas of discussion and the questions from the congressmen are revealing of the continued level of confusion, misunderstanding, and second-tier approach to Afghanistan. The intelligence community representative estimated that approximately 20,000 to 24,000 Taliban were active inside Afghanistan. The United States had 24,000 troops of all types on the ground during the same period, ISAF coalition partners had contributed another 10,000 and the fledgling Afghan National Army Forces numbered approximately 36,000. But despite the size and composition of ISAF, coalition, and ANA forces, the Taliban were gaining momentum. The convoluted command arrangements of NATO, ISAF, and Enduring Freedom continued to confound everyone, prompting more than one congressman to ask, somewhat exasperatedly, "Just who *is* in charge?" While the question concerned the military chain of command and the relationship between ISAF and Enduring Freedom, the sense of those in the hearing room was that the question was being applied to the entire Afghanistan effort. Toward the end of the two-hour session, one member of the committee asked, somewhat rhetorically, "Does it feel like an equal effort between Iraq and Afghanistan?" The truthful answer would have been a resounding "No!" in the summer of 2007, but the question was left hanging.[43]

The coalition, to include the United States, was still not supplying the required trainers for development of the Afghan National Security Forces, Pakistan continued to refuse to fully cooperate along the border, and the opium crop was back up to record levels. In fact the NSC paid considerable attention to the opium issue through the summer of 2007. The State Department's Bureau of INL had the lead and had produced a detailed, five-pillar strategy, which was explained in detail in a hundred-page "brief." The program's pillars included alternative crop development (referred to as "alternative development"), public information, eradication, demand reduction, and criminal prosecution. Unfortunately differences of opinion between Britain, the United States, and Karzai over eradication derailed any comprehensive implementation. Making matters even worse was a convoluted funding scheme that forced the State Department to rely on money from the Defense Department's own counternarcotics directorate. It is not surprising that execution was less than successful—eradication operations conducted by minimally trained Afghans under INL direction, without dedicated security forces, in the southern Afghanistan area under British military command and not fully supported by President Karzai. The most effective eradication tool, aerial spraying, was staunchly opposed by Karzai. He was bolstered in his stance by knowledge that the United Kingdom also was firmly against any aerial eradication efforts in Helmand. The aerial-spraying issue would continue to be debated for several more months but was essentially off the table. The opium problem would persist and continue to add to the Taliban's coffers and the broader problem of Karzai's legitimacy.

President Karzai visited Washington in early August 2007 and was hosted by President Bush at Camp David. President Bush reaffirmed U.S. support for Karzai's government. There was considerable concern, however, over the increasing violence of the Taliban. Twenty-three Korean missionaries had been taken hostage in July, and the negotiations for their release continued throughout Karzai's trip to Washington. Ultimately the South Korean government gave in to demands and agreed to withdraw its small force of two hundred soldiers from the ISAF coalition. Some reports also stated that the Koreans paid a $20 million ransom. Regardless of the details of the negotiations, it was clear the Taliban had gained momentum, that the coalition was under considerable stress, and that the insurgency was growing.

The "War Czar"

By the time the president made the Iraq surge decision in December 2006, there was a growing realization that improved coordination and execution of both the Iraq and Afghanistan wars was necessary from within the White House and across the cabinet. At about the same time, O'Sullivan, who had oversight of Iraq and Afghanistan, announced she would be departing from the NSC staff. As a result the president agreed to establish a position within the National Security Council staff of Assistant to the President and Deputy National Security Adviser for Iraq and Afghanistan.

In Washington, titles matter, and establishing the position as an "Assistant to the President" meant that whoever was named to the position would be equal in rank to the National Security Advisor himself, despite the "Deputy National Security Adviser" portion of the title. In effect the newly created position, dubbed the "War Czar" by the media, would report directly to the president and coordinate with Steve Hadley. It was a remarkable position intended to elevate the importance of the war efforts, increase the responsiveness of the cabinet and departments, and put somebody in the White House besides Hadley and the president himself who could focus the efforts and issue instructions in the name of the president.

The White House quietly approached several retired four-star generals, all of whom turned down the offer for various reasons. Ultimately the president selected an active-duty general officer, Lieutenant General Douglas Lute, then serving as the Director of Operations (J-3) on the Joint Staff.[44] Selecting a serving flag officer was somewhat unusual, although not unprecedented (Colin Powell had served as the National Security Advisor for President Ronald Reagan from 1987 to 1989 while a lieutenant general). Individuals serving in the Executive Office of the President, including the National Security Council staff, are not subject to the same Senate confirmation as senior members of the various departments and agencies. Lute's status as an active-duty general, however, meant that he would require Senate confirmation, not due to the position itself but because every flag officer serving in a three- or four-star billet is technically appointed, not permanently promoted, to the rank and must be reconfirmed by the Senate at each new position or assignment. The Senate was to reconfirm Lute's status as a lieutenant general based on his reassignment to the NSC. Had the president selected a retired officer or a civilian, no such confirmation would have been necessary. Lute's selection was a bit of a surprise within the policy community, as it was well known that he had not supported the Iraq surge option and was more aligned with Casey's intent to transfer more responsibility to the Iraqis while drawing down U.S. military presence and avoiding the perception of an occupation.[45]

In selecting Lute the president made clear that he expected sharper execution of policy and strategy. In fact the mandate of the War Czar included two specific tasks: continued policy development and policy implementation. The White House press release issued the day of Lute's initial selection by the president stressed implementation: "General Lute will be the full-time manager for the implementation and execution of our strategies for Iraq and Afghanistan, and will manage the interagency policy development process for these two theaters." Equally as interesting, the president's statement went on to say that "nothing is more important than getting Admiral [William J.] Fallon [then the

CENTCOM commander], General Petraeus, American commanders in Afghanistan, and Ambassadors Crocker and [William B.] Wood [in Afghanistan] what they need, and Douglas Lute can make sure that happens quickly and reliably."[46]

It was also clear that the focus was still squarely on Iraq, with Afghanistan remaining the supporting effort despite the president's February speech. It was interesting to note in the White House press release that General Petraeus, the commander in Iraq, was specifically named but General Dan McNeil, the other four-star U.S. theater commander, was relegated to "American commanders in Afghanistan." The day after the announcement, White House press secretary Tony Snow fielded a number of questions about the appointment. Throughout the press briefing Snow referred to Iraq repeatedly, but he never mentioned Afghanistan. The White House also released a separate fact sheet regarding Lute, stating that he was "taking on a vital mission at a critical time" and supplying a single, subordinate supporting statement: "The President's 'New Way Forward' for Iraq requires greater coordination and flexibility here at home. General Lute will handle, full-time, the implementation and execution of our strategies for Iraq and Afghanistan, and will lead policy development process for these two theaters."[47]

Lute was confirmed by the Senate with little fanfare on June 28, 2007, and began reorganizing the NSC Iraq and Afghanistan staff shortly thereafter. Much of the staff focused on Iraq was already in place. That for Afghanistan was not. Tony Harriman initially remained in place as the senior director for Afghanistan, but he was essentially an "Army of One." By late August Harriman had moved to the strategic plans office of the NSC and Lute had reached across the interagency and assembled a more robust six-person Afghanistan team with experience from the State and Defense Departments, CIA, and USAID. But despite the War Czar's focus on Iraq and Afghanistan, much of the policy oversight that had impact inside Afghanistan remained outside of Lute's mandate. NATO policy, fully enmeshed with ISAF force-generation and political issues, remained with its large and long-established European directorate. Pakistan, increasingly recognized as being equally important to the accomplishment of U.S. goals in Afghanistan as it was in the counterterrorism fight against Al-Qaeda, remained in the small South and Central Asia directorate, competing for attention with India and the president's aggressive and controversial U.S.-India Civil Nuclear Cooperation Initiative.[48]

Political Oversight

The focus remained on Iraq for the remainder of 2007 as the effects of the OIF surge were assessed and debated. All eyes were on General Petraeus and Ambassador Crocker when they testified, amid intense media coverage and political punditry, to the Senate Armed Services Committee on September 11, 2007, the sixth anniversary of Al-Qaeda's attacks.

In accordance with the long-standing traditions of the Senate—called the world's greatest deliberative body—the mood was not hostile, but neither was it particularly welcoming. The remarks of Senator (later Vice President) Joe Biden warned General Petraeus and Ambassador Crocker that "the American people will not support an indefinite war whose sole remaining purpose is to prevent the situation from becoming even worse." Senator Hillary Rodham Clinton chided Petraeus, claiming that the general's report on the situation in Iraq required a "willing suspension of disbelief."[49] And the future president, Senator Barack Obama, chose to provide his own version of testimony rather than questions for the witnesses. He stated, "Changing the definition of success to stay the course with the wrong policy is the wrong course for our troops and our national security. The time to end the surge and start bringing our troops home is now, not six months from now."[50]

Petraeus and Crocker remained unflappable throughout the session. Petraeus did not back away from his written testimony, in which he predicted that if the progress continued along the same trajectory, he could foresee reducing U.S. troop level to the presurge number of brigade combat teams by the summer of 2008 "without jeopardizing the security gains we have fought so hard to achieve."[51] In that testimony Petraeus emphasized a counterinsurgency approach: "We have employed counterinsurgency practices that underscore the importance of units living among the people they are securing, and accordingly, our forces have established dozens of joint security stations and patrol bases manned by Coalition and Iraqi forces in Baghdad and in other areas across Iraq."[52] But in the next paragraph he noted the increased offensive combat operations, going on to discuss the importance of the growth and development of the Iraqi security forces. While counterinsurgency continued to be the bumper sticker, the reality was a balanced approach of local counterinsurgency, targeted and violent offensive combat operations, and growing Iraqi security and governance capacity. Petraeus noted, "We employed non-kinetic means to exploit the opportunities provided by the conduct of our kinetic operations—aided in this effort by the arrival of additional Provincial Reconstruction Teams."[53]

Petraeus had provided recommendations through his chain of command the week prior to his congressional testimony. His recommendations had been captured in a paper titled "Security while Transitioning: From Leading to Partnering to Overwatch."[54] His recommendations included a time table for the reduction of the number of brigade combat teams (BCTs, task-organized brigades with attached support) over an eight-month period into the summer of 2008, but he did not offer any longer-term prediction of force reductions beyond the presurge levels targeted for summer 2008.

Six months before the high-intensity Petraeus-Crocker hearings, the Senate Foreign Relations Committee, chaired by Senator Biden, held a hearing on Afghanistan to follow up on President Bush's February speech. The subtitle of Biden's prepared opening remarks for March 8, 2007, was, "Success in Afghanistan is still possible[;] . . . if we surge forces anywhere, it should be in Afghanistan, not Iraq."[55] Biden outlined three necessary steps to improve the situation in Afghanistan: first, establish security, including expanding the Afghan National Security Forces; second, "get moving on reconstruction"; and third, "do counter-narcotics right." The only "counter" he mentioned was counternarcotics. He did not mention counterinsurgency or counterterrorism anywhere in his prepared remarks. In contrast to General Petraeus and Ambassador Crocker, the three witnesses were Assistant Secretary of State Richard Boucher, the recently retired former NATO military commander, General Jim Jones, and former ambassador James Dobbins. Not a single witness from the theater testified.

Perhaps adding to the confusion about the mission in Afghanistan, Assistant Secretary Boucher went well beyond the goals President Bush stated in February. In fact Boucher described a lofty vision of nation, and even region, building: "We have the strategic opportunity to help build a moderate, Muslim society that can support democratic development throughout the region. The transformation of Afghanistan from an essentially ungoverned territory into a land bridge linking South and Central Asia will bring unimagined opportunities to the people of the region and contribute to reducing tensions and internal political strife in neighboring countries."[56] He highlighted the $11.8 billion in additional funding requested by the Bush administration and how the funding would support reconstruction, security, counternarcotics, and law and order.

Perhaps most noteworthy, Boucher clearly linked Pakistan, and increased Pakistani cooperation, to any future success in Afghanistan. He did not go so far as to claim that Pakistan was a higher strategic priority for the United States, but he did note that any progress in Afghanistan required increased Pakistani efforts.

As 2007 drew to a close, the general trajectory was improving in Iraq, while exactly the opposite was happening in Afghanistan. Almost every security-sector metric was showing a negative trend, and August 2007 was the most violent month on record. The political maturation of the Karzai government had stalled, and the licit economy, while still expanding, was not enjoying the blistering expansion of the early part of the decade.

The situation in Pakistan was also of increasing concern. President Pervez Musharraf was embroiled in a battle for his political future. After months of pressure from the United States and other allies, Musharraf resigned from his position as chief of Army Staff and appointed the head of the intelligence service, General Ashfaq Kayani, as his replacement. Two weeks later, former prime minister Benazir Bhutto returned to Pakistan after reaching an amnesty agreement with Musharraf, but with the intent to reenter politics. Musharraf had fired the chief justice, who had opposed Musharraf's reelection, declared a state of emergency on November 3, and suspended the constitution. The situation was already extremely tense when Benazir was assassinated on December 27 after attending a political rally in Rawalpindi. A key ally in the war on terror, at least regarding Afghanistan, was coming apart at the seams.

South Asia was not getting better and in many areas was in fact getting worse. It was not the ideal situation for an economy-of-force theater.

Eight

The 2007 Baghdad Surge and the End of Combat Operations in Iraq

My priorities ... given to me by the commander in chief are: Focus on Iraq first. It's been that way for some time. Focus on Afghanistan second.
—Admiral Mike Mullen, USN, Chairman of the Joint Chiefs of Staff[1]

December 2006 was perhaps the most momentous month of the Iraq war. General Odierno, the newly assigned commander of Multinational Corps-Iraq, had decided that he did not see the Casey strategy as a path to victory in Iraq. The new counterinsurgency-doctrine manual that Generals Petraeus and Mattis had labored so long and so well to produce, Field Manual 3-24, was finally published. The new secretary of defense traveled to Iraq in the first days of his term in office to meet with the Iraqi minister of defense, along with Generals Pace, Abizaid, and Casey, during his visit to Baghdad on December 20, to discuss the new way ahead in Iraq. Finally, on the next to last day of the year, Saddam Hussein mounted the gallows where he had sent so many others to die and was hanged on December 30, 2006. The year 2007 would witness a new strategic effort in Iraq.

The Protection Strategy and the 2007 Baghdad Surge

The security situation in Iraq and particularly Baghdad is so grave, however, that political, economic, diplomatic, and reconciliation initiatives will fail unless a well-conceived and properly supported military operation secures the population first and quickly.
—Frederick W. Kagan[2]

The 2006 decision by President Bush to change national strategies in Iraq, which came to be known as "the surge," was viewed as a simple reinforcement of American forces. Yet the new strategic approach was in fact a complex integration of three significant efforts that coalesced into a single transformational force for Iraq. At the most basic level it included a modification to the tactical focus of coalition units engaged in combat all over Iraq—a new emphasis on protecting the Iraqi people. This aspect of the surge, commonly referred to as "securing the population," was an idea long prominent in counterinsurgency circles.[3] This called for coalition forces to move off of bases and live among the Iraqi people—at least until the security force units in the local area could perform all essential security tasks by themselves.

The second major element was a refined operational approach that shifted the focus of all major combat operations in Iraq from a priority on training the Iraqi military to a combined Iraqi and coalition effort designed to clean out pockets of insurgent activity, establish enduring security, protect key infrastructure, and build prosperity in neighborhoods. That operational focus was led by General Odierno, who focused on Baghdad and its surrounding "belts," which had not seen large combat operations since 2003. This required an increase in forces, because Baghdad was such a large area and had so many ethnically mixed neighborhoods.

The third change was the development within the White House of a new American national policy concerning Iraq. The president of the United States took personal responsibility for altering the effort in Iraq. In his speech to the nation on January 11, President Bush had noted, "The situation in Iraq is unacceptable to the American people—and it is unacceptable to me. Our troops in Iraq have fought bravely. They have done everything we have asked them to do. Where mistakes have been made, the responsibility rests with me. It is clear that we need to change our strategy in Iraq."[4] He had then explained, "in earlier operations, Iraqi and American forces cleared many neighborhoods of terrorists and insurgents—but when our forces moved on to other targets, the killers returned. This time, we will have the force levels we need to hold the areas that have been cleared."[5]

These three efforts required personal courage and renewed commitment, nearly five years into the Iraqi Freedom campaign. It was a clear testament to the dedication of America's military personnel and to President Bush that the

United States was able to make such a significant change in the face of widespread dismay about the situation in Iraq among the American people.[6]

> The surge did more than turn around the situation in Iraq—it made possible a major strategic victory in the broader war on terror. For the terrorists, Iraq was supposed to be the place where Al-Qaeda rallied Iraqis to drive America out. Instead, Iraq became the place where the Iraqis joined forces with America to drive Al-Qaeda out. As a result, Al-Qaeda suffered more than a military defeat in Iraq—it suffered an ideological defeat as well. Across the region, people saw that Al-Qaeda in Iraq could be vanquished, and that a future of terror was not fore-ordained.[7]

2007 had produced a significant improvement in the prosecution of the war in Iraq. The initial results of the initial operations inside Baghdad were mixed—some districts showed progress while others remained violence prone, but progress was clear and improved each month. In the two follow-on Operations conducted later the same year, deficiencies were corrected and obvious momentum began to build. The third offensive, known as operation Phantom Strike, was conducted for several weeks starting in mid-August, with the goal of coalition and Iraqi forces maintaining pressure on AQ-I operatives and other insurgent groups as they were flushed from sanctuaries in the capital. The fourth major offensive was labeled Operation Phantom Phoenix; it began just weeks before Odierno's departure in February 2008, and was designed to provide essential services and jump-start provincial government improvements in less-contested areas as well as expel the enemy.

> The key to the success of these operations was the combination of breadth and continuity. All of them struck multiple enemy safe havens and lines of communication at the same time—in contrast with previous U.S. military operations that had generally attacked enemy concentrations one at a time. Enemy groups could no longer move easily from one safe area to another and those that tried to move suffered serious losses as they dispersed. The rapid movement from one operation to the next denied the enemy time to regroup. As scattered insurgent leaders and fighters attempted to reconsolidate in new areas, Coalition forces hit them again and again.[8]

Keeping Up the Pressure

The added Marines in Anbar Province also demonstrated renewed commitment and encouraged Sunni Salvation Council members to continue recruiting volunteers to help secure their towns. Added to the effect of new facilities
projects and improvements in the local economy, these efforts convinced the
residents to increase their cooperation with the coalition forces even further
(primarily through revealing insurgents and their safe houses) in order to help
reduce violence. In June 2007 at the beginning of "the surge," General Petraeus had called security improvements in Anbar "breathtaking." He and other
commanders were able to walk freely in downtown Ramadi, which had been
a major battleground only months before. General Petraeus later testified that
that Anbar Province could be turned over to Provincial Iraqi Control by July
2008.[9] The positive trends in Anbar encouraged other anti-Al-Qaeda Sunnis
to join the Awakening movement. In May 2007 a Salvation Council of tribal
leaders was formed in Diyala Province. Beginning in early 2007, the town of
Amiriyah was slowly stabilized through the emergence of former Sunni insurgents cooperating with the coalition as a force called the "Amiriyah Freedom
Fighters." These fighters claim to have expelled AQ-I from their neighborhoods.[10] Even neighborhoods in Baghdad began to undergo similar transformations. Combat outposts, Joint Security Stations in partnership with the ISF, and
a population willing to come forward with information about AQ-I brought
the Iraqi capital to the point where 75 percent of its districts were considered
"secure," by late 2007. Prime Minister Maliki said on February 16, 2008, that
AQ-I had been largely driven out of Baghdad.[11]

Though the augmentation of the force in Iraq was the centerpiece of the
new strategy it was not the only significant factor in the decisive change in
the situation that eventually brought success. The effort in Iraq was conducted
both in depth and in breadth and fully engaged both conventional and special
operations force activities to produce a synergistic effect on the enemy. As
Fred Kagan wrote later, "Odierno worked with the U.S. special operations
forces under the command of Lieutenant General Stan McChrystal to make
sure they kept up the pressure on key leaders within the terrorist network.
Their precise and skillful attacks not only took out insurgent leaders but also
provided valuable additional intelligence that Odierno used to refine his plans.
And Odierno's operations to clear and hold key terrain would greatly facilitate the Special Forces' efforts by flushing key enemy leaders out of their safe

havens. Odierno's kinetic operations developed a positive synergy with the more traditional counterterrorism approach, making both much more effective than either could have been alone."[12] When General Odierno and his team finished their tour in February of 2008, civilian casualties were down 70 percent, and attacks on coalition forces had dropped to their lowest levels since 2004. In the Baghdad security districts, specifically, ethnosectarian attacks and deaths had decreased by 90 percent. The situation in Iraq had been "utterly transformed."[13]

General Petraeus appeared again before four committees of Congress on April 8 and 9, 2008, to discuss progress in Iraq. He testified that the assistance from the Sons of Iraq, coupled with "relentless pursuit" of AQ-I by U.S. forces, had "reduced substantially" the threat posed by AQ-I.[14] Whereas in his testimony the previous September General Petraeus could only be guardedly optimistic, in April 2008 his outlook was distinctly positive—reflective of the very real progress that had been made against AQ-I and with the Iraqi security forces for the Iraqi people.

Unfortunately even with the progress being made by MNF-I under Petreaus, Prime Minister Maliki was focused in the early months of 2007 on a very different agenda. His government was fraught with divisions and infiltrated by members who were far from cooperative; also, it faced a massive number of issues on which there was little consensus. As a former longtime exile and manager of guerilla movements against Saddam, he was secretive and ever wary of threats—particularly from other groups inside Iraq. General Petraeus in March had cajoled him into visiting Ramadi for the first time ever to show him the progress Sunni Iraqis were making, but it took a significant effort by Petraeus and Crocker to convince him that "interfering" in the military chain of command and turning a blind eye to efforts by Muqtada al-Sadr and even the Iranians in Iraq was extremely counterproductive to developing a unity government for all Iraqis. It was only after two highly successful Special Forces raids in Iraq in March revealed the depth of Iranian meddling in Iraq and the specific involvement of Hezbollah personnel and Iranian Revolutionary Guard al-Quds Force support in Iraq that Prime Minster Maliki saw the threat posed by some of his associates.[15]

The Taliban Pushes Back

While American forces in Iraq were developing and executing their surge and ISAF was controlling operations and establishing additional PRTs in Afghanistan, the Taliban was rebuilding its power base. Secretary Rumsfeld noted, "By early 2006, a reorganized Taliban insurgency had emerged in Afghanistan's east and south. Increasing numbers of Taliban fighters traveled into Afghanistan from Pakistan and retreated back across the border whenever coalition forces tried to engage them."[16] He soon reversed planned reductions in the size of the Afghan National Army and tried to get more U.S. Foreign Service Officers and economics experts to Afghanistan to help increase stability.[17] But by the end of 2007 the Taliban were ready to begin new, more powerful attacks during the 2008 fighting season; many of their reinforcements were coming back to Afghanistan from Pakistan.

In Helmand Province, the British contingent of ISAF had been fought to a stalemate in operations near the town of Garmsir by December 2007. Helmand was the heart of Pashtun Afghanistan,[18] and though the British had expected to secure the province easily when they arrived in 2006, they soon found they had far too few troops to do so. Afghan forces were sent as reinforcements, but their lack of training made them nearly ineffective. The following April the Taliban fought back hard. In response to the obvious lack of success, President Bush agreed to send additional Marines to Helmand, as a one-time commitment but also in hopes that the NATO allies would add their own reinforcements to support the ISAF commander, General Dan K. McNeil, USA.[19]

Combat continued to escalate through the late spring and summer of 2006, particularly in Helmand, Badghis, and Kunar Provinces. In May, ISAF forces (Norwegian and German, alongside ANA troops) conducted Operation Karez in Badghis Province in the north of Afghanistan, to destroy remaining Taliban in the area.[20] On June 13 the Taliban attacked Sarposa Prison in Kandahar to free some 1,200 prisoners (400 of whom were Taliban). The attack sent a clear signal that the Taliban was renewing the fight, and it also caused significant embarrassment for NATO, since it took place under the noses of security forces in one of the key cities of Afghanistan.[21] Then in September, the United States took the war to Pakistani soil when Special Forces conducted a heliborne raid near Jalal Khel.[22]

In early 2007 the British contingent of ISAF conducted several major operations designed to put pressure on the Taliban in advance of its spring offensive. The Taliban ambushed an American patrol in eastern Afghanistan on November 10, 2007, bringing the U.S. death toll for 2007 to a hundred and making 2007 the deadliest year to that point in the war for Americans in Afghanistan. The tide was clearly shifting away from ISAF. In the first five months of 2008, the number of U.S. troops in Afghanistan increased by over 80 percent, with a surge of 21,643 more troops, bringing the total number of U.S. troops in Afghanistan from 26,607 in January to 48,250 in June.[23]

The Iraqis Take Control

> Victory will not look like the ones our fathers and grandfathers achieved. There will be no surrender ceremony on the deck of a battleship. But victory in Iraq will bring something new in the Arab world—a functioning democracy that polices its territory, upholds the rule of law, respects fundamental human liberties, and answers to its people.
> —President George W. Bush, January 10, 2007[24]

The "Protection Strategy" of 2007 provided a way for the United States to develop a broad level of at least minimum security in Iraq. Such security was necessary if the war was to be won (the coalition having stayed in Iraq to build a government in 2003), but it was not sufficient to defeat the insurgency itself.[25] In order to develop the conditions identified by President Bush for victory in Iraq, the Iraqi government had to show itself capable of defending its borders, policing its territory, and protecting the basic elements assured the people in its constitution. That is, the Iraqi government was required to accept responsibility for the war, demonstrate its ability to lead, and provide for its citizens.

In 2004 the Interim Iraqi Government under Ayad Allawi had tried to accept responsibility but had had none of the tools required to affect the conflict's outcome. The first Iraqi national government, under Prime Minister Ibrahim Jafari in 2005, had been too weak to make any attempt at controlling events in Iraq.[26] Jafari lost power largely due to his inability to bring security to the streets of Iraq; he was succeeded in office by Nouri al-Maliki, another leader of the Dawa party, named through the efforts of the Ayatollah Ali al-Sistani in May 2006 to create an effective coalition government. Initially the government of Maliki showed a similar lack of fortitude, but in late November 2007 President Bush met with the Iraqi prime minister in Amman, Jordan, and exacted a pledge to act more aggressively against the threats to Iraqi security—including those posed by his coreligionist militias in the south of the country.[27]

Most of the fighting in Iraq up to 2007 had taken place in central, north-central, and northwestern Iraq. However the focus of the fight shifted suddenly when in March 2008 Maliki decided to take Basra back from the town's Shia militias. Basra, the third-largest city in Iraq, formed a crucial part of the country's transportation infrastructure (being on the Shatt al-Arab waterway and at the junction of the Tigris and Euphrates Rivers). It was the economic capital of Iraq and site through which flowed its most important natural resource—oil.

From late 2004 through 2005 the level of violence had increased in the city, while it was under British coalition control. Basra was affected by battles among competing militia groups jockeying for control of its rich infrastructure and potential profits. In 2006 the Iranian influence grew much stronger within the city, and the British forces became the victims of explosively formed penetrators (EFPs) from Iran, a shaped charge the use of which pushed them into bases, much as their American counterparts were doing at the same time. In mid-2007 the British contingent, which had controlled Basra Province since the initial invasion in 2003, withdrew from the city center to its main base at the airport on the outskirts of the city, a movement that was viewed as a victory for the militias.[28] At about the same time, the Iraqi government created a Basra Operations Command, led by Lieutenant General Mohan al-Freiji, who managed both the Iraqi army forces and the police in Basra, along the lines of the command-and-control model then in use in Baghdad. Later that summer, British forces officially handed over responsibility for their zone to General al-Freiji and the Iraqi government and departed Iraq.

Basra had shown evidence of growing infiltration by Iranian influence for some time, but after the British departure violence flared up significantly and it became clear that the government would have to act or be proven powerless in the face of Shia instability. Still, competition between Shia political factions and their respective militias escalated unchecked. This presented a serious challenge to the Iraqi government of Prime Minister Maliki, who faced the prospect of looking weak immediately prior to provincial elections in late 2008.

In response Maliki fired the Basra provincial governor, Mohammed Waeli, on July 28, about the time the British were handing over control of the province. Waeli was a member of a competing Shia political party known as the Islamic Virtue, or Fadhila, Party. Fadhila was a rival to the Sadrists, gathering its support mostly from the Shia poor in the south around Basra; in March 2007 it had withdrawn from Maliki's ruling Shia coalition and vowed to continue as an independent bloc. In defiance of Maliki, Waeli refused to give up his position. Nothing Maliki could do seemed to affect the situation in Basra.

Maliki's decision to act against the militias in Basra stemmed from economic, security, and political considerations. Widespread corruption, oil smuggling, and militia control of Iraq's shipping hub collectively posed a serious economic threat to a government beset by debt. Also, the security problems that resulted from escalating violence and militia control posed practical problems for the provincial elections scheduled for October. If the government security forces were unable to secure the city, they surely would not be able to secure the polling stations and prevent voter intimidation. Finally, the Maliki government needed to combat the growing threat of malign Iranian influence in Basra. The prime minister faced a no-confidence vote and needed to bolster his appearance as a strong, effective leader.[29] General Petraeus had been in discussions with Iraqi National Security Advisor Mowaffak al-Rubaie and General al-Freiji on March 21, 2008, when he first heard of the prime minister's intent to act quickly against Basra.[30] Petraeus and his staff were just starting to develop plans to address the problem when the Maliki told the MNF-I commander that Iraq would attack in Basra in a matter of days, not months. General Petraeus was quite concerned, but he approached the problem diplomatically and clearly agreed to render support.

The battle of Basra began on March 25, when the Iraqi army launched an operation code-named Saulat al-Fursan (meaning Charge of the Knights) to drive the Mahdi Army and other militia out of the city of Basra. The operation was the first major engagement planned and carried out primarily by the Iraqi army since the fall of Saddam. Unfortunately because it had been assumed the fight would be easy, the first five battalions were thrown into combat as soon as they arrived, only to face much more heavy resistance from Mahdi Army militia than expected; the offensive stalled, eventually requiring coalition air support and artillery fire. By the first week of April the fighting had degenerated into a standoff. Eventually a temporary cease-fire was brokered among the various Iraqi factions involved,[31] but by then some one thousand Iraqi soldiers had refused to fight, and their parent division, the 14th, had proven itself unsuitable for independent operations (it had been formed only five weeks before the operation began).[32] More than a thousand Iraqi casualties had occurred in six days of heavy fighting.[33] General Petraeus had immediately sent senior officers and advisers to Basra to assist the Iraqi military leadership. On April 1 the best division in the Iraqi army, the 1st Iraqi Army Quick Reaction Force (QRF) Division, with embedded Marine MTTs, arrived from its base in Anbar Province to reinforce the Iraqi division already in place.[34]

Once reinforced, the Iraqis planned and executed a more deliberate attack beginning on April 12, this time fully integrating the key lessons of the coalition operations in Baghdad, including the provision of humanitarian aid, a jobs program, and a significant national government investment in infrastructure improvements, announced by Maliki. The fighting continued with coalition support through the end of April and into the first weeks of May. Many of the Iraqi security force members who proved themselves unwilling to fight or incapable of it were dismissed; Major General Mohammed Jawad, who had commanded the 1st QRF Division, replaced General al-Freiji as the head of the Basra Operations Command. At the same time Prime Minister Maliki opened discussions with the local tribes and also began a highly successful recruiting campaign to attract residents of Basra into the Iraqi army. The operation was completed with a robust reconstruction effort that did much to improve living conditions in the city.

Operation Charge of the Knights was a critically important demonstration that the national Iraqi government was willing to confront and could successfully defeat major Shia militia groups outside Baghdad.[35] Although it started badly, due to rushed execution, poor initial assumptions, and poor preparation of forces, once redesigned in a more deliberate way it proved quite successful and showed how capable the Iraqi army could be in combat. Even more importantly, Nouri al-Maliki lived up to his promises to take action against his fellow Shia militiamen and took a leading role in the political and military aspects of the operation. Operation Charge of the Knights also showed that the coalition could stand in support and allow the Iraqis to take the lead fully in a major fight. All of these facts were crucial to the next phase of the campaign—the transition to full Iraqi leadership in the counterinsurgency effort.

Political Decisions in Iraq

Iraq's success in the counterinsurgency campaign was still measured by a series of benchmarks established in 2007—security-capacity building, ethnic power sharing, and improvements in reconciliation and justice.[36] Specifically, in the security realm the Iraqis had already provided forces and economic development schemes for the Baghdad Security Plan and had exercised sufficient military command and control to lead operations. In the political realm, however, the Maliki government needed to show progress on constitutional review, protection of minority rights, and a range of legislation concerning de-Ba'athification, distribution of hydrocarbon resources, provincial elections, amnesty, and militia disarmament. These were much more difficult issues than purely military ones, particularly in a weak coalition government.

The government developed (but did not pass) a hydrocarbon law in 2007, and it passed a budget for 2008, as well as on January 12 the Accountability and Justice Law, often also known as "de-Ba'athification reform," which opened the door for Sunni reconciliation. Maliki's leadership and willingness to tackle the militias in Basra did much to assist his government in accomplishing the benchmark tasks, however, and by July 2008 only three remained at unsatisfactory levels: militia disarmament, professionalization of the Iraqi police, and hydrocarbon resource distribution.[37] A Provincial Powers Act had been passed by the Iraqi parliament on February 13 but was not approved by the Presidency Council until October 2008; legislation concerning the status of Kirkuk and its oil resources would not be resolved before the provincial elections in January 2009. Still, much had improved in Iraq, and much progress had been made by its government as summer passed into fall in 2008.

In August 2007 President Bush and Prime Minister Maliki had agreed in principle to the development of a status of forces agreement (SOFA) between Iraq and the United States. The same month President Talabani, Vice Presidents Hashimi and Abd al-Mahdi, Kurdistan Regional Government President Barzani, and Maliki had called for an end to the Chapter VII (i.e., of the United Nations Charter) status under which the UN Security Council had established and maintained the coalition relationship in Iraq. These agreements had led in November 2007 to a "Declaration of Principles for a Long-Term Relationship of Cooperation and Friendship between the Republic of Iraq and the United States of America," a document that laid out a framework for the two countries to negotiate a SOFA and other related issues. Those negotiations began in earnest in early 2008. The SOFA and an associated security agreement were eventually approved by the Iraqi cabinet and the Iraqi Council of Representatives on November 27, 2008; on December 4, Iraq's Presidency Council endorsed that vote, approving the agreement on the Iraqi side.[38]

Prime Minister al-Maliki needed to prove to the Iraqi public before the next (2009) national election that the withdrawal of the American forces from

Iraq would happen in an appropriate manner. He saw the approval of the SOFA before the U.S. national election as an important political goal, because he had no way of knowing what the approach of the new administration might be following the departure of President Bush. Maliki also seemed to sense that Bush's involvement would be key to any such agreement (the two men had been conducting weekly VTCs for months), so he pressed for an agreement to be signed before the president left the Oval Office in January 2009.

Maliki also saw the SOFA as another chance to strike a stronger image with the Iraqi people and improve own his chances for reelection, as the official who had ended the "occupation" of Iraq. On December 14, 2008, President Bush and Prime Minister al-Maliki signed the Strategic Framework Agreement (SFA) and the SOFA. The SOFA gained most of the Iraqi and international media attention, while little attention was devoted to the SFA, though it involved a broader range of more crucial issues.

More extreme Shia organizations in Iraq, such as Muqtada al Sadr's Mahdi Militia, and some of the more conservative Sunni groups, like Harith al-Dari's Association of Muslim Scholars in Iraq (HEYET), all looked to the SOFA as an opportunity to gain something from the United States and, by simultaneously opposing the agreement, to de-legitimize the Maliki government prior to the upcoming elections. The Iraqi Kurds viewed the SOFA negotiations as a good way to delay any central government legislation concerning Kirkuk, hydrocarbon legislation, and greater federalism. With all of these diverging interests, development of the SOFA proved so complex that the government did not open it to public debate or referendum. A Department of Defense report later said, "With the entry into force and implementation of the Strategic Framework Agreement (SFA) and Security Agreement (SA), this period witnessed a historic transition in the nature of the relationship between the United States and Iraq. . . . [T]he SFA begins to normalize U.S.-Iraq relations through economic, diplomatic, cultural, and security ties, and it will serve as a foundation for a long-term bilateral relationship based on common goals and interests."[39]

American National Elections and Future Iraq Plans

Americans went to the polls in November 2008 in huge numbers to participate in one of the longest-argued and influential elections of their recent history. The election produced a number of firsts in U.S. presidential election history.

2007 Baghdad Surge and End of Combat Operations

It was the first election since 1952 in which neither the incumbent president nor vice president was a candidate. Governor Sarah Palin was the first woman nominated for vice president by the Republican Party, and for the first time in history both major party nominees were sitting U.S. senators. When Senator Barack Obama formally accepted the Democratic Party's nomination, he became the first African-American to be nominated for president by a major political party. Senator Obama won the election. With 365 electoral votes to Senator McCain's 173; Obama also had a 7 percent lead in the popular vote.[40] He became the first African-American president of the United States on January 20, 2009.

President Obama's election resolved several questions concerning the ongoing war in Iraq. First, it left no doubt that the majority of the American people accepted an early withdrawal based upon a schedule of events, not a more nebulous conditions-based approach. That schedule had been determined by the SOFA negotiations developed and approved by President Bush, but Obama's election ensured that the time table would not be delayed. Second, the election of President Obama established a new relationship among the leaders of the two countries, one that was not based on previous agreements. Finally, the election meant a shift of military priorities from Iraq to Afghanistan. That shift did not ignore the needs of Iraq, but commanders there would no longer have priority access to ever-diminishing resources. Indirectly it meant as well that Iraq would nearly disappear from major media coverage in the year to come, giving the Iraqi government freedom of movement.[41]

The outcome of the provincial elections in Iraq, also in January 2009, showed several important improving trends. Although the voter turnout was down slightly, the process was largely peaceful and was judged fair. In general the voting revealed a trend away from sectarian movements and toward more secular parties.[42] The election was also a victory for Maliki's State of Law party, which won the majority of votes in nine out of the fourteen provinces that held elections. It also added to the consolidation of power within the Iraqi federal government. The results were also "a significant milestone in the progress of Sunni reintegration and reconciliation with the Shia population and the Government of Iraq. In the 2005 provincial elections, less than 2% of the Sunni population voted . . . in al Anbar, an overwhelmingly Sunni province, roughly 40% of the population voted in 2009 compared to the 2% turnout in 2005."[43] Not surprisingly Prime Minister Nouri al-Maliki called the elections "a victory for all the Iraqis," an indicator of "the Iraqi people's trust in their government and in the elections," and "proof that the Iraqi people are now living in real security."[44] The U.S. ambassador to Iraq, Ryan Crocker, hailed it as "the most important election to take place since the fall" of Saddam Hussein.[45]

The End of the War in Iraq

> The great tragedy of Iraq is that no one really credits our soldiers for doing the near impossible: they went into the heart of the ancient caliphate, took out a genocidal monster, stayed on to foster consensual government, endured often poisonous attacks from critics at home, and triumphed at a cost less than during a major campaign in World War II.
>
> —Victor Davis Hanson[46]

In a little-heralded event largely lost in the New Year's celebrations around the world, a new U.S. embassy was formally opened in Baghdad on January 1, 2009;[47] even more importantly, on that same date, the Iraqi government officially assumed control of the "Green Zone" in Baghdad and effectively accepted responsibility of the war effort over the entire country.[48] Prime Minister Maliki declared, "This palace is the symbol of Iraqi sovereignty and its return is a message directed to the Iraqi people that Iraq's sovereignty has returned."[49] In another press report, Anthony Shadid of the *Washington Post* commented, "The war in Iraq is indeed over."[50]

The combat and violence did not end on that first day of 2009. In fact a massive suicide attack on the following day killed twenty-four prominent Sunnis and another the following day killed thirty-one. But the role of the United States in ongoing combat operations had shifted in a very important way. After the signing of the SOFA and the expressed, clear intentions of the incoming Obama administration made any long-term American commitment to retain the lead untenable, the requirement for the Iraqi government to take full responsibility for operations within its own borders was undeniable.

The impact in Iraq was felt more clearly with every passing day. On January 3 the U.S. military took a first step toward pulling combat troops from Iraqi cities, moving out of a Baghdad military base and handing it over to Iraq. The base had been set up in March 2007 to repel Shia militias from the largely Sunni Adhamiya District as a part of the surge. Brigadier General Robin Swan, deputy commander of U.S. forces in Baghdad, said the transfer of Forward

Operating Base Callahan was "tremendously significant."[51] The transfer of the FOB reflected both a narrowing of U.S. operations and the improvement in security in Baghdad.

President Obama entered office on January 20, 2009, with a significant agenda of change, yet high on his list of new initiatives was fulfillment of his campaign promise to end the war in Iraq and to shift national priorities back to the conflict in Afghanistan. He announced his resolve during his inaugural address, and one of his initial meetings, during his first day in office, was a face-to-face discussion with his secretary of defense, Robert Gates, and General Petraeus of changing the mission in Iraq.[52]

His predecessor in the Oval Office had said many times that the war on terrorism would not end with tumultuous parades and fancy ceremonies but would most likely be resolved under quiet, conditions-based circumstances. Bush's views on the end of the war in Iraq shifted over time but finally coalesced into a similarly staid vision.[53] Unlike the great ceremony held on the battleship USS *Missouri* in Tokyo Bay in 1945, the end of the Iraq war, after the transition to Iraqi sovereignty in 2004, could never have been a victory celebration but had to resemble more the ratification of the U.S. Constitution—a long series of uncertain steps, leading eventually to an uncertain agreement of principles and the enforcement of a new and tenuous social and political order. By January 2009 such a series of events had occurred (the Anbar Awakening, the strengthening of the Iraqi government, the signing of the SOFA, and the handover of the Green Zone and responsibility for the conduct of the war to the Iraqi government), making the presidential decision to withdraw military forces from Iraq a necessary but in no way decisive action. Symbolically, on the same day that the president was directing a new mission in Iraq, the Iraqi government and its security forces were assuming full responsibility for the formerly restive city of Ramadi, in Al Anbar Province. Clearly the situation on the ground in Iraq substantiated the reduction in troop levels and the effective termination of America's longest and most controversial struggle after twenty-nine years of conflict.

Less than two weeks later, the Iraqi people participated in a second national election, and in it for the first time in recent history the majority of Iraqi citizens voted. Sunni and Shiite, urban and rural, north and south, millions of Iraqis went to the polls to select from among some 14,000 candidates competing for 440 seats in fourteen of Iraq's eighteen provinces. Occurring without major incident and under the control of the Iraqi government (with the coalition in distant support), the election marked a significant step forward in Iraq's ability to demonstrate effective governance and security. One senior Marine officer said at the time, "One of the things I've always said was that we came here to 'give' them democracy. Even in the dark days my only consolation was that it was about freedom and democracy. After what I saw today, and having forgotten our own history and revolution, this was arrogance. People are not given freedom and democracy—they take it for themselves."[54]

In an address to service members at Camp Lejeune, North Carolina, on Friday, February 27, 2009, President Obama made the situation in Iraq very clear: "Our review is complete. . . . [T]he United States will pursue a new strategy to end the war in Iraq through a transition to full Iraqi responsibility. This strategy is grounded in a clear and achievable goal shared by the Iraqi people and the American people: an Iraq that is sovereign, stable, and self-reliant. To achieve that goal, we will work to promote an Iraqi government that is just, representative, and accountable, and that provides neither support nor safe-haven to terrorists. We will help Iraq build new ties of trade and commerce with the world. And we will forge a partnership with the people and government of Iraq that contributes to the peace and security of the region."[55] He made the future of U.S. forces in Iraq very clear as well: "Let me say this as plainly as I can: by August 31, 2010, our combat mission in Iraq will end."[56]

In January 2010, the fewest number of Iraqis had died than in any month period since 2003; the next month the number of Iraqis killed soared back to 258, but the number of Americans skilled in Iraq fell to 9—also the lowest to date since 2003. On April 7 the new American president flew announced to Iraq, where he visited with U.S. soldiers but also discussed the political situation in Iraq with Prime Minister al-Maliki and President Jalal Talibani. Many suspected he wanted to press them for continued progress. Obama noted while in Iraq, "We've made significant political progress in Iraq [but] there are a lot of unresolved issues that need to be dealt with."[57]

If the key element of sovereignty is the ability to protect the nation's people, Iraq's government had finally taken on the full measure of its responsibility. The United States was no longer at war with Iraq; it was no longer even the dominant partner in the effort to defeat the insurgency. Iraq was not fully at peace, but it was fully and democratically responsible for its own people and their security.

The war to remove Saddam Hussein ended when the Iraqi government that followed him was able to execute the responsibilities of a responsible nation-state; it was not a glorious event and could not even be precisely identified as a given point in time—American forces would remain in Iraq to advise and assist their Iraqi counterparts for months to come—but the decades-long opposition between the two nations was clearly at an end.[58] The conflict between Iraq and the United States had been a long war, one that spanned the gulf between the end of the Cold War era and the beginning of a new, more globalized and more networked century. In the same way that it had been conducted in a very different way than most Americans had envisioned, the war ended in a process that few Americans could really understand—but it ended with all of the major objectives achieved and with a very different future possible for the people of Iraq.[59]

Redoubling on the War in Afghanistan

Just as the war was winding down in Iraq, the American effort in Afghanistan had received new and greater emphasis.[60] By June 2008 the number of U.S. troops in Afghanistan had increased by over 80 percent, following President Bush's decision to surge over 21,000 more troops, bringing the total number to 48,250.[61] That June twenty-eight Americans were killed in Afghanistan, nearly equaling the twenty-nine American deaths in Iraq. The American commander in Afghanistan, General David McKiernan, who had commanded during the invasion of Iraq in 2003, said there were three main reasons for the increase in violence: a change in tactics by the insurgents to small attacks on more vulnerable targets, such as the civilian population, district centers, and convoys; the progress of Afghan and NATO forces in pushing into regions previously controlled by the Taliban, which had led to more fighting; and the "deteriorating situation with tribal sanctuaries across the border" in Pakistan.[62]

In September 2008 President Bush had announced a further increase of 4,500 troops.[63] But even before Bush's reinforcements could have any effect on the fighting, the Taliban increased its attacks against the Karzai government and ISAF. On June 13 as we have seen, Taliban fighters liberated some 1,200 prisoners from a Kandahar jail, causing a major embarrassment for ISAF in one of its most important security areas.[64] The following month, a coordinated Taliban attack by about two hundred guerrillas was launched on a remote ISAF base at Wanat, in Afghanistan's far eastern province of Nuristan. These developments revealed problems that were increasingly threatening the accomplishment of the American objectives in Afghanistan.

The July 2008 battle of Wanat, also known as Operation Rock Move, involved U.S. Army soldiers from the 2nd Battalion, 503rd Infantry Regiment, of the 173rd Airborne Brigade Combat Team. Several hundred Taliban fighters had surrounded their remote base and its observation post and had attacked it from the village and the surrounding farmland. The Taliban was reinforced by Pakistani militant and terrorist groups banded together from the surrounding region, including Kunar and in the Bajaur tribal agency in neighboring Pakistan. Some even believe that members of Al-Qaeda, the Kashmir-based Lashkar-e-Taiba, and Pakistan-based Hezb-i-Islami participated in the fight.[65] On the evening of July 12, members of the Taliban moved into Wanat and ordered the villagers to leave. Undetected by the Americans, they set up firing positions inside houses and a mosque that was next to; and overlooked the coalition base's perimeter.[66] They broke through the American defenses and entered the main base before being repulsed by artillery and close air support. Nine Americans were killed and twenty-seven wounded, along with four ANA soldiers. Those casualties were the largest losses in a single battle since the June 28, 2005, SEAL Team 10 raid in the same Kunar Province. That raid, led by Navy lieutenant Michael P. Murphy, had ended with nineteen Americans killed and the Medal of Honor being awarded posthumously to Murphy.[67]

Civilian deaths caused by allied operations had increased sympathy for the Taliban among local residents, who had allowed the fighters to move into the village. The American forces had noticed other warning signs. The day before the attack, the elders of Wanat had conducted a *shura* (a "consultation," or assembly) without the Americans' knowledge. The villagers had also begun pouring wastewater into an area near the post more frequently than they had to conceal the movement of Taliban within the village.[68] A 2009 U.S. Army report criticized the brigade and battalion commanders, citing a lack of supplies, equipment, and drinking water for troops in Wanat. The same report criticized the American commanders for a counterproductive approach to their military goals, stating that "the highly kinetic approach favored by TF Rock ... rapidly and inevitably degraded the relationships between the US Army and the Waigal (local) population."[69]

On September 3 the war spilled over on to Pakistani territory for the first time, when, as noted above, U.S. Army Special Forces helicopters attacked three houses in a village close to a known Taliban and Al-Qaeda stronghold near Jala Khel. The attack killed at least fifteen people, mostly civilian women and children.[70] Pakistan responded furiously, condemning the attack. The foreign ministry in Islamabad called the incursion "a gross violation of Pakistan's territory."[71] In response the Pakistani government announced disconnection of Pakistani supply routes to the ISAF forces in Afghanistan for an indefinite period.[72] It was understood that increasing the war effort in Afghanistan would produce more casualties, yet the counterattacks in strength by the Taliban and its allies and the increasingly hostile reactions of Afghan civilians and both the Afghan and Pakistani governments did not bode well for the effort to come.

Then, on September 11, 2008, seven years to the day after the attacks on the World Trade Center, militants killed 2 U.S. troops in the eastern part of Afghanistan, bringing the total number of American losses in the war to 113. That made 2008 the deadliest year for American troops in Afghanistan since the start of the war.[73] New approaches under new leadership in 2009 would be the only viable solutions for a campaign that was clearly losing the support of both populations involved.

Nine

Developing the Afghan Surge Strategy

B y the fall of 2008 consensus was forming across the political and military spectrum that the Baghdad surge was succeeding in reducing the level of violence in Iraq. Various local security initiatives across the country, such as the Sons of Iraq were also credited with bringing such a degree of stability to Iraq that the attention could shift to a long-term security and partnership arrangement. Whether the improvement in security in Iraq was the result of the surge, the ongoing "Anbar Awakening," ethnic cleansing, increasingly effective counterterrorism targeting by U.S. Special Operations Forces, or simply war weariness among the Iraqis remains debatable; the improvement in security seen in 2008 is not.

Back in January 2007, when President Bush announced the deployment of an additional five brigades to Iraq totaling more than 20,000 U.S. military forces, he also established six main objectives, in what the White House called "the New Way Forward." The six tenets Bush laid out were to reemerge in the Obama administration's strategy for Afghanistan and Pakistan, although the specific terminology would be changed, as we will see. Bush's goals included:

1. Let the Iraqis Lead
2. Help Iraqis protect the population
3. Isolate extremists
4. Create space for political progress
5. Diversify political and economic efforts
6. Situate the strategy in a regional approach.[1]

By August of 2008 progress had been demonstrated across all six objectives. The administration shifted the focus to securing a durable and lasting partnership with Iraq prior to the end of the Bush term in January 2009. Time was running short.

Focusing on the Longer Term in Iraq:
Strategic Framework and SOFA

Those who were working on the Afghanistan policy and strategy in 2008 saw the success of the Baghdad surge as an opportunity to refocus U.S. attention on Afghanistan and the deteriorating security situation there. Instead, much of the Bush administration's effort continued to be consumed by Iraq. Specifically, the Office of Iraq and Afghanistan in the National Security Council, the "War Czar's" office, prioritized securing a Strategic Framework Agreement and a security agreement (i.e., Status of Forces Agreement) with Iraq.[2]

The negotiations between the United States, led by Ambassador Ryan Crocker in Baghdad, and the Iraqis were tedious, occasionally contentious, and time-consuming. Almost daily video teleconferences between the U.S. embassy and the White House and State Department consumed hours of preparation and countless revisions of the negotiating documents. Each detail was debated, rewritten, and then debated some more. The calendar kept ticking toward January 20, 2009, when President Bush would relinquish the Oval Office to Barack Obama. Iraq, despite the perceived success of the surge, continued to consume the lion's share of the national security team's time. The situation in Afghanistan, meanwhile, continued to stagnate, if not deteriorate.

By the summer of 2008 coalition casualties in Afghanistan were approaching the same level as in Iraq, though coalition troop levels in Iraq were more than two and a half times those in Afghanistan. The year did not start off well. In January the iconic and upscale Serena Hotel in Kabul, despite extensive security measures, was attacked by Taliban, leaving six dead. In February Kandahar suffered a spectacular suicide bombing that left a hundred dead. In April the Taliban attacked the Victory Day parade, attempting to assassinate President Karzai. In June the Taliban stepped up the pressure in the south, as noted, attacking the Sarposa prison and freeing over a thousand prisoners. July continued the trend, with high-profile security incidents that included an attack on the Indian embassy in Kabul that killed fifty-eight, and the battle at

Combat Outpost Wanat—at the time the deadliest engagement in Afghanistan for the United States since 2001, with nine U.S. killed in action and twenty-seven wounded. The action at Wanat, discussed in chapter 8, included an estimated two to four hundred Taliban fighters, was a complex attack, and further reinforced the opinion that the security situation in Afghanistan was rapidly deteriorating.

A new U.S. commander of ISAF, General David McKiernan, arrived in the summer of 2008 and by October was keenly aware of the security challenges. In October, back in Washington for consultations, McKiernan requested twenty thousand additional U.S. forces. He explained to reporters in the Pentagon,

> We've seen an increased number of foreign fighters, non-Pashtun-speaking fighters in the East, increased levels of violence, people that generally don't feel secure, don't have freedom of movement. And so the additional military capabilities that have been asked for are needed as quickly as possible. And those are a range of assets. It's not just additional boots on the ground. It's enablers to go with them. But at the same time, I would tell you that it's not just a question about more soldiers. It's a question about more governance, about more economic aid, about more political assistance for the government of Afghanistan, as well as military capabilities.[3]

When asked about the prospects for resources following the 2008 U.S. presidential election, McKiernan replied "I think there's a common view that we need to do more; that Afghanistan has been an economy of force for the last several years. And so as resources become available, I think there's generally a uniform need—a uniform view that we need to shift some of those assets to Afghanistan."[4] The intent was to send about half of the reinforcements to the increasingly volatile southern provinces of Kandahar and Helmand. The remainder of the troops, about ten thousand, would be split between training the Afghan National Security Forces (ANSF) and combat missions in Regional Command–East.

Ultimately only one brigade of the four requested, or about three thousand troops, was approved in 2008, and it did not arrive until early 2009. For the remainder of 2008, at least, Afghanistan would continue to be the economy-of-force theater. The "good war" was not going well.

The 2008 Afghanistan Strategic Review

Despite the continued high-level focus on Iraq and the SFA and SOFA negotiations, Washington was slowly refocusing on Afghanistan. In September the National Security Advisor, Steve Hadley, held one of his periodic sessions focused on Afghanistan. The meeting reviewed the security situation, the state of the Afghan government, and the degree of reconstruction and development. At the conclusion of the meeting, Hadley summarized the state of affairs, concluding that if the United States was in fact waging a counterinsurgency fight and was essentially in a stalemate that, strategically, the United States, ISAF, and the Karzai government were losing. Though only four and a half months remained in the Bush presidency, a detailed assessment of the Afghan strategy was called for. A senior-level, unannounced, review—similar to the one run by former Deputy National Security Advisor J. D. Crouch that had ultimately recommended the Iraq surge—was suggested. At Hadley's instigation, on September 12, 2008, the Principals Committee recommended a comprehensive strategy review for Afghanistan. Before the end of the same week, President Bush ordered the review.

Lieutenant General Doug Lute, the "War Czar," convened a high-level interagency panel, formed around a nucleus of regular Deputies Committee attendees, to examine all aspects of the "next steps" for U.S. strategy for Afghanistan. Participants included Assistant Secretary of Defense for Asia and Pacific Affairs Jim Shinn and Assistant Secretary for Special Operations and Low Intensity Conflict Michael Vickers (who had extraordinarily deep ties to the Afghanistan mission, going as far back as the CIA support to the mujahedeen fighting the Soviet army in the 1980s); the Joint Staff's Director of Operations, Marine Lieutenant General James "Jay" Paxton, and the Director of Strategic Plans and Policy, Vice Admiral James "Sandy" Winnefeld; State Department Counselor Eliot Cohen and Assistant Secretary of State for South and Central Asia Richard Boucher; senior members of the National Intelligence Council; as well as representatives from the office of the vice president, outside experts, and of course the NSC's Afghanistan staff. The core group of interagency representatives and experts met for the first time on September 22, 2008, and then for more than eighteen times, usually for four hours at a time, and often twice in the same day, in a windowless fourth-floor secure room in the Old Executive Office Building.[5] The group invited Afghan participation and met with Minister of Defense Abdul Rahim Wardak and Director of the Independent Directorate for Local Governance Ghulam Jelani Popal. Former senior military commanders and ambassadors were brought in throughout the process, particularly to assist the group in understanding the assumptions that formed the underpinnings of the early strategy for Afghanistan. The incoming commander of U.S. Central Command, General Petraeus, spent several hours with the group. The Supreme Allied Commander of NATO, General John Craddock, participated for one day. The process was a rigorous examination of U.S. interests, assumptions, strategy, and plans for Afghanistan.

The early sessions were devoted to understanding the operating environment: the Afghan population, Afghan government, the Taliban, Al-Qaeda in Afghanistan, and the broader network of associated terrorists and insurgents. As the discussion pressed on, the participants found themselves increasingly discussing Pakistan. Long before the review concluded there was consensus that the way forward required a much more integrated and connected strategy linking Pakistan and Afghanistan. Despite a general disdain for the "Afg-Pak" shorthand, all participants agreed that the recommendations and conclusions had to address U.S. efforts and interests on both sides of the Durand Line in a fully integrated and coordinated way. Coincidentally the National Intelligence Council was in the final stages of releasing the National Intelligence Estimates (NIEs) for both Afghanistan and Pakistan, and the final debate concerning elements of the Pakistan NIE factored heavily in the discussions over Afghan strategy, as many of the reviewers for the two NIEs were participants the Afghanistan review. The impending Pakistan NIE was briefed in great detail.

As the debate stretched into October, the group also had to contend with the approaching end of the Bush administration. Time was indeed running short. All participants were committed to the intent of the study, but many recognized that the incoming administration—whether Republican or Democrat—would most likely want to start a fresh assessment. General Lute was keenly aware of this factor and deliberately structured the debates to yield both short- and long-term actions and recommendations. The short term was defined as "in the next 120 days," meaning actions that should or could be decided and implemented under President Bush's presidency. The long-term bin was not necessarily "long-term" in number of days or effects but rather in terms of what should or could be recommended to the incoming administration. Long-term actions were those that would require detailed discussion during the transition period between the outgoing and incoming administrations. The assumption was that the incoming administration would want to begin discussions and transition actions immediately after the November elections.[6]

The study team also wanted to capture lessons learned from 2001 to 2008, highlighting what had gone right in Afghanistan along with what had gone wrong, or at least had been less successful than expected. Some might cynically label this aspect of the review as trying to capture the legacy of the Bush administration's efforts in Afghanistan. In reality it was a sober assessment of U.S. collective efforts to stabilize Afghanistan and to offer a short history for the next administration to draw upon when formulating the way ahead for the next four years.

One of the major realizations of the study was that there was not simply one war being waged in a single theater in Afghanistan. Instead there were multiple, disparate campaigns, each answering to its own chain of command and all operating with slightly different objectives and on different time lines. Depending on how one might count, there were some nine or ten separate "wars" going on simultaneously.[7] There was the obvious and well-reported war—the international NATO-ISAF effort, then under command of a U.S. four-star, General McKiernan. At the same time, McKiernan was dual-hatted as the commander, U.S. Forces Afghanistan, with responsibility for the U.S.-centric Operation Enduring Freedom campaign, in existence since the outset of operations in October 2001, executed solely under the authority and leadership of the United States to pursue national counterterrorism objectives. This effort could be further subdivided into the overt and covert wars being pursued by the various special operations forces and commands in Afghanistan. The Combined Security Transition Command–Afghanistan (CSTC-A) was in charge of the largest of the train-and-equip missions for the ANSF, and, in a strange command-and-control arrangement, had some degree of operational and tactical control of U.S. and coalition support teams (and by extension, Afghan tactical forces) even after they had deployed out of the training base and into the fight.[8] The Afghan National Army and the Afghan National Police each fought independent operations under its own chain of command, as did the Afghan National Directorate of Security. The CIA also had ongoing operations throughout the country. It all added up to one huge violation of one of the fundamental principles of warfare—unity of command. Lute's team called it a "lack of coherence."

The study team also wrestled with the still prevalent doctrine of the time—"Clear, Hold, Build," and its extended version "Shape, Clear, Hold, Build, Transfer." In assessing the overall campaign plan it became clear that such short-hands didn't reflect the realities on the ground. Nor did they help foster coop-eration and coordination between the military and civilian efforts. As a better way of organizing the thinking, the group broke the efforts into two major phases: "clear-hold" and "hold-build." The intent was to show that many of the activities and actions required in the four-phase approach actually needed to occur simultaneously, or at least overlap for significant periods. It wouldn't be possible just to declare the "clear" mission a success and then immediately transition to a hold force. Instead the transition was more gradual, as condi-tions warranted, and might proceed at different speeds at different locations depending on many factors across the country. Indeed this idea was even more urgent when discussing the "hold-build" phase. Because of a lack of resources, both military and civilian, and of a clear and coherent plan, ISAF found itself clearing areas more than once—there was either insufficient force available to hold them or the clear-hold force was not retained in the area long enough for the civilian reconstruction, development, and governance efforts to take root. There was not enough security space for the development efforts—particular-ly local governance—to flourish. This repetitive cycle—clear, hold, clear some more, repeatedly—alienated the local population. In many cases commanders on the ground were reporting that it might have been better not to have en-tered a district at all than to arrive, conduct highly effective combat operations, and then withdraw, leaving a situation even more uncertain than it had been. Such actions also tended to further the distrust between many Afghans and their central government. The bottom line was that if clear-hold/hold-build was to be the strategy, more combat forces were immediately required, and more civilian assistance. But, with 100,000 troops still in Iraq, were such forces reasonably available? Should President Bush make deployment decisions that would not take effect until after the new president assumed office? And what about the role and responsibility of the Afghans themselves? Shouldn't the ANSF be capable of doing more?

The Afghan National Security Forces themselves were a major area of focus for the review team. If the United States, NATO, and the coalition partners were ever to depart Afghanistan, the Afghans themselves were going to need to be able to carry the security load. In October 2008 the Afghan National

Security Forces stood at just under 148,000 military and police: 68,000 army and 80,000 police.[9] Despite years of investment in the army, many units were not combat ready, the forces had been kept relatively small by agreement between the Afghans and the international supporters, and the distribution of what forces did exist was not weighted to the major areas of fighting in the south and east. The situation in the police was even worse. Most policemen, particularly the patrolmen, or "beat cops," had no training whatsoever. Almost all police were illiterate, and the train-and-equip efforts under CSTC-A were, by the command's own admission, several years behind those of the army. Granted, this lag was largely a result of inadequate resourcing for the train-and-equip mission, but it was also indicative of a lack of attention by both the Afghans and the West.

By any measure, the ANSF were not ready to take on a lead role in the security sector. Afghanistan simply lacked the capacity, and lack of capacity was not limited to the Afghan National Security Forces. There were only 33,000 total U.S. troops in Afghanistan in October 2008, split between ISAF and OEF missions, and about 30,000 coalition troops.[10] By comparison, during the same period the United States still had 148,000 soldiers in Iraq, along with about 7,000 coalition troops.[11] The civilian efforts were in a similar state. For years the U.S. embassy had requested significant increases in assistance funding to develop ministerial capacity, rule of law, and economic capacity. Much of each year's request was not supported in Washington.

In a nutshell, the review concluded that two overarching attributes best described the campaign in Afghanistan: a lack of coherence and a shortfall in capacity. These two descriptors covered the entire endeavor. Coherence was lacking in all sectors—security, governance, and economic development; coherence was also lacking across all major commands and organizations—ISAF, OEF, UNAMA, and within the U.S. and Afghan interagency processes. Capacity was lacking in the military efforts of ISAF and OEF, in the Afghan National Security Forces, and perhaps most importantly in the Afghan government at the central ministry, provincial, and district levels.

Ultimately the 2008 review (called the "Lute Review" by insiders) made nearly twenty major recommendations, split between Afghanistan and Pakistan and between near-term and long-term actions. Among the recommendations for Afghanistan were: significantly increase the U.S. military forces (i.e., an "Afghanistan surge," along with encouraging the NATO and coalition contributors to do the same), significantly increase efforts to grow and professionalize the Afghan National Security Forces, improve Afghan governance both in Kabul and at the district and provincial levels, reduce corruption across the board, reduce the opium poppy crop and heroin trafficking, and control the Afghanistan-Pakistan border. All of this would mean a "civilian surge" of diplomats and aid workers. The full-spectrum approach recommended by the Lute review equated to a push for a fully resourced counterinsurgency strategy.

For Pakistan the recommendations included additional efforts to reduce and eliminate the Taliban's safe havens as well as increased economic support.[12] More important perhaps than the details of the recommendations was the very explicit way the review linked Afghanistan and Pakistan. Rather than two distinct bilateral relationships, the review made clear that there was a symbiotic connection, whereby progress on one side of the border was inextricably linked to progress on the other side. Remarkably Afghanistan and Pakistan had not been treated as a single, unified theater since the beginning of Operation Enduring Freedom. The Lute review recommended that henceforth the two efforts be joined at the hip and under the oversight of a single policy coordinator—a change that would not be made until well after the Obama team was in place.

President Bush approved the final version of the report in late November 2008. He, more than any participant in the review, realized that his term was up. Bush decided not to publicly release the report's conclusions or recommendations, thinking that by doing so he might limit the incoming administration's willingness to consider its important recommendations. Unfortunately no detailed briefing of the review's findings to the transition team occurred until a week prior to the inauguration.[13]

During December 2008 the Afghanistan team began working on specific implementation plans for both the short-term and long-term recommendations. A small number of additional combat forces were authorized by the president to deploy to Afghanistan immediately, but the bulk of the surge request was put in abeyance, as the actual deployment decisions could wait for the new president to approve or disapprove. While there were many hints that president-elect Obama would support sustained efforts in the "good war" in Afghanistan and that he was showing an increased interest in Pakistan, the National Security Council staff frankly did not have a good feel for where the new president would take the policy. One good omen, at least perceived as such by the Afghan team, was that the new National Security Advisor, General (retired) Jim Jones, had decided to retain Doug Lute and nearly his entire team. There would be, it was thought, some continuity.

The Obama Administration and Afghanistan

Barack Obama held his first major foreign policy meeting two days after being sworn in, focusing on the situation in Iraq. His second major meeting was on Afghanistan, a day later. Candidate Obama had stated in July 2008 that Afghanistan had "to be our central focus, the central front, on our battle against terrorism." He was about to find out just how difficult the challenge of moving Afghanistan from back burner to central front would be.

President Obama entered office with a pending request for forces from General McKiernan awaiting action. President Bush, in quietly approving the Lute review's recommendations, had been particularly careful not to approve actions that could be held for the incoming president's decision. It wasn't a matter of passing along problems to his successor but rather extraordinary deference to the new president. Bush did not want to take any actions or decisions that could be perceived as an eleventh-hour attempt to box in the new president. A year later President Obama's press secretary, Robert Gibbs, characterized the deference instead as neglect, describing a request from the military commander as having languished "for more than eight months" in the previous administration until action was finally "filled by President Obama in March [2009]."[14] Gibbs, apparently, did not appreciate the latitude President Bush had been attempting to give his successor. Regardless, one of the first major decisions taken by the new president was to approve a sizeable portion of the 30,000 troops requested by McKiernan. By the end of March, Obama had decided he would send 17,000 combat troops and 4,000 additional soldiers as trainers. As for Pakistan, there was no immediate change to the U.S. approach.

As mentioned, the National Security Advisor retained the Bush Afghanistan team. He also recognized that the recommendation to merge Afghanistan and Pakistan was sound. However Jones now found out that changing the structure of the NSC staff was harder than it might seem. Despite agreement that Afghanistan and Pakistan required integrated management, oversight, and policy formulation, the Afghanistan and Pakistan offices remained separate for many months in the new administration. Far more effort was put into the appointment of the Special Representative for Afghanistan and Pakistan (SRAP), the formidable Richard Holbrooke, and the commencement of an Afghanistan-Pakistan Strategy Review, under the leadership of Holbrooke, the new undersecretary of Defense for Policy Michèle Flournoy, and former CIA analyst Bruce Riedel.

In the appointment of Holbrooke (and concurrently, Senator George Mitchell as the special envoy for Middle East Peace), Secretary of State Hillary Clinton stated that the new president "was sending a loud and clear signal that diplomacy is a top priority of your presidency, and that our nation is once again capable of demonstrating global leadership in pursuit of progress and peace."[15] She went on to state that Afghanistan and Middle East peace were "two of the biggest foreign policy challenges of our time." Clinton introduced Holbrooke with the following words:

> I next have the great personal pleasure of introducing the Special Representative for Afghanistan and Pakistan. Ambassador Holbrooke will coordinate across the entire government an effort to achieve United States' strategic goals in the region. This effort will be closely coordinated, not only within the State Department and, of course, with USAID, but also with the Defense Department and under the coordination of the National Security Council. It has become clear that dealing with the situation in Afghanistan requires an integrated strategy that works with both Afghanistan and Pakistan as a whole, as well as engaging NATO and other key friends, allies, and those around the world who are interested in supporting these efforts. It is such a great decision on the part of the Ambassador to respond to the call that the President and I sent out, asking that he, again, enter public service and take on this very challenging assignment. And we are grateful that he has.[16]

Holbrooke was given an extremely wide mandate that he would further expand and manipulate over the next two years. While Clinton's statement made clear that the SRAP would be "under the coordination of the National Security Council," Holbrooke almost immediately began establishing a parallel interagency team within his office in the State Department. Whether intentionally or not, the ever-expanding SRAP office would become the de facto center of gravity for the Afghanistan and Pakistan policy and strategy, wielding as much influence, if not authority, as the NSC staff and the National Security Advisor.

Holbrooke presaged his approach in his very first public remarks at the announcement ceremony. It is instructive to quote them at length here:

> Mr. President, Madame Secretary, Mr. Vice President, you've asked me to deal with Afghanistan and Pakistan, two very distinct countries with extraordinarily different histories, and yet intertwined by geography, ethnicity, and the current drama. This is a very difficult assignment, as we all know. Nobody can say the war in Afghanistan has gone well. And yet, as we speak here today, American men and women and their coalition partners are fighting a very difficult struggle against a ruthless and determined enemy without any scruples at all, an enemy that is willing to behead women who dare to teach in a school to young girls, an enemy that has done some of the most odious things on earth. . . . And across the border, lurks a greater enemy still: the people who committed the atrocities of September 11th, 2001. We know what our long-term objective is. I hope I will be able to fill out the mandate which Secretary Clinton has mentioned: to help coordinate a clearly chaotic foreign assistance program, which must be pulled together; to work closely with General Petraeus, CENTCOM, Admiral Mullen, and the Joint Chiefs of Staff, General McKiernan and the command in Afghanistan, to create a more coherent program. . . . If our resources are mobilized and coordinated and pulled together, we can quadruple, quintuple, multiply by tenfold the effectiveness of our efforts there. . . . In Pakistan the situation is infinitely complex, and I don't think I would advance our goals if I tried to discuss it today. I wish to get out to the region and report back to the Secretary, the Vice President, and the President. But I will say that in putting Afghanistan and Pakistan together under one envoy, we should underscore that we fully respect the fact that Pakistan has its own history, its own traditions, and it is far more than the turbulent, dangerous tribal areas on its western border. And we will respect that as we seek to follow suggestions that have been made by all three of the men and women standing behind me in the last few years on having a more comprehensive policy. So I thank you again for your confidence in me. I look forward to working for you, with you closely, and following a joint effort to do better than we have in the past. Thank you very much.[17]

The remarks were quintessential Holbrooke—a little bit of hyperbole, a little self-deprecation, a tendency to portray the challenge as nearly but not quite insurmountable, hints that if given whatever he asked he could "quadruple, quintuple, multiply by tenfold the effectiveness of" U.S. efforts in the region. And he peppered his short remarks with a few not-so-subtle jabs at the previous administration and the situation that faced the incoming team. It was only Day Three of the Obama administration, and the focus on Afghanistan and Pakistan was just getting started.

"Disrupt, Dismantle, and Defeat": A Strategy Emerges on February 2, 2009

Bruce Riedel, a long-time CIA analyst, former Deputy Assistant Secretary of Defense for Near East and South Asia, and author of a 2008 book on Al-Qaeda and South Asia, accepted an offer from President Obama to conduct an in-depth review of the strategy for Afghanistan and Pakistan.[18] Although the effort would be co-chaired by Michèle Flournoy and Richard Holbrooke, the effort soon became known as the "Riedel Review." Riedel reported to the NSC staff spaces in the Eisenhower Executive Office Building (EEOB) and settled into the office occupied until the change of administration by the senior director for South Asia. Despite the importance of the South Asia portfolio (less Afghanistan, which belonged to Lute), no replacement had yet been appointed by Obama, so the spacious office on the second floor was available.

Riedel arrived with much of the review already in his head—based largely on the book he had published the previous year. With almost no support staff, Riedel began crafting the Afghanistan Pakistan Strategy recommendations. Only a few meetings of the full formal review committee, including Holbrooke and Flournoy, ever occurred. When the committee did assemble, the meetings were held in the same room on the fourth floor of the Eisenhower Executive Office Building where the Lute review had been conducted in such lengthy and excruciating detail. The Riedel meetings were shorter and focused more on general policy questions, such as the primacy of Pakistan over Afghanistan, and the core emphasis on defeating Al-Qaeda. The approach wasn't flawed, but it was significantly different than the highly structured and detailed Lute review. What is interesting, and perhaps not surprising, is that Riedel came to many of the same conclusions as the Bush team.

White Paper of the Interagency Policy Group's Report on U.S. Policy toward Afghanistan and Pakistan

Executing and resourcing an integrated civilian-military counterinsurgency in Afghanistan

Resourcing and prioritizing civilian assistance in Afghanistan

Expanding the ANSF: Army 134k, Police 82k

Engaging the Afghan Government and bolstering its legitimacy

Encouraging Afghan government efforts to integrate reconcilable insurgents

Including provincial and local governments in our capacity building efforts

Breaking the link between narcotics and the insurgency

Mobilizing greater international political support of our objectives in Afghanistan

Bolstering Afghanistan-Pakistan cooperation

Engaging and focusing Islamabad on the common threat

Assisting Pakistan's capability to fight extremists

Increasing and broadening assistance in Pakistan

Exploring other areas of economic cooperation with Pakistan

Strengthening Pakistani government capacity

Asking for assistance from allies for Afghanistan and Pakistan

Released 27 March 2009 by the White House

Riedel concluded that the United States needed to shift strategic focus to Pakistan—a country with a Muslim-majority population of 180 million, an increasingly volatile and destructive insurgency of its own, and a military with an ever-growing number of nuclear weapons. At the same time, progress in Afghanistan was clearly linked to progress in Pakistan, and vice versa. Riedel also recommended that the United States recognize that it needed to deal with each country separately but with the region as one interconnected challenge: "Afg-Pak." Riedel also returned to and reemphasized the 9/11 rationale for entering Afghanistan and reengaging Pakistan—Al-Qaeda. In what would become an Obama mantra, Riedel succinctly stated that the United States must have a central strategic objective to "disrupt, dismantle, and eventually defeat al Qaeda." In order to succeed in Afghanistan, Riedel recommended, a fully resourced civil-military counterinsurgency strategy was needed. On the Pakistan side, he recommended increasing assistance to Pakistan's military in order to improve its counterinsurgency capacity.[19] Despite the rushed mechanics of the review and the limited number of meetings of the full review team, the recommendations were agreed to by the cochairs and most of the senior participants from across "the interagency." Holbrooke was fully on board, the principals—particularly Clinton and Gates—were in general agreement, and in short order so was the president. In fact, with the exception of the troop-level issue, there was little debate. Riedel generated the drafts, they were circulated by the NSC staff among the principals, a very few edits were made, and the recommendations were prepared for the president in an amazingly short period of time, considering the importance of the policy and strategy recommendations

In fact President Obama was up against a short deadline. In early April 2009 he was scheduled to attend his first major international forum, the NATO heads of state meetings in Strasbourg, France, and Kehl, Germany. In typical Washington fashion, the president needed a significant "deliverable"—a signature program, policy, or international agreement worthy of the office of the president. The Riedel review's recommendations provided the president with an opportunity to state a new U.S. policy and make his mark on NATO on a global stage.[20] The timing of the president's speech on March 27, 2009, was as much about ensuring that the president took a leadership stance in advance of the NATO meetings in order to minimize debate as it was about the specifics of the strategy. In a perfect world, Riedel and the review team would have taken more time and debated many of the major issues in more detail.

Several of the key recommendations, such as adopting a fully resourced civil-military counterinsurgency strategy in Afghanistan, remained points of friction in the Obama cabinet, particularly with the vice president. The troop request that was awaiting Obama's action as soon as he took office generated significant debate among the principals. Vice President Joe Biden was staunchly opposed to any significant increase in troop levels and advocated a smaller, counterterrorism-oriented strategy. The troop-level debates were conducted in parallel with the strategy review, as many in the Defense Department and the National Security Staff wanted an early decision in order to begin the necessary notification and mobilization procedures. Others in the cabinet were more cautious and wanted to wait for Riedel's team's recommendations. Ultimately as noted above, the president approved 17,000 additional combat troops and another 4,000 military personnel to serve as trainers and mentors. Despite the president's decision, many felt that the central "CT vs. COIN" debate was not fully resolved during the interagency debates or the decisions by the president.

Additionally none of the major recommendations, with perhaps the exception of increasing the U.S. military forces in Afghanistan as part of "executing and resourcing an integrated civilian-military counterinsurgency" campaign, had included any cost analysis, specifically of available civilian capacity for what Secretary Clinton would call the "civilian surge." In war-college terms, the recommendations may have been suitable and acceptable but perhaps not totally feasible. The recommendations assumed in many cases that necessary civilian personnel (with the appropriate skills, not just people), funding, time, and other resources were readily available.

Nonetheless and notwithstanding the lack of a resource assessment, the president liked the general reformulation of the policy refocus on Al-Qaeda, despite the fact that there were almost no Al-Qaeda members in Afghanistan and that intelligence suggested Bin Laden was in Pakistan (as was later borne out). He also was ready to move forward with what might appear as a shift of the main effort from the Department of Defense to the Department of State by endorsing the civilian surge and the focus on governance, institutional capacity building, and anticorruption efforts. He was willing to move more in the direction of civilian-military counterinsurgency, mainly because it appealed more to the "smart power" approach favored by Secretary Clinton, as opposed to an overarching military tactic.

In order to preempt the NATO meeting, Obama and his speechwriters latched onto the hastily crafted recommendations of the Riedel review, formally known as the Interagency Policy Group. Appearing in the tightly controlled theater on the fourth floor of the EEOB, President Obama delivered his first speech endorsing the new strategy for Afghanistan and Pakistan. Joined on the small stage by his Afg-Pak team—Secretaries Clinton and Gates, National Security Advisor Jones, SRAP Holbrooke, principal author Riedel, and CENTCOM commander Petraeus—Obama described the new way ahead for South Asia. The speech was nearly equally divided between Pakistan and Afghanistan. Although the president never uttered the word, there was an emphasis on counterinsurgency, as well as some aspects of nation building. In fact there was a little bit in the policy for everybody.

Obama attempted to make a clear link between Al-Qaeda and the need to increase efforts in Afghanistan. Early in the speech he stated, without establishing whether Al-Qaeda was present in Afghanistan, that "if the Afghan government falls to the Taliban—or allows al Qaeda to go unchallenged—that country will again be a base for terrorists who want to kill as many of our people as they possibly can."[21] He also made a compelling human-rights argument by highlighting the potential threats to women and girls: "For the Afghan people, a return to Taliban rule would condemn their country to brutal governance, international isolation, a paralyzed economy, and the denial of basic human rights to the Afghan people—especially women and girls. The return in force of al Qaeda terrorists who would accompany the core Taliban leadership would cast Afghanistan under the shadow of perpetual violence."[22] He then went on to outline the five core objectives of the new strategy:

- Disrupting terrorist networks in Afghanistan and especially Pakistan
- Promoting a more capable, accountable, and effective government in Afghanistan
- Developing Afghan security forces
- Enhancing civilian control and stable constitutional government in Pakistan and a vibrant economy that provided opportunity for the people
- Involving the international community to actively assist.

The real thrust of the speech was the focus on Al-Qaeda and the reaffirmation that the defeat of the terrorist network that had so brazenly attacked the United States was the "core goal." Obama stated emphatically that it was the intent of the United States to "disrupt, dismantle, and defeat Al-Qaeda and its safe havens in Pakistan and Afghanistan, and to prevent their return to either country in the future."[23] Calling attention to the safe havens and listing Pakistan first was a deliberate attempt to emphasize that the Al-Qaeda threat emanated principally from that country, not Afghanistan, but that if conditions were not significantly improved in Afghanistan that Al-Qaeda could reestablish

Roles and Missions of Headquarters

Headquarters	Level of Influence	Mission
ISAF	Strategic/ theater campaign (political–strategic– operational)	ISAF, in partnership with the Afghan government, conducts population-centric COIN operations, enables an expanded and effective ANSF, and supports improved governance and development in order to protect the Afghan people and provide a secure environment for sustainable stability.
IJC	Campaign (operational)/ Tactical	The combined team and supporting organizations, in close coordination, will conduct joint operations in key populated areas to disrupt insurgent activities, protect the people against enemy attacks, and maintain the conditions for social, economic, and cultural development.
NTM-A/ CSTC-A	Campaign (operational)/ Tactical	NTM-A/CSTC-A, in coordination with key stakeholders, generates the ANSF, develops capable ministerial systems and institutions, and resources the fielded force to build sustainable capacity and capability in order to enhance the Afghan government's ability to achieve stability and security in Afghanistan.
ISAF SOF & CFSOCC-A★	Campaign (operational)/ Tactical	ISAF SOF protects the population, enables the ANSF, and neutralizes malign influences in order to shape a secure environment for sustainable stability. CFSOCC-A★ plans and synchronizes direct and indirect special operations activities in support of COMISAF★★ COIN strategy by building ANSF capacity in order to protect the population and defeat the insurgency threatening the stability of the Afghan government.

★ Combined Forces Special Operations Component Command–Afghanistan
★★ Commander, ISAF

Report on Progress toward Security and Stability in Afghanistan and United States Plan for Sustaining the Afghanistan National Security Forces (Washington, D.C.: DoD, April 2010), p. 14, available at http://www.defense.gov/pubs/pdfs/Report_Final_SecDef_04_26_10.pdf.

its base of operations there. It was an approach that would likely gain approval in the United States, but Europe and NATO were less certain.

In fact there were mixed expectations in Europe regarding Obama's attendance at the summit and what issues he might push among the allies, particularly regarding Afghanistan. The Europeans generally liked Obama, and he was riding a crest of positive image into Europe and being embraced as the antithesis of George W. Bush. Despite not having near the experience in Europe that many of his predecessors had had, Obama was adopted as one of their own by the Europeans—an enlightened listener who endorsed soft-power approaches to the toughest of international challenges.[24] At the same time, Obama's counterparts were skeptical as he departed the United States and headed for the summit after a stopover in London. The global economy, well on its way to recession, was largely seen as an American problem foisted on Europe. Although he had inherited much of the economic mess from his predecessor, Obama was seen as the bearer of bad economic news, and many of his counterparts were not anxious to hear his prescriptions for fixing the economic woes that were by then attacking both sides of the Atlantic. Ahead of the summit there was much speculation that the allies would also not embrace the Afghanistan strategy Obama had laid out on March 27 in Washington. In fact expectations in the White House were low. There were no expectations that the allies would wholeheartedly embrace the new strategy for Afghanistan, and expectations were particularly low that troop-contributing nations would increase their force levels in the combat zone.[25] The British press in particular was predicting that the allies would resist U.S. pressure to "surge" in Afghanistan. Reports were circulating that the White House was scaling back requests of allies in order to not be disappointed when the Europeans responded.[26]

The result was far better than predicted or anticipated. By the time the summit adjourned, Obama had secured near-unanimous agreement on his strategy for Afghanistan, including pledges for additional military and civilian contributions. The allies had agreed to send an additional 5,000 troops, although most would be in training or mentoring, not combat, roles. Altogether, ten NATO members promised additional troops, training specialists, or finances, in addition to the 21,000 U.S. troops already ordered to deploy by Obama. Many of the additional NATO troops would arrive for short tours to support and protect the 2009 Afghan elections, a mission that gained wide support among the allies, as it was seen as promoting the peaceful spread of democracy rather than as outright combat. The pledges also included about

300 paramilitary troops, mostly from Italy and France, to train the Afghan police—the first time NATO had explicitly committed to a police training role.[27] Overall the summit was considered a resounding success by the Obama administration: pledges of more troops from the allies, more financial commitments, and a general endorsement of the new Afghanistan-Pakistan strategy (though Pakistan never came up at the summit).

But many skeptics remained, on both sides of the Atlantic. For years the Afghanistan strategies had seen revisions, followed by pledges of additional troops and development funds, and there had been several NATO plans. But the numbers of troops, particularly trainers for the ANSF, always lagged, and pledged funds never seemed to arrive in Kabul, the provinces, or the districts. Strategy speeches, pledges, and photo ops make for good public theater but don't win wars or convince enemies to surrender. By the end of April 2009 there were approximately 50,000 U.S. troops in Afghanistan, along with another 32,000 coalition soldiers, all under the command of U.S. General David McKiernan.[28] Perhaps the most significant change—bigger than the announced increases in U.S. and coalition troops, more powerful than the additional pledges of funds, even more impactful than President Obama's March 27 speech—was about to happen. In a completely unexpected move, McKiernan was removed from command and replaced by then-Lieutenant General Stanley McChrystal. The swift dismissal of McKiernan and his replacement by the foremost counterterrorism practitioner in the U.S. military would generate both action and unanticipated controversy.

Building Capacity: The ANSF Challenge

If there was one area, outside the domains of the Defense Department, where significant improvement could have made a real difference in Afghanistan, it was in the building of capacity on the Afghan National Security Forces. Planning for the long-term internal security for Afghanistan had always been difficult. Almost immediately after the fall of the Taliban there were disagreements and competing concerns among the coalition partners, the neighbors, and the Afghans themselves regarding the size, composition, roles, and missions of Afghanistan's own security forces. Despite considerable progress, many of the initial disagreements and concerns persisted (and are likely to remain contentious).

At the original Bonn Conference in December 2001, the Afghan delegation requested international assistance "in helping the new Afghan authorities in the establishment and training of new Afghan security and armed forces."[29] It also requested that the international community consider establishing a military assistance force under the auspices of the United Nations. In the meantime, the international community, particularly the United States, continued to rely upon the warlords and militias to maintain a semblance of order and security. Perhaps there was no other alternative, but most likely a combination of factors stalled the creation of viable Afghan National Security Forces.

The unique nature of the initial Operation Enduring Freedom military campaign, marked by a low-profile, small-footprint CIA and military cooperative campaign joined to and supporting the indigenous warlords, set the stage. A convoluted system of "lead nation" authorities for the various reconstruction, development, disarmament, and reintegration programs further confused the effort. The lack of an established, legitimate central government also added to the slow speed of establishing a standing Afghan army and police force. Lastly, despite the claims of victory and the rout of the Taliban leadership, significant pockets of resistance persisted throughout 2002.

In reviewing the situation in Afghanistan at the end of 2002, CARE International estimated that more than 200,000 armed militia continued to "rule local population through force of arms, control trade routes, and fight with each other for ever greater influence and power, causing scores of civilian deaths and thousands of displacements."[30] By late 2002 the senior U.S. commander on the ground, then General McNeill, was quoted as stating, "Until U.S. military trainers are able to help build a viable national army, warlords who helped the United States topple the Taliban regime last winter will continue to receive American support."[31]

For a variety of reasons, the training, development, and deployment of the ANSF was uneven and disjointed for nearly a decade. It was not for lack of effort by many talented and dedicated military professionals from many nations. It was primarily the result of inadequate focus, attention, and resources.

The Joint Coordination and Monitoring Board (JCMB), an international panel with oversight of the resourcing of reconstruction and development efforts in Afghanistan, did not agree to expansion of the ANA until February 2008, and then only to increase its size from 70,000 to 80,000. The Combined Security Transition Command–Afghanistan, a predominantly U.S. organization spawned from the Office of Military Cooperation and responsible for the training and equipping of the ANA, estimated at the time that the 80,000 troops would be fielded by the end of 2010. However CSTC-A's mission statement contained some potentially diametrically opposed goals. According to the Defense Department in 2008, "the long-term goal for the Afghan National Security Forces (ANSF) is to build and develop a force that is nationally respected; professional; ethnically balanced; democratically accountable; organized, trained, and equipped to meet the security needs of the country; and funded from the GIRoA [Government of the Islamic Republic of Afghanistan] budget."[32] To meet the security needs of Afghanistan with an 80,000-soldier force was a stretch. To do so and have it funded by GIRoA was an impossibility. U.S. funding for the ANA alone in fiscal 2008 stood at $1.711 billion—a figure that the Afghans could not expect to match for decades.

The police situation was even worse. The original target strength for the ANP was 62,000, but the JCMB had increased that target to 82,000 in May 2007. The problem was not the level of authorization but the degree of commitment from the international community to the training effort. In its January 2009 Report to Congress, the Defense Department admitted that the police training effort was woefully underresourced. The candid report spelled it out clearly: "Full PMT [Police Mentor Team] manning requires 2,375 total U.S. personnel. As of November 2008, 886 personnel were assigned—a paltry 37 percent of the critical training requirement. Thirty-one of the total 365 police districts had been trained via the [Focused District Development] program since its inception at the end of 2007."[33]

By September 2008 the JCMB once again increased the target for the ANA, from 80,000 to 134,000 (including a 12,000-person training account). CSTC-A projected the fielding of the 134,000 force by October 2013. The pattern continued over the next three years, as violence and instability increased in Afghanistan. Finally, in the most forward-leaning move in nearly a decade, NATO agreed to establish a consolidated NATO Training Mission–Afghanistan (NTM-A) and place both army and police training under one command. A U.S. three-star general was selected to command NTM-A and concurrently the American-centric CSTC-A. The creation of NTM-A raised the profile of the training and equipping mission, and it established its command structure—on paper at least—as an equal partner to the three-star operational command (ISAF Joint Command, also commanded by an American three-star general). Interestingly but also not surprisingly, the creation of NTM-A also paralleled the command arrangements the United States and NATO had established in Iraq in 2004—a full five years before!

In what could be seen as a sign of desperation, in the spring of 2009 (about five months prior to the stand-up of NTM-A) the commander of ISAF assigned to all U.S. maneuver forces the additional mission of providing police mentors in districts in which the U.S. forces were operating. It was estimated that such concurrent missions would provide the equivalent of approximately 1,278 of the missing mentors.[34]

By 2010 it appeared that the creation of the three-star NTM-A command and an infusion of resources had begun to make progress in fielding both the ANA and ANP. Under the exceptional leadership of Lieutenant General Bill Caldwell, NTM-A stepped up efforts to increase the quality and professionalism of the force as well as accelerate its overall growth in sheer numbers. Programs such as literacy training and "train the trainer" increased Afghan competence, quality, and prestige. But much more still needed to be accomplished to give Afghanistan the Afghan-based security it needed.

C2 Changes at the ISAF Level—2009

The most far-reaching and comprehensive changes to the NATO-ISAF command-and-control arrangements occurred in 2009. The United States had been working behind the scenes since 2007 to consolidate the command arrangements in Afghanistan, and in particular it wanted to dual-hat the four-star commander ISAF as commander, U.S. Forces during General McNeill's tenure in 2007. There had been continued resistance within NATO, particularly by the British, who did not want to abandon the alternating-commander arrangement. Ultimately NATO relented, and McNeill's successor, General David McKiernan, was named commander, U.S. Forces–Afghanistan concurrent with his ISAF duties. A major step toward unity of command had been achieved, although technically the U.S. counterterrorism and detainee operations missions remained outside McKiernan's authority, due to continued NATO objections.

In April 2009 the North Atlantic Council (NAC) approved the creation of NATO Training Mission–Afghanistan after endorsement of the concept by the NATO heads of state at the Strasbourg-Kehl Summit. NTM-A finally consolidated the international training and equipping mission for both the ANA and ANP under a single headquarters. CSTC-A remained essentially a U.S.-centric organization (mainly for funding authority reasons) but was fully subsumed into NTM-A, and the CSTC-A commander was made the NTM-A commander.

Four months later, on August 4, 2009, the NAC approved the recommendation of General McChrystal to create an operational-level three-star command. The ISAF Joint Command, or IJC, was initially formed from a U.S. corps headquarters nucleus, augmented by NATO allied staff, and commanded by U.S. Lieutenant General Dave Rodriguez. The IJC was to implement and coordinate the day-to-day combat operations and coordinate the civil-military aspects of the counterinsurgency campaign and thereby allow the ISAF commander and his staff to focus on long-term strategic issues, relations with the Afghan government, and coalition management.

Perhaps most importantly, the establishment of the two subordinate three-star operational headquarters eliminated one of the glaring C2 issues that had existed for many years. When IJC achieved initial operating capability in October 2009, NTM-A transitioned all of the ANSF mentoring missions, as well as the command and control for all of the ANA and ANP Operational Mentoring and Liaison Teams (OMLTs and POMLTs) to IJC. One headquarters, the IJC, now had complete responsibility for all of the coalition COIN maneuver and adviser missions in the area of operations. CSTC-A would no longer have direct (and sometimes contradictory) command authority over the OMLTs and POMLTs operating in the IJC's battlespace.

Another significant change occurred in mid-2010. On June 14 the ISAF commander split Regional Command–South into two areas and redesignated them as Regional Command–South and Regional Command–Southwest. The split was intended to improve command and control by allowing a regional-level operational commander to focus on Kandahar (RC-South), the cradle of the Taliban, and another to focus on Helmand (RC-Southwest), the breadbasket of Afghanistan and the opium poppy capital of the world. The Marine Expeditionary Brigade that had been operating in Helmand was increased in size and became I Marine Expeditionary Force (Forward). With the increased capabilities of the I MEF (FWD) and the increased focus of RC-South units in the Kandahar area, the ISAF commander's intent was to ultimately clear and then link the important Highway 1 (Ring Road) corridor across all of southern Afghanistan.

With a new, highly skilled commander, new command authorities, and the recommitment of the coalition partners, many looked to the 2011 campaign season as the new hope for Afghanistan.

Ten

Conflict Termination in Afghanistan

O n Monday, May 11, 2009, Secretary of Defense Robert Gates and Chairman of the Joint Chiefs of Staff Admiral Mike Mullen stood at the podium in the Pentagon ready to conduct a press conference. Gates had just returned from a trip to Afghanistan, ostensibly to review the situation on the ground and discuss the implementation of the president's new strategy before the year's "fighting season" got into full swing. Many of the reporters expected an update from the two leaders, as well as some comments about a high-profile incident that had just occurred at Camp Liberty in Iraq. Instead Gates announced that he had taken the extraordinary step of requesting that General David McKiernan, a veteran soldier with thirty-seven years of service, resign his command. Such a resignation would effectively end McKiernan's career.

Gates had reportedly been considering a change of leadership in Afghanistan for many months. Such a change in senior leadership would have been unusual for a number of reasons, not the least of which was that McKiernan had only assumed command in June 2008. In announcing his decision, Gates said:

> As I have said many times before, very few of these problems can be solved by military means alone. And yet, from the military perspective, we can and must do better. We have not been able to fully resource our military effort in Afghanistan in recent years, but I believe, resources or no, that our mission there requires new thinking and new approaches from our military leaders. Today we have a new policy set by our new president. We have a new strategy, a new mission, and a new ambassador.

> I believe that new military leadership also is needed. . . . After consultation with the Chairman of the Joint Chiefs of Staff and the commander of Central Command, and with the approval of the president, I have asked for the resignation of General David McKiernan.[1]

Gates stressed that he had made such a significant decision only after weighing all of the factors and consulting with Mullen and Petraeus. It was clear that Gates had not made the decision capriciously; nor had he been pressed into such a significant change by the White House. "By April 2009, the security situation continued to deteriorate to a point that threatened the existence of the Karzai government. Equally important was the fact that the Taliban's efforts to control the population through influence and intimidation were succeeding. Insurgent attacks were up 57 percent and US personnel killed in action increased by 24 percent from the previous year."[2] Ultimately, after several conversations at senior levels, "McKiernan was viewed as too cautious and conventionally minded."[3] As significant as the relief of McKiernan was, the naming of Lieutenant General Stan McChrystal as McKiernan's successor was to have more significant consequences, both intended and unintended.

Gates had the opportunity to select not just one but two new senior commanders to put in Afghanistan. The NATO command structure of ISAF had been recently modified to insert a three-star operational command to coordinate the combat operations and allow the ISAF commander to concentrate more on strategy, policy, coalition management, and dealings with President Karzai and the other Afghan leaders. McChrystal would be elevated to four stars from his current position as Mullen's director of the Joint Staff. Gates selected his own senior military assistant, Lieutenant General David Rodriguez, to be the operational-level commander for the ISAF Joint Command and concurrently serve as Deputy Commander, U.S. Forces Afghanistan. McChrystal had years of experience with highly classified covert and clandestine special operations and counterterrorism missions both in Iraq and Afghanistan. Rodriguez had two years in Regional Command–East with the 82nd Airborne Division commanding counterinsurgency operations. Rodriguez was most familiar with the operational and tactical challenges of the overt, ISAF war, the status of the ANSF, and dealing with the Afghan leadership. On paper it appeared to be a good match.

Earlier in the year, Karl Eikenberry, himself a former three-star general and former commander of coalition forces in Afghanistan, had been named U.S. ambassador to Kabul. Eikenberry was an interesting choice to be the senior U.S. diplomat in Afghanistan. A career soldier, Eikenberry had no formal diplomatic background. The closest equivalent had been his military service as an assistant army attaché in China, as both the commander of the Office of Military Cooperation (2002–2003) and the senior military coalition commander in Afghanistan from 2005 to 2007, and a short stint as the deputy chairman of the NATO Military Committee. His multiple military tours in Afghanistan had apparently impressed Richard Holbrooke and Secretary Clinton, who were both strong advocates of Eikenberry's nomination for the ambassadorship. Eikenberry was confirmed by the Senate in early April 2009 and sworn in as ambassador by Secretary Clinton before the end of the month. Eikenberry had attended the U.S. Military Academy, graduating in 1973—three years ahead of the two new senior military commanders in Afghanistan, McChrystal and Rodriguez.

Before Barack Obama was president, in fact even before he was the Democratic nominee, he stated that he admired Abraham Lincoln's approach to the presidency. In particular Obama liked the idea of forming a "team of rivals" around the president. In the summer of 2008, Obama told *Time*'s Joe Klein, "I don't want to have people who just agree with me. I want people who are continually pushing me out of my comfort zone."[4] After winning the presidency, Obama was true to his word. He did assemble a "team of rivals," and not just in his cabinet (e.g., Vice President Biden, Secretaries Clinton and Gates, Chief of Staff Rahm Emmanuel). By the summer of 2009 there was a second tier of "rivals" well below the cabinet level: Holbrooke, Petraeus, Eikenberry, and McChrystal. Lincoln's concept, adopted by Obama, was about to be put to the test, at least regarding the way ahead in Afghanistan.

McChrystal Assesses the Situation

When Secretary Gates announced the resignation of General McKiernan, stating that "we can and must do better," a reporter at the press conference asked Gates if he had any thoughts on how. In his reply the Secretary of Defense did not give any specific recommendations. He did say, however, what he expected from the new leadership team. "That's the challenge that we give to the new leadership," Gates said, referring to McChrystal and Rodriguez. "How do we do better? What new ideas do you have? What fresh thinking do you have? Are there different ways of accomplishing our goals? How can we be more effective? The admiral [Mullen] and I aren't the source of those ideas. General Mc-Chrystal and General Rodriguez are. And that's what we expect from them."[5]

General McChrystal arrived in Afghanistan in June 2009 and immediately began his assessment of the strategy. McChrystal set about doing exactly what Secretary Gates said was needed when Gates had pressed McChrystal's predecessor to resign—he applied a fresh set of eyes to the situation in Afghanistan. McChrystal had been given sixty days to conduct a review and report back to the secretary and the president. The sixty-day period served two purposes: buy McChrystal enough time to conduct a thorough assessment and tamp down the Washington rumor mill that McChrystal and Petraeus would immediately ask for a sizeable increase in military forces.[6] Whatever the rationale, a report was expected back in Washington by the end of the summer, including any recommended changes to the strategy announced a little more than two months earlier.

Gates had actually issued a formal directive to McChrystal dated June 26, 2009, instructing him to conduct an "initial assessment." General Petraeus immediately followed suit, issuing an order to Commander, U.S. Forces Afghanistan to complete the review. In a parallel tasking, the Supreme Allied Commander Europe (SACEUR) and NATO secretary general also issued similar directives. McChrystal seemed to have more than sufficient "top cover" to conduct a thorough and wide-ranging "multidisciplinary assessment of the situation in Afghanistan."[7] During the height of the summer fighting season, McChrystal assembled a team of outside academics to augment his small team of staff officers entrusted to conduct a thorough review, and he got busy.

McChrystal sought to answer three fundamental questions: Can ISAF achieve the mission? If so, how should ISAF go about achieving the mission? What is required to achieve the mission? As for the mission, McChrystal described the mission using the definition straight from the ISAF mandate: "ISAF, in support of GIRoA, conducts operations in Afghanistan to reduce the capability and will of the insurgency, support the growth in capacity and capability of the Afghan National Security Forces (ANSF), and facilitate improvements in governance and socio-economic development, in order to provide a secure environment for sustainable stability that is observable to the population."[8] However McChrystal expanded the mission by also stating, "Accomplishing this mission requires *defeating* [emphasis added] the insurgency, which this paper defines as a condition where the insurgency no longer threatens the viability of the state." Defeating the Taliban is a much more robust mission than reducing the capability and will of the insurgency. Defeating the enemy would require both a new strategy and significantly higher levels of resources.

McChrystal had perhaps unintentionally telegraphed his thinking and foreshadowed some of his recommendations when he issued a "Tactical Directive" to ISAF troops shortly after taking command. It was classified but the ISAF public affairs office released excerpts to the public in early July. McChrystal made clear that the "strategic goal is to defeat the insurgency threatening the stability of Afghanistan." He also reiterated that the strategy would be a population-centric approach to counterinsurgency and that the ability to win would be dependent on ISAF's "ability to separate insurgents from the center of gravity—the people." He also sought to address the continuing complaint of President Karzai about excessive civilian casualties by issuing strict guidance on the use of force and close air support. He concluded the directive on a sobering but positive note: "The challenges in Afghanistan are complex and interrelated, and counterinsurgencies are difficult to win. Nevertheless, we will win this war."[9]

When McChrystal delivered the "commander's initial assessment" on August 30 he boldly reported that "success is achievable, but it will not be attained simply by trying harder or 'doubling down' on the previous strategy. . . . The key take away from this assessment is the urgent need for a significant change to our strategy and way that we think and operate."[10] Although the president had never used the word "counterinsurgency" in his speech in March, the National Security Council staff had released the interagency white paper detailing the strategy, including "executing and resourcing an integrated civilian–military counterinsurgency." McChrystal clearly had a more robust definition in mind.

McChrystal's report and recommendations met both support and criticism when delivered to the senior policy makers on August 30. Rumors and low-level leaks were running rampant in Washington, causing considerable speculation as to just how radical McChrystal's recommendations would be. Almost immediately after the report was delivered, senior government officials gave background briefings to the media, but the classified, heavily protected report was not publicly released. In the background briefing, the officials highlighted the key points of McChrystal's assessment: more Afghan National Security Forces were required and needed to be recruited and trained faster; the overarching approach needed to be a full-scale, population-centric counterinsurgency campaign; greater emphasis needed to be placed on building Afghan government capacity and ensuring the government was considered legitimate by the citizenry; and significant changes were required within the ISAF military culture, in particular regarding overly aggressive force-protection measures and excessive risk adversity.[11] But the background briefers did not address whether or not McChrystal included any recommendations for increasing troop levels in Afghanistan. Nor did they point out that McChrystal's report only addressed Afghanistan, as his command and mandate did not include neighboring Pakistan.

The background briefings may have initially satisfied the media, but they did not soften the impact of the report among the administration. Some senior leaders thought McChrystal had been sent to Afghanistan to implement the strategy issued by the president on March 27, not conduct a wholesale reassessment and return with recommendations well beyond the boundaries established by Washington at the end of March. Some saw McChrystal's report as a brazen attempt to reopen the COIN-versus-CT debate in order to influence the resourcing for a much broader population-centric counterinsurgency campaign that moved Afghanistan back to the centerpiece of the overarching strategy. Such a construction of McChrystal's motives was misplaced. As commander of ISAF and U.S. Forces Afghanistan, McChrystal was constrained by his mandate to confine his assessment solely to that country. He was tasked by Secretary Gates, SACEUR, and NATO's secretary general to assess the situation in Afghanistan, and that's what he did. He was necessarily parochial in his analysis and recommendations, but that didn't satisfy many in Washington who thought the issue of the Afghanistan-Pakistan strategy was over and done with once the president made a speech and the heads–of–state–summit endorsed his approach. In early September the interagency began reviewing McChrystal's report. Clear divisions of opinion were forming, challenging McChrystal's recommendations, particularly regarding the need for significantly increasing the resources allocated to a comprehensive counterinsurgency strategy.

The debate broke into full public view on Monday, September 21, when the *Washington Post*'s Bob Woodward published a redacted copy of McChrystal's assessment that had been leaked. (The story had actually broken on Sunday, with the front-page *Washington Post* story following the next day.) Woodward summarized the report, although the redacted version was posted online at Washingtonpost.com. Woodward reported that "the top U.S. and NATO commander in Afghanistan warns in an urgent, confidential assessment of the war that he needs more forces within the year and bluntly states that without them, the eight-year conflict 'will likely result in failure.'"[12] Woodward went on to report McChrystal's opinion that "without more forces and the rapid implementation of a genuine counterinsurgency, defeat is likely." Perhaps most controversial to those in the administration who thought a strategy had already been agreed upon was McChrystal's prediction that "inadequate resources will likely result in failure. However, without a new strategy, the mission should not be resourced."

The leaked report and the *Washington Post's* reporting threw the spotlight squarely back on the Afghanistan-Pakistan strategy. Although the National Security Council had been debating the report since early in the month, the president was uncertain of the report and the impact on his previously declared strategy. On the morning of the same Sunday that the assessment was leaked, and undoubtedly knowing that the release of a redacted copy of the assessment was imminent, Obama said on CNN's "State of the Union" with John King, "But right now, the question is, the first question is, are we doing the right thing? Are we pursuing the right strategy?"[13] Given the president's remarks that Sunday and the breadth of McChrystal's assessment and recommendations, particularly regarding troop increases, it was not surprising that the president directed yet another review of the strategy. It would be the sixth major review in the course of a year.[14]

The 2009 Strategy Review: The Afghanistan Surge

The remainder of the fall of 2009 would be used for the second major Afghanistan strategy review of the year. This time, however, rather than call in Bruce Riedel with an essentially already written report, the president and the NSC staff directed the review. It was methodical, detailed, and not dominated by the prospect of a hard political performance like the NATO heads of state meeting the previous April. The president wanted a soup-to-nuts assessment, and he did not want to constrain the debate by placing limitations on resources prior to determining the course of action. In many regards, the review and debate proceeded along lines quite similar to the 2008 Lute review, which isn't surprising, as the former War Czar and his NSC staff were fully involved in the fall 2009 review.

The remainder of September, October, and November saw the Afghanistan-Pakistan team debating the pros and cons of a fully resourced counterinsurgency strategy versus a counterterrorism-centric strategy, and also a third option—dubbed "counterterrorism plus" by its strongest proponent, the vice president. The issue of troop levels remained undecided throughout this period as well. McChrystal reportedly offered the president and the Pentagon a range of options running from a low of 10,000 (focused almost entirely on training and mentoring the ANSF) to a high in excess of 45,000. No one thought the United States could afford the high end, as it still had sizeable troop levels in Iraq and commitments elsewhere in the world. The president remained wary of adding a significant number of troops, given that he had almost doubled U.S. force levels in Afghanistan already. The longer the debate took, the more skeptical and impatient the Afghans, Pakistanis, and the coalition partners became.

Also through the fall, the Afghan presidential election occurred, providing additional challenges and issues for the administration. The election was seen by many as flawed, manipulated, and illegitimate. Karzai had not attained a clear majority of the votes, and it appeared that a runoff election would be needed to determine whether Karzai or his rival, former foreign minister Abdullah Abdullah, would win. Ultimately Abdullah withdrew, stating that he did not think a second round of elections would be conducted without considerable corruption and voter fraud. Karzai prevailed, but many Afghans and much of the international community were dissatisfied—not necessarily with the Karzai's being declared the victor but with the degree to which the conduct of the election had been tainted. The Afghan election situation was cited by both sides as a rationale for a change in strategy. Those favoring a significantly increased COIN approach argued that population-centric, institutional-, and governmental-capacity-building factors made a fully resourced civilian-military counterinsurgency strategy the only way to help legitimize the Afghan government and bring stability to the country. Those favoring a counterterrorism-centered strategy, or at least counterterrorism-plus, cited the failings of the government as an indication that there was no reliable partner in the Afghan government and that a more narrowly focused strategy aimed at protecting the U.S. homeland and allies was a more prudent course of action. No one, it seemed, was willing to state that both objectives should be attempted simultaneously.

President Obama finally reached a decision at the end of November. The debate and review had been so contentious that he felt compelled to put his decision in writing for the principals so that there would be no equivocation or misunderstanding. He included clear definitions and objectives for both the military and civilian aspects of the strategy. He also made clear what the strategy did not include: it was not fully resourced counterinsurgency or nation building but rather "a narrower approach tied more tightly to the core goal of disrupting, dismantling, and eventually defeating al Qaeda and preventing al Qaeda's return to safe haven in Afghanistan or Pakistan."[15]

Obama's staff scheduled a nationally televised prime-time speech for December 1, 2009, at Eisenhower Auditorium at West Point. Obama stated clearly his main takeaway from McChrystal's report: "The status quo is not sustainable."[16] The president then announced his decision regarding the number of additional troops he would deploy. He had "determined that it is in our vital national interest to send an additional 30,000 U.S. troops to Afghanistan. After 18 months, our troops will begin to come home. These are the resources that we need to seize the initiative, while building the Afghan capacity that can allow for a responsible transition of our forces out of Afghanistan."[17] The president was trying to have it both ways, it seemed. He would support a sizeable, although not maximal, troop increase to support a mission to both beat back the Taliban and build capacity among the Afghans. However he also undercut the strategic influence such a decision might have by limiting the duration of the surge. "After eighteen months, our troops will begin to come home" sounded as though the president had set a date certain for the end of the war. Many listeners were astounded to think that the president had just set July 2011 as the new mark on the wall for the completion of the Afghanistan mission. Others were stunned that he would so clearly define for the insurgents just how long they needed to hold on until the United States, and therefore the coalition, would depart the battlefield. Knowing that the decision to set a time horizon was controversial, Obama offered his rationale:

> Finally, there are those who oppose identifying a time frame for our transition to Afghan responsibility. Indeed, some call for a more dramatic and open-ended escalation of our war effort—one that would commit

us to a nation-building project of up to a decade. I reject this course because it sets goals that are beyond what can be achieved at a reasonable cost, and what we need to achieve to secure our interests. Furthermore, the absence of a time frame for transition would deny us any sense of urgency in working with the Afghan government. It must be clear that Afghans will have to take responsibility for their security, and that America has no interest in fighting an endless war in Afghanistan.

The president laid out the three core elements of his strategy: a military effort to create the conditions for a transition, a civilian surge that reinforces positive actions by the Afghan government, and an effective partnership with Pakistan. Once again, however, he delivered a major policy speech about the strategy in Afghanistan, and never in the more than 4,500 words used to describe the strategy did he ever say the word "counterinsurgency." The new strategy required a military surge, a civilian surge, and an eye on the calendar.

Finishing Combat in Iraq

On February 17, 2010, Secretary of Defense Gates announced that as of September 1, 2010, the name of Operation Iraqi Freedom would be changed to New Dawn.[18] It was both symbolic of the new approach to Iraq operations and a foreshadowing of the significant changes to come in 2011. The American forces in Iraq were giving up the lead role in military operations and placing the onus of the fight squarely in Iraqi hands.

That did not mean that the United States was no longer addressing terrorists, only that the Iraqi government was to be given the credit or blame for future successes and failures. On April 18, 2010, U.S. and Iraqi forces killed Abu Ayyub al-Masri, the leader of Al-Qaeda in Iraq, in a joint American and Iraqi operation near Tikrit.[19] Prime Minister Nouri al-Maliki announced the killings of Abu Omar al-Baghdadi and al-Masri at a news conference in Baghdad and showed reporters photographs of their bloody corpses. General Odierno praised the operation, saying, "The death of these terrorists is potentially the most significant blow to al-Qaeda in Iraq since the beginning of the insurgency. There is still work to do but this is a significant step forward in ridding Iraq of terrorists."[20]

Even with the Iraqis in the lead, the conflict remained deadly. In June Iraq's Central Bank was bombed in an attack that left fifteen people dead and

brought much of downtown Baghdad to a standstill. The attack was claimed
to have been carried out by the Islamic State of Iraq. This attack was followed
by another attack on Iraq's Bank of Trade building, which killed twenty-six
and wounded fifty-two people.[21] In late August 2010 insurgents conducted a
major attack, with at least twelve car bombs simultaneously detonating from
Mosul to Basra, killing at least fifty-one people. These attacks coincided with
the U.S. withdrawal of combat troops, and it may have been a last-ditch effort
on the part of the insurgents to compel the Americans to stay and fight.[22] But
even such attacks did not delay the departure of American combat units from
Iraq. The last U.S. combat brigades departed Iraq in the early morning of August
19, 2010. Some 50,000 personnel remained in the country to provide support
for the Iraqi military.[23] These troops were required to leave Iraq by 31 December 2011 under an agreement between the U.S. and Iraqi governments.[24]
State Department spokesman P. J. Crowley stated, "We are ending the war . . .
but we are not ending our work in Iraq. We have a long-term commitment
to Iraq."[25]

On August 31, 2010, Obama announced from the Oval Office the official
end of Operation Iraqi Freedom. In his address he covered his plans for ending
operations in Afghanistan, the use of soft power by the United States, the effect
the war had had on the United States economy, and the legacy of America's
ongoing wars in Iraq and Afghanistan. He said,

> The United States has paid a huge price to put the future of Iraq in
> the hands of its people. We have sent our young men and women to
> make enormous sacrifices in Iraq, and spent vast resources abroad at a
> time of tight budgets at home. We have persevered because of a belief
> we share with the Iraqi people—a belief that out of the ashes of war,
> a new beginning could be born in this cradle of civilization. Through
> this remarkable chapter in the history of the United States and Iraq, we
> have met our responsibility. Now, it is time to turn the page.[26]

On the same day in Iraq, at a ceremony at Saddam Hussein's former Al
Faw Palace in Baghdad, General Odierno stated that the new era "in no way
signals the end of our commitment to the people of Iraq." Speaking in Ramadi
earlier in the day, Secretary Gates had said that U.S. forces "have accomplished
something really quite extraordinary here, [but] how it all weighs in the bal-

ance over time I think remains to be seen." When asked by reporters if the seven-year war had been worth fighting, Gates commented, "It really requires a historian's perspective in terms of what happens here in the long run." He noted the Iraq war "will always be clouded by how it began," referring to Saddam Hussein's supposed possession of weapons of mass destruction. "This is one of the reasons that this war remains so controversial at home."[27] Saying the war was over did not end the tragedy, however; seven days later, two U.S. troops were killed and nine wounded in an incident at an Iraqi military base.[28] The key to continued progress in Iraq was facilitating the development of Iraqi security forces to the point at which they could become self-reliant. Part of that effort was significant American arms sales to the Iraqi military.

On September 1, 2010, as promised, the United States formally shifted to a supporting role in Iraq. In a unanimous vote on Wednesday, December 15, 2010, the United Nations Security Council lifted restrictions imposed in 1990 after the invasion of Kuwait, because "the situation is dramatically different today than when the measures were taken." The council noted that Iraq now was a partner to international treaties and conventions on nuclear non-proliferation and chemical and biological weapons and had the confidence of the International Atomic Energy Agency. The Security Council also voted to return control of Iraq's oil and natural gas revenues to the Iraqi government and its people as of June 30, 2011, and to end all remaining activities under the Oil-for-Food program.[29] Iraq was left to determine its own future with the United States and the world.

On December 16, after a meeting between Prime Minister al-Maliki and President Obama in the Oval Office, the United States folded its flag in Baghdad and announced the official end of the war—eight years, eight months, and twenty-six days after it began.[30] The United States was no longer at war in Iraq; it was no longer the dominant partner in the effort to defeat the insurgency. Iraq was not fully at peace, but it was fully and democratically responsible for its own people and their security. The war to remove Saddam Hussein ended when the Iraqi government that succeeded him was able to execute the responsibilities of a responsible nation-state. It was not a glorious event and could not even be precisely identified in time—American forces would remain in Iraq to advise and assist their Iraqi counterparts for months to come—but the opposition between the two nations was clearly at an end. Conflict between Iraq and the United States had been a long war that spanned the gulf between the end of the Cold War and the beginning of a new, more globalized, and more networked century. Just as it had been conducted in a very different way from what most Americans had envisioned, the war ended through a process that few Americans fully understood, but it ended with all of the major objectives achieved and with a very different, and much improved, future possible for the people of Iraq.

2011—Finally an End Game in Iraq

On January 15, 2011, three U.S. soldiers were killed in Iraq. One of the troops was killed on a military operation in central Iraq, but the other two were deliberately shot by one or two Iraqi soldiers during a training exercise.[31] On June 6 five U.S. troops were killed in an apparent rocket attack on Camp Victory, located near Baghdad International Airport.[32] On June 29 three U.S. soldiers were killed in a rocket attack on a base located near the border with Iran. With the three deaths, June 2011 became the bloodiest month in Iraq for the U.S. military since June 2009, with fifteen U.S. soldiers killed, only one of them outside combat.[33]

With the collapse of the negotiations over an extension of the SOFA agreement granting immunity from Iraqi prosecution for Americans beyond 2011, on October 21, President Obama announced at a White House press conference that all remaining U.S. troops and trainers would leave Iraq by the end of the year as previously scheduled, bringing the mission in Iraq to an end that year.[34] The final convoy of American soldiers left Iraq on December 18, 2011. As scheduled, all American forces returned to the United States by Christmas, ten long years after the attacks in New York City and Washington, D.C.

The war had been horribly costly. The casualty figures confirmed 4,485 American deaths and 31,921 military personnel wounded by hostile fire as of December 2011. Deaths of civilian employees of U.S. government contractors were estimated to have exceeded 2,000. Iraqi deaths from war-related violence, according to Iraq Body Count, were at least 103,775—some estimates of Iraqi casualties raised that figure to over 150,000. The financial cost of the war to the United States was estimated to be more than $805 billion. Against such huge costs, the benefits of bringing down Saddam Hussein were rather meager. In Iraq, oil production had fallen from 2.58 million barrels per day before the war to 2.37 million in the summer of 2011; electricity had increased from a prewar nationwide average of 3,958 megawatts per day to 6,990 in the same period; available water supplies rose from 12.9 million people having access to potable water in 2003 to approximately 24 million by 2011. Still, in prewar Iraq, 6.2 million Iraqis had been served by adequate sewerage, whereas by 2011 approximately 20 million people had it. But these advances had to be balanced against the cost of approximately 1.3 million internal refugees displaced inside Iraq and some 1 million Iraqis living abroad, mainly in Syria and Jordan, because they had been forced from their homes by the fighting.[35]

The United States left an Iraq that was still reeling from internal problems. Additionally the Iraqi government in 2011 was both decidedly more friendly with the Iranian government than the Americans had hoped and far less cordial with the Saudis and Kuwaitis. America was safer without Saddam's threats, but by 2011 the global security situation had changed significantly. Democracy was clearly a powerful influence in the greater Middle East, and changes seemed to be under way in Libya, Egypt, Yemen, and Syria. But Iran was still working to develop nuclear weapons and remained a vocal source of international concern.

Whither the Taliban? Executing the Surge while Waiting for the Drawdown

After the December 2009 speech by President Obama, the main effort in Afghanistan had shifted to devising ways and identifying means to implement the plan for withdrawal. As 2010 began McChrystal had clear instructions, the Pentagon was moving forward on deploying 30,000 additional forces to the theater, and the State Department was attempting to surge civilians into Afghanistan. It looked as though the United States and NATO finally had a clear way forward. All that was needed now was some time to implement the plan. There were still eighteen months before the July 2011 deadline. Despite the appearance of an accepted strategy, however, the team of rivals was apparently not quite ready to agree on the playbook.

In late January 2010 the *New York Times* ran a front-page story by Eric Schmitt entitled, "U.S. Envoy's Cables Show Worries on Afghan Plans." Eikenberry had sent the cables in November, at the height of the strategy debate in the National Security Council. In them he had challenged the assumption that President Karzai and the Afghan government were or could be adequate partners of the United States. Eikenberry also challenged the viability of the military surge. In short, the senior U.S. diplomat in Afghanistan did not think Washington could succeed with a strategy that called for strong partnering with the Karzai government and argued that the United States could not financially afford the military surge and a fully resourced counterinsurgency campaign.

The leak of the classified cables and their publication completely undermined Eikenberry's effectiveness as ambassador. It also made it nearly impossible for him to be seen as the full and complete diplomatic partner of McChrystal. Eikenberry was almost diametrically opposed to everything McChrystal had recommended. There clearly was not, and now could not be, any relationship between them similar to the vaunted "Crocker-Petraeus" team credited with turning around Iraq. Despite the resultant freezing of relations between Eikenberry and Karzai and the potential rift with McChrystal, Eikenberry, almost unbelievably, neither resigned nor was recalled by the president. He stayed in place in Kabul until a normal two-year diplomatic tour was complete, not leaving until July 25, 2011, when he was succeeded by Ryan Crocker.

Even Richard Holbrooke, who when initially introduced as the special representative had said he could "multiply by tenfold the effectiveness of our efforts," had significant reservations about the military surge, preferring to pursue a diplomatic track for reconciliation coupled with an increased focus on Afghan governance and infrastructure.[36]

2010 Combat Operations in Afghanistan—Operation Moshtarak

Beginning in the fall of 2009 ISAF soldiers from Princess Patricia's Canadian Light Infantry began training about four hundred Afghan National Army recruits. In January 2010 coalition forces launched several "shaping" operations to prepare a large assault, Operation Moshtarak, on the key town of Marjah anticipated in mid-February 2010. Those shaping operations included special-operations raids designed to capture or kill known Taliban leaders in the area and target weapons caches. The Afghan public was warned of the upcoming operation; General McChrystal and British major general Nick Carter, the commander of ISAF Regional Command–South, hoped thereby to reduce collateral casualties among the Afghan population. This was a new doctrinal approach in Afghanistan and a reflection of lessons learned in the more heavily populated areas of Iraq.[37]

For the first time in the campaign, Afghan troops constituted about 60 percent of the total force involved and were given a leading role in the operation. When the ISAF coalition units were included, the total number of troops assigned to attack Marjah reached 15,000, including 3,500 U.S. Marines, 2,000 British soldiers, and forces from Denmark, Estonia, and Canada.[38] Moshtarak was described as the largest operation conducted in Afghanistan since the fall of the Taliban in 2001.

Marjah had been controlled for two years by the Taliban and drug traffickers.[39] It was the last remaining major Taliban stronghold in southern Helmand and was considered both a center for assembling roadside bombs and a key supply center for opium poppies—a lucrative revenue source for Taliban.[40] The Afghan government announced its intention to reopen schools, restore civil liberties, and enforce a ban on poppy cultivation, something it had failed to do in other areas of the country. The operation was the first in Helmand since the surge of 30,000 U.S. troops and of British reinforcements in late 2009 and early 2010. More importantly Moshtarak was a significant attempt to export to Afghanistan techniques and doctrines used successfully in Iraq. "The slogan of the new U.S. strategy is 'Clear, Hold, Build,' and it has the declared intention of not withdrawing after expelling or killing the Taliban, but of winning the support of local people by protecting them and providing services such as roads, clean water and electricity."[41]

In many ways the operation was patterned after the 2004 American attack on Fallujah. As had happened in the Fallujah operation, hundreds of civilian families fled Marjah ahead of the abundantly publicized military operation. On February 12 President Karzai gave his personal approval for the operation, after Afghan officials conducted last-minute negotiations with insurgents. Then on February 13, Chinook and Cobra helicopters inserted a force of British, Afghan, and French troops into the city. The advance was slowed by home-made explosives and other land mines in poppy fields.[42] By nightfall, it was claimed by ISAF sources that Marines "appeared to be in control" of the center of Marjah.[43] On February 18 Afghan soldiers raised their national flag over the badly damaged bazaar in Marjah, which had been the target of ISAF and Afghan army attacks, after succeeding in their third attempt to drive back Taliban snipers. Despite that initial success, however, General McChrystal some ninety days after the offensive began called the offensive in Marjah a "bleeding ulcer."[44]

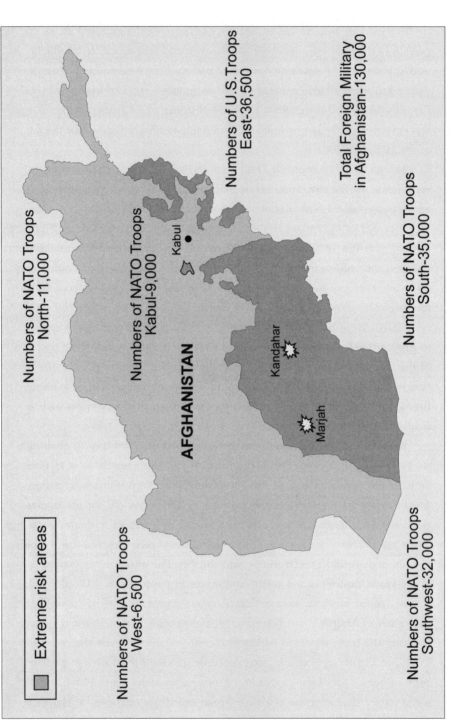

Numbers of NATO Troops
North-11,000

Numbers of U.S. Troops
East-36,500

Total Foreign Military
in Afghanistan-130,000

Numbers of NATO Troops
Kabul-9,000

Kabul

Numbers of NATO Troops
South-35,000

AFGHANISTAN

Kandahar

Marjah

Extreme risk areas

Numbers of NATO Troops
West-6,500

Numbers of NATO Troops
Southwest-32,000

The 2010 Surge Battles

First of all, like most military operations of its size, Moshtarak suffered from imponderables that plagued its execution. Most unfortunately twelve civilians, ten of them from the same family, were killed when civilian houses in Marjah were struck by two rockets fired by a NATO High Mobility Artillery Rocket System (HIMARS). All use of the rocket system was quickly stopped by commanders, and General McChrystal telephoned Karzai to apologize for what he called an "unfortunate incident." Later McChrystal called for an investigation.[45]

After twelve days of heavy fighting, on February 25 the Afghan flag was raised on a building at the Marjah bazaar by Mohammad Gulab Mangal, governor of Helmand Province, and witnessed by Brigadier General Larry Nicholson, the commander of the U.S. Marines in southern Afghanistan. The ceremony, with security provided by Marine snipers on the roofs of buildings, was attended by only several hundred of the city's inhabitants. By mid-March the conflict in Marjah had left thirty-five civilians dead, thirty-seven injured, and fifty-five houses destroyed—without specification as to which side had killed how many civilians. Except for some small pockets of resistance, the Taliban had been driven out of the town, but many inhabitants were still struggling to return to some kind of normality. The promised rapid aid had yet to materialize in any meaningful way.[46]

According to American and Afghan commanders, the number of insurgents in the area dropped by about half after the assault. About a quarter of the four hundred Taliban fighters estimated to have been in Marjah at the beginning of the operation were killed; another quarter, including some of the commanders, apparently fled Afghanistan or retreated to other provinces. In Marjah itself some combat continued through the remainder of the fighting season.[47] Unfortunately by June 2010, four months after the start of the operation, security was still lacking for local people who were cooperating with ISAF troops, and there were numerous gun battles. The former Taliban stronghold had been intended as "a showpiece of what a judicious combination of Western military might and a ramping up of Afghan government services could accomplish. Instead, it has become something of a cautionary tale."[48] Insurgents continued to undermine the daily lives of the local population through intimidation. The fighting at Marjah has been viewed as the "high water mark" of the McChrystal COIN policy.[49]

Civil-Military Relations in the United States

By June, General McChrystal was in hot water, and not because of the Marjah campaign, which was proceeding more or less as he had planned, including the increases in violence and casualties. It was once again a media report that broke up the team. In a *Rolling Stone* article, McChrystal and his staff were portrayed as dismissive of and disrespectful to senior Washington leaders, in particular Vice President Biden. In a swift move President Obama relieved McChrystal on June 23 and immediately asked General David Petraeus to be his replacement. Petraeus, with his counterinsurgency success in Iraq still fresh in everyone's mind, quickly agreed. It was clear that even with a presidential decision, a publicly agreed strategy, and a prime-time policy speech, the success of a strategy is dependent upon the personalities responsible for its execution. The team of rivals was perhaps not much of a team after all.

One pair that did seem to be in synch was that of Secretary Clinton and Secretary Gates. They publicly appeared to be in agreement on the need for an integrated civilian-military counterinsurgency campaign in Afghanistan tied to a diplomatic and military commitment to Pakistan. It was the steadfast agreement in principle between these two key cabinet figures that held the strategy together throughout 2010 and laid the foundation for that year's NATO summit at Lisbon.

Operation Moshtarak was well understood to be a test of the population-centric COIN approach's viability in Afghanistan; unfortunately it did not prove as successful as anticipated. Instead the operation only showed how different Afghanistan was from Iraq and that the solutions needed there would have to reflect the reality in the country and not just be cookie-cutter approaches transposed from Iraq. The operation having been well publicized, many people, including in Afghanistan, were well aware of its poor results. It did not develop into the hold and build stages as hoped, largely because the ANA and ANP were not sufficiently professional to develop longer-term security in the district.

The final major operation in 2010 was a combined U.S. and Afghan military offensive, called Operation Hamkari, focusing on the province of Kandahar. The Kandahar offensive was originally planned for the summer but was launched only after the Muslim holy month of Ramadan ended in September. It included a series of tactical operations in and around the city of Kandahar and also its surrounding districts, including the towns of Malajat, Zhari, Arghandab, and the Horn of Panjwayi. Hamkari was a key test of the Afghan National Security Forces' ability to fight. In the event it was credited with putting severe pressure on insurgent operations and increasing security in some key areas, such as Panjwayi, but unlike previous operations, Hamkari did not result in any significant gains. It may in fact have been so difficult and costly that it discouraged further such operations.[50]

Thus 2010 closed out with little more to show at the operational level. For General Petraeus, who had replaced McChrystal in the midst of Operation Moshtarak's most important phase, the summer offensive only reconfirmed the need to find a better solution for Afghanistan. In fact McChrystal inherited a very bad situation that resulted from many years of misdiagnoses and inappropriate remedies. Accordingly his initial assessment was bleak. . . . McChrystal presented the president with a momentous policy decision that called for an extensive American commitment to include a permanent surge of as many as 40,000 additional troops. The goal seemed to be building a reasonably modern Afghan state where one never existed."[51] State building in Afghanistan was indeed the key question, and it would continue to plague the coalition to the end.

Petraeus that summer still had great expectations for population-centric COIN; he wrote in July, "We must never forget that the center of gravity in this struggle is the Afghan people; it is they who will ultimately determine the future of Afghanistan." But by the fall he was less optimistic. Operation Hamkari did not produce the results he had hoped for and exacerbated problems with President Karzai. By the end of 2010 Petraeus may have "abandoned the notion that he will ever win over the population in those Taliban strongholds."[52] This may have been a turning point in the war. Karzai and Obama may have adopted the same pessimistic view of a COIN solution in Afghanistan in the last months of 2010.

When the allies met in November, President Karzai convinced Obama and the senior U.S. leadership that December 2014 was a more reasonable, and politically attractive, date than July 2011 for transition to an Afghan lead in security. This was not a subtle change; it was a dramatic shift in the terms of a deadline. Obama could state that he would begin the drawdown of the 33,000 surge forces in July 2011, but now full transition to Afghan security lead would continue through the end of 2014. This change bought the ISAF military leadership at least two more fighting seasons, additional time to grow the ANSF to more than 350,000 soldiers and police, and the diplomatic side more time to craft a political settlement, or at least some early steps toward reconciliation.

The NATO Lisbon summit gave maneuver room to Obama and validated Karzai's recommendation of 2014 as the transition target date. The summit declaration stated that the "ISAF mission in Afghanistan remains the Alliance's key priority. . . . We reaffirm our long-term commitment to Afghanistan. . . . The process of transition to full Afghan security responsibility and leadership in some provinces and districts is on track to begin in early 2011, following a joint Afghan and NATO/ISAF assessment and decision. Transition will be conditions-based, not calendar-driven, and will not equate to withdrawal of ISAF-troops. Looking to the end of 2014, Afghan forces will be assuming full responsibility for security across the whole of Afghanistan."[53]

The twelve months following Obama's West Point speech should have been marked by a clear strategy, a focus on generating and delivering the military and civilian surge forces, and progress on the diplomatic front for a political settlement and on reconciliation. Instead it had been another year of fits and starts, of bold statements, sensational media leaks, and another NATO summit. In mid-December the Obama team would suffer perhaps its greatest loss: Special Representative Richard Holbrooke, the larger-than-life diplomat at the very center of the integrated civilian-military counterinsurgency strategy and the most ardent proponent of reconciliation, died suddenly of a torn aorta.

Holbrooke's importance to the efforts in Afghanistan and Pakistan cannot be overstated. He was the driving force for a regional approach, the main proponent of increased infrastructure and development projects in both Afghanistan and Pakistan, and he had been pressing hard, both publicly and clandestinely, for reconciliation with the Taliban. He was outspoken, often in disagreement with some aspects of the policies he was tasked to execute. Even those who did not agree with his positions had, sometimes begrudgingly, to admire his tenacity and audacity. His previous successes, particularly the Dayton Accords that had brought a degree of peace to Bosnia, led many to hope that he could broker a similar conclusion in Afghanistan. His untimely death left a significant void on the civilian side of the civilian-military counterinsurgency strategy.

It took the Obama administration several months to find a replacement. In February 2011, Secretary Clinton spoke at the Asia Society's inaugural Richard C. Holbrooke Memorial Address in New York City. Although the naming of retired Ambassador Marc Grossman as special representative was an important element of Clinton's speech, she went on to emphasize and reiterate the major components of the Obama administration's Afghanistan-Pakistan strategy.

Clinton reaffirmed in strong terms that the core goal of the United States remained to disrupt, dismantle, and defeat Al-Qaeda. Clinton's speech was a nuanced twist on the pillars of the strategy, however; it publicly acknowledged for perhaps the first time that a negotiated settlement was a main objective of the administration. The secretary laid out not two surges but three: a military surge (the 33,000 troops approved by Obama more than a year earlier), a civilian surge, and an "intensified diplomatic push," which she described as efforts to pursue reconciliation and political accommodation.[54] Clinton intimated that the Taliban should come to the negotiating table: "Today, the escalating pressure of our military campaign is sharpening a similar decision for the Taliban: Break ties with al-Qaida, renounce violence, and abide by the Afghan constitution, and you can rejoin Afghan society; refuse and you will continue to face the consequences of being tied to al Qaeda as an enemy of the international community. They [Taliban] cannot wait us out. They cannot defeat us. And they cannot escape this choice."[55] The speech did not attract significant international coverage, but among the policy community in Washington it was read closely. Most recognized the shift of emphasis toward negotiating a political settlement and reconciliation.

By March 2011 both the military and civilian surges were in place. U.S. forces stood at 100,000, along with 42,000 coalition forces and 280,000 ANSF. There were also approximately 90,000 private defense contractors operating in the country. There had indeed also been a civilian surge in Afghanistan; the total number of civilians stood at 1,150 (compared to 360 in March 2009), although the bulk of the civilians were located at the U.S. embassy in Kabul.[56]

2011 or 2007, Part II?

Interestingly throughout 2010 and into 2011 General Petraeus continued to build upon the counterinsurgency strategy that General McChrystal had put in place. Although some violence indicators continued to go up, initially there was guarded optimism that "fragile and reversible" gains were being made. That Petraeus built upon McChrystal's COIN approach is not surprising. Both were staunch advocates of a population-centric approach to counterinsurgency. Both had advocated strong kinetic combat operations against insurgents coupled with Special Operations Forces targeting high-value insurgent and terrorist leaders. But beyond this, the similarity between the overall strategy the Afghan strategy in 2011 and that in Iraq in 2007, and between Petraeus's personal approaches to the two theaters, is striking.

On his first day in command in Iraq in February 2007 Petraeus had issued a letter to the troops declaring, "We serve in Iraq at a critical time."[57] The letter went on to state that "the enemies of Iraq will shrink at no act, however barbaric. They will do all that they can to shake the confidence of the people and to convince the world that this effort is doomed. . . . Together with our Iraqi partners, we must defeat those who oppose a new Iraq." He wrote that he appreciated the sacrifices of the troops and their families and concluded by saying that it was an honor to serve with MNF-I.

On his first day in command in Afghanistan, Petraeus issued an almost identical letter to the troops of ISAF: "we serve in Afghanistan at a critical time."[58] ISAF was fighting "an enemy willing to carry out the most barbaric of attacks," and "our enemies will do all that they can to shake our confidence and the confidence of the Afghan people." It was imperative to "secure and serve the people of Afghanistan," and to do so ISAF would "carry out a comprehensive civil-military counterinsurgency campaign." The effort "nonetheless does require killing, capturing, or turning the insurgents." He concluded again with an expression of appreciation for the sacrifices of the troops and their families. The two letters' similarities were no mere coincidences. Petraeus had resolved to do in Afghanistan what he had done in Iraq.

For a commander to issue such a letter is not remarkable in itself. But what perhaps is remarkable is how similar the strategy in place in Afghanistan in 2011 was to that adopted for Iraq in early 2007. The specific mode of implementation was unique to Afghanistan, and the roles of the coalition, NATO, and the Afghans were significantly different, but the overall strategies, after more than half a dozen assessments and "strategic reviews" between 2008 and 2011, were quite similar (see the figure).

One has to ask, if the strategies were essentially the same, why has progress been so uneven in Afghanistan? The answer, probably, mostly involves resourcing. If the same level of resources could have been applied in both theaters simultaneously, could similar progress have been made in both theaters? It is, of course, a moot point, but one worth considering as the United States looks across the uncertainties of the Arab Spring, North Korea, and the challenges posed by Iran and Syria.

National Goals in Iraq and Afghanistan

Goals for Iraq 2007

1. Let the Iraqis lead
2. Help Iraqis protect the population
3. Isolate extremists
4. Create space for political progress
5. Diversify political and economic efforts
6. Situate the strategy in a regional approach.

Goals for Afghanistan 2011

1. Transition to Afghan lead
2. Help the ANSF protect the population
3. Separate the Taliban from the people, break links to Al-Qaeda
4. Pursue reconciliation (through the "diplomatic surge")
5. Build infrastructure, economic capacity, and governance
6. Pursue a multilateral, regional solution.

Combat in Afghanistan during the Tenth Year of the War

> We've got our teeth in the enemy's jugular now, and we're not
> going to let go.
>
> —General David Petraeus[59]

In the year 2011 many Americans expected to see operational improvements in the Afghan campaign. McChrystal had apparently hardened the coalition and focused operations in the most important areas, while also improving the synchronization of conventional and special forces. Petraeus was expected to make even more improvements, bringing his magic COIN touch from Iraq to Afghanistan. He acknowledged that expectation in an article published in October 2010 in *Army* magazine: "We have begun to see some encouraging progress, however, amid the tough fighting. From just early April through early August, more than 375 middle- and upper-level Taliban and other extremist element leaders were killed or captured, and some 1,500 of their rank-and-file were taken off the battlefield. . . . Amplified commitment and urgency now characterize our effort to implement the comprehensive civil military counterinsurgency campaign."[60] Unfortunately aside from a single great victory over Al-Qaeda, such hopes never materialized in 2011.

Operation Neptune Spear

Intelligence analysts identified a possible hiding spot of Osama bin Laden, a house in Pakistan. President Obama, CIA director Panetta, and the American national security team put forth a concerted, highly classified and highly compartmentalized effort (that is, restricted access) to determine if bin Laden was at the site and to develop options for ending his leadership of Al-Qaeda.

Shortly after 1 a.m. on Monday, May 2, 2011, an American SEAL team of the Joint Special Operations Command (JSOC) carried out a Central Intelligence Agency operation code-named Neptune Spear to kill Osama bin Laden in Abbottabad, Pakistan.[61] The attack, ordered and closely monitored by President Obama, was supported by CIA operatives on the ground.[62] The raid on bin Laden's compound was launched from Afghanistan in a very risky manner designed not to alert the Pakistanis for fear they would reveal the raid to bin Laden. After the raid the SEALs took bin Laden's body to Afghanistan for positive identification, and then to an aircraft carrier, where it was buried at sea.

Although it did little to affect the actual conduct of combat operations in Afghanistan, the death of bin Laden extinguished the hated symbol of the campaign for many around the globe. It showed that the United States could persevere in its national strategic objectives and clearly announced that the Obama administration would conduct operations wherever necessary to combat terrorism. The raid was a superb tactical success; whatever its effect on the ground in Afghanistan, it had a telling one on support for the war within the United States—Americans were thrilled and proud at the death of the Al-Qaeda leader. But they soon began to question the need for continued operations in Afghanistan if the leadership of Al-Qaeda could no longer support a resurgent Taliban. The raid also so angered the Pakistanis that they reduced their support for crucial ISAF logistics convoys moving through their territory.

Taliban Operations

The enemy did not wait for Petraeus to initiate his 2011 COIN plan. The first battle of 2011 was again in Kandahar, but it was an attack by Taliban forces throughout the heartland of Helmand Province. Early in the morning of May 7, forty to sixty militants attacked the provincial governor's office from nearby buildings, using rocket-propelled grenades, guns, and other weapons.[63] The battle, which was the kickoff of the normal Taliban spring offensive in 2011,

The Afghan Border Region with Pakistan

began less than a week after American forces killed Osama bin Laden in Pakistan; it was clearly designed to show that the Taliban had not been beaten. The Taliban suffered some forty total deaths and over fifty wounded but demonstrated that despite heavy losses since 2001, it remained a threat to coalition and Afghan forces. The battles also showed that Taliban morale had not been decisively affected by the death of bin Laden and that the Taliban was far from "on the ropes."

July 2011—End of the Beginning or Beginning of the End?

On June 22 President Obama walked to the podium in the East Room of the White House to give a much-anticipated speech announcing his decision on the drawdown plans for Afghanistan. He reiterated once again the central focus on Al-Qaeda, but this time he could do so with the confidence gained from the killing of bin Laden the previous month. He recounted that he had "ordered an additional 30,000 American troops into Afghanistan. When I announced this surge at West Point, we set clear objectives: to refocus on Al-Qaeda, to reverse the Taliban's momentum, and to train Afghan security forces to defend their own country."[64] He now announced what everyone was waiting to hear: "We will be able to remove 10,000 of our troops from Afghanistan by the end of this year, and we will bring home a total of 33,000 troops by next summer, fully recovering the surge." He made clear that the United States and allies would be transitioning to a support role and that "by 2014, this process of transition will be complete, and the Afghan people will be responsible for their own security."

There could be no doubt that the United States was on the road to withdrawing from Afghanistan. Despite assurance that the pace and slope of the withdrawal would be determined by conditions on the ground, it was also clear that the 2014 date was firm. Obama also made clear that the United States was putting additional emphasis on reconciliation and a political settlement, just as Secretary Clinton had back in February. But Obama also stated what was becoming increasingly obvious—that the national and global economic situation was making it increasingly difficult for the United States to continue to pursue the strategy it had adopted in Afghanistan and Pakistan. Obama ended his remarks with a message clearly aimed at the domestic U.S. audience: "Above all, we are a nation whose strength abroad has been anchored in opportunity for our citizens here at home. Over the last decade, we have spent a trillion dollars on war, at a time of rising debt and hard economic times. Now, we must invest in America's greatest resource—our people. We must unleash innovation that creates new jobs and industries, while living within our means. . . . America, it is time to focus on nation building here at home."

The president had made clear that the goal was to withdraw the entire surge by the end of 2012, and to shift the entire combat operation to the Afghans by 2014. Once again he had given a major policy speech on the strategy for Afghanistan. Once again in it he never used the word "counterinsurgency." Many were now wondering, the nation having killed the mastermind of the 9/11 attacks on the U.S. homeland, whether the president's "overarching goal" had shifted from "disrupt, dismantle, and defeat al Qaeda in Afghanistan and Pakistan, and to prevent its capacity to threaten America and our allies in the future" to one of "get out of Afghanistan by 2014."

On July 18, 2011, General John R. Allen, USMC, assumed command of both the International Security Assistance Force and U.S. Forces Afghanistan (USFOR-A) from General Petraeus, who returned to the United States to become the director of the CIA. Allen had been Petraeus's deputy and temporary successor at CENTCOM; the two men knew and respected each other. Also easing the transition was the fact that General Allen had previously served in Iraq from 2006 to 2008, as commanding general, 2nd Marine Expeditionary Brigade and had been a key figure in the Anbar Awakening. Petraeus had not accomplished much in his year in command in Afghanistan, and some would say that because he did not develop a strong working relationship with President Karzai he actually set the campaign back a few steps.[65] There can be no doubt that he was unable to work the great changes in Afghanistan that his service in Iraq had seemed to herald at his arrival in Kabul. Afghanistan had again demonstrated that it was a different place from Iraq, had different issues, and needed different solutions.

On August 6, 2011, Taliban fighters shot down a U.S. helicopter, killing several Afghan troops and thirty Americans, including seventeen members of SEAL Team 6, the unit that had killed Osama bin Laden, although none of the deceased had participated in that operation. In the last week of October an ANA soldier opened fire on Australian troops, shooting eleven people and killing three, along with an Afghan army interpreter. The ANA soldier was killed during the ensuing gunfight. It was the bloodiest incident for Australian forces since 2001 and the worst for the Australian Defense Force since the Vietnam War.[66] The attack weakened trust between Australian and ANA forces and led to the confiscation of weapons from ANA soldiers for several days. A similar attack occurred just ten days later, on November 9, when an ANA soldier opened fire and wounded three Australians and two Afghan soldiers.[67]

Later the same month, on November 26, with tensions between the United States and Pakistan extremely high after Neptune Spear, an ISAF attack on Pakistani forces killed twenty-four soldiers. It was the biggest attack on Pakistan's armed forces since 9/11.[68] Pakistan quickly blocked NATO supply routes and ordered all Americans to leave Shamsi Airfield. Although Secretary General Anders Fogh Rasmussen said the attack was "tragic" and "unintended,"[69] the Pakistani government made it clear that the incident would have serious consequences for cooperation between Pakistan and members of the alliance, including the United States.

Several coordinated attacks struck three Afghan cities—Kabul, Kandahar, and Mazar-i-Sharif—almost simultaneously on December 6, a day after an international conference on Afghanistan in Bonn, Germany. The attacks killed at least sixty Shiite Afghans, including many children, and wounded an estimated two hundred. Lashkar-i-Jhangvi, a Pakistan-based Deobandi extremist group allied to Al-Qaeda, claimed responsibility for the attacks, which many feared had been an attempt to further destabilize Afghanistan by adding a new dimension of strife to a country battered by a decade of war.[70]

By the fall of 2011, there were some 97,000 U.S. troops in the war zone, with the number gradually falling under the pullout plan announced by the president. When the 2012 drawdown was complete, President Obama directed, "U.S. troops would continue leaving Afghanistan at a 'steady pace' as Afghan forces assume more responsibility for the country's security."[71] But seeing the size of the problem in Afghanistan and the poor readiness of the Afghan security forces, General Allen still wanted to halt troop withdrawals after the 2012 reductions and maintain troop levels at 68,000 through all of 2013; he wanted the drawdown to resume "sometime in 2014, the year Afghans are scheduled to assume lead responsibility for securing the country."[72] Allen could see already that more needed to be done to build capacity in Afghanistan in the face of still very credible Taliban capabilities.

The Way Ahead in Afghanistan with No War in Iraq

Despite a slowdown in Taliban activity, 2012 witnessed a number of extremely high-profile events that seemed to discredit the efforts of ISAF to help bring a peaceful end to the conflict in Afghanistan. On February 22, 2012, members of the Afghan security forces working at Bagram Base reported seeing U.S. personnel there set fire to copies of the Koran. Their comments resulted in outraged Afghans besieging Bagram, and during the eight days of protests that followed, nearly thirty people were killed, including two American soldiers, allegedly killed by one of their Afghan counterparts.[73] Large demonstrations also occurred in Kabul.

Although the ISAF commander in Afghanistan, General Allen, publicly apologized and ordered an investigation and NATO security forces worked hard to stop the demonstrations from spiraling out of control, the domestic impact in Afghanistan was severe. In fact on February 24 President Barack Obama apologized for the Koran burnings to help stem the violence.[74] Furious Afghans attacked and besieged NATO bases at Mihtarlam and Kapisa, and the Taliban exploited the anti-U.S. sentiment: "You should bring the invading forces military bases under your brave attack, their military convoys, kill them, capture them, beat them, and teach them a lesson that they will never again dare to insult the Holy Koran."[75]

Then on March 11, 2012, Staff Sergeant Robert Bales allegedly left his base and killed sixteen civilians, including nine children, in their homes in the Panjwai district of Kandahar Province. Several hundred local Afghans responded by protesting at the nearby American military base, Camp Belambay. "President Hamid Karzai condemned the attacks, calling them in a statement an 'inhuman and intentional act' and demanding justice."[76] Other Afghan leaders also demanded that the United States and NATO act, suspicious as to whether the crime would receive proper treatment in a U.S. court. Shukria Barakzai, an Afghan member of parliament, said, "Afghan blood cannot be spilled in vain. . . . We really need a proper, very official court for that guy."[77] American and ISAF commanders apologized again and promised a full investigation. Secretary of Defense Leon Panetta stated that the soldier "will be brought to justice and be held accountable" and that the death penalty "could be a consideration."[78] The Taliban vowed revenge, and the mood of Afghans toward the coalition grew even angrier.

Even with these powerfully negative incidents, during March and April of 2012 the United States and Afghanistan reached two agreements that recast the framework for U.S. involvement in Afghanistan beyond 2014, when the last foreign combat troops were due to leave the country. First an agreement to transfer control of the Parwan Detention Facility outside Bagram air base to the Afghanistan government was signed on March 9, 2012, by General Allen and Abdul Rahim Wardak, the Afghan defense minister.[79] The agreement shifted overall responsibility for the facility to the Afghan government but also created a six-month window to gradually transfer detainees to Afghan oversight, managed by a joint U.S.-Afghan commission.

The second agreement gave Afghan military units greater control of controversial night raid operations, which were by then increasingly unpopular with the Afghans. That document was signed on April 7, 2012. General Allen noted, "Today we are one step closer to the establishment of the U.S.-Afghan strategic partnership. Most importantly, today we are one step closer to our shared goal and vision of a secure and sovereign Afghanistan."[80] According to press reports, that agreement meant "giving Kabul a veto over the operations despised by most local people and clearing the way for a wider pact securing a U.S. presence. . . . Their conduct had been one of the biggest hurdles in negotiations on a broader strategic pact governing a future U.S. role in the country, including advisers and Special Forces soldiers, to help safeguard stability for at least a decade.[81]

The detainee accord and the shift of the Afghan military to manage military operations in the country mirrored advances developed in Iraq prior to the development of the Strategic Framework Agreement of 2008. A similar arrangement for Afghanistan was already in negotiations. According to the *New York Times,* the agreement, finalized on April 22, pledged "American support for Afghanistan for 10 years after the withdrawal of combat troops at the end of 2014."[82] The agreement was a prerequisite for any ISAF withdrawal and was also "meant to reassure the Afghan people that the United States will not abandon them, to warn the Taliban not to assume that they can wait out the West, and to send a message to Pakistan, which American officials believe has been hedging its bets in the belief that an American departure would leave the Taliban in charge."[83]

Even as the key strategic agreement was being finalized, the fighting season in Afghanistan began, with militants from the Haqqani network conducting major attacks in Kabul and three provincial capitals on April 15. Though the Afghan security forces acquitted themselves well, President Karzai blamed ISAF for what he called an intelligence failure.[84] The 2012 fighting season was understood to be the key transition point to demonstrate the ability of the Afghans to take responsibility for the war; it was ISAF's last good chance strengthen the Afghan National Security Forces and assist in a significant counteroffensive against the Taliban before the ANSF took the lead in operations and in establishing security in the country.

Analysts at STRATFOR noted,

> The politically motivated April 15 attacks were tactically ineffective, despite being thoroughly planned, coordinated and supplied. The ANSF contained the attackers and ultimately killed 36 of the 37 while sustaining only 15 deaths in return (four civilians and 11 security personnel). This was accomplished with limited ISAF support, including some helicopter support, a demonstration of the outcome the ISAF desires for the strategy shift it has implemented over the last year. The ISAF's focus has been shifting from counterinsurgency operations to a concerted effort to establish a large, trained and cohesive indigenous security force that can assume all security responsibilities after the planned 2014 withdrawal. With foreign forces slated to start drawing down later this year, the 2012 spring fighting season is the last chance for the ISAF to enforce its strategy and lay the groundwork for the successful transfer of control.[85]

So by the beginning of 2012, even given the slow pace of development, the fact that there was only the campaign in Afghanistan to deal with made many in the U.S. military optimistic about the future of the war there. Foreign policy analysts John Nagl and Michael O'Hanlon wrote, "Despite the sense of hopelessness in Afghanistan, there is progress—and there is a plan. We hardly are guaranteed a successful outcome, and progress on the political and anticorruption fronts is still needed. But our odds of attaining at least the core of our strategic goals are reasonably good if we remain patient over the next three years and work to build up and support the Afghan troops, who will bear responsibility for their nation's future."[86]

General John Allen's most significant contributions to the campaign may be more subtle to discern than the surge and less contentious than the leaked assessments of his predecessors but will perhaps be the most enduring. Allen had deftly restructured and accelerated the transition to Afghan lead security responsibility while continuing to manage the combat phases of the operation and planning for, and beginning execution of, the removal of ISAF forces from Afghanistan in order to maximize the support available from ISAF to the ANSF. His mission was characterized by some in Afghanistan as *simultaneously win the war and redeploy*. The two requirements seemed diametrically opposed, akin to winning an election while announcing immediate retirement. In the summer of 2012 Allen appeared to be balancing the two competing requirements masterfully, all the while maintaining a critical and positive relationship with President Karzai and the other senior Afghan leaders. Getting out of a war is far harder than getting into one. Getting out of one while still trying to fight it—and win it—is a monumental challenge. Still, even after only a year in command, General Allen had demonstrated the essential skills that many of his predecessors lacked and he seemed up to the enormous task at hand.

A Strategy for Ending the War

> We have traveled through more than a decade under the dark cloud of war. In the pre-dawn darkness of Afghanistan, we can see the light of a new day on the horizon.
>
> —President Barack Obama[87]

On May 1, 2012, President Obama traveled to Afghanistan to clarify the way ahead for the conflict there. He first signed with President Karzai a strategic agreement outlining cooperation between their two countries for a ten-year period following withdrawal, scheduled for 2014, of the U.S.-led international force. Then in a speech reminiscent of the one he had given outlining the end of the war in Iraq in February 2009, President Obama spoke to the both the American and Afghan people, outlining the fundamentals of a strategy designed to end the war and build an "enduring partnership" between the United States and Afghanistan.[88]

Obama made the trip exactly one year after the killing of Al-Qaeda leader Osama bin Laden, and he gave his speech in Bagram Air Base at about the same time of the day that the Navy SEALs had carried out the raid on bin Laden's compound in Abbottabad, Pakistan. The significance of the date and the strategy was clear. "The tide has turned," Obama said. "We broke the Taliban's momentum. We've built strong Afghan Security forces. We devastated al Qaeda's leadership, taking out over 20 of their top 30 leaders. And one year ago, from a base here in Afghanistan, our troops launched the operation that killed Osama bin Laden," he said. "The goal that I set—to defeat al Qaeda, and deny it a chance to rebuild—is within reach."[89]

The president outlined his new commitment to assist the Afghan people, as well as troop reductions and clear restrictions on American military involvement that were designed to ensure success for an effort he characterized as, "As they stand up, we stand alongside."[90] Obama promised America would not develop a lasting military presence and specified that future U.S. military efforts in Afghanistan would be limited to accomplishing only two narrow security missions beyond 2014: counterterrorism and continued training. Both of these missions and the decade of promised assistance were designed to give Afghanistan the opportunity to stabilize and create a new nation. "We will not build permanent bases in this country, nor will we be patrolling its cities and mountains. That will be the job of the Afghan people," he said.[91]

Obama also revealed that his administration had been in negotiations with the Taliban (separate and distinct from Al-Qaeda) and that the United States was pursuing a negotiated peace. Obama stressed that remaining members of the Taliban had a choice to be "part of this future if they break with al Qaeda, renounce violence, and abide by Afghan laws."[92] With a decade-long commitment for assistance, clear limitations on the use of foreign military force, and the door open to negotiations, Obama and Karzai hoped to develop a formula for a lasting peace after 2014. The conditions were again ripe to develop an end to hostilities; much work remained, but with clear goals and a time line established to guarantee the United States would not abandon the Afghan people, there was every reason to believe that peace might eventually return to Afghanistan.

Only time would tell, but Afghanistan had beaten many in its long history. It was a country unlike any other, with its own unique destiny to fulfill.

Eleven

A Final Assessment
Fighting Two Wars

Fighting multiple wars simultaneously makes it hard to succeed. The time and attention that military commanders were obliged to devote to Iraq distracted them from Afghanistan. Consequently, what started out in 2001 as a quick mission to topple the Taliban and eradicate Al-Qaeda bases from Afghanistan turned into a decade-long war that seems destined to produce few tangible benefits for the United States. We will never know for sure what might have happened in Afghanistan had we not invaded Iraq, but it is clear that we seriously underestimated the difficulty—both militarily and politically—of waging two wars.

—Linda J. Bilmes[1]

On October 21, 2011, President Barack Obama announced that "after nearly nine years, America's war in Iraq will be over. The coming months will be a season of homecomings. Our troops in Iraq will definitely be home for the holidays."[2] The last American forces departed from Iraq in December 2011, finally making the Afghan war the first foreign-policy priority of the United States after a decade of combat. By that time the American effort in Afghanistan was transitioning as well, from a period characterized by an Iraq-like surge to the eventual reduction in forces and withdrawal that would effectively end the involvement of the U.S. combat forces in the region. Operation Enduring Freedom had become the main effort of America's war against Al-Qaeda, but only after the American president had announced that his military forces would begin to leave Afghanistan in 2014.

The decision to leave Iraq was made after talks designed to develop a new bilateral agreement between the United States and Iraq (to replace the Strategic Framework Agreement of 2008) fell apart without any commitment by the Iraqis to grant American forces assigned there immunity from prosecution under Iraqi law. Effectively the Iraqi government of Prime Minister al-Maliki refused to allow the American forces to continue operating independently in Iraq, and the Obama administration could do little else than effect a full withdrawal. President Obama, having pledged to end the war during his campaign, was in no way inclined to press on with American support against the wishes of the Iraqi government. The lack of agreement was also influenced, to at least some degree, by an increasing warming of relations between the Maliki government in Iraq and Iranian government of Mahmoud Ahmadinejad. Still, all five of the major objectives identified by the Bush administration (an Iraq that was peaceful, united, stable, democratic, and secure)[3] could be seen to be in place by 2011, and very little more was likely to be produced by the continued presence of American troops.

With the Iraq war at its end and the end-state goals well in sight for the start of an American withdrawal from Afghanistan in 2014, the world could begin to assess the meaning of the decade of war that had enflamed America and the Middle East since 9/11. The American campaigns in Iraq and Afghanistan had changed the way the United States was viewed around the world and the way it dealt with a number of friends and allies across the globe; the campaigns had also changed the way the country thought about war, as another generation of American citizens had met the horrors of combat and its awful aftermath in a way no previous citizenry had felt such pain since the middle of the previous century. Iraqi Freedom and Enduring Freedom had altered American foreign policy and changed the global balance of power.

The lessons of the two wars will certainly affect the United States for decades; they need to be well understood and well accommodated. This study is not intended as a definitive analysis of the successes and failures of the war in Afghanistan. Rather it is specifically designed to consider how the decision to conduct two major campaigns affected the success of each and whether such a decision should ever be undertaken voluntary by the United States in the future.

A Just War

The attacks on the World Trade Center and the Pentagon of September 11, 2001, had changed many of the most fundamental aspects of strategic decision making in the United States, and the attitudes of American policy makers toward war had changed as well. The impact of the 9/11 attacks, like the impact of those that had occurred at Pearl Harbor some sixty years previously, changed overnight the normally isolationist-pacifist mind-set of the American people, first to shock, and second to anger, and eventually to a fatalistic acceptance of war.

During the first few days following the attacks, the administration of President George W. Bush had taken stock of the events and formulated a national response that included waging interventionist war against not only the perpetrators of the attacks and their supporters and hosts but other nations that posed like threats. President Bush used the term "war" in the first days following the attacks—what *kind* of war still needed to be determined.

Enduring Freedom combat operations began with air strikes on Taliban targets in Afghanistan on October 7, 2001, just three weeks following the attacks in New York City. The United States led an impressive coalition of more than sixty-eight nations in this effort; all united against the Al-Qaeda perpetrators of the terrorist attacks and their supportive Taliban hosts. In fact NATO even considered the attacks justification for invoking Article V of the alliance charter—it was perhaps the most emotionally unified coalition since the Second World War. That coalition soon included the Afghan Northern Alliance, an indigenous coalition of Tajiks, Pashtuns, Hazaras, Uzbeks, Turkmen, and others.[4]

By late October 2001 the U.S.-led coalition forces had destroyed most of the opposing Taliban air defenses and had executed a series of highly successful missions including, striking at the Taliban leader, Mullah Omar, in the Taliban capital of Kandahar. Coalition Special Operations Forces linked up with groups of anti-Taliban militia, coordinated fire support, and provided significant financial and logistical assistance to instigate attacks on the key areas of Afghanistan under Taliban control. On November 9 the coalition began an attack on the key city of Mazar-i Sharif and only three days afterward began the final attack on the Afghan capital, Kabul. The Taliban however had been so damaged by the coalition that it evacuated the city without a fight. Very quickly thereafter all of the western Afghan provinces fell to anti-Taliban forces.

By November 16 the Taliban's last stronghold in northern Afghanistan was under attack by forces of the Northern Alliance. By that point the Taliban had been forced back to its original heartland in southeastern Afghanistan, near Kandahar. By November 13 Al-Qaeda and the Taliban had been corralled into a pocket in the Tora Bora area, near the Pakistani border. Within weeks they were reduced to isolated pockets of fighters, or had fled to Pakistan.[5] By mid-December the Taliban had been evicted from the Afghan capital, which was then in the hands of the Northern Alliance.

Though the campaign had been directed largely in the same manner as previous conventional campaigns, the operational concept employed in Afghanistan to this point was clearly unconventional. Enduring Freedom's unique and highly successful approach was driven largely by the circumstances of time and distance in Afghanistan.[6] Though Osama bin Laden and many of his supporters would eventually escape from the Tora Bora pocket, the 2001 phase of the operation in Afghanistan was a highly effective example of the integrated employment of Special Operations Forces, strategic firepower, and indigenous forces to topple a regime. Some of the lessons eventually learned by the American military in Afghanistan, such as the use of Provincial Reconstruction Teams, would change how the planning and fighting in Iraq were conducted. But for most of the following ten years the combat operations in Afghanistan would be a backwater, in terms of American interest, and the initial gains won so laudably would soon be squandered by a shift of focus to the war in Iraq.

The Strategic Impact of 9/11 and the Iraq Campaign

Though there are people who believe that the cost of war is never justifiable, the campaign in Afghanistan will always stand out as one of the very few conflicts in history that was avidly supported in its initial stages by most of the nations of the world. In the aftermath of the terrorist attacks that occurred on September 11, 2001, nearly seventy nations actively voiced support for a response against the Taliban and Al-Qaeda. The Taliban had been vilified in the international press and had twice before been sanctioned by the United Nations.[7] This was initially therefore both a just and internationally popular war. So why and how did its support wane—and yet still involve forty-nine nations and nearly 130,000 troops as the Iraq war ended in late 2011?

Essentially the war in Afghanistan was an American-led international response to the 9/11 attacks, with the strategic objective of regime change and installation of a new government in Kabul inhospitable to Al-Qaeda. It was immediately obvious that such a strategic objective would not require significant conventional combat but that some method of restoring a modicum of Afghan governance would need to be part of the solution. The Afghan people were not enemies of the United States, and Afghanistan itself was not an opponent in a traditional war; here was a new variation on conflict, pitting numerous nation-states against an unpopular government and a nonstate, terrorist organization. As a new variation of war with special characteristics, the Enduring Freedom campaign justified different approaches and encountered new, unanticipated problems. These problems would have been manageable had the war remained the first national priority; but once the effort in Afghanistan was relegated to secondary importance, they became chronic. The 2003 invasion of Iraq shifted many of the best commanders, best units, and best intentions of the United States to Mesopotamia.

Although the focus of American leaders quickly shifted to Iraq, the rest of the world had misgivings about invading that country and remained more interested in keeping the pressure on Al-Qaeda in the Afghan-Pakistan region. This disparity of focus grew over time, particularly as the war in Iraq grew more costly and less predictable after 2004. The effect was that the two campaigns lost much of the synergy that existed originally within the global coalition, and though many nations did send troop contingents to Iraq, those units were normally small in size and restricted in mission, which only reduced the forces available to keep the pressure against Al-Qaeda strong. Plus, it was evident from the beginning that the coalition accrued no benefit from what should have been mutually supporting attacks in the two countries on a common enemy: Al-Qaeda's losses in Iraq seemed to have no negative impact on Al-Qaeda generally. Thus it should have been clear that the two movements were not unitary. Some even have said that the invasion of Iraq actually bolstered Al-Qaeda recruiting globally, as many young Muslim men saw the American-led invasion as a direct threat to the sacred lands of their faith.

The Enduring Nature of War: The Furnace of Combat

Lieutenant General John Kelly, who had served as the top Marine commander in Iraq in 2008-2009, penned a letter to friends and family in November 2010: "Our Robert was killed in action, protecting our country, its people, and its values from a terrible and relentless enemy. He went quickly, thank God he did not suffer. In combat that is as good as it gets and we are thankful. We are a broken hearted, but proud family. He was a wonderful and precious boy living a meaningful life. He was in exactly the place he wanted to be, doing exactly what he wanted to do, surrounded by the best men on this earth." The body was met at Dover Air Force Base by Kelly's other son, a Marine captain, and was brought to Arlington National Cemetery for burial with the heroes of so many past wars. Lieutenant Kelly had previously served two combat tours in Iraq.[8]

The campaign in Afghanistan had some characteristics in common with previous wars, but it also demonstrated a few new challenges that may mark the normally immutable nature of war over the century to come. First and most undeniably, although many failed to understand the difficulty of fighting in such varied and difficult terrain, combat in Afghanistan was bone-crushingly exhausting and brutal. Some young Americans were put in places so remote and so dominated by the enemy that they were under fire for the majority of the time they remained "in country." The heat (or extreme cold), dust, loneliness, frustration, worry, lack of sleep, and fear all combined to make every day harder than the previous one. The continual nights on watch and days on patrol, waiting for the eerie stillness to be shattered by gunfire and the explosions of improvised explosive devices, seemed unending and often even pointless. Inexplicably violent combat always overstimulated soldiers and Marines and then left them empty and drained. Remaining constantly on alert made some wonder how far they could go and still survive as the same people who had left America just months before. One soldier wrote, "It's as though the very act of touching the soil draws the life slowly out of you with each step."[9]

For many the relentless ache of combat anxiety was increased by a dark foreknowledge—a great number of those who fought in Afghanistan had previously served in combat there or had served similarly in Iraq, so they knew how bad it could be. One's first exposure to war terrifies; knowing what to expect makes a return trip even more forbidding. Staff Sergeant Salvatore Giunta, who was awarded the Medal of Honor in Kunar Province, Afghanistan, described combat there in this way:

There were more bullets in the air than stars in the sky. A wall of bullets at every one at the same time with one crack and then a million other cracks afterward. They're above you, in front of you, behind you, below you. They're hitting in the dirt early. They're going over your head. Just all over the place. They were close—as close as I've ever seen. . . .

You do everything you can. You don't think. You just react. Everyone knows. This isn't our first rodeo, and this isn't everyone's first time getting shot at. This is a newer experience, and this is a different way than it's ever come in, but everyone knows exactly what they need to do. If they're shooting? Shoot back. If there's cover, you find it. It's just all self-preservation at that point. Everyone's just giving it back as hard as we can, because the more we shoot, hopefully the less they shoot.[10]

Unfortunately, after 2003 the war in Afghanistan was deeply affected by the ongoing combat operations in Iraq, and it suffered by neglect, particularly in the period from 2006 through 2008, when the intensity of the combat there was little known outside the country but just as terrible for those that endured it.

Eventually as in Iraq, the U.S. government redoubled its military effort in Afghanistan by conducting a surge of forces designed to take the rising momentum back from the enemy and turn the tide of the fighting in its own favor. As a result the number of American and allied casualties actually increased significantly in 2009 (in the year after coalition casualties in Iraq began to be dramatically reduced), peaking at over 700 dead in 2010. Over 1,800 American men and women lost their lives fighting in Afghanistan through 2011; over 14,000 Americans sustained wounds during the fighting as well. Nearly 4,500 Americans had died in Iraq over the course of that war; over 32,000 had been wounded. Twenty-seven other countries also saw their citizens die in Afghanistan (twenty-two for Iraq) over the course of the fighting.

Uniformed military members were not the only victims of these two campaigns. Over 5,000 Afghans died as a result of combat in the first five years of the war. In 2007 the United Nations Assistance Mission in Afghanistan began keeping better count of civilian casualties; it recorded 1,500 deaths in 2007 and 2,100 in 2008 (a 40 percent rise from the previous year).[11] Just over 2,400 Afghan civilians died in 2009, and 2,700 were killed in 2010. In the first half of 2011, there had already been nearly 1,500 Afghans killed as a result of the increased fighting in their country.[12] Each year after 2007 represented an increasing toll of civilian deaths and a similar rise in less obvious destruction of personal property and family prosperity. No one will ever know how many Iraqis were killed as a result of the fighting in their country between 2003 and 2011, but some estimate the number was over 50,000.[13]

The Changing Character of War

Although the nature of war has endured despite the passage of time, the creativity of man, and even the dynamic development of technology, at least a few characteristics of the combat in Afghanistan and Iraq did signal significant changes in the landscape of warfare. Certainly the impact of information on the execution of military operations only continues to grow as information systems improve in speed and portability. Similarly globalization has come to demonstrate the interlinked nature of nations around the world and has also shown that conflict anywhere in the globe has an impact on nations besides those actually doing the fighting.

Some have posited that the twenty-first century has ushered in the end of the Westphalian era.[14] They would view the increases in globalization, the spread of ethnic diasporas, the global economic challenges of 1997 and 2009, and the rise of global insurgent movements such as Al-Qaeda as indications that the nation-state itself may be losing preeminence on the world stage. The wars in Iraq and Afghanistan certainly pointed to a lack of resilience in international borders and demonstrated the importance of international organizations with global reach. Much more will have to occur before the international legal framework moves past nation-centricity and nation-states are removed from their predominant place on the world stage. Still, there have been other indications that the character of war has changed in the past decade.

What war looks like at any point in time and space (its "face," shape, practice, dynamics, intensity, and scope) reflects the nature of the societies waging it at that time and in that particular region. War also reflects society's dynamics, the economic, political, social, cultural, and technological norms that influence life, and it is affected by who fights, why they fight, and how they fight. The campaigns in Iraq and Afghanistan in these respects clearly demonstrate at least two significant changes in the character of war. The most obvious of the factors inherent in these two conflicts that demonstrate the continuing evolution of war's essential characteristics were the involvement of nonstate actors and the blending of conventional- and irregular-warfare techniques in combat.

The Taliban and Al-Qaeda: State and Nonstate Actors

Twentieth-century warfare was dominated by contests between nation-states. Ultimately the war in Afghanistan was different from many that preceded it in one significant respect: the conflict was directed by a nation-state against a network or group of individuals, not another nation-state. This difference had both policy and legal implications; it also restricted the use of some of the traditional tools of American warfighting and made it much more difficult to identify and accomplish specific and measurable end-state objectives. Objectives in war heretofore had traditionally been framed as nation-state effects, such as army capitulation, seizure of a capital, or acceptance of sanctions. None of these were likely in the case of Al-Qaeda or even the Taliban, neither of which had a firm base to be controlled or even an easily identifiable force structure to be attacked and defeated. Al-Qaeda was America's enemy worldwide, and members of the group fought in both Afghanistan and Iraq. This "common enemy" was one aspect of the conflict that linked the efforts in both nations; even though there was no evidence that Al-Qaeda was actually operational in Iraq prior to the 2003 invasion, the Bush administration believed it to have been working in at least tacit cooperation with Saddam Hussein.

Although its name means "the base," the fact that Al-Qaeda had ultimately no territory and no organized army made it difficult for the United States to bring any pressure to bear on it that was nonkinetic—in other words, at least initially the only way America could fight the group was to find and kill its members. Not knowing who they were or where they were made this difficult, yet not impossible. The real problem was that Al-Qaeda recruited replacements almost as quickly as the United States killed its members. The more dominating the American presence in the region was made, to enable it to kill members of Al-Qaeda, the more young men were attracted to its message and its training camps. It took years before the United States was able to form a message that helped dissuade new members from joining the group, and much of that message's appeal was actually drawn from the errors of Zarqawi in Iraq as he targeted coreligionist Shiites.

For years Osama bin Laden, the leader of Al-Qaeda, was able, even while on the run, to transmit messages that sent his words around the world and into receptive Muslim minds everywhere, while the United States only seemed to further alienate those most likely to become his recruits. To date, the United States still struggles to form and disseminate a credible global message in its favor.

The Taliban in itself was also a problem for the United States. Though once the principal part of the Afghan government, it was at its most basic simply a conservative Muslim movement whose extreme policies, although barbaric, were rarely illegal. Though it had no territory or organized army to focus American combat power against, the area around Kandahar remained its central breeding ground throughout the decade. Though unpopular even among most Muslims, it still attracted recruits, even inside Afghanistan, at least in part because its repressive policies were strictly enforced and gave a semblance of stability to Afghanistan during the years it was in power in Kabul.

The Blending of Conventional- and Irregular-Warfare Techniques in Combat

Both campaigns began with modern firepower and maneuver dominating the conduct of operations; both shifted after a certain period to be dominated by irregular warfare; and when the Afghanistan campaign ceases, both will have ended with a mix of conventional and irregular capabilities to terminate hostilities. Though this blending is not unique in history (even during the Second World War—perhaps the best known example of conventional combat in modern times—there were irregular campaigns, in the former Yugoslavia, for example) and there have been irregular facets of conventional campaigns (the integration of the Maquis resistance forces into the conventional assault on France in 1944, for example). Still, the full integration of irregular and conventional capabilities and techniques exhibited by American forces in both Iraq and Afghanistan represented a new way of warfare at the tactical and operational levels.

With the adaptability and flexibility gained by the significant assimilation of Reserve and National Guard forces with their conventional, regular counterparts and the superb integration of a wide range of special operations capabilities with conventional forces, the capacity of the American forces in Iraq and Afghanistan reached a level never attained by other militaries. Where those improvements were additive to the teamwork that resulted from close cooperation of military forces with counterparts from the State and Justice Departments and federal intelligence agencies (principally the CIA), the product was the refinement of a new American way of war. That new way of war brought greater capability to the tactical twenty-first-century battlefield in a way that advanced sensors and intelligence systems radically changed the twentieth-century battlefield during the first U.S.-Iraq war in 1990–91.

By 2011 in Afghanistan, small numbers of American units were having effects on the enemy and the surrounding population that far exceeded the impact of any similarly sized units in history. This greatly increased human and skill-set capacity will be hard to sustain as budget cuts and a return to domestic priorities reduce the impetus for integration across the American government and also the ability of the military to bring diverse forces together with telling effect. But if it can be maintained, at least in certain units, it will remain a game changer in the combat scenarios of the future.

The Keystones of Counterinsurgency

The conflicts in Iraq and Afghanistan amply demonstrated that some factors should be viewed as characteristically important to the successful prosecution of a counterinsurgency effort. Three factors inherent in the two campaigns stand out as particularly important: the important roles of sanctuary nations, the crucial impact of host-nation leadership, and the influence of domestic factors on the prosecution of long-term military campaigns.

The Role of Pakistan as a Sanctuary

Sanctuary has frequently played an important and negative role in counterinsurgency warfare. America had supported the Afghan mujahedeen insurgents against the Soviets from the sanctuary of Pakistan, so in 2001 American leaders knew well, in advance, that Pakistan could significantly influence their efforts to combat the Taliban (which had strong ties to the Pakistani Inter-Services Intelligence Agency (ISI)—the equivalent in some ways of the American Central Intelligence Agency). In fact the CIA and the ISI had worked very well together during the previous effort to oust the Soviets from Afghanistan. Thus the American campaign in Afghanistan had a Pakistani component from its earliest days.

For its part Pakistan had had interests in Afghanistan since the 1940s, when the Pakistanis had recruited Pashtun tribal *lashkars* (militias) from both Pakistan and Afghanistan to fight the Indians in Kashmir in 1948. Pakistan had played an increasingly strong role in Afghanistan since the 1970s, when it had committed itself to a northward thrust to ward off the influence of the Soviet Union.[15] The ISI continued to run operations in the Federally Administered Tribal Area (FATA) and in Afghanistan well into the conflict, believing it necessary to counter Indian influence and to set up a future Afghan government that would add strategic depth for Pakistan.

Thus the border area—the infamous, poorly demarcated Durand Line—remained a complicating factor throughout the later years of the conflict in Afghanistan. It reached a painful peak with the killing of some twenty-four Pakistani soldiers on November 26, 2011, an incident that nearly ended U.S.-Pakistani cooperation in the war. Taliban support ran back and forth across the border, ISAF and Afghan forces were constrained from crossing it, and the Pakistanis rarely picked up the chase on their side. American and ISAF logistical supplies also had to cross the border, often the targets of local Taliban bombings.[16] Similar flows of Shia militia support from Iran plagued the U.S. effort in Iraq. In any future counterinsurgency campaign a much greater focus—military, economic, and diplomatic—needs to be exerted in order to isolate the enemy from such sanctuary.

Host-Nation Leadership

President Hamid Karzai came to power in Afghanistan on the wings of the United States. Karzai began the war leading a group of Pashtun fighters from Quetta, Pakistan, conducting operations against the Taliban.[17] Karzai was later selected by prominent Afghans to serve as the first chairman of the Interim Administration of Afghanistan during the December 2001 Bonn Conference. The 2002 *loya jirga* then chose him for a two-year term as interim president; he was elected president of Afghanistan in his own right in both 2004 and 2009.

Like Karzai, Iraqi Prime Minister al-Maliki had also fought against his own government. He began his political career as a dissident against Saddam Hussein in the late 1970s and rose to prominence after fleeing a death sentence into exile. During his exile he became a senior leader of the Dawa political party and built relationships with Iranian and Syrian officials whose help he sought in overthrowing Saddam.[18] His first government was approved by the Iraqi National Assembly on May 20, 2006; his second cabinet, in which he served as interior minister, defense minister, and national security minister, was approved on December 21, 2010.

Both Karzai and Maliki were dependent upon the United States and its allies to develop security in their countries, even to safely conduct the very elections that brought them to power. But both leaders also voiced differences with the United States, and both courted American enemies (principally Iran) in their nationalist quests for stability. The United States completely reformed both the Iraqi military and the Afghan military and police; America also brought new foreign investment, as well as hundreds of billions of dollars of U.S. aid to both countries;[19] yet al-Maliki eventually refused to extend the Status-of-Forces Agreement to permit continued American military involvement in his country, and he supported Iran and Syria in ways that ran counter to U.S. regional interests. Karzai was not as contrary, but he did complain frequently about excessive use of force by ISAF and accepted money and other support from Iran, even while his American ally was attempting to isolate Tehran.[20] Many analysts would point out that Karzai was also a far less competent national leader than even the controversial al-Maliki. One author noted, "Although a flawed structure might succeed if run by a talented leader, a fragile state could not easily survive with a badly designed government in the hands of a poor leader. This is unfortunately what the Afghans experienced under Karzai's presidency."[21]

The fact remains that national leaders must place their real efforts in areas that align with their own national interests. Though they may solicit and use American aid and security support, the leaders of nations fighting domestic insurgencies need to remain sovereign, and eventually they want the United States to withdraw. For all these reasons they make difficult partners. In both the Iraqi and Afghan cases such predictable difficulties were compounded by staggering levels of corruption, as both the Iraqi and Afghan governments struggled to develop ethical leaders at all levels while their nations were awash in American cash.

The Domestic Context and Prolonged Campaigns

After ten years of war, some six thousand American dead in Iraq and Afghanistan, and the death of Osama bin Laden, many people in the United States seriously questioned why the war was continuing. Many had stated that the war would not end with a triumphant surrender and parades; it was obvious that other criteria would determine when the United States would stop sending its men and women to fight in places so distant and for goals so remote from its own domestic needs. Once the American economy suffered its "downturn" starting in 2008, many analysts began to question why so much money—reportedly $443 billion—could be spent in Afghanistan at such a time. It is no wonder that the key phrase in the presidential speech of June 22, 2011, announcing the drawdown of U.S. forces from Afghanistan, was, "It is time to focus on nation building here at home."[22]

The killing by Special Forces of Osama bin Laden on May 2, 2011, after the initial euphoria, certainly reduced domestic support for the war; many Americans had come to believe that the Al-Qaeda chief was not just an enemy leader but in fact the real source of the conflict. After all, his policies had been the motivation behind the 9/11 attackers. With his death, the deaths of many of his subordinate leaders, and the assessment by some that Al-Qaeda had been reduced significantly in its ability to menace the United States, the rationale for continued combat and the deaths of young Americans to build an Afghan state seemed insignificant. Defense Secretary Bob Gates later said that the U.S. commander on the ground at the time, General David Petreaus, favored a slower withdrawal that would have kept more troops in place to consolidate fragile gains against the Taliban. The "advantages and disadvantages" of a range of options were debated in White House deliberations, including "not only the situation on the ground in Afghanistan but also political sustainability here at home."[23] Another key Pentagon policy official, Michèle Flournoy, said during the summer of 2011, "Our strategy in Afghanistan is working as it was designed. The momentum has shifted to coalition and Afghan forces, and together we have degraded the Taliban's capability and achieved significant security gains. . . . Those gains have been achieved mostly in the southern part of Afghanistan, and they are enabling key political initiatives to make progress. . . . We have begun a transition process that will, ultimately, put Afghans in the lead for security nationwide by 2014."[24]

In many ways the most constructive assessment that can be derived from the conflicts in Iraq and Afghanistan should focus on the ability of nation-states, particularly wealthy industrial countries, to wage prolonged theater campaigns. In their most essential forms, these conflicts have been a series of significant major combat operations conducted over an exceedingly long period of time, all focused toward a single overarching (but often forgotten) end—the reduction of the threat to the world posed by Al-Qaeda and affiliated terrorist organizations.

Operation Iraqi Freedom was designed to topple Saddam Hussein from power and change the government in Iraq to one that would be less threatening to the region and inhospitable to terrorists. It was designed to maximize advanced firepower and swift maneuver to defeat the Iraqi military but failed through its own unexpectedly rapid success to develop the conflict-termination conditions conducive to the establishment of a replacement government in Iraq. These conditions of instability then led to a subsequent, unnamed, but very different operation from 2004 to 2009 focused necessarily more on irregular warfare and counterinsurgency than on conventional maneuver and firepower actions.

Iraqi Freedom continued through three distinct phases, struggling to transform itself from a combat operation to a post-hostilities, peace-enforcement operation, to a true counterinsurgency operation designed to protect the Iraqi population from internal threats. This transition process was traumatic for the United States and its extremely capable professional military. Clearly one of the most difficult challenges that any military must face in the service of its nation is to be able to continually assess progress and adapt to changing circumstances, despite procurement and doctrine development processes that lag far behind the realities of the frontline fighter.

Each of these issues has had similar effects during the fighting in Afghanistan. Operation Enduring Freedom also suffered under a gradual and poorly maintained evolution from a special forces–centric operation to an ill-defined irregular warfare operation as a part of a counterinsurgency campaign. Afghanistan also required the rotations of hundreds of units on nine-to-twelve-month tours, and it also required a great deal of development of insight until individual soldiers and Marines could understand the environment in which they were expected to fight and win.

In 2011 George Freidman wrote, "Some in Afghanistan have claimed that the United States has been defeated, but that is not the case. The United States may have failed to win the war, but it has not been defeated in the sense of being compelled to leave by superior force. It could remain there indefinitely, particular as the American public is not overly hostile to the war and is not generating substantial pressure to end operations. Nevertheless, if the war cannot be brought to some sort of conclusion, at some point Washington's calculations or public pressure, or both, will shift and the United States and its allies will leave Afghanistan."[25] In order to maintain the strategic momentum toward a successful solution to the conflict, the Afghan government must maintain a strategic partnership wherein the United States continues providing security and economic assistance after 2014. Karzai needs to repair the image of weakness that plagued his government, and the Afghan security forces need to move demonstrably into command operationally (as had their counterparts in Iraq three years before). The promises that have been made to rural Afghans need to be moderated but honored. Finally, relations among Pakistan, Afghanistan, and the United States need be addressed and improved.[26]

Still, on the other hand, the duration of the fighting did provide some benefits to the United States. "The protracted nature of the conflict played to America's advantage, surprisingly, as new commanders were able to learn from previous examples and personal experiences even as they adapted to a changing situation and a fluid enemy."[27] Eventually, by 2007, Iraqi Freedom was employing new techniques, new doctrine, and new enabling technologies to protect the fledgling Iraqi government that had managed to take shallow root over the preceding three years. Enduring Freedom, under ISAF command, did much the same for the government of Hamid Karzai, the ANA, and the ANP.

Defining Success

Defense Secretary Gates said in June 2011: "If you define success the way I think we should, which is that we have prevented the Taliban from forcefully overthrowing the government of Afghanistan; that the Afghan security forces can secure their own territory and prevent al-Qaida or other extremist groups from coming back and using it as a safe haven. I believe that's an achievable mission by the end of 2014, and I think we're making good headway in that direction."[28] Frederick Kagan asked a key question in late 2011: "If we abandon our current efforts in Afghanistan either by accepting defeat or by declaring success before actually achieving it, what will prevent al Qaeda and its affiliates from re-establishing their bases there and resuming their efforts to attack and kill Americans?"[29]

President Obama made his administration's national security goals in Afghanistan very clear in 2009, saying,

> Our overarching goal remains the same: to disrupt, dismantle, and defeat Al-Qaeda in Afghanistan and Pakistan, and to prevent its capacity to threaten America and our allies in the future. To meet that goal, we will pursue the following objectives within Afghanistan. We must deny Al-Qaeda a safe haven. We must reverse the Taliban's momentum and deny it the ability to overthrow the government. And we must strengthen the capacity of Afghanistan's security forces and government so that they can take lead responsibility for Afghanistan's future.[30]

Yet Professor Joe Collins noted in 2009, "Since 2004, the Taliban has clearly done more to regain its lost status than the coalition has done to advance its objectives. Among the key strengths possessed by the Taliban are a few thousand dedicated cadres, excellent funding from the drug trade and Persian Gulf charities, and the luxury of an unimpeded sanctuary in a neighboring country. Hampering the combat endeavor are the half-hearted efforts of most North

Atlantic Treaty Organization (NATO) nations and the complex decision mechanisms associated with the International Security Assistance Force (ISAF)."[31]

Success came to the Iraq War in 2011 as a little-heralded departure of military forces from a fledgling and barely stable democracy. The former regime had been removed irrevocably, but much remained to be done to ensure that the nation would continue to progress. A similar definition might still be in store for Afghanistan, yet it is likely that that country, as it has so many times before, will demonstrate more differences from Iraq than similarities. What is certain is that Americans cannot expect the romantic image of unconditional surrender ceremonies on battleships to be the norm in modern conflict. The fighting in Afghanistan will likely grow more sporadic as Afghanistan stops being the focus of international attention and as foreign forces depart; eventually the violence will return to pre-Taliban levels, but true security will only come to the country if the Afghans succeed in building a new, more effective nation-state.

Operational Advances

At the operational level of war, a number of improvements made the United States and its NATO allies more capable against their enemies. Three specific advances merit special focus. The Provincial Reconstruction Team, an innovation that helped link military and development efforts in Afghanistan, was a reflection of the importance of gaining the support of the people in a counterinsurgency effort. Later, PRTs were created in Iraq. Military Transition Teams (later Embedded Training Teams, and for coalition forces, Operational Mentor Liaison Teams) provided a way of developing the security forces of Afghanistan and Iraq to increase stability in those countries. Finally, the operational employment of National Guard and reserve component forces was critical to every success in Afghanistan and Iraq.

Provincial Reconstruction Teams

The first in importance among these advances for Afghanistan has to be the creation of the provincial reconstruction team. The PRT was designed to tailor reconstruction assistance to local needs, and because most of them were NATO-led, to the providing nation. By 2010 there were twenty-seven PRTs in Afghanistan, operated by twenty-one allied nations (including the United

States, which was leading thirteen teams). "PRTs have been an overwhelmingly positive development. They have, however, exacerbated civil-military tensions within the U.S. government and led to recurring problems with international financial institutions and NGOs, who are still not used to having combat forces in the 'humanitarian space.' While many objected to the military flavor of these teams, the need for large scale security elements dictated that role. Regional Commanders after 2003 controlled maneuver forces and PRTs in their region. The concept of PRTs was exported to Iraq, where they were under State Department management."[32] While some believe that PRTs created a parallel government structure that actually impeded the handover of responsibility to the GIRoA and local Afghan governments, most analysts view the concept as a true strength of the American effort.

Military Transition Teams

MTTs were created to accelerate the development of the Iraqi and Afghan military, police, and border security forces. In concept an MTT is a small element of senior enlisted personnel and field-grade officers (generally from staff sergeant to lieutenant colonel) who act within the structure of a host-nation unit to train and mentor developing domestic leaders and impart tactics, techniques, and procedures necessary for the unit to function in the war. The relative seniority of the team members ensures that the team is sufficiently experienced to properly mentor and train its foreign counterparts. MTTs were formed from all components of the U.S. military, including the regular army, the Army Reserve, the Army National Guard, and the active and reserve U.S. Marine Corps, Navy, and Air Force. Most Iraqi MTTs comprised from ten to sixteen members; however, the number of members in a team ranged from as few as three to as many as forty. Coalition forces normally operated in Afghanistan as OMLTs. They served largely the same functions as the American MTTs; twenty-seven nations pledged to contribute to the OMLT program.[33]

MTTs eventually served with every type of unit and in nearly every region of both Iraq and Afghanistan. Some of their best work was done with police units, which required very different skills than were normally associated with combat units. There can be no doubt that the rapid development and increased combat readiness of units all across Iraq and Afghanistan were due in large part to the role played by these MTTs. Members of MTTs often saw as much fighting as their more traditionally assigned peers in combat units. As an example, the Medal of Honor citation for Sergeant Dakota Meyer, USMC, an MTT member in Afghanistan, reads in part:

> While serving with Marine Embedded Training Team 2-8, Regional Corps Advisory Command 3-7, in Kunar Province, Afghanistan, on 8 September 2009. Corporal Meyer maintained security at a patrol rally point while other members of his team moved on foot with two platoons of Afghan National Army and Border Police into the village of Ganjgal for a predawn meeting with village elders. Moving into the village, the patrol was ambushed by more than 50 enemy fighters firing rocket propelled grenades, mortars, and machine guns from houses and fortified positions on the slopes above. Disregarding intense enemy fire now concentrated on their lone vehicle, Corporal Meyer killed a number of enemy fighters with the mounted machine guns and his rifle, some at near point blank range, as he and his driver made three solo trips into the ambush area. During the first two trips, he and his driver evacuated two dozen Afghan soldiers, many of whom were wounded. When one machine gun became inoperable, he directed a return to the rally point to switch to another gun-truck for a third trip into the ambush area where his accurate fire directly supported the remaining U.S. personnel and Afghan soldiers fighting their way out of the ambush. Despite a shrapnel wound to his arm, Corporal Meyer made two more trips into the ambush area in a third gun-truck accompanied by four other Afghan vehicles to recover more wounded Afghan soldiers and search for the missing U.S. team members. Still under heavy enemy fire, he dismounted the vehicle on the fifth trip and moved on foot to locate and recover the bodies of his team members. Corporal Meyer's daring initiative and bold fighting spirit throughout the 6-hour battle significantly disrupted the enemy's attack and inspired the members of the combined force to fight on. His unwavering courage and steadfast devotion to his U.S. and Afghan comrades in the face of almost certain death reflected great credit upon himself and upheld the highest traditions of the Marine Corps and the United States Naval Service.[34]

The "Operational Reserve"

No one can doubt the importance or the success of the use of reserve and National Guard forces in Iraq and Afghanistan. The force committed could not

have been deployed, employed, sustained in theater, or redeployed upon rotation without the assistance and skillful integration of the reserve and Guard
forces of the U.S. military. From the early months of the fighting, mobilization augmentees, critical-skill specialists, and transportation units from these
components were important to the successful execution of the largely active-
component efforts in Afghanistan and Iraq. After 2004 the reserve and Guard
mix of the deployed force began to grow, and large non-active-duty units
began to shoulder important tactical missions right alongside their regular-
component neighboring units.

Few Americans realize how many reserve and National Guard forces have
fought in combat since September 2001. The figures are impressive. According to the National Guard Bureau, the first three of its personnel deployed to
Afghanistan arrived in December 2001. By April 2004 when the conflict in
Iraq had started its second phase, there were 5,000 reserve and Guard personnel in Afghanistan. That total exceeded 9,500 in May 2005 and, after a slump,
exceeded 10,000 in the same month four years later. By 2012 there were over
16,000 reserve and National Guard soldiers in Afghanistan. The numbers for
Iraq topped 10,000 in March 2003, exceeded 50,000 in September 2004, and
reached an all-time peak of nearly 70,000 in March 2005. The Iraq numbers
do not reflect forces in neighboring Kuwait, which at their peak numbered
some 25,000.[35] Frequently the commitment from the reserve and Guard only
increased as the focus of effort turned from offensive combat to combat support during redeployment; in every sense of the word, those soldiers, and their
sailor, airmen, and Marine counterparts, were fundamental to every success
gained by the United States.

Tactical Innovations

At the tactical level, the United States proved itself to be a powerful innovator
and a technical powerhouse. Though its decision to rotate units remains controversial, there can be no doubt that the process helped units to improve each
time they were deployed into similar circumstances, normally with improved
weapons systems, body armor, and detection systems. Tactical intelligence
gathering also improved significantly over the course of the two conflicts,
though this owed as much to individual-unit learning as it did to institutional
improvements fostered by the Army or Marine Corps.

The majority of American and allied combatants killed and wounded were victims not of direct contact with the enemy but of improvised explosive devices and suicide bombers. One key success story was the rapid acquisition and fielding of IED resistant "Mine Resistant Ambush Protected" (MRAP) vehicles. Largely as a result of the sizeable numbers of American fighting men and women killed by IEDs in Iraq, on May 8, 2007, Secretary of Defense Robert Gates stated that the acquisition of MRAPs was the Department of Defense's highest acquisition priority.[36] Within a year the positive impact of a vehicle that could withstand the effects of an IED attack was already evident.[37] For many the rapid acquisition of the MRAP proved both American resourcefulness and the dedication of the American government to protecting the lives of its combatants. Even though the longer-term impacts of buying so many heavy, expensive vehicles may make them appear fiscally and operationally short-sighted, for the purpose for which they were designed the fielding of the MRAP was a tactical success story. Opponents of the MRAP accurately noted that it reinforced the risk-averse tendencies of many commanders and actually precluded the effective-relationship-building efforts that formed a key part of the prevailing COIN approach; still, the vehicle was an important signal that individual lives were the most valued of all America's treasure.

A second resounding success involved the enormous improvements in combat medical transport and initial care on the battlefield. Field "medevac" procedures and expeditionary medical care improved tremendously over the course of the decade, and many combatants survived firefights and IEDs in Iraq or Afghanistan due primarily to advances in that medical care. The "golden hour" (i.e., recognition of the need for treatment very soon after the event) became a standard for care that saved huge numbers of the injured from wounds that would have been mortal in any other war in history. Interthe-ater strategic transport through the Landstuhl Regional Medical Center in Germany to world-class medical facilities at the Walter Reed Army Medical Center, the Bethesda Naval Hospital, or the Brooke Army Medical Center in Texas saved the lives of thousands. Because of these improvements, thousands remain alive today who would have perished only a few years before.

The Other Elements of National Power

As these two complex campaigns continued, it became very obvious to American officials that some traditional methods of wielding national power were not sufficiently developed to be of much use, particularly in Afghanistan. The use of economic tools to improve the quality of life of the average Afghan (as a way of weaning from other loyalties toward an endorsement of the central government in Kabul and its NATO allies) was soon seen as far from effective. This was primarily due to the heavy hand of corruption in Afghan political life and culture, but the effect of economic tools was also lessened by the rudimentary nature of life in the rural provinces of Afghanistan. There the standard of living was among the lowest in the world, and the infrastructure that was part and parcel of government economic improvement was just too hard to develop.

The effectiveness of economic tools might have been improved had the rule of law within Afghan culture disincentivized corruption. However even multiyear efforts to bring national and provincial legal processes to the Afghan hinterland proved ineffective against the long-standing dominance of tribal law. It became obvious that in the case of the rule of law, American approaches proved nonexportable to Afghanistan.

With the exception of the Bonn Agreement, diplomacy too, normally a strength of the United States and its allies, proved relatively weak against nonstate actors. This was the result of several complex problems: the absence of established platforms for international dialog or negotiations made non-personal diplomacy difficult; fear of the ill effects of negotiations (the need to identify oneself and to concede on some points of diametric difference) often made face-to-face meetings impossible. Al-Qaeda had no representatives with which other nations could conduct diplomatic relations. Also, as is so often the case in war, some nations were conducting multiple, covert diplomatic efforts that made standard approaches very difficult. One has only to consider the diplomatic entanglements with Iran during this same period and their effects on the campaigns in both Iraq and Afghanistan to see how difficult and ineffective diplomatic efforts often were during the two wars.[38]

Two Campaigns and Their Effect on Global Security

Many changes will undoubtedly result from the decade-long interventions by the United States in Iraq and Afghanistan. Unfortunately the United States has a rather clear historical tendency not to internalize important lessons or to forget them once the passage of time dulls their urgency.

Obviously some of even the most important lessons were not immediately learned because, even as it was leaving Iraq and trying desperately to find exit space in Afghanistan, the Obama administration decided to deploy U.S. military power in Libya to prevent the Libyan leader, Mohammar Gaddafi, from killing his own countrymen who had risen up against his decades-old regime after successful democratic uprisings in neighboring Tunisia and Egypt. President Obama sent aircraft, cruise missiles, and nonmilitary aid to support the anti-Gaddafi forces under a NATO command structure dominated by American assets.

Members of the Taliban, having beaten the Soviets with U.S. aid in the 1980s, will undoubtedly always see the departure of coalition forces from Afghanistan after 2014 as a demonstration of their skill; some of them may even claim a victory over the United States. Some in the international community will make this assertion as well. As long as no future terrorist organizations menace the global population from Afghanistan, most Americans will see the campaign as a successful retaliation for the attacks of September 11, 2001, and as a useful effort to kill bin Laden and destroy his heinous Al-Qaeda organization while helping Afghans reject the Taliban and install a more moderate and more popular government system; though many will question whether America stayed in Afghanistan far too long.

Iran will be a clear winner of the two U.S. interventions, as Saddam Hussein was a much worse thorn in its side than he was a threat to the United States. With a relatively weak, and some would say pro-Iranian, government in place in Baghdad, Iran at last has a fairly secure, nonthreatening western border for the first time in half a century. Iran will also benefit from the government established in Afghanistan, which will at a minimum reduce the flows of migrant peoples and drugs from western Afghanistan into the Iranian Republic.

Pakistan may be the biggest loser in the entire region, as its interference in the U.S. effort in Afghanistan lost it the only ally it might have forged against the growing power of the Indian state to its east and so weakened its own fragile governance capacity that it lost the minimal control it had established over the brewing dissatisfaction of Pashtuns in the FATA. Pakistan had hoped to develop strategic depth in Afghanistan, but it most likely will reap increased instability and the loss of the only influential friends that it had in the twentieth century. The ability of the United States to conduct strategic raids inside Pakistani territory had by 2011 so weakened the Pakistani government and so shredded its relations with the United States that both "accounts" may be insolvent in the second decade of the twenty-first century.

Lessons of Fighting Two Theater Campaigns

The decision to conduct major campaigns in Afghanistan and Iraq clearly affected the success of each, and it should be clear that such a decision should not be undertaken voluntarily by the United States in any future conflict.

The most valuable assessments that can be derived from the conflicts between the United States and Iraq and Afghanistan should focus on the ability of a nation-state, particularly a wealthy industrial country, to wage two simultaneous theater campaigns. At their most essential levels, both of these conflicts were conducted focused toward a single overarching (but often forgotten) end—regime change, aimed at the reduction of the threat of terrorism, which had been posed initially by Osama bin Laden's Al-Qaeda group (then resident in Afghanistan and nurtured by its government the Taliban) and by Saddam Hussein, the president of Iraq.

With the paradigm shift resulting from the terrorist attacks of September 11, 2001, and threats to the U.S. homeland taking on a new priority, the ongoing threats foolishly posed by Saddam Hussein became impossible to ignore. The leaders of Iraq and the United States failed to understand each other, and the two nations were driven toward combat. Operation Iraqi Freedom was designed to change the government in Iraq to one that would be less threatening to the region and less hospitable to terrorists. Like its predecessor, Enduring Freedom, it was designed to maximize advanced firepower and swift maneuver to defeat the Iraqi military, and like Enduring Freedom, its own unexpectedly rapid success highlighted a failure to address conflict termination. It then morphed into combat operations characterized more by irregular warfare and counterinsurgency than by conventional warfighting.

Clearly one of the most difficult challenges that any military must face in the service of its nation is the ability to continually assess progress and to adapt to changing circumstances, even with procurement and doctrine development processes that lag far behind the realities of the frontline fighter.

One of the key challenges in the adaptation process is the periodic transition of forces that must take place in order to fight a long-term modern war. Gone are the days when armies went off to war and did not return until the fighting was done. Modern forces must be rotated over any conflict period that exceeds twenty-four months, and although nations always hope to resolve conflicts in periods less than that, it is now logical to anticipate that modern war will require troop rotation policies to maintain capability in excess of that time frame. In Iraq, forces settled into a deployment wave that witnessed major influxes of forces in the early spring and a lull in effective combat due to extreme weather conditions in the Middle East until the late summer. This made American forces predictable and provided an unnecessary advantage to the enemy. The seasonal differences made the peak of combat in Afghanistan much more restricted, essentially forcing every annual campaign into a long spring and summer firefight. Still the effect of unit rotations in and out of Iraq and Afghanistan was numbing. Some units, and many soldiers and Marines, made more than five combat deployments in a decade.

Eventually by 2007, Iraqi Freedom was employing new techniques, new doctrine, and new enabling technologies to protect the new Iraqi government. Those lessons were later applied in Afghanistan with less dynamic results, primarily because the terrain was more difficult in Afghanistan, the border region more porous, and the government in Kabul much less effective as a partner. Whereas the Iraqi government of Nouri al-Maliki was able to profit from the surge around Baghdad, President Karzai never really turned the increased size of American forces or of his own ANA or ANP to his advantage against the Taliban.

Inevitable Comparisons between the Two Campaigns

Fighting in Afghanistan in the 1980s and the 2000s

In the 1980s, the United States studied the conflict between the Russians and the Afghans in order to help the Afghans win in that campaign. Americans understood the difficulty of the terrain, the porous nature of the border, the powerful influence of the Pakistanis, and the hardy, warlike nature of many Afghan tribes. Additionally it understood Afghanistan has never been a coherent nation-state, with a central government fully capable of providing security for the all the peoples who reside within its borders. All of these factors remained important for the new conflict that Americans fought in Afghanistan in the 2000s. Some officials even played important roles in both wars. Was there a failure to learn? Were these complicating factors "wished away" during planning for Enduring Freedom? Or were they simply too difficult to overcome or too pervasive to avoid, even with foresight? Although the planning for Operation Enduring Freedom never included any significant stability operations (the initial objective was simply to oust the Taliban), it must be judged that these geostrategic aspects of Afghanistan were simply too daunting and that the United States simply proceeded with its subsequent nation-building objectives with only its overwhelming combat power and technological advantages as mitigation. These advantages ultimately proved weak in the face of the nature of war in Afghanistan. The United States should have understood that it cannot change the fundamental nature of the Afghan state in a way that could prevent a group like Al-Qaeda from residing there in the future. The conflicts in Iraq and Afghanistan should also attenuate the expectations of those who believe that liberal democracy can quickly take root and flourish in the Middle East and Central Asia.

The Surges

The successful use of a "surge" strategy in Iraq by President Bush in 2007 led President Obama to approve a similar augmentation of forces for Afghanistan in 2010. The 2007 surge of about 20,000 troops in Iraq was focused almost exclusively on Baghdad (and to a lesser degree on the city of Ramadi). It was designed to dampen the incidence of sectarian violence there and allow the Iraqi central government to restore order primarily in the one city in Iraq that mattered. The surge in Afghanistan was larger (some 33,000 men), but it was spread over much more terrain and not aligned with a true center of gravity.[39] Also, the surge in Afghanistan occurred before the host-nation security forces there were fully prepared to assist in attaining its operational goals. The surge in Iraq was considered highly successful, if not central to the end-game accomplishment; the surge in Afghanistan did not generate significant operational results.

Petreaus I and II, Crocker I and II

Unlike almost any other pair of wars, the same team of strategic leaders had turns at directing the war in both Iraq and Afghanistan. David Petreaus commanded MNF-I in Iraq from 2007 to 2009 and ISAF in Afghanistan from 2010 to 2011. Ryan Crocker served as the U.S. ambassador to Afghanistan in 2003 and to Iraq from 2007 to 2009, and then again to Afghanistan starting in 2010. Obviously the two men served together in Iraq over the same period. Overall Petreaus was considered highly successful in Iraq. He refocused the strategy there to take advantage of new advances in COIN doctrine and techniques and refocused his forces on the correct center of gravity (Baghdad and its environs) in order to make a telling operational impact on the enemy he faced. He was, of course, ably supported by subordinate commanders, including the highly talented Ray Odierno. Petreaus was not as successful in Afghanistan. He did not have nearly the same number of forces at his disposal (in a larger and more geographically difficult area of operations) and did not have the advantage of national command of all his assigned forces. Still his impact on the war in Afghanistan was clearly underwhelming.

Ryan Crocker brought significant cultural and diplomatic expertise to all three of his assignments during the period (as well as his assignment as U.S. ambassador to Pakistan earlier in the decade). He improved relations between the host-nation leaders (Maliki in Iraq and Karzai in Afghanistan) and the United States, even as the U.S. presence in their countries was accompanied by a variety of problems bound to infuriate any host nation (principally civilian casualties and collateral damage). Also he did much to coordinate the use of diplomatic, economic, legal, and informational tools in support of wartime national goals. He was certainly tremendously successful as a wartime ambassador in Iraq, and his performance in Afghanistan was nearly as noteworthy. Yet the U.S. goals he worked for remained elusive in Afghanistan through 2012. These factors reinforce the differences between Iraq and Afghanistan and point again to the ultimate conclusion that Afghanistan presents special problems that should caution any nation about the risks of waging war there.

Inevitable Questions

Given the lessons of recent history, it seems now that the United States would have been prudent to have withdrawn its forces from Afghanistan in 2005 after the departure of David Barno and Zal Khalilzad from Kabul. The American financial outlay and, more importantly, loss of life after 2006 did not warrant the gains made in Afghanistan after that time. Only the death of Osama bin Laden in 2010 reached a level of significance commensurate with the cost to America after 2006, and there is every reason to believe that his death would have occurred as quickly, or even more quickly, had the United States not been so deeply involved with activities inside Afghanistan and had placed the full weight of its global power instead on the hunt for the leader of Al-Qaeda next door in Pakistan.

It is equally evident that the United States did a poor job of conduct-ing two nearly simultaneous campaigns in two distant theaters of operation against the same major enemy. America failed to leverage its great economic and military power to crush Al-Qaeda after the fall of the Taliban. It also failed to manage the negative tide of international opinion, which actually favored recruitment for Al-Qaeda in the years after 2002, thereby increasing the size of its enemy. American logistical forces, its special operators, and its tactical units performed superbly under extremely difficult conditions, but as a nation, as the sole superpower, the United States appeared almost diffident strategically.

Finally, at the most basic level, the national command authority of the United States never attempted to manage the two fronts of its global war as coordinated efforts focused on a single strategic goal—the hobbling of inter-national terrorism. That goal would have taken time in any case, perhaps even ten years, but America did not address the sources of global terrorism or the methods of global reach that made its enemy so formidable in any synchro-nized way through its prosecution of the campaigns in Afghanistan and Iraq.

As previously noted the chairman of the Joint Chiefs had received what he thought was crystal clear guidance in 2008: focus on Iraq first; focus on Afghanistan second. What was not precise was just how far to elevate the first priority and economize on the second. In this regard, the guidance must come from the very top of the U.S. policy apparatus, the president. Without strong and firm guidance—"commander's intent," in military parlance—the depart-ments and agencies of the U.S. government are left to themselves to decide where to economize and by how much. The lack of senior-level attention to Afghanistan from 2006 through 2008, essentially the period that the United States attempted to outsource the Afghan campaign to NATO, potentially contributed to the rapid deterioration of the situation on multiple fronts: se-curity, governance, and development. When fighting a two-front war or mul-tiple campaigns, sufficient attention is required for each effort if both are to succeed. For the campaign in Afghanistan, being the economy-of-force theater went beyond simply logistics and tactics—it also included less attention from the top as leaders attempted to coordinate the two efforts. There must be a clear understanding of the trade-offs between theaters when one is clearly the priority and the other is merely an economy of effort.

The U.S. military learned a great deal in the crucible of combat. America made significant structural security reforms over ten years, and the international community banded together fairly well to combat global terrorism, but no significant defeat has yet been dealt to the motive force of the terrorist enemy. That will only occur when international organizations come together to develop international policing and legal processes strong enough to prevent terrorists from crossing international borders a second time.

Afghanistan, Iraq, and the United States

Democracy in Iraq will never mirror democracy in the United States; neither will the form of government in Afghanistan ever move far from tribal dominance. But governance in both countries has improved since the dark days before the U.S. invasions. Still, though democratic reform is a great boon, the war disrupted both local societies and killed untold thousands of civilians. The costs of the two wars to the United States has also been high in both financial and human terms, and America certainly lost significant prestige and respect around the world as a result of its missteps in both. The conflicts involving Afghanistan, Iraq, and the United States witnessed tremendous changes in the military capacity and doctrine of the American forces and in the execution of its national security strategy. The wars ushered in new approaches toward the Muslim world and opened the door to significant domestic changes within America as well. They were watershed events in many ways.

Once the management of the insurgency in Iraq had been accepted successfully by the Iraqi government, the United States assumed a military-support posture in that country. Very quickly thereafter, it also shifted its priorities back to the still-ongoing conflict in Afghanistan, which became the main military effort under the Obama administration. During that shift, the administration ended the use of the phrase "global war on terror," effectively de-linking the conflict in Iraq from the larger effort against global extremism and terrorism.

The transformation of the Iraqi and Afghan security forces was one of the best outcomes of the war. The Iraqi army was remade completely (albeit with coalition assistance in a Western mold), with proper tactical command and control, appropriate education and training for key commanders and staff, and newly empowered small-unit leaders. Additionally, at least at the higher levels, joint approaches were introduced and harmonized to improve the effectiveness of the entire defense organization. In Afghanistan the changes were larger numerically but far less progressive, as the Afghan army and police were far from capable in any modern conventional sense at the beginning of the decade; although the size of the ANA and ANP expanded more significantly their capabilities never reached that of their Iraqi counterparts. After ten years of methodical improvements they were both larger and more capable forces, and the command-and-control capacities of both had been strengthened; the stability of both their nations will rest almost entirely on their skills.

The American defense establishment also made some significant changes as the war progressed. Irregular warfare (defined as struggle among state and nonstate actors for legitimacy and influence over the relevant populations, to include counterinsurgency) came to be viewed as equal in importance to conventional combat among military professionals.[13] Thus, counterinsurgency finally was understood to deserve the same level of training effort and resources as did conventional warfare. The traditional American way of war evolved by the end of the decade to include more than massed combat power and techno-logical solutions; it had fully incorporated nontraditional actors, information operations, and the integration of other government agencies within its nor-mal approaches. The American way of war was still unique, but it had adapted to the norms of a new century.

Lessons of Fighting Two Theater Campaigns

The decision to conduct major campaigns in Afghanistan and Iraq clearly af-fected the success of each, and it should be clear that such a decision should not be undertaken voluntary by the United States in any future conflict.

The most valuable assessments that can be derived from the involvement of the United States in Iraq and Afghanistan should focus on the ability of a nation-state, particularly a wealthy industrial country, to wage two simultane-ous theater campaigns. At their most essential levels, both of these conflicts were conducted focused toward a single overarching (but often forgotten) end—regime change, aimed at the reduction of the threat of terrorism, which had been posed initially by Osama bin Laden's Al-Qaeda group (then resident in Afghanistan and nurtured by its government the Taliban) and by Saddam Hussein, the president of Iraq.

These two wars witnessed striking successes and puzzling defeats. Both offensive operations (in 2001 and in 2003) were brilliantly executed. But both were followed by disappointingly ineffective transitions to vaguely defined "post-hostilities operations." Overall the American strategies for conventional operations were superb, but those developed for stability operations were far less effective. Operational decision making improved significantly as the wars progressed, until by 2007 the American forces and their NATO allies were employing very sophisticated modes of operational integration that dominated the tempo of the fight and significantly reduced the opportunities for insurgents to act in a proactive manner. The critical political, strategic, and operational decisions that dramatically affected the outcomes of both wars will be instructive for years to come.

Whenever national leaders (particularly Americans) determine that they must conduct two simultaneous military efforts in different geographical areas, they must understand that prosecuting them requires that priorities be established and resource decisions kept in order so that the two efforts can develop the desired security outcomes. When those campaigns are waged as counterinsurgencies, those same leaders should additionally understand that their vision and strategic decisions must be for the longer term—longer, in fact, than their terms in office—durations that all too often grow increasingly difficult to sustain under domestic pressures. And when those campaigns involve anything more that the defeat of the enemy, when the desired outcomes include the building of national capacities, those leaders must be fully aware that their odds of developing such successful conclusions rest mightily on the host-nation leaders they partner with and the willingness of any other nation to give sanctuary and succor to the insurgents. Conducting multiple military efforts is a challenge for only the most dire of strategic circumstances.

Notes

Preface

1. U.S. Government, *The National Military Strategy of the United States of America: A Strategy for Today, a Vision for Tomorrow* (Washington, D.C., 2004), 3.
2. According to the U.S. Marine Corps, a *campaign* is a series of related military operations aimed at accomplishing a strategic or operational objective within a given time and space. A *campaign plan* describes how time, space, and purpose connect these operations. Usually a campaign is aimed at achieving some particular strategic result within a specific geographic theater. A war or other sustained conflict sometimes consists of a single campaign, sometimes of several. If there is more than one campaign, they can run either in sequence or—if there is more than one theater of war—simultaneously. U.S. Navy Dept., *Campaigning*, MCDP 1-2 (Washington, D.C.: Headquarters U.S. Marine Corps, August 1, 1997), 3.
3. Colin S. Gray, "War: Continuity in Change, and Change in Continuity," *Parameters* 40, no. 2 (Summer 2010), 6.

Prologue

1. Hashim Shukoor and Nancy A. Youssef, "Helicopter Taliban Downed Was Carrying Navy SEALs," McClatchy Newspapers, August 6, 2011, http://www.mcclatchydc.com/2011/08/06/119718/taliban-down-us-helicopter-in.html#ixzz1UI7HTnnJ.
2. MSNBC.com staff and news service reports, "31 US Troops, Mostly Elite Navy SEALs, Killed in Afghanistan," August 6, 2011, http://www.msnbc.msn.com/id/44043847/ns/world_news-south_and_central asia/?gt1=43001.
3. Amy Belasco, *The Cost of Iraq, Afghanistan, and Other Global War on Terror Operations since 9/11,* Report RL33110 (Washington, D.C.: Congressional Research Service, March 29, 2011), 1.
4. By 2011 many in the Muslim world were convinced that the policies of the United States were imperial, anti-Islamic, and commonly misrepresent-

ed by American officials to seem less aggressive than they were intended to be. America had lost the public relations war by invading Iraq, ignoring Pakistani sovereignty and establishing bases in several Central Asian nations.

Chapter 1: Fighting Two Enemies

1. Michael Gerson, "The Necessary Three-Front War," *Washington Post,* April 30, 2008, http://www.washingtonpost.com/wp-dyn/content/article /2008/04/29/AR2008042902549.html.
2. U.S. Government Printing Office, "Public Law 107-40:——Authorization for Use of Military Force," http://www.gpo.gov/fdsys/pkg/PLAW -107publ40/content-detail.html.
3. U.S. Government Printing Office, "Public Law 107-243:——Authorization for Use of Military Force against Iraq Resolution of 2002," http:// www.gpo.gov/fdsys/pkg/PLAW-107publ243/content-detail.html.
4. Language denouncing Iraq activities such as "continuing to possess and develop a significant chemical and biological weapons capability, actively seeking a nuclear weapons capability, and supporting and harboring terrorist organizations." Also other references to factual inaccuracies, such as: "members of al Qaida, an organization bearing responsibility for attacks on the United States, its citizens, and interests, including the attacks that occurred on September 11, 2001, are known to be in Iraq; whereas Iraq continues to aid and harbor other international terrorist organizations, including organizations that threaten the lives and safety of United States citizens."
5. Peter Antill, Peter Dennis, *Stalingrad 1942* (Oxford, U.K.: Osprey, 2007), 7.
6. A two-front war is a conflict wherein the fighting takes place on two geographically separated fronts. It is usually executed by two or more separate forces simultaneously, or nearly simultaneously, in the hope that the opponent will be forced to split its fighting force to deal with both threats, therefore reducing the opponent's odds of success.
7. Wesley K. Clark, *Winning Modern Wars: Iraq, Terrorism, and the American Empire* (New York: PublicAffairs, 2003), 130.
8. Antulio J. Echevarria II, *"An American Way of War or Way of Battle?"* (Carlisle, Pa.: U.S. Army War College, Strategic Studies Institute, n.d.), http:// www.strategicstudiesinstitute.army.mil/pdffiles/pub662.pdf.
9. Examples of less than altruistic national objectives are expansion in the Mexican War and revenge and expansion in the Spanish American War, to name only two instances.
10. See Russell F. Weigley, *The American Way of War: A History of United States Military Strategy and Policy* (New York: Macmillan, 1973).
11. Echevarria, *American Way of War,* 2.
12. That UN-sanctioned intervention operation was led by Australia. See John R. Ballard, *Triumph of Self-determination: Operation Stabilise and United Nations Peacemaking in East Timor* (Westport, Conn.: Praeger Security International, 2008).

13. American Forces Press Service, "Afghanistan Still Crucial to U.S. Interests, Obama Says," June 28, 2010, http://www.globalsecurity.org/military/library/news/2010/06/mil-100628-afps04.htm.

14. For many, the fact that the stated military policy of the United States in 2001 had been that it was prepared to fight two near-simultaneous major military operations at the same time (then conceived to be Iraq and North Korea) seemed ludicrous after 2005. See Thom Shanker and Eric Schmitt, "Pentagon Weighs Strategy Change to Deter Terror," *New York Times,* July 5, 2005, http://www.nytimes.com/2005/07/05/politics/05strategy.html?adxnnl=1&pagewanted=print&adxnnlx=1325164877-wG7PbvNaYtrBC2hl39NHDQ.

15. Dana J. Pittard, "Thirteenth Century Mongol Warfare: Classical Military Strategy of Operational Art?" (course paper Army Command and General Staff College, School of Advanced Military Studies, Fort Leavenworth Kans., May 5, 1994).

16. Robert M. Epstein, *Napoleon's Last Victory and the Emergence of Modern War* (Lawrence: University Press of Kansas, 1994).

17. The siege of Charleston was one of the major battles of the American Revolutionary War. It was the beginning of the shift in strategic focus by the British toward fighting in the southern colonies. It also saw the biggest loss of troops suffered by the American army in the war.

18. Bruce W. Menning, "Operational Art's Origins," *Military Review* 77, no. 5 (September–October 1997), 32–47, quoting James J. Schneider, "War Plan RAINBOW 5," *Defense Analysis* (December 1994), 289–92.

19. Peter Hopkirk, *The Great Game* (London: Oxford University Press, 1990), 263–64.

20. Terence R. Blackburn, *The Extermination of a British Army: The Retreat from Cabul* (Midland, Tex.: APH, 2008), 121.

21. See Michael Barthorp, *Afghan Wars and the North-West Frontier 1839–1947.* (London: Cassell, 2002).

22. See D. S. Richards, *The Savage Frontier: A History of the Anglo-Afghan Wars* (London: Pan Books, 2003).

23. August 19 later became Afghan Independence Day.

24. David Greenberg, "Blundering into Afghanistan: The Great Game Has Repeatedly Foiled the Great Powers," *Slate*, September 20, 2001, http://www.slate.com/id/115851/.

25. Robert M. Gates, *From the Shadows: The Ultimate Insider's Story of Five Presidents and How They Won the Cold War* (New York: Simon & Schuster, 2006), 145.

26. Martin Ewans, *Afghanistan: A Short History of Its People and Politics* (New York: HarperCollins, 2002), 196.

27. Mohammed Daud Khan overthrew the monarchy of his first cousin, Mohammed Zahir Shah, to become the first president of Afghanistan in 1973. He ruled the country until his assassination in 1978 by the PDPA.

28. Robert D. Kaplan, *Soldiers of God: With Islamic Warriors in Afghanistan and Pakistan* (New York: Vintage Departures, 2001), 115.

29. Barnett R. Rubin, *The Fragmentation of Afghanistan* (New Haven, Conn.: Yale University Press, 1995), 20.

30. Michael Kort, *The Soviet Colossus: History and Aftermath* (Armonk, N.Y.: M. E. Sharpe, 2001), 309.

31. Peter Bergen, *Holy War Inc* (New York: Free Press, 2001), 68.

32. Olivier Roy, *Islam and Resistance in Afghanistan* (Cambridge: Cambridge University Press, 1990), 118.

33. Bruce J. Amstutz, *Afghanistan: The First Five Years of Soviet Occupation* (Washington, D.C.: National Defense University Press, 1986), 127.

34. Lester W. Grau and Michael A. Gress, *The Soviet-Afghan War: How a Superpower Fought and Lost* (Lawrence: University Press of Kansas, 2002), 26.

35. Roy, *Islam and Resistance in Afghanistan,* 191.

36. Amstutz, *Afghanistan,* 43.

37. Peter R. Blood, ed. *Afghanistan: A Country Study* (Washington: U.S. Government Printing Office [hereafter GPO] for the Library of Congress, 2001), 103.

38. Roy, *Islam and Resistance in Afghanistan.*

39. Central Intelligence Agency, "*The Soviet Invasion of Afghanistan: Five Years After*" (Washington, D.C.: Directorate of Intelligence, May 1985), 1, http://www.gwu.edu/~nsarchiv/NSAEBB/NSAEBB57/us5.pdf.

40. Tim Weiner, *Blank Check: The Pentagon's Black Budget* (New York: Warner Books, 1990), 149.

41. See George Crile, *Charlie Wilson's War: The Extraordinary Story of the Largest Covert Operation in History* (New York: Atlantic Monthly, 2003).

42. Oswald Johnston, "Refugees inside Afghanistan to Get U.S. Aid," *Los Angeles Times,* May 9, 1985, http://articles.latimes.com/1985-05-09/news/mn-6690_1_refugee-aid.

43. Niel S. Annen, "Echoes of the Soviet Surge: The West's War in Afghanistan Increasingly Resembles the Soviet Union's, *Foreign Policy* (March 2, 2011), http://www.foreignpolicy.com/articles/2011/03/02/echoes_of_the_soviet_surge.

44. Mark Urban, *War in Afghanistan* (New York: St. Martin's, 1990), 251.

45. Philip Taubman, "Soviet Lists Afghan War Toll: 13,310 Dead, 35,478 Wounded," *New York Times,* May 26, 1988, http://www.nytimes.com/1988/05/26/world/soviet-lists-afghan-war-toll-13310-dead-35478-wounded.html.

46. Lester W. Grau, "Breaking Contact without Leaving Chaos: The Soviet Withdrawal from Afghanistan," *Journal of Slavic Military Studies* 20, no. 2 (June 2007), 235.

47. David G. Fivecoat, "Leaving the Graveyard: The Soviet Union's Withdrawal from Afghanistan" (unpublished paper, National War College, Washington, D.C., April 2012), 4.

48. Rafael Reuveny and Aseem Prakash, "The Afghanistan War and the Break-down of the Soviet Union," *Review of International Studies* 25 (1999), 696.

49. See Seth G. Jones, *In the Graveyard of Empires: America's War in Afghanistan* (New York: W. W. Norton, 2009).

50. Victor Davis Hansen, "A Familiar Western Experience in Ancient Afghanistan," in *Afghan Endgames: Strategy and Policy Choices for America's Longest War*, ed. Hy S. Rothstein and John Arquilla (Washington, D.C.: Georgetown University Press, 2012), 17–38. See also Christian Caryl, "Bury the Graveyard," *Foreign Policy* (July 26, 2010), http://www.foreignpolicy.com/ articles/2010/07/26/bury_the_graveyard, as well as Thomas J. Barfield, *Afghanistan: A Cultural and Political History* (Princeton, N.J.: Princeton University Press, 2010).

51. Rothstein and Arquilla, *Afghan Endgames*, 29.

52. See John Prados, ed., "Volume II: Afghanistan: Lessons from the Last War," *National Security Archive,* October 9, 2001, http://www.gwu.edu/~nsarchiv/ NSAEBB/NSAEBB57/us.html.

Chapter 2: The Attacks of 9/11 and the Decision to Go to War in Afghanistan

1. U.S. Government, *Final Report of the National Commission on Terrorist Attacks upon the United States* (Washington D.C.: GPO, n.d. [2004]) [hereafter *9/11 Commission Report*], 60, and endnote 48, 468, http://govinfo.library.unt .edu/911/report/911Report.pdf, accessed December 11, 2010.

2. "Perry: U.S. Eyed Iran Attack after Bombing," United Press International, http://www.upi.com/Security_Terrorism/Briefing/2007/06/06/perry _us_eyed_iran_attack_after_bombing/7045/, accessed December 11, 2010.

3. U.S. Department of State, *Report of the Accountability Review Board–Executive Summary* (Washington, D.C.: January 8, 1999), http://www.state.gov/ www/regions/africa/board_overview.html.

4. U.S. District Court, Southern District of New York, *Indictment # S(9) 98 Cr. 1023,* http://fl1.findlaw.com/news.findlaw.com/hdocs/docs/binladen /usbinladen1.pdf.

5. *Report of the Joint Inquiry into the Terrorist Attacks of September 11, 2001 by the House Permanent Select Committee on Intelligence and the Senate Select Committee on Intelligence* (Washington, D.C.: December 2002) [hereafter *Joint Inquiry*], 286, http://www.gpoaccess.gov/serialset/creports/pdf/fullreport_errata .pdf.

6. The ten programs and the lead agencies were outlined to the joint inquiry by Richard Clarke as apprehension, extradition, rendition, and prosecution (Department of Justice); disruption (CIA); international cooperation (State); preventing terrorist acquisition of weapons of mass destruction (National Security Council); consequence management (Department of Justice/Federal Emergency Management Agency); transportation security (Department of Transportation); protection of critical infrastructure and

cybersystems (National Security Council); continuity of operations (National Security Council); countering the foreign terrorist threat in the United States (Department of Justice); and protection of Americans overseas (Departments of State and Defense).

7. Hugh H. Shelton, *Without Hesitation: The Odyssey of an American Warrior* (St. Martin's, October 2010), 343–51. See also Steve Coll, *Ghost Wars: The Secret History of the CIA, Afghanistan, and Bin Laden, from the Soviet Invasion to September 10, 2001* (Penguin, 2004), 643. Karamat and Prime Minister Nawaz Sharif were both infuriated when the missiles were finally detected. According to Coll, "When Pakistani authorities learned that two of the missiles had fallen short and hit inside Pakistani territory, they denounced the attack in public and in private."

8. *Joint Inquiry,* 230–31.

9. Ibid., 232.

10. Even with strong evidence of Al-Qaeda involvement there are some who are reluctant to hold bin Laden culpable. See "The Trail of Evidence & the Warnings," *Frontline,* http://www.pbs.org/wgbh/pages/frontline/shows /binladen/bombings/, and, "USS Cole Attack Verdicts Upheld," *BBC News,* February 26, 2005, http://news.bbc.co.uk/go/pr/fr/-/2/hi/middle _east/4300015.stm.

11. *9/11 Commission Report,* 191.

12. Ibid.

13. Ibid., *The Military, Staff Statement No. 6.,* 4.

14. *9/11 Commission Report,* 194.

15. Shelton, *Without Hesitation,* 342.

16. Coll, *Ghost Wars,* 386.

17. U.S. Department of State Information, memo, "Pushing for Peace in Afghanistan," n.d., National Security Archive, George Washington University, Washington, D.C., www.gwu.edu/~nsarchiv/.

18. *9/11 Commission Report,* 183.

19. "George W. Bush for President 2000 Campaign Brochure, *4President.org,* http://www.4president.org/brochures/georgewbush2000brochure.htm, accessed November 26, 2010.

20. Condoleezza Rice, "Campaign 2000: Promoting the National Interest," *Foreign Affairs* (January/February 2000), http://www.foreignaffairs.com /articles/55630/condoleezza-rice/campaign-2000-promoting-the -national-interest.

21. George W. Bush, *Decision Points* (New York: Crown, 2010), 205.

22. George W. Bush, "A Period of Consequences" (speech delivered at The Citadel, Charleston, S.C., September 23, 1999), http://www.citadel.edu /pao/addresses/pres_bush.html.

23. Ibid.

24. *9/11 Commission Report, National Policy Coordination, Staff Statement No. 8.,* 9.

25. National Security Council, memorandum, "Presidential Policy Initiative/

Review: The Al Qaida Network," January 25, 2001, National Security Archive, George Washington University, Washington, D.C., www.gwu.edu /~nsarchiv/.

26. Ibid.

27. Also available from the National Security Archive, George Washington University, Washington, D.C., www.gwu.edu/~nsarchiv/.

28. Coll, *Ghost Wars,* 566.

29. Ibid., 564.

30. *9/11 Commission Report,* 203.

31. Ibid., 204–205.

32. Ibid., 206.

33. Benjamin S. Lambeth, *Air Power against Terror* (Santa Monica, Calif.: RAND, 2005), 5-6.

34. Lieutenant General Michael DeLong, with Noah Lukeman, *Inside CENT-COM: The Unvarnished Truth about the Wars in Afghanistan and Iraq* (Washington, D.C.: Regnery, 2004), 18.

35. Bush, *Decision Points,* 134.

36. The Senate unanimously approved the resolution, voting ninety-eight to none, with two "not present" (Sen. Jesse Helms and Sen. Larry Craig). The House voted 420 to one, with ten "not voting." The lone "nay" vote was Rep. Barbara Lee, a Democrat representing California's Ninth District (Berkeley to Castro Valley).

37. Bob Woodward, *Bush at War* (New York: Simon & Schuster, 2003), 79–80.

38. Bush, *Decision Points,* 184.

39. Woodward, *Bush at War,* 61.

40. Ibid.

41. Gary C. Schroen, *First In: An Insider's Account of How the CIA Spearheaded the War on Terror in Afghanistan* (New York: Ballantine, 2005), 15–16.

42. Bush, *Decision Points,* 186.

43. Ibid., 187.

44. Woodward, *Bush at War,* 91.

45. Ibid., 87.

46. Bush, *Decision Points,* 194.

47. *9/11 Commission Report,* 337. Bush, *Decision Points,* 194. See also Donald P. Wright et al. *A Different Kind of War: The United States Army in Operation ENDURING FREEDOM October 2001–September 2005* (Fort Leavenworth, Kans.: Combat Studies Institute Press, May 2010), 46. Franks would continue to revise and update the OEF plan, and much of the Phase IV detail was not added until several weeks into the start of combat operations. In fact Franks did not publish the final version of the OEF plan until late November 2001. (See Wright, *Different Kind of War,* 48.)

48. Michael R. Gordon, "Scarcity of Afghan Targets Leads U.S. to Revise Strategy," *New York Times,* September 19, 2001, http://www.nytimes.com/2001/09/19/international/19MILI.html.

49. Lambeth, *Air Power against Terror*, 52–53.
50. Wright, *Different Kind of War*, 43–44. The Russians, while supportive of the U.S. intentions to go after Al-Qaeda and the Taliban, were less than optimistic about the outcome. One Russian general remarked to U.S. interlocutors, "I have to say you're really going to get the hell kicked out of you." Woodward, *Bush at War*, 103.
51. Ibid., *Bush at War*, 29.
52. Lambeth, *Air Power against Terror*, 54–72. Lambeth provides an excellent and detailed account of the preparatory movements of the U.S. military.
53. Ibid., 83.
54. Bob Woodward and Dan Balz, "Combating Terrorism: 'It Starts Today,'" *Washington Post*, February 1, 2002; A01.
55. SOCCENT (Special Operations Command, Central) was the special operations headquarters for General Frank's combatant command, responsible for all special operations activities in the Afghan operations area.
56. Wright, *Different Kind of War*, 48.
57. SOCOM was Special Operations Command, the global headquarters for all American special operations forces and activities, headquartered in Tampa near CENTCOM.
58. Wright, *Different Kind of War*, 62.
59. Lambeth, *Air Power against Terror*, 78–80.
60. Ibid., 61.
61. Wright., *Different Kind of War*, 75.
62. Ibid., 73, 95.
63. DeLong, *Inside CENTCOM*, 164.
64. Bush, *Decision Points*, 220, 205.

Chapter 3: The Opening Gambit

1. "The forces the United States and its allies had trained and armed now fought each other in complex coalitions for control of Afghanistan. Though the United States did not take part in this war directly, it did not lose all interest in Afghanistan. Rather, it was prepared to exert its influence through allies, particularly Pakistan. Most important, it was prepared to accept that the Islamic fighters it had organized against the Soviets would govern Afghanistan. There were many factions, but with Pakistani support, a coalition called the Taliban took power in 1996. The Taliban in turn provided sanctuary for a group of international jihadists called Al-Qaeda, and this led to increased tensions with the Taliban following jihadist attacks on U.S. facilities abroad by Al-Qaeda." See George Friedman, "The 30-Year War in Afghanistan," *Stratfor*, June 29, 2010, http://www.stratfor.com/weekly/20100628_30_year_war_afghanistan?ip_auth _redirect=1#ixzz1h5sphQg1.
2. Bush, *Decision Points*, 194.
3. Wright, *Different Kind of War*, 4. See also Christopher N. Koontz, ed., *Enduring Voices: Oral Histories of the U.S. Army Experience in Afghanistan, 2003–*

2005 (Washington, D.C.: U.S. Army Center of Military History, 2008).

4. See Richard Clarke, classified NSC memo to Condoleezza Rice, January 25, 2001, *The National Security Archive, George Washington University,* http:// www.gwu.edu/~nsarchiv/NSAEBB/NSAEBB147/clarke%20memo.pdf.

5. Richard C. Clarke "A Strategy for Eliminating the Threat from the Jihadist Networks of Al Qaida; Status and Prospects," *National Security Archive, George Washington University,* http://www.gwu.edu/~nsarchiv/NSAEBB /NSAEBB147/clarke%20attachment.pdf.

6. Ibid.

7. Bush, *Decision Points,* 188.

8. Forrest L. Marion, "Building USAF 'Expeditionary Bases' for Operation Enduring Freedom–Afghanistan, 2001–2002," *Air & Space Power Journal* (18 November 2005), http://www.au.af.mil/au/cadre/aspj/airchronicles/cc/ marion.html.

9. Woodward, *Bush at War,* 148.

10. Bush, *Decision Points,* 194.

11. Commission on the Intelligence Capabilities of the United States Regarding Weapons of Mass Destruction, *Report to the President of the United States* (Washington, D.C., 31 March 2005).

12. The CENTCOM area of responsibility covered the "central" area of the globe and comprised twenty countries. In addition to Afghanistan, CENTCOM was responsible for U.S. military activities in Bahrain, Egypt, Iran, Iraq, Jordan, Kazakhstan, Kuwait, Kyrgyzstan, Lebanon, Oman, Pakistan, Qatar, Saudi Arabia, Syria, Tajikistan, Turkmenistan, United Arab Emirates, Uzbekistan, and Yemen.

13. The mission assigned to Schroen was simple: "Go find the al Qaeda and kill them. . . . Get bin Laden." Woodward, *Bush at War,* 139–41.

14. Sharon Weinberger, "The CIA, Siberia and the $5m Bar Bill: A Federal Court Case Reveals a Bizarre Tale of Post-9/11 Operations in Afghanistan," *New York Post,* August 17, 2009, http://www.nypost.com/p/news/ opinion/opedcolumnists/item_Kl183f4pzMzHx2MwItC6cK#ixzz1hBP v4xsa.

15. Woodward, *Bush at War,* 143.

16. George Bush, *Selected Speeches of President George W. Bush, 2001–2008,* 65–75, http://georgewbush-whitehouse.archives.gov/infocus/bushrecord/ documents/Selected_Speeches_George_W_Bush.pdf.

17. Woodward, *Bush at War,* 154.

18. "Strikes Target Taliban's Air Defenses," *St. Petersburg Times,* October 8, 2001, http://www.sptimes.com/News/100801/Worldandnation/Strikes _target_Taliba.shtml.

19. Michael Kilian and Colin McMahon, "Strikes Target Taliban Troops," *Chicago Tribune,* October 23, 2001, www.chicagotribune.com/chi-0110230274 oct23,0,4831702.story.

20. Wright, *Different Kind of War,* 63.

21. Ibid., 64.

22. Tommy Franks, *American Soldier* (New York: Regan Books, 2004), 255–56, 286–87.

23. Wright, *Different Kind of War*, 10.

24. Abdul Rashid Dostum was a former pro-Soviet fighter during the Soviet war in Afghanistan and is considered by many to be the leader of Afghanistan's Uzbek community. He later grew close to Hamid Karzai and became the chief of staff to the commander in chief of the Afghan National Army.

25. Tony Karon, "Rebels: Mazar-i-Sharif Is Ours," *Time,* November 9, 2001, http://www.time.com/time/nation/article/0,8599,183885,00.html #ixzz1hHxg5XmK.

26. U.S. Army Center for Military History, *The United States Army in Afghanistan, Operation ENDURING FREEDOM, October 2001–March 2003,* CMH Pub 70-83-1, 15.

27. Ibid.

28. David Rohde, "A Nation Challenged: The Front Line—Waging a Deadly Stalemate on Afghanistan's Front Line," *New York Times,* October 28, 2001, http://www.nytimes.com/2001/10/28/world/nation-challenged -front-line-waging-deadly-stalemate-afghanistan-s-front-line.html; "Massive American Bombing on Taliban Front Lines," *Fox News,* November 5, 2001, http://www.foxnews.com/story/0,2933,38013,00.html# ixzz1h72zEQZk.

29. Friedman, "30-Year War in Afghanistan."

30. JSOC normally worked for SOCOM, not CENTCOM, but was well practiced at working for other combatant commanders.

31. Major General Dell Dailey, USA, commanded Task Force Sword, but his forward commander for operations was Brigadier General Gregory Trepon, USAF.

32. Wright, *Different Kind of War*, 14.

33. Austin Mansfield, "Enduring Freedom Task Force Earns Presidential Unit Citation," Story Number NNS041208-06, Navy.mil, December 8, 2004, http://www.navy.mil/search/print.asp?story_id=16216&VIRIN=&ima getype=0&page=1. See also "JTF2: Canada's Super-Secret commandos," *CBC News,* July 15, 2005, http://www.cbc.ca/news/background/cdn military/jtf2.html.

34. This section is based on "Unclassified Documents from Marine Task Force 58's Operations in Afghanistan," *Strategy Page,* http://www.strategypage .com/articles/tf58/default.asp.

35. Though it had been previously exercised, this was the first time operational combat command of Navy and Marine forces afloat had been given to a Marine Corps general. Mattis had been forward deployed in Egypt for Exercise Bright Star, as had General Franks.

36. Ibid.

37. Wright, *Different Kind of War*, 19.

38. "Execution 25 November to 25 December," *Strategy Page,* http://www .strategypage.com/articles/tf58/execution.asp.

39. Wright, *Different Kind of War,* 21.

40. "Taliban Lose [*sic*] Grip on Mazar-i-Sharif, *Guardian,* 7 November 2001, http://www.guardian.co.uk/world/2001/nov/07/afghanistan.terrorism1.

41. Wright, *Different Kind of War,* 21.

42. *Center for Military History, The United States Army in Afghanistan,* 19.

43. Wright, *Different Kind of War,* 20.

44. Peter Bergen, "The Battle for Tora Bora: How Osama bin Laden Slipped from Our Grasp—The Definitive Account," *New Republic,* December 22, 2009, http://www.tnr.com/print/article/the-battle-tora-bora.

45. Ibid.

46. Bergen, "Battle for Tora Bora."

47. Ibid.

48. Ibid.

49. Mike Mount, "Document Suggests bin Laden Escaped at Tora Bora," CNN, March 24, 2005, http://articles.cnn.com/2005-03-24/us/pentagon .binladen_1_tora-bora-bin-john-stufflebeem?_s=PM:US.

50. Bergen, "Battle for Tora Bora."

51. Matthew Forney "Inside the Tora Bora Caves," *Time,* December 11, 2001, http://www.time.com/time/world/article/0,8599,188029,00.html #ixzz1hIRBZoul.

52. Bergen, "Battle for Tora Bora."

53. Wright, *Different Kind of War,* 27.

54. A *loya jirga* is a mass meeting, or grand council, usually held in preparation for major events such as choosing a new king, adopting a constitution, or discussing important national matters, as well as for solving disputes, in Pashtun areas of Afghanistan and Pakistan.

55. The resolution in total can be found at Afghanistan International Security Assistance Force, http://www.nato.int/isaf/topics/mandate/unscr/ resolution_1386.pdf.

56. Wright, *Different Kind of War,* 182.

57. See the UN New Center Summary Report, *United Nations,* http://www .un.org/News/dh/latest/afghan/un-afghan-history.shtml.

58. See the Japanese Ministry of Foreign Affairs Summary report at *Ministry of Foreign Affairs of Japan,* http://www.mofa.go.jp/region/middle_e/afghan istan/min0201/.

59. See UN New Center Summary Report.

60. Thomas Barfield, "Afghan Paradoxes," in Rothstein and Arquilla, *Afghan Endgames,* 40.

61. Barfield, "Afghan Paradoxes," 53.

62. Franks, *American Soldier,* 268.

63. One example of a linked policy decision designed for Enduring Freedom was the establishment of the holding facility at Guantanamo Bay, Cuba, in January 2002.

64. Franks, *American Soldier,* 329.

65. Ibid., 331.

66. Ibid, 329.

67. President Bush and General Franks were both Texans, and they got along quite well.

68. Carl Conetta, *Strange Victory: A Critical Appraisal of Operation Enduring Freedom and the Afghanistan War,* Research Monograph 6 (Cambridge, Mass.: Commonwealth Institute, Project on Defense Alternatives, 30 January 2002), 4–5.

69. "Operation Enduring Freedom—Afghanistan," GlobalSecurity.org, http://www.globalsecurity.org/military/ops/enduring-freedom-plan.htm.

70. Bradley Graham, "Pentagon Plans a Redirection in Afghanistan," *Washington Post,* 20 November 2002, A.1.

71. Wright, *Different Kind of War,* 30.

72. Ibid., 31.

73. Ibid., 32.

74. Ibid.

75. Ibid., 35.

76. "Operation Anaconda Costs 8 U.S. lives," *CNN,* March 4, 2002, http://articles.cnn.com/2002-03-04/world/ret.afghan.fighting_1_shahi-kot-afghan-forces-qaeda-and-taliban?_s=PM:asiapcf.

77. Wright, *Different Kind of War,* 32.

78. Ibid., 37–38.

79. Ibid., 39.

80. Ibid., 40–41.

81. Petty Officer Roberts was awarded the Bronze Star. His citation read in part, "Petty Officer First Class Neil Roberts was standing in the rear by the open exit ramp when the first rounds struck. With the severed line spraying hydraulic fluid everywhere and the chopper jerking this way and that, Roberts lost his balance and fell to the snowy ground below. Roberts collected himself, activated his emergency beacon, and then took stock. His only weapons were a pistol and two hand grenades. Unfortunately his light machine gun had not fallen out of the chopper, too. Three Al-Qaeda fighters began moving in. Roberts crawled toward better cover, engaging the terrorists with the pistol and grenades. He soon ran out of ammunition. Nobody knows what happened next. Images broadcast by a Predator unmanned aerial vehicle showed three men dragging him away. A rescue team later recovered his body. Roberts had been shot to death." See "Neal Roberts," NavySEALs.com, http://www.navyseals.com/neil-roberts.

82. Technical Sergeant John A. Chapman, Senior Airman Jason D. Cunningham, Private First Class Matthew A. Commons, Sergeant Bradley S. Crose, Specialist Marc A. Anderson, and Sergeant Phillip Svitak. See the Department of Defense summary report, "Executive Summary of the Battle of Takur Ghar," *U.S. Department of Defense,* May 24, 2002, http://www.defense.gov/news/May2002/d20020524takurghar.pdf.

83. See also Malcolm MacPherson, *Roberts Ridge* (New York: Bantam Dell, 2005), and Sean Naylor, *Not a Good Day to Die* (New York: Penguin, 2005).
84. Wright, *Different Kind of War*, 44.
85. Elaine Grossman, "Was Operation Anaconda Ill-Fated from Start? Army Analyst Blames Afghan Battle Failings on Bad Command Set-Up," *Inside the Pentagon*, July 29, 2004, 1, http://www.dnipogo.org/grossman/army _analyst_blames.htm.
86. Conetta, *Strange Victory*, 4–5.
87. Ibid.
88. Ibid., 3.
89. See John R. Ballard, *From Storm to Freedom: America's Long War with Iraq* (Annapolis, Md.: Naval Institute Press, 2010), 108.
90. Franks, *American Soldier*, 342.
91. Ibid., 349–51.
92. Ibid., 355–56.
93. Harlan Ullman, *Shock and Awe: Achieving Rapid Dominance* (Washington, D.C.: Center for Advanced Concepts and Technology, 1996).
94. Franks, *American Soldier*, 370.
95. Ibid., 366.
96. Michael R. Gordon and Bernard E. Trainor, *Cobra II: The Inside Story of the Invasion and Occupation of Iraq* (New York: Pantheon Books, 2006), 44.
97. Ibid., 44.
98. Ibid., 50–51.
99. Ibid.

Chapter 4: Iraq and the Iraqi Freedom Campaign

1. Franks, *American Soldier*, 431.
2. Richard Clarke, *Against All Enemies: Inside America's War on Terror* (New York: Free Press, 2004), 32.
3. Woodward, *Bush at War*, 99.
4. Franks, *American Soldier*, 268.
5. See Bergen, "Battle for Tora Bora."
6. United Nations Security Council Resolution 1386 was adopted unanimously on December 20, 2001. It reaffirmed the previous resolutions on the situation in Afghanistan and authorized the establishment of the International Security Assistance Force to assist the Afghan Interim Authority in the maintenance of security in Kabul and surrounding areas.
7. The UN-sponsored Bonn Conference led to the appointment of the Afghan Interim Administration under the chairmanship of Hamid Karzai. The Interim Administration was scheduled to govern for only six months before being replaced by a Transitional Administration. The move to this second stage would require the convening of a traditional Afghan *loya jirga*. The *loya jirga* elected Karzai as the new head of state in June 2002 and appointed the Transitional Administration, which, in turn, would run

the country for a maximum of two more years until a fully representative government could be elected.

8. George W. Bush, "State of the Union Address," January 29, 2002.

9. Unlike in Afghanistan, an attack into Iraq without proximate provocation required the United States to deploy a large and highly visible force. So if America was to go to war on its own time line it would be necessary to do so with great secrecy and to deploy the force against the Iraqi regime quickly.

10. Lutfullah Mashal, "An Escalating, High-Altitude Showdown: The US and Allies Have Killed Hundreds, but Enemy Ranks Have Been Renewed," *Christian Science Monitor,* March 8, 2002, http://www.csmonitor.com/2002/0308/p01s04-wosc.html.

11. Michael Barone, "The Road to Baghdad," *U.S. News & World Report,* June 17, 2002, as well as Gerry J. Gilmore, "Bush: West Point Grads Answer History's Call to Duty," American Forces Press Service, http://www.defenselink.mil/news/newsarticle.aspx?id=43798.

12. Thomas E. Ricks and Vernon Loeb, "Bush Developing Military Policy of Striking First: New Doctrine Addresses Terrorism," *Washington Post,* June 10, 2002, A01.

13. Gregory Fontenot, E. J. Degen, and David Tohn, *On Point: The United States Army in Operation Iraqi Freedom* (Annapolis, Md.: Naval Institute Press, 2005), 29.

14. Elliot Blair Smith, "U.S. Helping Create an Army in Afghanistan," *USA Today,* November 28, 2002, http://www.usatoday.com/news/world/2002-11-26-afghan-usat_x.htm.

15. NSPD 24 has yet to be made public.

16. Donald P. Wright and Timothy R. Reese, *On Point II: The United States Army in Operation Iraqi Freedom, May 2003–January 2005—Transition to the New Campaign* (Fort Leavenworth, Kans.: Combat Studies Institute Press, 2008), 70.

17. In addition to Lieutenant General McKiernan as the land component commander and Lieutenant General Buzz Moseley as the air component commander, Marine lieutenant general Earl Hailston served as the Marine component commander, Vice Admiral Tom Keating as the naval and maritime component commander, and Army brigadier general Gary Harrell as the joint special operations component commander.

18. Franks, *American Soldier,* xvi, and Bush, *Decision Points,* 223.

19. See Ballard, *From Storm to Freedom,* 129.

20. Jim Lacey, *Takedown: The 3rd Infantry Division's Twenty-One-Day Assault on Baghdad* (Annapolis, Md.: Naval Institute Press, 2007), 45.

21. Ibid., 49.

22. Ibid., 58.

23. Gordon and Trainor, *Cobra II,* 209.

24. General Franks said several times, "The key is speed . . . speed kills, the enemy." Franks, *American Soldier,* 466.

25. Lacey, *Takedown*, 89. This was particularly serious because the major supply base for the continuing operations of V Corps (Objective Rams) was just to the west of Najaf and within easy striking distance—it had to be protected if the advance were to continue successfully toward Baghdad.

26. See Nicholas E. Reynolds., *Basrah, Baghdad, and Beyond: U.S. Marine Corps in the Second Iraq War* (Annapolis, Md.: Naval Institute Press, 2005), 92; Gordon and Trainor, *Cobra II*, 304–5; and Lacey, *Takedown*, 119–21. General Franks had a very different perspective; see Franks, *American Soldier*, 508–509.

27. Rick Atkinson, "General: A Longer War Likely, Logistics, Enemy Force Reevaluation," *The Washington Post*, March 28, 2003, A01. The article said in part, "The Army's senior ground commander in Iraq, Lt. Gen. William S. Wallace, said today that overextended supply lines and a combative adversary using unconventional tactics have stalled the U.S. drive toward Baghdad and increased the likelihood of a longer war than many strategists had anticipated."

28. Kevin M. Woods and Michael R. Pease, *The Iraqi Perspectives Report: Saddam's Senior Leadership on Operation Iraqi Freedom from the Official U.S. Joint Forces Command Report* (Annapolis, Md.: Naval Institute Press, 2006), 32.

29. The entire corridor of the corps rear area was divided into two areas of operations, one for each division. Fontenot, Degen, and Tohn, *On Point*, 214.

30. The Iraqi commander of the Republican Guard II Corps, Lieutenant General Hamdani, had hoped to defend Karbala with a division, but he was directed to keep his forces on the eastern side of the Euphrates River to defend Baghdad. Lacey, *Takedown*, 134.

31. Woods and Pease, *Iraqi Perspectives Report*, ix.

32. See Ballard, *From Storm to Freedom*, 140.

33. General Franks would later claim the title "thunder run" as his own reference to a similar tactic used during the Vietnam War. See Franks, *American Soldier*, 517.

34. Reynolds, *Basrah, Baghdad, and Beyond*, 106.

35. While passing through the Saddam City sector of Baghdad the Marines began to observe Iraqis looting in large numbers but could do little at the time to prevent it.

36. Lieutenant General Jay Garner, interview, "Frontline: War, Truth and Consequences," Public Broadcasting Service (PBS), http://www.pbs.org/wgbh/pages/frontline/shows/truth/interviews/garner.html

37. Ibid.

38. Charles H. Ferguson, *No End in Sight: Iraq's Descent into Chaos* (New York: PublicAffairs, 2008), 124–26.

39. L. Paul Bremer III, with Malcolm McConnell, *My Year in Iraq: The Struggle to Build a Future of Hope* (New York: Simon & Schuster, 2006), 6–7.

40. Elaine Halchin, *The CPA: Origins, Characteristics and Institutional Authorities* (Washington, D.C.: Congressional Research Service, April 29, 2004), 4.

41. Wright and Reese, *On Point II*, 29.
42. Franks had been offered the job as chief of staff of the U.S. Army by Secretary Rumsfeld, but he declined and pressed for retirement instead. See Franks, *American Soldier*, 531–32.
43. For the discussion in Washington, see Bremer, *My Year in Iraq*, 39, and Douglas J. Feith, *War and Decision: Inside the Pentagon at the Dawn of the War on Terrorism* (New York: Harper, 2008), 431–32.
44. Ibid.
45. Then called the Supreme Council of the Islamic Revolution in Iraq (SCIRI), renamed in June 2007 as the Islamic Supreme Council of Iraq (ISCI).
46. Kenneth Katzman, *Iraq and Al Qaeda*, Report RL32217 (Washington, D.C.: Congressional Research Service, April 28, 2008), CRS-9, http://fpc.state.gov/documents/organization/105195.pdf.
47. Secretary Rumsfeld coined the term "dead-enders." See, for example, "Rumsfeld Blames Iraq Problems on 'Pockets of Dead-Enders,'" *USA Today*, June 18, 2003, http://www.usatoday.com/news/world/iraq/2003-06-18-rumsfeld_x.htm. He refused to use the terms "insurgency" or "guerilla war," even when commanders like General Abizaid felt them correct; see "DOD News Briefing: Mr. Di Rita and Gen. Abizaid," *DefenseLink*, 16 July 2003, http://www.defenselink.mil/transcripts/2003/tr20030716-0401.html.
48. Bremer, *My Year in Iraq*, 225–28.
49. Ballard, *From Storm to Freedom*, 159.
50. More properly known as the "Law of Administration for the State of Iraq for the Transitional Period," the TAL provided the only framework for law in Iraq until the new constitution could be written. It can be found at: http://www.iraqcoalition.org/government/TAL.html.
51. Wright, *Different Kind of War*, 181.
52. Unanimously approved by all nineteen NATO members, the commitment marked the first time in its history that NATO had accepted responsibility for a mission outside the North Atlantic area.
53. D'arcy Doran, "U.S. General: Groups Supply Afghan Rebels," Associated Press, April 29, 2002, http://www.afghanistannewscenter.com/news/2003/april/apr302003.html.
54. Wright, *Different Kind of War*, 184.
55. Barbara Starr, "U.S. Remains on Trail of bin Laden, Taliban Leader," CNN, March 14, 2002, http://articles.cnn.com/2002-03-14/us/ret.osama.whereabouts_1_mullah-mohammed-omar-taliban-leader-bin?_s=PM:US.
56. Rory Carroll, "Perilous Fight against Shadowy Enemy," *Guardian*, April 8, 2002, http://www.guardian.co.uk/world/2002/apr/09/afghanistan.comment. See also "Afghanistan: United Kingdom Deploys Commando Battlegroup," *CDI* [Center for Defense Information] *Terrorism Project*, April 2, 2002, http://www.cdi.org/terrorism/uk-battlegroup-pr.cfm.

57. Wright, *A Different Kind of War*, 185.

58. Individual combat actions within Jacana included Operations Ptarmigan, Snipe, Condor, and Buzzard.

59. Richard Norton-Taylor, "Scores Killed by SAS in Afghanistan," *Guardian*, July 5, 2002, http://www.guardian.co.uk/world/2002/jul/05/september 11.afghanistan.

60. General Dan K. McNeill, interview, Contemporary Operations Study Team, Combat Studies Institute, Fort Leavenworth, Kans., June 16, 2008, 4, cited in Wright, *Different Kind of War*, 189–90.

61. Ibid., 192.

62. Wright, *Different Kind of War*, 187–88.

63. Jim Garamone, "Coalition Forces Complete Operation Mountain Sweep," American Forces Press Service, Washington, DC, August 26, 2002, http://www.globalsecurity.org/military/library/news/2002/08/mil-020826-dod02.htm.

64. Hy Rothstein, "America's Longest War," in Rothstein and Arquilla, *Afghan Endgames*, 62.

65. Wright, *Different Kind of War*, 181.

66. Joseph J. Collins, *Understanding War in Afghanistan* (Washington, D.C.: National Defense University Press, 2011), 28–29, available at http://purl.fdlp.gov/GPO/gpo11115.

67. *DOD Dictionary of Military and Associated Terms,* Joint Publication 1-02 (Washington, D.C., 2001), as quoted in William Flavin, *Civil Military Operations: Afghanistan* (Carlisle, Pa.: U.S. Army Peacekeeping and Stability Operations Institute, 23 March 2004), v.

68. Wright, *Different Kind of War*, 193.

69. Although a logistician with no formal experience in CA—his response when offered the position was, "Great, what is that?"; Major General David E. Kratzer, interview, 47th Military History Detachment, Camp Doha, Kuwait, July 16, 2002, 1, cited in Wright, *Different Kind of War*, 206. General Mikolashek thought Kratzer, who at least knew Afghanistan, would make a better commander of the CJCMOTF than a civil-affairs officer. This was only one case where members of the regular Army and Marine Corps demonstrated that they did not really understand, or did not trust, elements of their own reserve components early in the war.

70. Wright, *Different Kind of War*, 194, citing Kratzer, interview, July 16, 2002, 5.

71. Ibid., citing Flavin, *Civil Military Operations,* 21.

72. More typically such functions were accomplished by Civil Military Operations Centers (CMOCs), but that term was considered inappropriate and too expansive early on in Afghanistan.

73. Wright, *Different Kind of War*, 194.

74. Ibid., 195.

75. Ibid., 199.

76. Bill Skinner and Ryan Chilcote, "'Operation Mountain Sweep' Nets Taliban Weapons," CNN, August 26, 2002, http://articles.cnn.com/2002-08

-26/world/afghan.operation_1_al-qaeda-financier-caches-taliban -documents?_s=PM:asiapcf.

77. Security Council, "Official Records of the Security Council," Fifty-seventh year, 4638th meeting, New York, Wednesday, 30 October 2002, http://www.securitycouncilreport.org/atf/cf/%7B65BFCF9B-6D27 -4E9C-8CD3-CF6E4FF96FF9%7D/Afgh%20Spv4638.pdf.

78. "U.S. Special Forces in Afghanistan Kill One Attacker," *USA Today*, November 8, 2002, http://www.usatoday.com/news/world/2002-11-08 -afghan-attacker_x.htm.

79. Ahmad Masood, "Afghans Start Work on Key East–West Road Project," Reuters, November 10, 2002, http://reliefweb.int/node/113122.

80. Colonel George P. Maughan, interview, Contemporary Operations Study Team, Combat Studies Institute, Fort Leavenworth, Kans., August 24, 2007, cited in Wright, *Different Kind of War,* 225–26.

81. Major General David E. Kratzer, telephone interview, Contemporary Operations Study Team, Combat Studies Institute, Fort Leavenworth, Kans., July 5, 2007, cited in Wright, *Different Kind of War,* 226.

82. Ali Jalali, interview, Contemporary Operations Study Team, Combat Studies Institute, Fort Leavenworth, Kans., 1 June 2007, 7–8, cited in Wright, *Different Kind of War,* 226.

83. Wright, *Different Kind of War,* 226.

84. Dennis Skocz, telephone interview notes, by Contemporary Operations Study Team, Combat Studies Institute, Fort Leavenworth, Kans., September 17, 2007, 1, cited in Wright, *Different Kind of War,* 226–27.

85. Ibid., 227.

86. Colonel Michael Stout, "Afghanistan: Effects Based Operations as a 'Road-map to Transition,'" U.S. Army War College Briefing, cited in Wright, *Different Kind of War,* 227.

87. Colonel Michael Stout, 352nd CA Command, interview, Contemporary Operations Study Team, Combat Studies Institute, Fort Meade, Md., May 22, 2007, cited in Wright, *Different Kind of War,* 227.

88. Ibid.

89. Ibid.

90. Lieutenant Colonel Carl E. Fischer, interview, Contemporary Operations Study Team, Combat Studies Institute, Fort Leavenworth, Kans., January 18, 2007, 4, cited in Wright, *Different Kind of War,* 228.

91. Deborah Alexander, USAID Field Program Manager for Afghanistan, interview, Center for Military History, November 15, 2002, cited in Wright, *Different Kind of War,* 229.

92. Major General John R. Vines, interview, Contemporary Operations Study Team, Combat Studies Institute, Fort Leavenworth, Kans., June 27, 2007, 6, cited in Wright, *Different Kind of War,* 228.

93. Wright, *Different Kind of War,* 229, citing CJTF-180, Memorandum for the Commander (ATTN: CJCMOTF LNO to CJTF180), "OHDACA Status Report as of 1 January 2003, 5 January 2003."

94. Matt Mientka, "US Medics Reach Out in Afghanistan," *U.S. Medicine* (December 2002) http://www.usmedicine.com/article.cfm?articleID =550&issueID=45.

95. For the history of ISAF see *Afghanistan: International Security Assistance Force,* http://www.isaf.nato.int/history.html, as well as Kennedy Hickman, "Current Conflicts: International Security Assistance Force," *About.com: Military History,* http://militaryhistory.about.com/od/afghanistan/p/ISAF.htm.

96. Chris Lawrence, "CNN Tonight: War Plan Pitch; Afghanistan Exit Strategy; Tiger's P.R. Nightmare; White House Crashers; Wall Street vs. Main Street; Where are the Jobs?" CNN, December 2, 2009, http://transcripts .cnn.com/transcripts/0912/02/ctn.01.html.

97. "US Troops Attacked in Afghanistan, Expect More Clashes," *Afghanistan News Center,* April 15, http://www.afghanistannewscenter.com/news /2002/april/apr152002.html.

98. David M. Halbfinger, "Threats and Responses: The Military, Pilots Apologize to Relatives of Canadians They Bombed," *New York Times,* January 24, 2003, http://www.nytimes.com/2003/01/24/us/threats-responses -military-pilots-apologize-relatives-canadians-they-bombed.html.

99. Luke Harding and Matthew Engel, "US Bomb Blunder Kills 30 at Afghan Wedding, Pentagon Admits One of Its Bombs Was 'Errant,'" *Guardian,* July 1, 2002, http://www.guardian.co.uk/world/2002/jul/02/afghanistan .lukeharding.

100. "Afghan Insurgency Originates in Pakistan, says Top US General," *VOA News,* July 30, 2003, http://www.voanews.com/english/news/a-3-a-2003 -07-30-13-Afghan-66322792.html?refresh=1.

101. Address to the National Defence College in Islamabad, on February 12, 2004; see *Calcutta Telegraph,* February 12, 2004, http://www.telegraphindia .com/1040213/asp/foreign/story_2891333.asp, reprinted in *Seattle Times* as "Militants Might Use Pakistan to Launch Attacks, Leader Says," http:// seattletimes.nwsource.com/html/nationworld/2001857030_terror 13.html.

102. "From 2003–05, the U.S. team led by Ambassador Khalilzad and General Dave Barno focused on teamwork and organization for COIN and stability operations. Barno unified the field commands and divided the country into regional commands, where one colonel or general officer would command all maneuver units and PRTs." Collins, *Understanding War in Afghanistan,* 33.

Chapter 5: Fighting Two Wars

1. "President Outlines War Effort: Remarks by the President to the George C. Marshall ROTC Award Seminar on National Security," 17 April 2002, Office of the Press Secretary, The White House, Washington, D.C., http:// www.whitehouse.gov/news/releases/2002/04.

2. Wright, *Different Kind of War,* 237.

3. David W. Barno, "Fighting the Other War," *Military Review* (September–October 2007), http://usacac.leavenworth.army.mil/CAC/milreview/English/SepOct07/barnoengseptoct07.pdf.

4. Lieutenant General David W. Barno (Retired), interview, Contemporary Operations Study Team, Combat Studies Institute, Fort Leavenworth, Kans., January 29, 2009, 2–3; Colonel David W. Lamm (Retired), interview, Contemporary Operations Study Team, Combat Studies Institute, Fort Leavenworth, Kans., September 28, 2009.

5. Lieutenant General (Retired) John R. Vines, interview, Contemporary Operations Study Team, Combat Studies Institute, Fort Leavenworth, Kans., June 27, 2007, 19.

6. Barno, "Fighting the Other War," 33.

7. Koontz, *Enduring Voices,* 17.

8. Barno, "Fighting the Other War," 32.

9. Ahmed Rashid, *Descent into Chaos: The United States and the Failure of Nation Building in Pakistan, Afghanistan, and Central Asia* (New York: Viking, 2008), 247.

10. Wright, *Different Kind of War,* 240; Rashid, *Descent into Chaos,* 242.

11. Ali Jalali, former Afghan Minister of Interior, interview, with David W. Lamm, Near East South Asia Center for Strategic Studies, Washington, D.C., July 12, 2011.

12. Wright, *Different Kind of War,* 233.

13. David W. Lamm, "Success in Afghanistan Means Fighting Several Wars at Once," *Armed Forces Journal,* November 2005, 1.

14. Barno, "Fighting the Other War," 34.

15. Koontz, *Enduring Voices,* interview with Lieutenant General Barno, 15.

16. Wright, *Different Kind of War,* 243.

17. Ibid., 15.

18. Tucker B. Mansager, "Interagency Lessons Learned in Afghanistan," *Joint Force Quarterly* (First Quarter 2006), 82.

19. Barno, "Fighting the Other War," 34.

20. Ibid.

21. Barno, "Fighting the Other War," 34.

22. Ibid.

23. Wright, *Different Kind of War,* 244.

24. Ibid.

25. Wright, *Different Kind of War,* 244.

26. Ibid., 245, citing Barno, interview, by Center for Military History, November 21, 2006, 8.

27. Ibid.

28. Barno, "Fighting the Other War," 35.

29. Wright, *Different Kind of War,* 246.

30. Ibid., 247.

31. Ibid.

32. Koontz, *Enduring Voices,* 144.

33. Carlotta Gall, "Afghanistan: Taliban Leader Vows Return," *New York Times,* November 13, 2004, http://query.nytimes.com/gst/fullpage.html?res=9F 05E5DB173FF930A25752C1A9629C8B63.

34. Owais Tohid, "Taliban Regroups: On the Road," *Christian Science Monitor,* June 27, 2003, http://www.csmonitor.com/2003/0627/p06s01-wosc.html ?related.

35. Scott Baldauf and Owais Tohid, "Taliban Appears to Be Regrouped and Well-Funded, a New Hierarchy of Leaders Has Emerged across Parts of Afghanistan," *Christian Science Monitor,* May 8, 2003, http://www.csmonitor .com/2003/0508/p01s02-wosc.html.

36. Ibid.

37. Carlotta Gall, "Afghanistan: Taliban Leader Vows Return," *New York Times,* November 13, 2004, http://query.nytimes.com/gst/fullpage.html?res=9F 05E5DB173FF930A25752C1A9629C8B63.

38. Sayed Salahuddin, "Afghan Govt Says Ousts Taliban from Dai Chopan; Taliban Holdouts Destroyed," Reuters, September 3, 2003, http://www .freerepublic.com/focus/f-news/975077/posts.

39. Ibid.

40. Ibid.

41. Ibid.

42. Koontz, *Enduring Voices,* 138.

43. Barno, "Fighting the Other War," 39.

44. Wright, *Different Kind of War,* 280; Koontz, *Enduring Voices,* 133.

45. Barno, "Fighting the Other War," 40.

46. Lamm, "Success in Afghanistan," 2; Wright, *Different Kind of War,* 285.

47. Barno, "Fighting the Other War," 40.

48. Koontz, *Enduring Voices,* 285–86.

49. Lamm, "Success in Afghanistan," 2.

50. Ali Jalali, interview.

51. A similar incident occurred in 2003, but at that time Deputy Secretary of State Richard Armitage did not support the removal of Ismail Khan, because he concluded that such a move would destabilize Afghanistan.

52. Ambassador Zalmay Khalilzad, discussion with David, Lamm, Combined Forces Command–Afghanistan, September 23, 2003.

53. Ibid.

54. Barno, "Fighting the Other War," 38–39.

55. David Lamm, staff meeting notes, Combined Forces Command–Afghanistan, August 23–September 23, 2004,

56. Ibid.; Wright, *Different Kind of War,* 301–2.

57. David Lamm, staff meeting notes," Combined Forces Command–Afghanistan, September 24–November 5, 2004.

58. Ibid.

59. General Barno's personal role in the election proved to a critical one. In mid-July, under pressure from Ambassador Khalilzaid and members of

the coalition, Hamid Karzai announced that General Fahim Kahn, one of Afghanistan's strongest warlords, was being removed as the vice-presidential candidate on the Karzai ticket and replaced by Ahmed Zia Massoud, the brother of the hero Ahmed Shah Massoud. Fahim's removal could have caused significant political issues; perhaps Fahim could even have prevented the election had he chosen to do so. He had significant militia forces and heavy weapons, including tanks, just minutes from the presidential palace. However, the psychologically wounded Fahim met with both Barno and General Hillier the day after the announcement. The coalition generals had an open discussion with him, pointing out that he would be free to pursue a political career in a suit rather than a uniform after his forces were demobilized and disarmed. Barno was also able to play to Fahim's pride, by noting that retired General Wesley Clark was running in the U.S. presidential primaries at that time as well. David Lamm, staff meeting notes, Combined Forces Command–Afghanistan, June 29–July 28, 2004.

60. Lamm, "Success in Afghanistan," 2.
61. Ibid.
62. Koontz, *Enduring Voices,* 116.
63. Wright, *Different Kind of War,* 199.
64. UN General Assembly Security Council, "The Situation in Afghanistan and Its Implications for International Peace and Security," 18 March 2002, cited in Wright, *Different Kind of War,* 200.
65. Wright, *Different Kind of War,* 229.
66. Ibid., 201.
67. Ibid., 229.
68. Ibid.
69. Flavin, *Civil Military Operations,* xvi.
70. Krantzer, interview, July 16, 2002, 5, cited in Wright, *Different Kind of War,* 196.
71. Wright, *Different Kind of War,* 230.
72. Major Christopher M. Chambers, Deputy Director, OEMA (ANA Reconstruction Team, CJTF-180), "Recruiting for the Afghan National Army," briefing, October 3, 2002.
73. Staff Sergeant Tyler Ekwell, 401 CA BN, CHLC 11, interview, Center for Military History, 28 October 2002.
74. Wright, *Different Kind of War,* 230.
75. Ibid., 231.
76. Heike Hasenauer, "America and the War on Terror," *Soldiers,* September 2003, 25.
77. OMC-A, "Building the Afghan National Army," briefing, January 2003.
78. Lieutenant General Karl Eikenberry, interview, Contemporary Operations Study Team, Combat Studies Institute, Fort Leavenworth, Kans., November 27, 2006, 3, cited in Wright, *Different Kind of War,* 231.
79. Eikenberry, interview, 10, cited in Wright, *Different Kind of War,* 232.

80. Colonel Timothy Reese, interview, Contemporary Operations Study Team, Combat Studies Institute, Fort Leavenworth, Kans., June 26, 2007, cited in Wright, *Different Kind of War,* 232.
81. Eikenberry, interview, 5–6, cited in Wright, *Different Kind of War,* 232.
82. Wright, *Different Kind of War,* 233–34.
83. Ibid., 262.
84. Colonel David Lamm, interview, Contemporary Operations Study Team, Combat Studies Institute, Fort Leavenworth, Kans., September 20, 2007, 4; Barno, interview, 21 November 2006, 48.
85. Wright, *Different Kind of War,* 299.
86. Christopher Griffin, "A Working Plan: Hope Isn't the Only Strategy for Afghanistan," *Armed Forces Journal* (April 2007), http://www.armedforces journal.com/2007/04/2587549.
87. Wright, *A Different Kind of War,* 301.
88. Lieutenant General Carl Eikenberry, "Remarks at CFC-A Change of Command," May 3, 2005, www.defense.gov/news/newsarticle/aspx?id =31741.
89. David Lamm, staff meeting notes, Combined Forces Command–Afghanistan, March 27–May 16, 2005.
90. Ibid.
91. Ibid.
92. Ibid.,
93. Paul Wiseman, "Revived Taliban Waging 'Full-Blown Insurgency,'" *USA Today,* June 20, 2006, http://www.usatoday.com/news/world/2006-06 -19-taliban-afghanistan-cover_x.htm?csp=34.
94. "Taleban Vow to Defeat UK Troops," *BBC News,* 7 June 2006, http:// news.bbc.co.uk/2/hi/south_asia/5057154.stm.
95. Ibid.
96. Wiseman, "Revived Taliban Waging 'Full-Blown Insurgency.'"
97. Bill Roggio, "Three Days of Operation Mountain Thrust in Kandahar," *Long War Journal,* June 14, 2006, http://www.longwarjournal.org/ archives/2006/06/three_days_of_operat.php#ixzz1hpbL3zzs.
98. MSNBC.com News Services, "NATO: 200 Taliban Dead in Afghan Offensive, Fighting in South Inflicts Heavy Losses; 80 Captured; 4 NATO Soldiers Killed," *MSNBC,* September 3, 2006, http://www.msnbc.msn. com/id/14653529/.
99. ISAF Press Release, "Operation Wyconda Pincer Draws Down in Farah Province," Press Release 2006-179, September 23, 2006, http://www .nato.int/isaf/docu/pressreleases/2006/Release_23Sept06_179.htm.
100. CTV.ca News, "Soft Approach Working in Operation Baaz Tsuka," CTV, December 22, 2006, http://www.ctv.ca/CTVNews/World/20061222/ baaz_tsuka_061222/#ixzz1i2CnSZLh.
101. Wright, *Different Kind of War,* 342.
102. Seth G. Jones, *In the Graveyard of Empires: America's War in Afghanistan* (New York: W. W. Norton, 2009), 244.

103. Ibid., 245.

104. Ibid., 246.

105. Barno, "Fighting the Other War," 42.

106. Jones, *In the Graveyard of Empires,* 250.

107. United Nations Department of Safety and Security, *Half-Year Review of the Security Situation in Afghanistan* (New York: August 13, 2007), "Country Wide Incidents by Week: 2007"; Rich Atkinson, "The Single Most Effective Weapon against Our Deployed Forces," *Washington Post,* September 30, 2007, http://www.washingtonpost.com/wp-dyn/content/article/2007/09/29/AR2007092900750.html. VSSA, Afghanistan 2007; UNAMA, *Afghanistan: Annual Report on Protection of Civilians in Armed Conflicts* (n.p.: 2008); International Security Assistance Force, "Troop Numbers and Contributions, North Atlantic Treaty Organization, Afghanistan Report 2009," http://www.isaf.nato.int/troop-numbers-and-contributions/index.php; Anthony H. Cordesman, *The Afghan-Pakistan War: The Air War* (Washington, D.C.: Center for Strategic and International Studies, May 12, 2009), http://www.humansecuritygateway.com/documents/CSIS_AfPak War_AirWar.pdf

108. Ibid.

109. Cordesman, "Afghan-Pakistan War." See also James L. Jones, *NATO's Role in Afghanistan* (Washington, D.C.: Council on Foreign Relations, Washington Club, October 4, 2006), http://www.cfr.org/afghanistan/natos-role-afghanistan-rush-transcript-federal-news-service/p11605.

110. Jones, *In the Graveyard of Empires,* 243.

111. Ibid., 254.

112. Barno, "Fighting the Other War," 43.

113. Ibid.

Chapter 6: The Casey Strategy in Iraq, from Fallujah to Tal Afar

1. "This is a revolution against the occupation force until we get independence and democracy," al-Sadr's spokesman, Ahmed Shaybani, said in a telephone interview with Jackie Spinner of the *Washington Post.* See her "Cleric's Attack Tests Iraqi Leaders, Rebel Cleric Declares 'Revolution' against U.S. Forces in Iraq," August 6, 2004.

2. "A large number of aggressors, later confirmed to be members of the radical Shiite cleric Muqtada al-Sadr's Muqtada Militia, attacked the city of Najaf's main police station at 1 a.m. and were quickly repelled by the Iraqi police. Later, at 3 a.m., they attacked again, this time with heavy machine guns, rocket propelled grenades, mortars and small arms. Iraqi National Guardsmen from the 405th Battalion, 50th Iraqi Brigade, were notified and arrived on the scene and helped the IPs successfully defend the station from the Anti-Iraqi Forces." Chago Zapata, "11th MEU Battles Anti-Iraqi Forces in An Najaf," *Marine Corps News,* August 11, 2004. See also Spinner, "Cleric's Attack Tests Iraqi Leaders."

3. In the immediate aftermath of resettlement in Fallujah, Iraq held its first national elections in January 2005; this was in effect a semi-plebiscite for the Allawi government and a big indicator of popular sentiment. In Fallujah, where little or no significant reconstruction had begun at the time of the election, nearly one-third of the residents stood in long lines to vote. Elsewhere in al-Anbar Province Sunnis were intimidated, because every Iraqi who voted had his or her right index finger marked with blue dye, and insurgents had claimed all such fingers would be cut off; fewer than 18,000 people went to the polls. But in Fallujah a significant percentage felt safe enough to vote.

4. George Packer, "Letter from Iraq: The Lesson of Tal Afar—Is It Too Late for the Administration to Correct Its Course in Iraq?" *New Yorker*, April 10, 2006, 52.

5. Dan Murphy, "US Strategy in Iraq: Is It Working? Major Sweeps Show Results in Western Iraq. But Insurgents Keep Adapting and Attacking," *Christian Science Monitor*, June 21, 2005, 1.

6. As in Afghanistan, linked to this kinetic lever but still conducting somewhat independent, yet coordinated, operations was Joint Special Operations Command, whose mission was dominated by the fight against Al-Qaeda in Iraq and other linked terrorist activities.

7. Coordination between the various commands in Iraq was not always optimal. Philip Zelikow noted: "There's all kinds of tensions going on between Abizaid and Casey, and also even within Baghdad between the Multi-National Force command headed by Gen. Casey and the Corps command headed by Gen. Vines, then Gen. Chiarelli and now headed by Gen. Odierno. And actually the Multi-National Force headquarters and the Corps headquarters are in different locations. And a lot of what the Multi-National Force headquarters does is generate PowerPoint slides to use in briefing Washington, but the Corps is actually the people who have their fingers on what's going on in the field every day." Philip Zelikow, interview, PBS, http://www.pbs.org/wgbh/pages/frontline/endgame/interviews/zelikow.html.

8. H. R. McMaster, *Dereliction of Duty: Lyndon Johnson, Robert McNamara, the Joint Chiefs of Staff, and the Lies That Led to Vietnam* (New York: Harper Collins, 1997).

9. Packer, "Letter from Iraq," 50.

10. Ibid., 53.

11. Ibid., 54.

12. Ibid.

13. According to GlobalSecurity.org: "In this assault, the insurgents took heavy losses, 118 dead and 137 captured, before being driven out of the city. By September 13, the operation had been responsible for the deaths of numerous suspected terrorists and the detainment of 341 individuals. In addition, 22 weapons caches were uncovered, including mortar systems.

Colonel McMaster claimed that the operation also included the capture
of many associates of Zarqawi. Examination of the western part of the city
revealed that certain buildings had been rigged for destruction upon the
entrance of coalition troops. One building contained barrels of chemicals
that were intended to explode. After reconnaissance detected the threat,
the area was cleared and the building was demolished. Operation Restoring Rights continued through October, with raids along the border
between Iraq and Syria. During a 5-day-period in mid-October, more
than 10,000 pounds of explosives were uncovered and destroyed." Global
Security.org, http://www.globalsecurity.org/military/ops/oif-restoring
-rights.htm.

14. Packer, "Letter from Iraq, 54.
15. Ibid.
16. Ibid., 56.
17. Condoleezza Rice had replaced Colin Powell as secretary of state in No-
    vember 2004. She had of course been the administration's "point man"
    on Iraq for some time as the president's National Security Advisor, but in
    response to less than detailed responses to queries about the situation in
    Iraq from Rumsfeld's Defense Department, she began to gather her own
    information in order to make the international message concerning Iraq
    clearer.
18. Secretary of State Condoleezza Rice, "Iraq and U.S. Policy, Testimony be-
    fore the Senate Committee on Foreign Relations," available at http://foreign
    .senate.gov/testimony/2005/RiceTestimony051019.pdf.
19. Zelikow, interview.
20. Bob Woodward, "Doubt, Distrust, Delay: The Inside Story of How Bush's
    Team Dealt with Its Failing Iraq Strategy," *Washington Post,* September 7,
    2008, A1.
21. From Zelikow, Condoleezza Rice and the State Department immediately
    began to espouse a new approach toward winning the war based upon
    McMaster's "clear, hold, build" concept. It was not yet a national strategy—
    Secretary Rumsfeld flatly denied its use—and initially the White House
    did not fully understand the subtle differences in approach. Still, Zelikow's
    transporting of the concept back to the Washington bureaucracy would
    finally help the idea prosper, when via another route altogether the evolv-
    ing approaches to winning in Iraq would reach up over the months from
    the ranks to key members of the defense establishment in Washington,
    through academia, and through the network of retired military officers.
22. Fouad Ajami, *The Foreigner's Gift* (New York: Simon & Schuster, 2006),
    295–98.
23. David H. Petraeus, "Battling for Iraq," *Washington Post,* September 26,
    2004, B07.
24. Glenn Kessler, "Weapons Given to Iraq Are Missing, GAO Estimates 30%
    of Arms Are Unaccounted For," *Washington Post,* August 6, 2007, A01.

25. The constitutional review committee was created by the Iraqi parliament on September 25, 2006, but it did not develop any changes to the document over the first three years of its existence.

26. Thomas E. Ricks, *The Gamble: General David Petraeus and the American Military Adventure in Iraq, 2006–2008* (New York: Penguin, 2009), 32.

27. General Petraeus had even written in September 2005, "18 months after entering Iraq, I see tangible progress. Iraqi security elements are being rebuilt from the ground up. The institutions that oversee them are being reestablished from the top down. And Iraqi leaders are stepping forward, leading their country and their security forces courageously in the face of an enemy that has shown a willingness to do anything to disrupt the establishment of the new Iraq." Petraeus, "Battling for Iraq," B07.

28. Ballard, *From Storm to Freedom,* 192.

29. In his testimony before the Senate Armed Services Committee on February 27, 2007, the director of the Defense Intelligence Agency, General Michael Maples, called AQ-I "the largest and most active of the Iraq-based terrorist groups." See Lieutenant General Michael D. Maples, U.S. Army, "Current and Projected National Security Threats to the United States," *The Investigative Project on Terrorism,* http://www.investigativeproject.org /documents/testimony/268.pdf.

30. Kenneth Katzman, *Iraq and Al Qaeda,* Report RL32217 (Washington, D.C.: Congressional Research Service, April 28, 2008), CRS-11, http:// fpc.state.gov/documents/organization/105195.pdf.

31. UN High Commissioner for Refugees, Division of Operational Services, *2006 Global Trends: Refugees, Asylum-seekers, Returnees, Internally Displaced and Stateless Persons* (New York, June 2007, revised July 16, 2007), 13.

32. Department of Defense, *Measuring Stability and Security in Iraq,* Report to Congress (Washington, D.C., November 2006), 24.

33. See Ballard, *From Storm to Freedom,* 195.

34. Ellen Knickmeyer and Jonathan Finer, "Insurgent Leader Al-Zarqawi Killed in Iraq," *Washington Post,* June 8, 2006, A1, http://www.washing tonpost.com/wp-dyn/content/article/2006/06/08/AR2006060800114 .html.

35. Katzman, *Iraq and Al Qaeda.*

36. Knickmeyer and Finer, "Insurgent Leader Al-Zarqawi Killed," A1.

37. Jonathan Finer and Michael Abramowitz, "In Baghdad, Bush Pledges Support to Iraqi Leader, Visit Aimed at Buttressing Newly Formed Government," *Washington Post,* June 14, 2006, A01.

38. James A. Baker and Lee H. Hamilton, co-chairs; with Lawrence S. Eagleburger, Vernon E. Jordan, Jr., Edwin Meese III, Sandra Day O'Connor, Leon E. Panetta, William J. Perry, Charles S. Robb, Alan K. Simpson, *The Iraq Study Group Report: The Way Forward—A New Approach* (New York, Vintage Books, 2006), 32.

39. Ibid., 48.

40. See *Michael J. Totten's Middle East Journal,* http://www.michaeltotten.com /archives/001514.html.
41. Ballard, *From Storm to Freedom,* 198–99.
42. Anthony Loyd, "Murder of Sheikh Provokes Sunnis to Turn on Al-Qaeda; Ramadi, Stronghold of the Insurgents, Has Turned against Al-Zarqawi," *Times,* February 10, 2006, http://www.timesonline.co.uk/tol/news /world/iraq/article729206.ece.
43. Ibid.
44. Ballard, *From Storm to Freedom,* 201.
45. In May of 2006 some 80 percent in al-Anbar saw civil war as likely, up from 50 percent in January. See Carter Malkasian, "Local Opposition to Al Qaeda in Iraq," in Center for Technology and National Security Policy, National Defense University, *Exit Strategies and Military to Civilian Transitions Conference Report,* February 11–12, 2009.
46. Todd Pitman, "Sunni Sheiks Join Fight vs. Insurgency," *Washington Post Online Edition,* March 25, 2007, http://www.washingtonpost.com/wp -dyn/content/article/2007/03/25/AR2007032500600.html. On September 13, 2007, Sheikh Sittar was killed by an AQ-I suicide bomber, but the council continued to function under his brother, Sheikh Ahmad al-Rishawi. The latter, along with Governor Mamoun Rashid al-Awani and other tribal figures, visited Washington, D.C., in November 2007 to discuss the progress of security in al-Anbar province.
47. Ricks, *Gamble,* 69.
48. Ibid.
49. Martin Fletcher, "Fighting Back: The City Determined Not to Become Al-Qaeda's Capital; A Power Struggle Is Taking Place in the Sunni Triangle, with Tribal Leaders and Coalition Forces Aligning against a Common Enemy," *Times,* November 20, 2006, http://www.timesonline.co.uk/tol /news/world/iraq/article642374.ece?token=null&offset=0&page=1.
50. As described in the U.S. Institute for Peace website, the Iraq Study Group, "was undertaken at the urging of several members of Congress with agreement of the White House. A final report was released to Congress, the White House, and the public on December 6, 2006. Leadership of the group was provided by two distinguished cochairs: James A. Baker, III, former secretary of state and honorary chairman of the Baker Institute, and Lee H. Hamilton, former congressman and director of the Woodrow Wilson International Center for Scholars. The balance of the bipartisan group was comprised of Americans who have distinguished themselves in service to their nation: Robert M. Gates, Vernon E. Jordan, Jr., Edwin Meese III, Sandra Day O'Connor, Leon E. Panetta, William J. Perry, Charles S. Robb, and Alan K. Simpson.
51. *Iraq Study Group Report,* 13.
52. Ibid., 20.
53. Ibid., 10.

54. For example, see David S. Cloud and Eric Schmitt, "More Retired Generals Call for Rumsfeld's Resignation," *New York Times,* April 14, 2006, http://www.nytimes.com/2006/04/14/washington/14military.html?_r=1&oref=slogin

55. Although only a few of the key decision makers inside the Defense Department changed in the immediate aftermath of the resignation of Rumsfeld, the tone and activity of the Pentagon changed dramatically.

56. The meeting room inside the Pentagon where the chiefs of the military services often meet formally is known as "the Tank." Members of the Joint Chiefs of Staff at the time included General Peter Pace, USMC, as chairman; Admiral Ed Giambastini, USN, as the vice chairman; General Pete Schoomaker, USA, as chief of staff of the Army; General James Conway, USMC, as commandant of the Marine Corps; Admiral Mike Mullen, USN, chief of Naval Operations; and General Mike Moseley, USAF, Air Force chief of staff.

57. Specifically the report called for "a surge of seven Army brigades and Marine regiments to support clear-and-hold operations that begin in the spring of 2007 is necessary, possible, and will be sufficient to improve security and set conditions for economic development, political development, reconciliation, and the development of Iraqi Security Forces (ISF) to provide permanent security." The formal title of the actual report was "Choosing Victory, A Plan for Success in Iraq, Phase I Report." It can be found at http://www.aei.org/docLib/20070105_ChoosingVictoryFINAL cc.pdf

58. The four "elements of the new approach" announced by the president were security, politics, economics and regional engagement.

59. See Ballard, *From Storm to Freedom,* 208.

60. Lieutenant General Raymond T. Odierno, "The Surge in Iraq: One Year Later," Heritage Lecture 1068, March 13, 2008, http://www.heritage.org /Research/NationalSecurity/hl1068.cfm.

Chapter 7: Parallel Campaigns

1. During the same period in late 1983 and early 1984 Donald Rumsfeld served as President Reagan's special envoy to the Middle East and worked extensively on the situation in Lebanon. After his first trip to Beirut as envoy, Rumsfeld cabled Secretary of State George Schultz that "I wish we hadn't gone in. We need to be looking for a reasonably graceful way to get out." By the end of March 1984, Rumsfeld's mission was complete and U.S. troops were out of Lebanon. He concluded that "the withdrawal of American troops, our inability to match actions with our public statements and our hopes, and a lack of firmness by the administration in the face of congressional pressure had contributed to the outcome." Donald H. Rumsfeld, *Known and Unknown: A Memoir* (New York: Sentinel, 2010), 22, 31.

2. David Cloud and Greg Jaffe, *The Fourth Star: Four Generals and the Epic Struggle for the Future of the United States Army* (New York: Three Rivers, 2009), 48–51.

3. General John R. Galvin, "Uncomfortable Wars: Toward a New Paradigm," *Parameters* 16, no. 4 (Winter 1986), 6 [italics original].

4. Ibid., 3.

5. U.S. Army Command and General Staff College, *Low Intensity Conflict,* Field Circular 100-20 (Fort Leavenworth, Kans., May 30, 1986), v, available at www.vietnam.ttu.edu/star/images/137/1370316001a.pdf.

6. Ibid.

7. U.S. Army and U.S. Air Force, *Military Operations in Low Intensity Conflict,* Field Manual 100-20/Air Force Publication 3-20 (Washington, D.C., December 5, 1990), foreword.

8. Ibid., paras. 1-5 and 2-8 through 2-9.

9. For a short discussion of U.S. involvement in insurgencies and counterinsurgencies, see Michael O'Hanlon, *America's History of Counterinsurgency,* Brookings Counterinsurgency and Pakistan Paper Series 4 (Washington, D.C., June 2009).

10. Colonel Gregory Wilson, "Anatomy of a Successful COIN Operation: OEF-PHILIPPINES and the Indirect Approach," *Military Review* (November–December 2006, 4.

11. Ibid., 6.

12. Ibid., 11.

13. For an exceptional review of OEF-P see Richard Swain, PhD, "Case Study: Operation Enduring Freedom Philippines" (U.S. Army Counterinsurgency Center, October 2010).

14. Wright, *Different Kind of War,* 238.

15. Lieutenant General David W. Barno, USA (Ret.), "Fighting the 'Other War': Counterinsurgency Strategy in Afghanistan, 2003–2005," *Military Review* (September–October 2007), 32–44.

16. Robert Burns, "Mullen: Afghanistan Isn't Top Priority," *USA Today,* posted online December 11, 2007, http://www.usatoday.com/news/washington/2007-12-11-3963072919_x.htm.

17. Cloud and Jaffe, *Fourth Star,* 207–208.

18. The White House, *National Strategy for Victory in Iraq* (Washington, D.C., November 2005), available at http://www.washingtonpost.com/wp-srv/nation/documents/Iraqnationalstrategy11-30-05.pdf.

19. See Ballard, *From Storm to Freedom,* 212.

20. One of the most frequently quoted phrases found in *On War* is Clausewitz's comment, "Now, the first, the grandest, and most decisive act of judgment which the statesman and general exercises is rightly to understand in this respect the war in which he engages, not to take it for something, or to wish to make of it something which, by the nature of its relations, it is impossible for it to be." *On War,* chapter 1, part 27.

21. Ricks, *Gamble*, 111.
22. FOBs, or forward operating bases, were coalition military compounds, normally isolated from the rest of Iraq, where most soldiers and Marines lived when they were not conducting limited-duration forays. They provided safe havens for the coalition but also left the Iraqis to fend for themselves in the days, and most nights, when coalition forces were not present in the towns.
23. Lieutenant General Raymond T. Odierno, "The Surge in Iraq: One Year Later" (Heritage Lecture 1068, March 13, 2008), available at http://www.heritage.org/Research/NationalSecurity/hl1068.cfm.
24. See Ballard, *From Storm to Freedom*, 214.
25. Linda Robinson, *Tell Me How This Ends: General David Petraeus and the Search for a Way Out of Iraq* (New York: PublicAffairs, 2008), 148.
26. Ibid., 149.
27. Six of the eighteen key benchmarks were related in some way to reconciliation and governance reform in Iraq; see ibid., 170.
28. See GlobalSecurity.org, http://www.globalsecurity.org/military/ops/oif-phantom-thunder.htm.
29. See Ballard, *From Storm to Freedom*, 219.
30. Katzman, *Iraq and Al Qaeda*, CRS-13.
31. Ibid.
32. Ibid.
33. See Ballard, *From Storm to Freedom*, 221.
34. Frederick W. Kagan and Kimberly Kagan, "The Patton of Counterinsurgency," *Weekly Standard*, March 10, 2008, http://www.weeklystandard.com/Content/Public/Articles/000/000/014/822vfpsz.asp.
35. See "Operation Fardh Al-Qanoon," *ISW: Institute for the Study of War*, http://www.understandingwar.org/operation/operation-fardh-al-qanoon.
36. Kagan and Kagan, "The Patton of Counterinsurgency."
37. Odierno's III Corps staff was replaced in Iraq the staff of the XVIII Airborne Corps on February 15, 2008. General Austin turned over command of MNC-I to Lieutenant General Charles Jacoby in 2009.
38. Bob Woodward, *The War Within: A Secret White House History, 2006–2008* (New York: Simon & Schuster, 2008), 206–7.
39. Rumsfeld, *Known and Unknown*, 691.
40. "President Bush Discusses Progress in Afghanistan, Global War on Terror" (remarks to the American Enterprise Institute, Mayflower Hotel, February 15, 2007), available at http://georgewbush-whitehouse.archives.gov/news/releases/2007/02/print/20070215-1.html.
41. Ibid.
42. National Security Council, "Fact Sheet: Increasing Support to Help the People of Afghanistan Succeed," February 15, 2007, available at http://georgewbush-whitehouse.archives.gov/news/releases/2007/02/print/20070215.html
43. Personal notes of the author.

44. Sheryl Gay Stolberg, "Bush Picks General to Coordinate War Policy," *New York Times,* May 16, 2007, http://www.nytimes.com/2007/05/16 /washington/16warczar.html.

45. Ibid.

46. The White House, "President Bush Names Lieutenant General Douglas Lute as Assistant to the President and Deputy National Security Advisor for Iraq and Afghanistan," news release, May 15, 2007, http://georgew bush-whitehouse.archives.gov/news/releases/2007/05/20070515-9.html.

47. The White House, "Fact Sheet: Lieutenant General Douglas E. Lute— Experience and Authority," May 15, 2007, available at http://georgew bush-whitehouse.archives.gov/news/releases/2007/05/print/20070515 -10.html.

48. The NSC South and Central Asia directorate had a staff of three, with one director tasked to oversee both Pakistan and India affairs. The U.S.-India Civil Nuclear Cooperation Initiative, or "123 Agreement," was a signature accomplishment of the Bush administration. Considerable controversy and debate both in the United States and India resulted in protracted debate and political maneuvering in both countries. The final agreement was not confirmed by the U.S. Senate until October 1, 2008 (by a vote of 86–13); it was operationalized nine days later.

49. "Clinton Spars with Petraeus on Credibility," *New York Sun,* September 12, 2007, http://www.nysun.com/national/clinton-spars-with-petraeus -on-credibility/62426/.

50. Ibid.

51. David Petraeus, *Report to Congress on the Situation in Iraq,* September 10–11, 2007, available at http://www.defense.gov/pubs/pdfs/Petraeus-Testimony 20070910.pdf.

52. Ibid.

53. Ibid.

54. The title of Petraeus's 2007 recommendation paper is in itself interest- ing, considering the ISAF approach in Afghanistan after his assumption of command. The ISAF approach by late 2010 became "Shape, Clear, Hold, Build, Transfer."

55. Joseph Biden, "Opening Statement in the Senate Foreign Relations Com- mittee Hearing on Afghanistan: Time for a New Strategy?" March 8, 2007, available at http://foreign.senate.gov/imo/media/doc/BidenStatement 070308.pdf.

56. Richard A., Bouchard, "Moving Forward in Afghanistan," March 8, 2007, available at http://foreign.senate.gov/imo/media/doc/BoucherTestimony 070308.pdf.

Chapter 8: The 2007 Baghdad Surge and the End of Combat Operations in Iraq

1. Karen DeYoung and Jonathan Weisman, "Obama Shifts the Foreign Policy Debate," *Washington Post,* July 23, 2008, A08, retrieved June 23, 2011.

2. Frederick W. Kagan, *Choosing Victory: A Plan for Success in Iraq, Phase One Report* (Washington, D.C.: American Enterprise Institute, December, 2006). The publication lists the following members of the Iraq Planning Group at AEI: Frederick W. Kagan; Jack Keane, General, U.S. Army (Ret.); David Barno, Lieutenant General, U.S. Army (Ret.); Danielle Pletka; Rend al-Rahim; Joel Armstrong, Colonel, U.S. Army, (Ret.); Daniel Dwyer, Major, U.S. Army (Ret.); Larry Crandall; Larry Sampler; Michael Eisenstadt; Kimberly Kagan; Michael Rubin; Reuel Marc Gerecht; Thomas Donnelly; Gary Schmitt; Mauro De Lorenzo; and Vance Serchuk.

3. For just one example of several well-known authors who developed studies of counterinsurgency that made the population a prized objective, see David Galula, *Counter-Insurgency Warfare: Theory and Practice* (London: Pall Mall, 1964), and Galula, *Pacification in Algeria, 1956–1958* (Santa Monica, Calif.: RAND, 1963, repr. 2006).

4. "President Bush Speaks to the Nation about Iraq, January 10, 2007," available at http://www.cnn.com/2007/POLITICS/01/10/bush.transcript /index.html.

5. Ibid.

6. Ballard, *From Storm to Freedom,* 210.

7. Marc A. Thiessen, ed., *A Charge Kept: The Record of the Bush Presidency, 2001–2009* (Washington, D.C.: GPO, 2009), 14.

8. Kagan and Kagan, "Patton of Counterinsurgency."

9. Ibid., CRS-14.

10. Ballard, *From Storm to Freedom,* 220.

11. Katzman, *Iraq and Al Qaeda,* CRS-14.

12. Kagan and Kagan, "Patton of Counterinsurgency."

13. Kagan and Kagan, "Patton of Counterinsurgency."

14. "Iraq and Al Qaeda, CRS-14."

15. Ibid., 166–67.

16. Rumsfeld, *Known and Unknown,* 687.

17. Ibid., 689–90.

18. Helmand was also the center of Afghan opium production—which provided significant funding to the Taliban. Garmsir was surrounded by opium poppy farms, and coalition planners believed they could reduce funding for the Taliban by pacifying the area.

19. Ann Scott Tyson, "British Troops, Taliban in a Tug of War over Afghan Province in One Town, a Small Force Battles for Yards of Ground," *Washington Post,* March 30, 2008, http://www.washingtonpost.com/wp-dyn /content/article/2008/03/29/AR2008032902033_pf.html.

20. Avnina Berglund, "Telemark Battalion in New Combat with Taliban," *Aftenposten,* May 27, 2008, http://www.aftenposten.no/english/local/ article2448302.ece.

21. M. Karim Faiez and Henry Chu, "Deadly Taliban Assault Frees 1,000 Prisoners," *Los Angeles Times,* June 14, 2008, http://articles.latimes.com/2008 /jun/14/world/fg-prison14.

22. Pir Zubair Shah, Eric Schmitt and Jane Perlez, "American Forces Attack Militants on Pakistani Soil," *New York Times*, September 4, 2008, http://www.nytimes.com/2008/09/04/world/asia/04attack.html.

23. JoAnne O'Bryant and Michael Waterhouse, *U.S. Forces in Afghanistan,* Report for Congress (Washington, D.C.: Congressional Research Service, July 15, 2008).

24. George Bush, "President's Address to the Nation," January 10, 2007, available at http://georgewbush-whitehouse.archives.gov/news/releases/2007/01/20070110-7.html.

25. Ballard, *From Storm to Freedom,* 225.

26. Jafari and his Shia United Iraqi Alliance party led the Iraqi government from April 7, 2005, to May 20, 2006, by bringing together a political coalition based on the Jafari's own Islamic Dawa Party and Supreme Council for the Islamic Revolution in Iraq (SCIRI) party.

27. Michael Abramowitz and Sudarsan Raghavan, "Bush Rejects Troop Reductions, Endorses Maliki, President Calls Prime Minister 'the Right Guy for Iraq' after Summit in Jordan," *Washington Post,* December 1, 2006, A24.

28. Marisa Cochrane, "The Battle for Basra, March 2003–May 31, 2008," *Weekly Standard,* Iraq Report 9, June 23, 2008, 4, http://www.understandingwar.org/report/battle-basra.

29. See Ballard, *From Storm to Freedom,* 227.

30. Ricks, *Gamble,* 278–79.

31. Interestingly the cease-fire was developed with Iranian support from the leader of the Iranian al-Quds force, Qassem Suleimani; Cochrane, "Battle for Basra," 9.

32. Cochrane, "Battle for Basra," 9.

33. Sudarsan Raghavan and Sholnn Freeman, "U.S. Appears to Take Lead in Fighting in Baghdad, U.S. Forces Battle Mahdi Army in Sadr City, Aircraft Target Basra," *Washington Post,* April 1, 2008, http://www.washingtonpost.com/wp-dyn/content/article/2008/04/01/AR2008040100833.html.

34. Cochrane, "Battle for Basra," 10.

35. See Ballard, *From Storm to Freedom,* 228.

36. The eighteen benchmarks to gauge success in Iraq were drafted in coordination with Iraqi leaders and inserted into congressional bill HR 2206, "U.S. Troop Readiness, Veterans' Care, Katrina Recovery, and Iraq Accountability Appropriations Act, 2007." HR 2206 was passed by Congress in mid-May 2007 and signed into law by President Bush on May 25, 2007.

37. Karen DeYoung, "U.S. Embassy Cites Progress in Iraq, Most Congressionally Set Benchmarks Met, Report Finds," *Washington Post,* July 2, 2008, A08.

38. See Ballard, *From Storm to Freedom,* 230.

39. Department of Defense, *Measuring Stability and Security in Iraq* (Washington, D.C., March 2009), iii. Report to Congress in accordance with the Department of Defense Supplemental Appropriations Act 2008 (Section 9204, Public Law 110-252).

40. See the Federal Election Commission's official results tally at "2008 Official Presidential General Election Results," *Federal Election Commission,* http://www.fec.gov/pubrec/fe2008/2008presgeresults.pdf.

41. See Ballard, *From Storm to Freedom,* 232.

42. Claire Russo, "Capitol Hill Briefing Notes: Provincial Elections in Iraq," February 19, 2009, http://www.understandingwar.org/print/525.

43. "Capitol Hill Briefing Notes: Provincial Elections in Iraq."

44. Hélène Frade and Lucas Menget, "Maliki Hails Iraqi Vote as 'a Victory,'" *France 24,* February 1, 2009, http://www.france24.com/en/20090201 -maliki-hails-iraq-vote-victory-provincial-elections-polls-close.

45. "Provincial Elections Test Iraq's Move towards Democracy," *PBS News Hour Extra,* http://www.pbs.org/newshour/extra/features/world/jan-june 09/iraq.html.

46. Victor Davis Hanson, "The Good—Part III," *PJ Media,* http://pajamas media.com/victordavishanson/784/.

47. For explanation of the above subhead see the excellent Dominic J. Caraccilo and Andrea L. Thompson, *Achieving Victory in Iraq: Countering an Insurgency* (Mechanicsburg, Pa.: Stackpole Books, 2008).

48. See Ballard, *From Storm to Freedom,* 233.

49. Amit R. Paley, "Green Zone Handed Off with Little Fanfare, Embassy Ceremony Hints at Uncertainty," *Washington Post,* January 2, 2009, 12.

50. Anthony Shadid, "In Iraq, the Day After: The War, in a Sense, Is Over. But a New Struggle Begins as Citizens Ask the Inevitable Question: What Next?," *Washington Post,* Friday, January 2, 2009, A01.

51. Tim Cocks, "US Starts Pullout, Transfers Base to Iraq," *Boston Globe,* January 4, 2009.

52. General Odierno participated in the meeting via VTC from Baghdad. See Peter Baker and Thom Shanker, "Obama Meets with Officials on Iraq, Signaling His Commitment to Ending War," *New York Times,* January 22, 2009.

53. Bush had identified the objectives of the war in several ways, but most consistently he described three determining factors. He said in 2005, "victory will be achieved when the terrorists and Saddamists can no longer threaten Iraq's democracy, when the Iraqi security forces can provide for the safety of their own citizens, and when Iraq is not a safe haven for terrorists to plot new attacks against our nation." George W. Bush, "Remarks by President Bush on the War on Terror" (Park Hyatt Philadelphia, Philadelphia, Pennsylvania, December 12, 2005).

54. Major General John F. Kelly, USMC, e-mail, February 1, 2009.

55. President Barack Obama, "Responsibly Ending the War in Iraq" (speech given at Camp Lejeune, North Carolina, Friday, February 27, 2009), available at http://www.whitehouse.gov/the_press_office/Remarks-of-President -Barack-Obama-Responsibly-Ending-the-War-in-Iraq/.

56. Ibid.
57. Cable News Network, "Obama Makes Surprise Visit to Iraq," April 7, 2009, http://cnnwire.blogs.cnn.com/2009/04/07/obama-makes-surprise-visit-to-iraq-2/.
58. See Ballard, *From Storm to Freedom*, 238.
59. Ibid.
60. Secretary Gates: "I know we talk about a 10-year war in Afghanistan, but the truth of the matter is, after we'd ousted the Taliban in 2002 and also al-Qaida from Afghanistan, the U.S. sort of turned its attention away from Afghanistan and really didn't turn back with the full resources, a full strategy and so on, until really early in 2009." "Gates: I Was 'Strong Advocate' for Afghanistan Surge to End in Summer 2012," interview, *PBS Newsmaker*, air date June 23, 2011, available at http://www.pbs.org/newshour/bb/politics/jan-june11/gates_06-23.html.
61. O'Bryant and Waterhouse, *U.S. Forces in Afghanistan*.
62. "9 U.S. Soldiers Killed in Taliban Assault on Base," *Seattle Times*, July 14, 2008, http://seattletimes.nwsource.com/html/nationworld/2008050103_afghan14.html.
63. Luis Martinez, "President Bush Announces Modest Troop Cuts" *ABC News*, September 9, 2008, http://abcnews.go.com/Politics/story?id=5761814&page=1.
64. "Militants Attack Afghan Prison with Car Bomb, Free 870 Inmates," *Fox News*, June 14, 2008, http://www.foxnews.com/story/0,2933,366701,00.html#ixzz1ZdaCF3Y8.
65. Bill Roggio, "Joint al Qaeda and Taliban Force behind Nuristan Base Attack," *Long War Journal*, July 14, 2008, http://www.longwarjournal.org/archives/2008/07/joint_al_qaeda_and_t.php#ixzz1bcJwibB7.
66. Eric Schmitt, "Afghan Officials Aided an Attack on U.S. Soldiers," *New York Times*, November 3, 2008, http://www.nytimes.com/2008/11/04/world/asia/04military.html?partner=rssnyt&emc=rss.
67. U.S. Army Combat Studies Institute, *Wanat: Combat Action in Afghanistan, 2008* (Fort Leavenworth, Kans.: Combined Studies Institute Press, 2010), available at http://www.cgsc.edu/carl/download/csipubs/Wanat.pdf. See also Gary Williams, *Seal of Honor: Operation Red Wings and the Life of Lt. Michael P. Murphy, USN* (Annapolis, Md.: Naval Institute Press, 2011).
68. Ibid.
69. Thomas E. Ricks, "Wanat (VIII): An Army Report Finds a Major COIN Failure," *Foreign Policy*, July 23, 2009, http://ricks.foreignpolicy.com/posts/2009/07/23/wanat_viii_an_army_report_finds_a_major_coin_failure.
70. Pir Zubair Shah and Jane Perlez, "NATO Gunships Attack Taliban Stronghold in Pakistan Tribal Area," *New York Times*, September 3, 2008, http://www.nytimes.com/2008/09/03/world/asia/03iht-attack.1.15858867.html.

71. Simon Tisdall and Saeed Shah, "Pakistan Reacts with Fury after Up to 20 Die in 'American' Attack on Its Soil," *Guardian,* September 3, 2008, http://www.guardian.co.uk/world/2008/sep/04/pakistan.
72. Nasrullah Afridi, "Pakistan Cuts Supply Lines to Nato Forces," *International News of Pakistan,* September 6, 2008, http://www.thenews.com.pk/TodaysPrintDetail.aspx?ID=17051&Cat=13&dt=9/6/2008.
73. "2008 Marks Deadliest Year for U.S. Troops in Afghanistan," *Cable News Network,* September 11, 2008, http://edition.cnn.com/2008/WORLD/asiapcf/09/11/afghan.troop.deaths/.

Chapter 9: Developing the Afghan Surge Strategy

1. See remarks by the president, January 10, 2007.
2. See Office of the Press Secretary, "Fact Sheet: The Strategic Framework Agreement and the Security Agreement with Iraq," December 4, 2008, available at www.whitehouse.gov/news/releases/2008/12/print/20081204-6.html.
3. "DoD News Briefing with General McKiernan from the Pentagon," U.S. Department of Defense news transcript, October 1, 2008, available at http://www.defense.gov/utility/printitem.aspx?print=http://www.defense.gov/Transcripts/Transcript.aspx?TranscriptID=4297.
4. Ibid.
5. Bob Woodward, *Obama's Wars* (New York: Simon & Schuster, 2010), 4–44.
6. Eventually, the report was divided into "Next 90 days" and "Future" recommendations because of the short period remaining for the Bush administration when the report was finalized in late November 2008.
7. Woodward, *Obama's Wars,* 43–44.
8. CSTC-A was established by in April 2006, by renaming the U.S. Office of Military Cooperation–Afghanistan and its successor the Office of Security Cooperation–Afghanistan. CSTC-A retained the dual army/police mission that had been earlier held by both OSC-A and OMC-A.
9. Ian S. Livingston and Michael O'Hanlon, *Afghanistan Index: Tracking Variables of Reconstruction and Security in Post-9/11 Afghanistan* (Washington, D.C.: Brookings Institution, October 31, 2011), 6, available at www.brookings.edu/afghanistanindex.
10. Ibid., 5.
11. Ian S. Livingston and Michael O'Hanlon, *Iraq Index: Tracking Variables of Reconstruction and Security in Post-Saddam Iraq* (Washington, D.C.: Brookings Institution, October 28, 2011), 13, available at www.brookings.edu/iraqindex.
12. Woodward, *Obama's Wars,* 43–44.
13. There were two other significant strategy reviews under way at about the same time, but these concluded in January 2009. The Joint Chiefs of Staff had a small team of officers working in the Pentagon to assess the strategy in Afghanistan. When General Petraeus assumed command of CEN-

TCOM he also set up a strategy review, headed by then–Colonel H. R. McMaster. Both strategy reviews came to similar conclusions as the Lute review, particularly that a more fully resourced counterinsurgency strategy was called for in Afghanistan. Also like the Lute review, neither was widely reported.

14. Press Secretary Robert Gibbs, briefing, October 22, 2009, available at http:// www.whitehouse.gov/the-press-office/briefing-white-house-press -secretary-robert-gibbs-102209-0.

15. "Remarks by Secretary Hillary Rodham Clinton," January 22, 2009, U.S. Department of State, Washington, D.C., available at http://www.state.gov /secretary/rm/2009a/01/115297.htm

16. Ibid.

17. Ibid.

18. Woodward, *Obama's Wars*, 88–89.

19. Ibid., 99–110.

20. White Paper of the Interagency Policy Group's Report on U.S. Policy toward Afghanistan and Pakistan, http://www.whitehouse.gov/blog/09/03/27/ A-New-Strategy-for-Afghanistan-and-Pakistan/.

21. "Remarks by the President on a New Strategy for Afghanistan and Pakistan," March 27, 2009, Office of the Press Secretary, White House, Washington, D.C., March 27, 2009, http://www.whitehouse.gov/blog/09/03/27 /A-New-Strategy-for-Afghanistan-and-Pakistan/.

22. Ibid.

23. Ibid.

24. Robert Marquand, "On Eve Of NATO Summit, Obama's Style Poses Inherent Challenge for Europe," *Christian Science Monitor*, April 2, 2009.

25. Howard LaFranchi, "On European Trip, Rock Star Obama Faces Skeptical Allies," *Christian Science Monitor*, March 31, 2009.

26. Ian Traynor, "NATO Summit: Europe Resists US Pressure on Afghanistan 'Surge,'" *Guardian*, April 2, 2009.

27. Richard Wolf, "NATO Allies Endorse Obama's Afghan Plan," *USA Today*, April 4, 2009, http://www.usatoday.com/news/world/2009-04-04-nato -summit_N.htm.

28. Livingston and O'Hanlon, *Afghanistan Index*.

29. "Agreement on Provisional Arrangements in Afghanistan Pending the Re-establishment of Permanent Government Institutions," *United Nations*, http://www.un.org/News/dh/latest/afghan/afghan-agree.htm.

30. "Policy Brief: CARE International in Afghanistan. January 2003," *CARE Canada*, http://care.ca/sites/default/files/files/publications/Afghanistan PolicyBrief_Jan03.pdf.

31. David Zucchino, "General Values Alliance with Afghan Warlords," *Los Angeles Times*, November 4, 2002. Interestingly, the same *Los Angeles Times* article went on to state, "McNeill, a three-star general, also said he has been assured by the Pentagon that he will continue to be given sufficient resources in Afghanistan if the Bush administration decides to attack Iraq."

32. *Progress towards Security and Stability in Afghanistan: Report to Congress* (Washington, D.C.: DoD, June 2008), 14.
33. Ibid., January 2009, 9.
34. Ibid., June 2009, 35.

Chapter 10: Conflict Termination in Afghanistan

1. "Press Conference with Secretary Gates and Admiral Mullen on Leadership Changes in Afghanistan from the Pentagon," U.S. Department of Defense news transcript, May 11, 2009, available at www.defense.gov/transcripts/transcript.aspx?TranscriptID=4424.
2. Rothstein, "America's Longest War," 62.
3. Ibid., 63.
4. Joe Klein, "Joe Klein: Obama's Team of Rivals," *Time,* June 18, 2008, www.time.com/time/printout/0,8816,1816476,00.html.
5. "Press Conference with Secretary Gates and Admiral Mullen on Leadership Changes in Afghanistan from the Pentagon."
6. Woodward, *Obama's Wars,* 124–25. See also "DoD News Briefing with Geoff Morrell from the Pentagon Briefing Room, Arlington, Va.," U.S. Department of Defense news transcript, June 8, 2009, available at www.defense.gov/Transcripts/Transcript.aspx?TranscriptID=4430.
7. General Stanley McChrystal, "Commander's Initial Assessment," August 30, 2009, Headquarters, International Security Assistance Force. Kabul, Afghanistan.
8. See the NATO ISAF mission statement at http://www.isaf.nato.int/mission.html.
9. General Stanley McChrystal, "Tactical Directive," July 6, 2009, Headquarters, International Security Assistance Force, Kabul, Afghanistan.
10. McChrystal, "Commander's Initial Assessment," 1-1.
11. Ann Scott Tyson, "General: Afghan Situation 'Serious,'" *Washington Post,* September 1, 2009.
12. Bob Woodward, "McChrystal: More Forces or 'Mission Failure,'" *Washington Post,* September 21, 2009.
13. "State of the Union with John King." September 20, 2009, CNN Transcripts, 9:00 a.m., available at www.cnn.com/TRANSCRIPTS/0909/20/sotu.01.html; Eric Schmitt and Thom Shanker, "General Calls for More U.S. Troops to Avoid Afghan Failure," *New York Times,* September 21, 2009.
14. The five concluded reviews were: Lute's November 2008 review, Mullen's January 2009 review, Petraeus's January 2009 review, Riedel's review, and McChrystal's assessment. All had generally endorsed a more fully resourced civilian-military counterinsurgency campaign in Afghanistan.
15. Woodward, *Obama's Wars,* 387.
16. "Remarks by the President to the Nation on the Way Forward in Afghanistan and Pakistan," Office of the Press Secretary, White House, December 1, 2009.

17. Ibid.
18. Kristina Wong, "Exclusive: War in Iraq to Be Given New Name," *ABC News,* February 18, 2010. The official memorandum can be viewed at: http://a.abcnews.go.com/images/Politics/08144-09.pdf.
19. "2 Most Wanted Al Qaeda Leaders in Iraq Killed by U.S., Iraqi Forces," FOXNews.com, April 19, 2010, http://www.foxnews.com/world/2010 /04/19/iraqi-al-qaeda-leader-killed-countrys-intelligence-team-pm -maliki-says/#ixzz1gETY4ExD.
20. Ernesto Londoño, "Two Top Leaders of the Insurgent Group Al-Qaeda in Iraq Are Killed in Raid," *Washington Post,* April 20, 2010, A05.
21. Khalid D. Ali and Timothy Williams, "Car Bombs Hit Crowds outside Bank in Baghdad," *New York Times,* June 20, 2010, A4.
22. Anthony Shadid, "Coordinated Attacks Strike 13 Iraqi Cities," *New York Times,* August 25, 2010, A1.
23. Richard Engel, Charlene Gubash, and Alex Johnson, "Last Full U.S. Combat Brigade Leaves Iraq, Final Fighting Force Rolls into Kuwait; 50,000 Americans to Remain," *MSNBC News,* August 19, 2010, http://www .msnbc.msn.com/id/38744453/ns/world_news-mideastn_africa/#.Tu SyjlbfXTo.
24. Ernesto Londoño, "Operation Iraqi Freedom Ends as Last Combat Soldiers Leave Baghdad," *Washington Post,* August 19, 2010, http://www.washington post.com/wp-dyn/content/article/2010/08/18/AR2010081805644 .html?sid=ST2010081805662.
25. Leo Standora, "War Is Over: Last U.S. Combat Troops Leave Iraq; 50,000 Remain as Advisers," *New York Daily News,* August 19 2010, http://www .nydailynews.com/news/national/war-u-s-combat-troops-leave-iraq-50 -000-remain-advisers-article-1.202559#ixzz1gEXvBmIA.
26. "President Obama's Address on Iraq," *New York Times,* August 31, 2010, http://www.nytimes.com/2010/09/01/world/01obama-text.html ?ref=world&pagewanted=1.
27. Michael R. Gordon and Elisabeth Bumiller, "In Baghdad, U.S. Officials Take Note of Milestone," *New York Times,* September 2, 2010, A4.
28. Steven Lee Myers, "G.I. Deaths Are First for U.S. after Combat Mission's End," *New York Times,* September 8, 2010, A10.
29. Margaret Besheer, "UN Security Council Lifts Some Restrictions on Iraq, Voice of America," *Voice of America News,* December 15, 2010, http:// www.voanews.com/english/news/UN-Security-Council-Lifts-Some -Restrictions-On-Iraq-111951129.html.
30. Julian E. Barnes, Sam Dagher, and Nathan Hodge, "U.S. Closes Its Mission on Uncertain Note," *Wall Street Journal,* December 16, 2011, 6.
31. John Leland, "3 U.S. Service Members Killed in Iraq," *New York Times,* January 16, 2011, A8.
32. Muhanad Mohammed, "Five U.S. Troops Killed in Iraq Attack," Reuters, June 6, 2011, http://www.reuters.com/article/2011/06/06/us-iraq -violence-us-idUSTRE7551QG20110606.

33. Tim Craig and Ed O'Keefe, "U.S. Military Sees Iran behind Rising Troop Deaths in Iraq," *Washington Post,* June 30, 2010, http://www.washington post.com/world/3-us-troops-killed-in-iraq-adding-to-deadly-month /2011/06/30/AGrDQprH_story.html.

34. "Remarks by the President on Ending the War in Iraq," October 21, 2011, The White House, http://www.whitehouse.gov/the-press-office /2011/10/21/remarks-president-ending-war-iraq.

35. Associated Press, "Iraq: Key Figures since the War Began," *Washington Post,* December 3, 2011, http://www.washingtonpost.com/world/middle-east /iraq-key-figures-since-the-war-began/2011/12/03/gIQAPZ2tOO_ story.html.

36. Nicholas D. Kristof, "What Holbrooke Knew," *New York Times,* May 14, 2011, www.nytimes.com/2011/05/15/opinion/15kristof.html.

37. Caroline Wyatt, "Restraint the New Tactic for UK Troops in Afghanistan," *BBC News,* January 28, 2010, http://news.bbc.co.uk/2/hi/uk_news /8484205.stm.

38. "Operation Moshtarak: At a Glance," *Aljazerra,* February 13, 2010, http:// www.aljazeera.com/news/asia/2010/02/201021343536129252.html.

39. Sharif Khoram, "Marjah: Heroin and Taliban Nexus in the Eye of a Storm," *Daily Times,* February 09, 2010, http://www.dailytimes.com.pk/default .asp?page=2010\02\09\story_9-2-2010_pg20_10.

40. "Afghanistan offensive on Taliban in Helmand," *BBC News,* February 13, 2010, http://news.bbc.co.uk/2/hi/south_asia/8513849.stm.

41. Patrick Cockburn, "Operation Moshtarak: Biggest Offensive since 2001 under Way Allies and Afghans Join Forces to Seize Stronghold, but What Will Be the Ultimate Outcome?" *Independent,* February 14, 2010, http:// www.independent.co.uk/news/world/asia/operation-moshtarak-biggest -offensive-since-2001-under-way-1899127.html.

42. "Nato launches major Afghan assault," *Aljazerra,* February 13, 2010, http:// www.aljazeera.com/news/asia/2010/02/201021222455527806.html.

43. Marie Colvin, "Taliban Leaders Flee as Marines Hit Stronghold," *Times,* February 14, 2010, http://article.wn.com/view/2010/02/14/Taliban_ leaders_flee_as_marines_hit_stronghold/.

44. Dion Nissenbaum, "McChrystal Calls Marjah a 'Bleeding Ulcer' in Afghan Campaign," *McClatchy Newspapers,* May 24, 2010, http://www.mc clatchydc.com/2010/05/24/94740/mcchrystal-calls-marjah-a-bleeding .html#ixzz1fsdO1owj.

45. Saeed Shah, "U.S. Apologizes for Killing of 12 Afghan Civilians," *McClatchy Newspapers,* February 14, 2010, http://www.mcclatchydc.com /2010/02/14/84853/the-mistaken-killing-of-12-afghan.html#ixzz 1fxZ4dNoP.

46. IRIN, "AFGHANISTAN: Marjah Residents Take Stock after Offensive," Kabul, 16 March 2010, http://www.globalsecurity.org/military/library /news/2010/03/mil-100316-irin01.htm.

47. Dexter Filkins, "Half of Town's Taliban Flee or Are Killed, Allies Say," *New York Times,* February 16, 2010, A1.
48. Laura King, "Test of Counterinsurgency Strategy in Afghanistan, Exhibit A: The Flagging Operation in Helmand Province," *Los Angeles Times,* June 25, 2010, http://articles.latimes.com/2010/jun/25/world/la-fg-afghani stan-marja-20100625.
49. Rothstein, "America's Longest War," 76.
50. Gareth Porter, "Kandahar Gains Came with 'Brutal' Tactics: The District Governor in Arghandab, Shah Muhammed Ahmadi, Acknowledged That Entire Villages Had Been Destroyed," International Press Service, December 21, 2010, http://www.rawa.org/temp/runews/2010/12/21/kandahar -gains-came-with-brutal-tactics.html#ixzz1gzfcBYHV.
51. Rothstein, "America's Longest War," 65.
52. Porter, "Kandahar Gains Came with 'Brutal' Tactics."
53. "Lisbon Summit Declaration," NATO press release, November 20, 2010.
54. U.S. Department of State, "Remarks at the Launch of the Asia Society's Richard C. Holbrooke Memorial Addresses," February 18, 2011, available at http://www.state.gov/secretary/rm/2011/02/156815.htm.
55. Ibid.
56. Livingston and O'Hanlon, *Afghanistan Index,* 4–9.
57. General David Petraeus, "To the Soldiers, Sailors, Airmen, Marines, and Civilians of Multi-National Force–Iraq," Headquarters, Multinational Force–Iraq. February 10, 2007.
58. General David Petraeus, "To the Soldiers, Sailors, Airmen, Marines, and Civilians of NATO's International Security Assistance Force," Headquarters, International Security Assistance Force/United States Forces–Afghanistan. July 4, 2010.
59. Rod Nordland, "An Uncharacteristically Upbeat General in Afghanistan," *New York Times,* January 24, 2011, http://atwar.blogs.nytimes.com /2011/01/24/an-uncharacteristically-upbeat-general-in-afghanistan/.
60. David H. Petraeus, "Setting—and Capitalizing on—Conditions for Progress in Afghanistan," *Army,* October 2010, 85–94, http://www.ausa.org /publications/armymagazine/archive/2010/10/Documents/Petraeus _1010.pdf
61. Helene Cooper, "Obama Announces Killing of Osama bin Laden," *New York Times,* May 1, 2011, http://thelede.blogs.nytimes.com/2011/05/01 /bin-laden-dead-u-s-official-says/.
62. Greg Miller, "CIA Spied on bin Laden from Safe House," *Washington Post,* May 5, 2011, http://www.washingtonpost.com/world/cia-spied-on -bin-laden-from-safe-house/2011/05/05/AFXbG31F_story.html.
63. Kristen Chick, "Kandahar Assaults Underscore Vulnerabilities in Afghan War Effort, Taliban Attacks Continued for a Second Day in Kandahar, Despite a Yearlong Effort by NATO and Afghan Forces to Drive the Taliban Out of the Southern Province," *Christian Science Monitor,* May 8, 2011,

http://www.csmonitor.com/World/terrorism-security/2011/0508/
Kandahar-assaults-underscore-vulnerabilities-in-Afghan-war-effort.

64. "Remarks by the President on the Way Forward in Afghanistan," Office of the Press Secretary, The White House, June 22, 2011.

65. See, for example, "Karzai and Petraeus At Odds over Afghan Strategy," *National Public Radio*, http://www.npr.org/blogs/thetwo-way/2010/11/15/131326062/karzai-and-petraeus-at-odds-over-afghan-strategy.

66. Australian Associated Press, "Nato Confirms Death of Aussie Diggers," *Sydney Telegraph,* October 30, 2011, http://www.dailytelegraph.com.au/news/breaking-news/nato-cofirms-death-of-aussie-diggers/story-e6freuyi-1226180573552.

67. Sally Sara, "Afghan Soldier Shoots 3 Diggers," *ABC News*, November 09, 2011, http://www.abc.net.au/news/2011-11-09/soldiers-shot/3653744.

68. Sebastian Abbot, "NATO Attack Allegedly Kills 24 Pakistani Troops," *Guardian,* November 26, 2011, http://www.guardian.co.uk/world/feed article/9966283.

69. Reuters, "NATO's Rasmussen Says Pakistani Deaths Unintended," *MSNBC,* November 27, 2011, http://www.msnbc.msn.com/id/45451912/t/natos-rasmussen-says-pakistani-deaths-unintended/#.Tu4fnlbfXTo.

70. Rod Nordland, "Rare Attacks on Shiites Kill Scores in Afghanistan," *New York Times,* December 7, 2011, 1.

71. Adam Entous and Julian E. Barnes, "Commander Seeks Delay in U.S. Troop Drawdown," *Wall Street Journal,* December 7, 2011, 11.

72. Ibid.

73. Kevin Sieff, "U.S. Probe of Koran Burning Finds 5 Troops Responsible, Officials Say; Afghans Demand Trial," *Washington Post,* March 2, 2012, http://www.washingtonpost.com/world/us-probe-of-koran-burning-finds-5-soldiers-responsible-afghan-clerics-demand-public-trial/2012/03/02/gIQAwJqYmR_story.html.

74. Agence France-Presse (AFP), "Obama Forced to Apologise to Karzai for Koran Burnings in Afghanistan," *Australian,* February 24, 2012, http://www.theaustralian.com.au/news/world/obama-forced-to-apologise-to-karzai-for-koran-burnings-in-afghanistan/story-e6frg6so-1226280166800.

75. "Two NATO Troops Killed by Afghan Soldier," *Herald Sun,* Melbourne, Australia, February 24, 2012, http://www.heraldsun.com.au/news/more-news/two-nato-troops-killed-by-afghan-soldier/story-e6frf7lf-1226280004891.

76. Taimoor Shah and Graham Bowley, "Army Sergeant Accused of Slaying 16 in Afghan Villages," *New York Times,* March 11, 2012, http://www.nytimes.com/2012/03/12/world/asia/afghanistan-civilians-killed-american-soldier-held.html.

77. Londoño, Ernesto, Afghans Voice Rage over Civilian Deaths as US Defends Mission, *Boston Globe,* March 13, 2012, http://www.bostonglobe.com/news/world/2012/03/12/afghans-voice-rage-over-civilian-deaths-defends-mission/5fe1tEOA7IjFnkXPY7AH4K/story.html.

78. Ibid.
79. Rod Nordland, "U.S. and Afghanistan Agree on Prisoner Transfer as Part of Long-Term Agreement," *New York Times,* March 9, 2012, http://www .nytimes.com/2012/03/10/world/asia/us-and-afghanistan-agree-on -detainee-transfer.html.
80. "Afghanistan and US sign 'night raid' deal," *Al Jazeera,* April 8, 2012, http:// www.aljazeera.com/news/asia/2012/04/2012488573337183.html.
81. Reuters, "Afghanistan Gets Veto Power over NATO Night Raids," *MSNBC News,* April 8, 2012, http://worldnews.msnbc.msn.com/_news /2012/04/08/11083361-afghanistan-gets-veto-power-over-nato-night -raids?lite.
82. Alissa J. Rubin, "With Pact, U.S. Agrees to Help Afghans for Years to Come," *New York Times,* April 22, 2012, http://www.nytimes.com/2012/04/23 /world/asia/us-and-afghanistan-reach-partnership-agreement.html ?_r=1&ref=asia.
83. Ibid.
84. Laura King, "Karzai Faults Afghan Intelligence—and NATO—in Attacks," *Los Angeles Times,* April 16, 2012, http://latimesblogs.latimes.com/world_ now/2012/04/karzai-faults-afghan-intelligence-and-nato-in-attacks .html.
85. STRATFOR, "ISAF Plans for Spring Offensive," April 20, 2012, http:// us4.campaign-archive1.com/?u=74786417f9554984d314d06bd&id=f0e5 104d8b&e=88257c8faf.
86. John Nagl and Michael O'Hanlon, "Afghan Strategy Begins to Make Gains," *Politico.com,* December 6, 2011, http://www.politico.com/news /stories/1211/69881.html.
87. Kevin Sieff and Scott Wilson, "Obama Signs Pact in Kabul, Surprise Trip Also Marks bin Laden's Death," *Washington Post,* May 2, 2012, 1. See also The White House, "Remarks by President Obama in Address to the Na- tion from Afghanistan," Bagram Air Base, Afghanistan, May 1, 2012, http:// www.whitehouse.gov/the-press-office/2012/05/01/remarks-president -obama-address-nation-afghanistan.
88. Mark Landler, "Obama Signs Pact in Kabul, Turning Page in Afghan War," *New York Times,* May 2, 2012, 1.
89. "Remarks by President Obama in Address to the Nation from Afghanistan."
90. Ibid.
91. Ibid.
92. Ibid.

Chapter 11: A Final Assessment

1. Linda J. Bilmes, "What Have We Learned? As Iraq War Winds Down, the Conflict Offers Expensive Lessons," *Boston Globe,* December 7, 2011, 15.
2. CNN Wire Staff, "Obama: Iraq War Will Be Over by Year's End; Troops Coming Home," October 21, 2011, http://articles.cnn.com/2011-10-21

/middleeast/world_meast_iraq-us-troops_1_iraq-war-operation-new
-dawn-iraq-and-afghanistan-veterans?_s=PM:MIDDLEEAST.

3. National Security Council, *National Strategy for Victory in Iraq* (Washington, D.C., November 2005), 3, available at http://www.washingtonpost.com /wp-srv/nation/documents/Iraqnationalstrategy11-30-05.pdf. The plan also called for an Iraq that "is a partner in the global war on terror and the fight against the proliferation of weapons of mass destruction, integrated into the international community, an engine for regional economic growth, and proving the fruits of democratic governance to the region." Iraq at the time was clearly not very well integrated into the international community and was far from an engine for regional economic growth.

4. The Northern Alliance was more correctly known as the United Islamic Front for the Salvation of Afghanistan (UIF, in Pasto, the Jabha-yi Muttahid -i Islami-yi Milli bara-yi Nijat-i Afghanistan). It was a military-political umbrella organization created in 1996 under the leadership of Defense Minister Ahmad Shah Massoud. The organization united all ethnic groups of Afghanistan fighting against the Afghan Taliban, bin Laden's Al-Qaeda, and their supporters in neighboring Pakistan.

5. See "Operation Enduring Freedom: Afghanistan," GlobalSecurity.org, n.d., http://www.globalsecurity.org/military/ops/enduring-freedom-plan.htm.

6. Solid analysis of the Enduring Freedom campaign can be found in Wright, *Different Kind of War.*

7. United Nations Security Council Resolution 1267 of October 15, 1999, was followed by UNSCR 1333 of December 19, 2000. Both condemned "the continuing use of the areas of Afghanistan under the control of the Afghan faction known as Taliban, which also calls itself the Islamic Emirate of Afghanistan (hereinafter known as the Taliban), for the sheltering and training of terrorists and planning of terrorist acts." The UN also deplored "the fact that the Taliban continues to provide safehaven to Usama bin Laden and to allow him and others associated with him to operate a network of terrorist training camps from Taliban-controlled territory and to use Afghanistan as a base from which to sponsor international terrorist operations." The Security Council had previously deplored the terrorist acts committed in East Africa by Al-Qaeda in UNSCR 1189 of August 13, 1998, but that resolution did not mention Afghanistan or Al-Qaeda specifically.

8. See "Robert Michael Kelly, First Lieutenant, United States Marine Corps," Arlington National Cemetery Website, http://www.arlingtoncemetery.net /rmkelly.htm. See also "DOD Identifies Marine Casualty," Office of the Assistant Secretary of Defense (Public Affairs) news release, http://www .defense.gov/releases/release.aspx?releaseid=14048.

9. *Poor Bastards Club,* http://mywarstories.blogspot.com/.

10. Tim Hetherington, "Medal of Honor Winner Salvatore Giunta on Bravery, Brotherhood, and the Korengal," *Vanity Fair,* November 11, 2010, 12. Staff Sergeant Giunta's Medal of Honor citation reads in part: "Specialist

Salvatore A. Giunta distinguished himself conspicuously by gallantry and intrepidity at the risk of his life above and beyond the call of duty in action with an armed enemy in the Korengal Valley, Afghanistan, on October 25, 2007. While conducting a patrol as team leader with Company B, 2d Battalion (Airborne), 503d Infantry Regiment, Specialist Giunta and his team were navigating through harsh terrain when they were ambushed by a well-armed and well-coordinated insurgent force. While under heavy enemy fire, Specialist Giunta immediately sprinted towards cover and engaged the enemy. Seeing that his squad leader had fallen and believing that he had been injured, Specialist Giunta exposed himself to withering enemy fire and raced towards his squad leader, helped him to cover, and administered medical aid. While administering first aid, enemy fire struck Specialist Giunta's body armor and his secondary weapon. Without regard to the ongoing fire, Specialist Giunta engaged the enemy before prepping and throwing grenades, using the explosions for cover in order to conceal his position. Attempting to reach additional wounded fellow soldiers who were separated from the squad, Specialist Giunta and his team encountered a barrage of enemy fire that forced them to the ground. The team continued forward and upon reaching the wounded soldiers, Specialist Giunta realized that another soldier was still separated from the element. Specialist Giunta then advanced forward on his own initiative. As he crested the top of a hill, he observed two insurgents carrying away an American soldier. He immediately engaged the enemy, killing one and wounding the other. Upon reaching the wounded soldier, he began to provide medical aid, as his squad caught up and provided security. Specialist Giunta's unwavering courage, selflessness, and decisive leadership while under extreme enemy fire were integral to his platoon's ability to defeat an enemy ambush and recover a fellow American soldier from the enemy."

11. "2,100 Civilians Killed in Afghanistan in 2008: UN," Reuters, http://www.abc.net.au/news/2009-02-04/2100-civilians-killed-in-afghanistan-in-2008-un/282520.

12. See UNAMA's Annual Report, http://unama.unmissions.org/Portals/UNAMA/Documents/2011%20Midyear%20POC.pdf.

13. For rough estimates since Iraqi sovereignty see Iraq Coalition Casualty Count, http://icasualties.org/Iraq/IraqiDeaths.aspx.

14. The Treaty of Westphalia was actually a series of peace treaties signed in 1648 ending the Thirty Years' War (1618–48). More importantly, the peace initiated a new system of political order in central Europe based upon the concept of a sovereign state. This system led to the dominance of the nation-state in modern political affairs.

15. David C. Isby, *Afghanistan: Graveyard of Empires: A New History of the Borderlands* (New York: Pegasus Books, 2010), 90–91.

16. See, for example, "U.S. Supply Convoy Hijacked In Pakistan," *CBS News*, February 11, 2009, http://www.cbsnews.com/8301-224_162-4594768.html.

17. See Eric Blehm, *The Only Thing Worth Dying for: How Eleven Green Berets Forged a New Afghanistan* (New York: Harper, 2010.) Biography, *Academy of Achievement,* http://www.achievement.org/autodoc/page/kar0pro-1.

18. See the Dawa Party's "Leader Description," available at http://islamicdawa party.com/?module=home&fname=leaderdesc.php&id=78. See also the BBC's profile on al-Maliki at http://www.bbc.co.uk/news/world-middle-east-11733715.

19. See Belasco, *Cost of Iraq, Afghanistan, and Other Global War on Terror Operations since 9/11.*

20. Ben Arnoldy, "Why Karzai Readily Admits Receiving Bags of Iranian Cash?," *Christian Science Monitor,* October 25, 2010, http://www.csmonitor .com/World/Asia-South-Central/2010/1025/Why-Karzai-readily -admits-receiving-bags-of-Iranian-cash.

21. Thomas Barfield, "Afghan Paradoxes," in Rothstein and Arquilla, *Afghan Endgames,* 53.

22. Mark Landler and Helene Cooper, "Obama Will Speed Pullout From War in Afghanistan," *New York Times,* June 23, 2011, A1.

23. Dan De Luce, "Waning Public Support Weighed on Afghan Move: Gates," American Forces Press Service, Washington, D.C., June 23, 2011.

24. Lisa Daniel, "Flournoy: Afghanistan Drawdown Matches Strategy," American Forces Press Service, Washington, D.C., June 23, 2011.

25. George Friedman, "Pakistan, Russia and the Threat to the Afghan War," *StratFor,* http://www.stratfor.com/weekly/20111129-pakistan-russia-and -threat-afghan-war.

26. Linda Robinson, "Is There Hope for Afghanistan?" *ForeignPolicy.com,* November 29, 2011, http://afpak.foreignpolicy.com/posts/2011/11/29/is _there_hope_for_afghanistan.

27. Kagan and Kagan, "Patton of Counterinsurgency."

28. "Gates: I Was 'Strong Advocate' for Afghanistan Surge to End in Summer 2012," interview, *PBS Newsmaker,* air date June 23, 2011, available at http:// www.pbs.org/newshour/bb/politics/jan-june11/gates_06-23.html.

29. Frederick Kagan, "DEBATE PREP: Is This the Only Path to Victory in Afghanistan?," *CNN Security Blogs,* http://security.blogs.cnn.com/2011 /11/07/debate-prep-is-this-the-only-path-to-victory-in-afghanistan/.

30. "Remarks by the President in Address to the Nation on the Way Forward in Afghanistan and Pakistan," West Point, New York, December 1, 2009, available at http://www.whitehouse.gov/the-press-office/remarks-president -address-nation-way-forward-afghanistan-and-pakistan.

31. Joseph J. Collins, "Afghanistan: The Path to Victory," *Joint Force Quarterly,* no. 54 (3rd Quarter, 2009), 59.

32. Collins, *Understanding War in Afghanistan,* 35.

33. "Fact Sheet: NATO's Operational Mentor and Liaison Teams (OMLTs)," October 2009, available at http://www.nato.int/isaf/topics/factsheets /omlt-factsheet.pdf.

34. Medal of Honor citation, available at http://www.marines.mil/community /Pages/MedalofHonorSgtDakotaMeyer-Citation.aspx.
35. E-mail from G3, Army National Guard staff member on April 26, 2012.
36. Tom Vanden Brook, "Gates Lauds MRAPs as Iraq Bombings Spike," *USA Today,* January 20, 2008, http://www.usatoday.com/news/world/iraq /2008-01-20-gates_N.htm.
37. Tom Vanden Brook, "Roadside Bombs Decline in Iraq," *USA Today,* June 22, 2008, http://www.usatoday.com/news/world/iraq/2008-06-22-ieds _N.htm.
38. See for example, "Iran's Role in Iraq, Nuclear Ambitions Cloud U.S. Policy," *PBS NewsHour,* April 16, 2008, http://www.pbs.org/newshour/bb /middle_east/jan-june08/iran_04-16.html.
39. In Iraq 20,000 were added to a total force of nearly 165,000; in Afghanistan, 33,000 were added to only 119,000.

Selected Bibliography

Books

Baker, James A., and Lee H. Hamilton, cochairs; with Lawrence S. Eagleburger, Vernon E. Jordan Jr., Edwin Meese III, Sandra Day O'Connor, Leon E. Panetta, William J. Perry, Charles S. Robb, and Alan K. Simpson. *The Iraq Study Group Report: The Way Forward—A New Approach.* New York: Vintage Books, 2006.

Ballard, John R. *Fighting for Fallujah: A New Dawn for Iraq.* Westport, Conn.: Praeger Security International, 2006.

———. *From Storm to Freedom: America's Long War with Iraq.* Annapolis, Md.: Naval Institute Press, 2010.

Bergen, Peter. *Holy War Inc.* New York: Free Press, 2001.

Bremer, L. Paul, III, with Malcolm McConnell. *My Year in Iraq: The Struggle to Build a Future of Hope.* New York: Simon & Schuster, 2006.

Briscoe, Charles H. *All Roads Lead to Baghdad: Army Special Operation Forces in Iraq.* Fort Bragg, N.C.: USASOC History Office, 2006.

Bush, George W. *Decision Points.* New York: Crown, 2010.

Caraccilo, Dominic J., and Andrea L. Thompson. *Achieving Victory in Iraq: Countering an Insurgency.* Mechanicsburg, Pa.: Stackpole Books, 2008.

Chandrasekaran, Rajiv. *Imperial Life in the Emerald City: Inside Iraq's Green Zone.* New York: Alfred A. Knopf, 2006.

Clark, Wesley K. *Winning Modern Wars: Iraq, Terrorism, and the American Empire.* New York: PublicAffairs, 2003.

Clarke, Richard. *Against All Enemies: Inside America's War on Terror.* New York: Free Press, 2004.

Cloud, David, and Greg Jaffe. *The Fourth Star: Four Generals and the Epic Struggle for the Future of the United States Army.* New York: Three Rivers, 2009.

Coll, Steve. *Ghost Wars: The Secret History of the CIA, Afghanistan, and Bin Laden, from the Soviet Invasion to September 10, 2001.* New York: Penguin, 2004.

Collins, Joseph J. *Understanding War in Afghanistan.* Washington, D.C.: National Defense University Press, 2011. http://purl.fdlp.gov/GPO/gpo11115.

Crile, George. *Charlie Wilson's War: The Extraordinary Story of the Largest Covert Operation in History.* New York: Atlantic Monthly, 2003.

DeLong, Lieutenant General Michael, with Noah Lukeman. *Inside CENTCOM: The Unvarnished Truth about the Wars in Afghanistan and Iraq.* Washington, D.C.: Regnery, 2004.

Dobbins, James F. *After the Taliban: Nation-Building in Afghanistan.* Washington, D.C.: Potomac Books, 2008.

Feifer, Gregory. *The Great Gamble: The Soviet War in Afghanistan.* New York: Harper, 2009.

Feith, Douglas J. *War and Decision: Inside the Pentagon at the Dawn of the War on Terrorism.* New York: Harper, 2008.

Fontenot, Gregory, E. J. Degen, and David Tohn. *On Point: The United States Army in Operation Iraqi Freedom.* Annapolis, Md.: Naval Institute Press, 2005.

Ferguson, Charles H. *No End in Sight: Iraq's Descent into Chaos.* New York: PublicAffairs, 2008.

Franks, Tommy. *American Soldier.* New York: Regan Books, 2004.

Gannon, James. *Obama's War: Avoiding a Quagmire in Afghanistan.* Washington, D.C.: Potomac Books, 2011.

Gates, Robert M. *From the Shadows: The Ultimate Insider's Story of Five Presidents and How They Won the Cold War.* New York: Simon & Schuster, 2006.

Goodson, Larry P. *Afghanistan's Endless War: State Failure, Regional Politics, and the Rise of the Taliban.* Seattle: University of Washington Press, 2001.

Gordon, Michael R., and Bernard E. Trainor. *Cobra II: The Inside Story of the Invasion and Occupation of Iraq.* New York: Pantheon, 2006.

Grau, Lester W., and Michael A. Gress. *The Soviet-Afghan War: How a Superpower Fought and Lost.* Lawrence: University Press of Kansas, 2002.

Hafez, Mohammed M. *Suicide Bombers in Iraq: The Strategy and Ideology of Martyrdom.* Washington, D.C.: United States Institute of Peace, 2007.

Hashim, Ahmed S. *Insurgency and Counter-Insurgency in Iraq.* Ithaca, N.Y.: Cornell University Press, 2006.

Hopkirk, Peter. *The Great Game.* London: Oxford University Press, 1990

Isby, David C. *Afghanistan: Graveyard of Empires: A New History of the Borderlands.* New York: Pegasus Books, 2010.

Iraq Study Group (U.S.), James Addison Baker, Lee Hamilton, and Lawrence S. Eagleburger. *The Iraq Study Group Report.* New York: Vintage Books, 2006.

Jalali, Ali Ahmad, and Lester W. Grau. *The Other Side of the Mountain: Mujahideen Tactics in the Soviet-Afghan War.* Quantico, Va.: U.S. Marine Corps, Studies and Analysis Division, 1999.

Jones, Seth G. *In the Graveyard of Empires: America's War in Afghanistan.* New York: W. W. Norton, 2009.

Kaplan, Robert D. *Soldiers of God: With Islamic Warriors in Afghanistan and Pakistan.* New York: Vintage Departures, 2001

Koontz, Christopher N., ed., *Enduring Voices: Oral Histories of the U.S. Army Experience in Afghanistan, 2003–2005*. Washington, D.C.: U.S. Army Center of Military History, 2008.

Lacey, Jim. *Takedown: The 3rd Infantry Division's Twenty-One-Day Assault on Baghdad*. Annapolis, Md.: Naval Institute Press, 2007.

Lambeth, Benjamin S. *Air Power against Terror*. Santa Monica, Calif.: RAND, 2005.

MacPherson, Malcolm. *Roberts Ridge*. New York: Bantam Dell, 2005.

Marr, Phebe. *The Modern History of Iraq*, 2nd. ed. Boulder, Colo.: Westview, 2004.

Metz, Steven. *Iraq and the Evolution of American Strategy*. Washington, D.C.: Potomac Books, 2008.

Murray, Williamson, and Robert H. Scales, Jr. *The Iraq War: A Military History*. Cambridge, Mass.: Harvard University Press, 2003.

Naylor, Sean. *Not a Good Day to Die*. New York: Penguin, 2005.

Neumann, Ronald E. *The Other War: Winning and Losing in Afghanistan*. Washington, D.C.: Potomac Books, 2009.

Rashid, Ahmed. *Descent into Chaos: The United States and the Failure of Nation Building in Pakistan, Afghanistan, and Central Asia*. New York: Viking, 2008.

Reynolds, Nicholas E. *Basrah, Baghdad, and Beyond: U.S. Marine Corps in the Second Iraq War*. Annapolis, Md.: Naval Institute Press, 2005.

Richards, D. S. *The Savage Frontier: A History of the Anglo-Afghan Wars*. London: Pan Books, 2003.

Ricks, Thomas E. *Fiasco: The American Military Adventure in Iraq*. New York: Penguin, 2006.

———. *The Gamble: General David Petraeus and the American Military Adventure in Iraq, 2006–2008*. New York: Penguin, 2009.

Robinson, Linda. *Tell Me How This Ends: General David Petraeus and the Search for a Way Out of Iraq*. New York: PublicAffairs, 2008.

Rothstein, Hy S., and John Arquilla. *Afghan Endgames: Strategy and Policy Choices for America's Longest War*. Washington, D.C.: Georgetown University Press, 2012.

Roy, Olivier. *Islam and Resistance in Afghanistan*. Cambridge: Cambridge University Press, 1990.

Rubin, Barnett R. *The Fragmentation of Afghanistan*. New Haven, Conn.: Yale University Press, 1995.

Rumsfeld, Donald H. *Known and Unknown: A Memoir*. New York: Sentinel, 2010.

Schroen, Gary C., *First In: An Insider's Account of How the CIA Spearheaded the War on Terror in Afghanistan*. New York: Ballantine, 2005.

Shelton, Hugh H. *Without Hesitation: The Odyssey of an American Warrior*. New York: St Martins, October 2010.

Tanner, Stephen. *Afghanistan: A Military History from Alexander the Great to the War against the Taliban*. Philadelphia: Da Capo, 2009.

Urban, Mark. *War in Afghanistan*. New York: St. Martin's, 1990.

Weigley, Russell F. *The American Way of War: A History of United States Military Strategy and Policy*. New York: Macmillan, 1973.

West, Francis J. *The Strongest Tribe: War, Politics, and the Endgame in Iraq*. New York: Random House, 2008.

———. *The Wrong War: Grit, Strategy, and the Way Out of Afghanistan*. New York: Random House, 2011.

West, Francis J., and Ray L. Smith. *The March Up: Taking Baghdad with the 1st Marine Division*. New York: Bantam, 2003.

Williams, Gary. *Seal of Honor: Operation Red Wings and the Life of Lt. Michael P. Murphy, USN*. Annapolis, Md.: Naval Institute Press, 2011.

Woods, Kevin M. *The Mother of All Battles: Saddam Hussein's Strategic Plan for the Persian Gulf War*. Annapolis, Md.: Naval Institute Press, 2008.

Woods, Kevin M., and Michael R. Pease. *The Iraqi Perspectives Report: Saddam's Senior Leadership on Operation Iraqi Freedom from the Official U.S. Joint Forces Command Report*. Annapolis, Md.: Naval Institute Press, 2006.

Woodward, Bob. *The Commanders*. New York: Simon & Schuster, 1991.

———. *Bush at War*. New York: Simon & Schuster, 2002.

———. *Plan of Attack*. New York: Simon & Schuster, 2004.

———. *State of Denial: Bush at War, Part III*. New York: Simon & Schuster, 2006.

———. *The War Within: A Secret White House History, 2006–2008*. New York: Simon & Schuster, 2008.

Wright, Donald P., et al. *A Different Kind of War: The United States Army in Operation ENDURING FREEDOM October 2001–September 2005*. Fort Leavenworth, Kans.: Combat Studies Institute Press, May 2010.

Wright, Donald P., and Timothy R. Reese. *On Point II: The United States Army in Operation Iraqi Freedom, May 2003–January 2005—Transition to the New Campaign*. Fort Leavenworth, Kans.: Combat Studies Institute Press, 2008.

Articles and Papers

Barno, David W. "Fighting the Other War." *Military Review* (September–October 2007), 32–44.

Bergen, Peter. "The Battle for Tora Bora: How Osama bin Laden Slipped from Our Grasp—The Definitive Account." *New Republic* (December 22, 2009). http://www.tnr.com/print/article/the-battle-tora-bora.

Collins, Joseph J. "Afghanistan: The Path to Victory." *Joint Force Quarterly* no. 54 (3rd Quarter 2009).

Conetta, Carl. *Strange Victory: A Critical Appraisal of Operation Enduring Freedom and the Afghanistan War*. Research Monograph 6. Cambridge, Mass.: Commonwealth Institute, Project on Defense Alternatives, 30 January 2002.

Feith, Douglas J. "Why We Went to War in Iraq." *Wall Street Journal*, July 3, 2008, 11.

Gray, Colin S. "War: Continuity in Change, and Change in Continuity." *Parameters* 40, no. 2 (Summer 2010).

Kagan, Frederick W. *Choosing Victory: A Plan for Success in Iraq, Phase One Report*. Washington, D.C.: American Enterprise Institute, December 2006.

Kagan, Frederick W., and Kimberly Kagan. "The Patton of Counterinsurgency." *Weekly Standard,* March 10, 2008, 26.

Katzman, Kenneth. *Iraq and Al Qaeda.* Report RL32217. Washington, D.C.: Congressional Research Service, April 28, 2008.

O'Bryant, Joanne, and Michael Waterhouse. *U.S. Forces in Afghanistan.* Report RS22633. Washington, D.C.: Congressional Research Service, July 15, 2008.

Packer, George. "Letter from Iraq: The Lesson of Tal Afar—Is It Too Late for the Administration to Correct Its Course in Iraq?" *New Yorker,* April 10, 2006, 51–52.

Rafael Reuveny and Aseem Prakash, "The Afghanistan War and the Breakdown of the Soviet Union." *Review of International Studies* no. 25 (1999).

Government/Organizational Documents

Obama, President Barack. "Responsibly Ending the War in Iraq." Speech given at Camp Lejeune, North Carolina, Friday, February 27, 2009. http://www.whitehouse.gov/the_press_office/Remarks-of-President-Barack-Obama-Responsibly-Ending-the-War-in-Iraq/.

Rice, Secretary of State Condoleezza. "Iraq and U.S. Policy, Testimony before the Senate Committee on Foreign Relations." http://foreign.senate.gov/testimony/2005/RiceTestimony051019.pdf.

Taguba, Major General Antonio M. "Article 15-6 Investigation of the 800th Military Police Brigade." The "Taguba Report" on Treatment of Abu Ghraib Prisoners in Iraq. http://news.findlaw.com/hdocs/docs/iraq/tagubarpt.html#ThR1.9.

U.S. Army Combat Studies Institute. *Wanat: Combat Action in Afghanistan, 2008.* Fort Leavenworth, Kans.: Combined Studies Institute Press, 2010.

U.S. Congress. Senate Committee on Armed Services. *Defense Organization: The Need for Change: Staff Report to the Committee on Armed Services.* Senate. Washington, D.C., 1985.

U.S. Government. *The National Military Strategy of the United States of America: A Strategy for Today, a Vision for Tomorrow.* Washington, D.C., 2004.

———. *Final Report of the National Commission on Terrorist Attacks upon the United States.* Washington, D.C.: U.S. Government Printing Office, 2004.

U.S. Government Printing Office. "Public Law 107-243: Authorization for Use of Military Force against Iraq Resolution of 2002." http://www.gpo.gov/fdsys/pkg/PLAW-107publ243/content-detail.html.

White House. *National Strategy for Victory in Iraq.* Washington, D.C., November 2005.

Internet Sources

British Broadcasting Corporation (BBC). http://news.bbc.co.uk/hi/english/world/.

Cable News Network. www.cnn.com/.

iCasualties.org. http://icasualties.org/.

National Security Archive at The George Washington University. http://www
.gwu.edu/~nsarchiv/index.html.

New York Times. www.nytimes.com/aponline/, and www.nytimes.com/library/
world/asia/.

United Nations. www.un.org/News/ossg/hilites.htm.

Index

About the Authors

John R. Ballard, PhD, is the dean of faculty and academic programs at the National War College; he commanded the U.S. Marine Corps' 4th Civil Affairs Group in Iraq during 2004–2005. **David W. Lamm** previously served as Commander, U.S. Army Central Command, Kuwait (2000–2002), and as Chief of Staff, Combined Forces Command, Afghanistan (2004–2005); he is now the deputy director of the Near East South Asia Center for Strategic Studies. **John K. Wood** is an associate professor at the Near East South Asia Center for Strategic Studies; he served from 2007 to 2009 as senior director for Afghanistan on the National Security Council in Washington, D.C.